Successful Restaurant Design

Successful

Restaurant

Design

SECOND EDITION

Regina S. Baraban   Joseph F. Durocher, Ph.D.

JOHN WILEY & SONS, INC.

New York • Chichester • Weiheim • Brisbane • Singapore • Toronto

Library of Congress Cataloging-in-Publication Data:

Baraban, Regina S.
  Successful restaurant design / by Regina S. Baraban and Joseph F. Durocher.—2nd ed.
      p. cm.
    Includes index.
    ISBN 0-471-35935-1 (cloth : alk. paper)
    Restaurants—Design and construction. I. Durocher, Joseph F., 1948- II. Title

    TX945 .B26 2000
    647.95'068'2—dc21   00-043382

Printed in the United States of America.

10 9 8

Book design and text composition HRoberts Design

Acknowledgments

Throughout the research and writing of the 2nd Edition of Successful Restaurant Design, many designers, architects, restaurateurs, and photographers generously contributed their time and expertise. To all of them, we are grateful.

Special thanks to the experts who shared their insights on design in Chapter seven, and to all of the behind-the-scenes-folks who worked to set up interviews, obtain photography, and keep the paperwork flowing.

We'd also like to acknowledge our family and friends, who for too long had to hear us say, "No, not this weekend. We have to work on the book." To Harry Scheckman, Regina's dad . . . Gladys would be proud. And to our daughters Debra, Lori, and Gail, let's go eat in some of these great restaurants and toast to the memory of grandma and grandpa Durocher.

Contents

Chapter 5: Design Implementation: Back to Front Through Management's Eyes — **133**

Chapter 6: Mini-Case Solutions   **171**

Chapter 7: Speak Out on Design

Bill Aumiller and Keith Youngquist, Principals
Aumiller Youngquist, PC, Architecture and Interior Design

Larry Bogdanow, Principal
Bogdanow Partners Architects, PC

William V. Eaton, President and COO
Cini-Little International, Inc.

Pat Kuleto, Designer-Owner
Pat Kuleto Restaurants, Inc.

Henry Meer, Chef-Owner
City Hall Restaurant and the Cub Room

Drew Nieporent, President
Myriad Restaurant Group

Richard Melman, Chairman of the Board
Lettuce Entertain You Enterprises, Inc.

Mary Sue Milliken and Susan Feniger, Chef-Owners
Border Grill and Ciudad

Morris Nathanson, Principal
Morris Nathanson Design, Inc.

Jeffrey Beers, Principal
Jeffrey Beers International

Steven Pannone, Creative Director
Girvin Design, Inc.

David Rockwell, Principal
Rockwell Group

Adam Tihany, Principal
Adam D. Tihany International Ltd.

James Webb, Principal
Webb Foodservice Design Consultants, Inc.

Andrew Young, Principal
Andrew Young & Co., Inc.

Preface

The story goes like this. Once upon a time we compared libraries. One of us had books on design and architecture, some of which focused on front-of-the-house spaces in restaurants; the other had a multitude of texts on restaurant management and back-of-the-house design. The books that covered the back of the house said nothing about the front, and vice versa. As we began to review one another's books—now in a combined library—we realized that one set of books looked at the restaurant only from the front door to the kitchen entrance. The other books started at the receiving dock and stopped at the same kitchen door. None of them clearly showed how the front and back of the house worked together. That's where our work on the first edition of *Successful Restaurant Design* began.

We didn't write a technical manual, nor did we create a lavish coffee-table book with lots of color pictures. Rather, we produced a guide to help readers understand how a restaurant works, back and front, because we believe this understanding is essential to good restaurant design. In addition to the basics of design, we incorporated insights into dozens of restaurant projects, from simple taco operations to complex full-service restaurants and cafeterias. Since 1989, *Successful Restaurant Design* has been used by many students, designers, and restaurateurs as they approached the process of designing restaurants.

The second edition of *Successful Restaurant Design* builds on the foundation laid in the first. During the intervening years, we've done our homework. Collectively, we've written hundreds of articles about both back- and front-of-the-house topics, and we've visited countless restaurants. We've become even more convinced of our thesis that restaurant design is a process, a set of interactive steps that can't be reduced to fail-safe formulas.

In this edition, we have expanded our coverage of the core issues related to designing restaurants. We also asked designers and restaurateurs to speak their mind about design. We discuss the issues and solutions for 35 distinct restaurant designs. Some of these are single-unit operations, while others are prototypes for chains—some small and some large—each intended to pique your interest, to promote discussion, and to make you think about design as more than fabric on the seats or paint on the wall.

Lastly, we emphasize that design has to be experienced. Neither pictures nor words can express the cosseting feel of the chairs in Le Cirque Las Vegas, the boisterous sights and sounds of celebration at Ciudad, the delicate aromas of fresh-baked bread at Beacon, the enticing coolness of oysters at Legal Sea Foods raw bar, the enormity of the jellyfish lamps in Farallon, or the delicate mingling of flavors in the salmon tartare at Next Door Nobu. Restaurant design is dynamic, and our support of the second edition of *Successful Restaurant Design* is also dynamic. Just point your favorite browser to "Successful Restaurant Design;" you should find us there with links to design firms and reference materials, updates to existing and new restaurants that we visit, and a special instructional support section for educators and students.

Successful Restaurant Design

Where Design Begins

The restaurant can be compared to any complex system that depends on all its parts to function correctly. Metaphorically speaking, it is like a desktop computer. What people see are the monitor, keyboard, and CPU box, along with peripherals such as printers and scanners. The keyboard is a simple input device, while the monitor and printer are output devices. What makes the computer work is the seamless, complex interaction of the internal hardware components of the CPU and the software—both the operating system and the various programs. If any of the hardware or software components fails to work properly, the computer crashes.

The same holds true for the individual parts of a restaurant. The front and back of the house are meaningless without one another. All spaces in the restaurant should be considered not only on their own terms but also with respect to how well they perform in relation to the whole. This means that the front and the back of the house (even if they are designed by different parties) must work together seamlessly.

All too often, however, the two halves of the restaurant are designed by separate people looking at the space from different doors: the foodservice consultant from the back door and the interior designer or architect from the front. Each ends his involvement at the swinging door between the two spaces.

The fact is that both sides of the door are influenced by the restaurant concept and by one another. If the front of the house is not designed to support the back of the house, or the back of the house is not designed to carry out the concept expressed in the front of the house, then the operation suffers. For instance, picture a classical kitchen with a full battery of ranges, ovens, steamers, broilers, and so on, all geared to produce a comprehensive menu for a gourmet restaurant. A typical fast-food interior design scheme would be an obvious mismatch with this classical kitchen and would result in financial disaster for the restaurant.

Another mismatch example is the inclusion of a bank of deep-fat fryers in the kitchen of a café serving spa cuisine. The deep-fat fryers are a costly and space-wasting mistake because fried foods are infrequently found on this type of menu.

Unfortunately, mismatches occur often because the restaurant concept and

The secret to a good relationship of concept, menu, and design is to conduct a careful market study and menu analysis before determining specific design elements in either the kitchen or the dining area.

the menu are not fully developed prior to design programming. The secret to a good relationship of concept, menu, and design is to conduct a careful market study and menu analysis before determining specific design elements in either the kitchen or the dining area.

Successful restaurant design should be based on a complete feasibility study that covers the following ten areas:

- type of restaurant
- the market
- concept development
- menu
- style of service
- speed of service
- the per-customer check average
- general ambience
- management philosophy
- budget

This will help achieve an integrative design process that results in a good match of front and back of the house. These points should be considered at the start of a project, before arriving at layouts and specifications.

The Type of Restaurant

One of the first decisions made about any foodservice space concerns the type of restaurant. Defining restaurant type is not easy. On a simplistic level, one might say, "I want to open a sit-down restaurant." But what exactly does that mean from a design perspective? For example, that sit-down restaurant could fall within any of the following categories:

- freestanding or within an existing structure
- independent or chain
- eat-in only or with a take-out station
- theme or nontheme
- ethnic or generic

The type of restaurant can also encompass market segment classifications such as fast food, coffee shop, hotel dining, family restaurant, entertainment restaurant, and corporate cafeteria.

The direct correlation between the type of restaurant and choice of kitchen equipment is obvious. A Chinese restaurant, for example, calls for different equipment than a seafood family dinner house. Every Chinese restaurant needs, for example, specific ranges designed to hold a wok. But front-of-the-house design elements are not nearly as easy to determine. A Chinese restaurant may hint at a particular color palette and design theme, but not all successful Chinese restaurants are festooned with red dragons and smiling Buddhas (Figure 1.1).

The Market

The importance of conducting a thorough market analysis before embarking on a restaurant design cannot be overemphasized. The most spectacular design, the most delectable food, and the finest service can fail to save an establishment that doesn't meet the needs of the marketplace. A good market analysis looks at four main components: potential customers, competition, location, and the economic environment. They are all interrelated, but each should be thoroughly analyzed.

POTENTIAL CUSTOMERS

Identifying the demographic and psychographic profiles of potential customers is crucial for restaurant design success. Demographic information can be fairly easy to obtain. Data such as family income, age distribution, education levels, and home ownership describe part of the picture about potential customers. Such data are available from the U.S. Census Bureau and local economic devel-

FIGURE 1.1

Subtle thematic references can, at times, be more effective than overdone clichés. Here the artwork and table setting in an Asian restaurant set the stage for diners.
(Photo by Joseph Durocher.)

opment offices (Figure 1.2). A number of online services sell data for any market. Users can choose the exact size of the geographic market from which they intend to draw customers and receive the data via mail or over the Internet.

But the psychographic information—which reveals consumer behaviors—tells an even more compelling story. Psychographics reveal how often the targeted customers actually dine out, how much they spend when they dine away from

FIGURE 1.2

This U.S. population estimate for 2001 projects potential customers per age group. When looked at over time, population projections can also anticipate potential labor shortages.

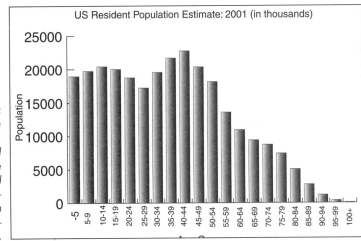

home, and identifies the type of restaurants they frequent. Some of these data can be obtained through consumer surveys, although those are costly. Credit card companies such as American Express sell detailed data on the purchasing habits of consumers, broken down by geographic markets. Another useful source of customer purchase behavior in restaurants is the Restaurant Growth Index, published yearly by *Restaurant Business* magazine. Yet another important source is the annual *Restaurant Industry Operations Report* published by the National Restaurant Association and Deloitte & Touche, LLP.

In some situations, the customers to be served at one meal are totally different from those served at another. This is particularly true of hotel restaurants (Figure 1.3). In all-suite hotels, for instance, breakfast is usually included in the price of the room and served almost exclusively to hotel guests, but lunch usually draws a local business crowd. Many popular restaurants in urban areas serve lunch to a neighborhood business clientele and dinner to a far-flung group of patrons who journey to the restaurant from around the city.

In such instances, design needs to suit diverse groups of customers if the restaurant is to succeed. A room designed as an attractive backdrop rather than an imposing statement can accommodate different tastes. Changing certain elements for each meal period, such as tabletop appointments or lighting levels, can also alter the mood of a room. Flexibility is a crucial design factor in both kitchen and dining areas for establishments that serve a wide spectrum of customers.

FIGURE 1.3 *The inviting, modern design of this hotel restaurant attracts hotel guests for all three meals, local businesspeople for lunch, and some destination diners for dinner. The seating area around the wood-fired oven is particularly appealing to single diners throughout the day.* (Photo by Joseph Durocher.)

THE COMPETITION

Sizing up the competition is critical to a good market analysis. It starts with the identification of both the primary and secondary competition. Primary competitors are those restaurants located in close proximity that offer the same type of food and service as the proposed restaurant. In rural settings, identifying the primary competition is easy, but in suburban and urban settings, this can be challenging. For example, a proposed restaurant in the northern Chicago suburbs will compete with all of the similar restaurants that lie along the driving route of commuters as they head home from work.

Secondary competitors encompass the different types of restaurants located nearby. Even widely divergent types—fast food and gourmet, coffee shop and eatertainment extravaganzas—should be considered potential competitors. However, the *major* secondary competitors are those restaurants that have a check average and style of service similar to a proposed restaurant.

Next, the trick is to determine how many restaurants the market can support and how well a particular type of restaurant can compete in a given area. To figure out the potential for market growth, we again recommend reference to the *Restaurant Business* Restaurant Growth Index. These data show those geographic areas where the propensity to dine away from home exceeds the capacity of restaurants to meet that demand—likewise, areas that are oversaturated with restaurants.

Both data gathering and data analysis can be complex. Studies should indicate the financial health of competing restaurants and their volume of business. Shopping the competition by checking out their parking lots and observing their waiting area during meal periods can provide important details about an operation's popularity.

Every effort should be made to find out what developments are planned for the neighborhood in question. In some cases, choosing to locate a restaurant close to others is a good strategy. The chain-restaurant row adjacent to suburban malls is one example of where clustering restaurants tends to work well. The challenge is to create a unique identity for each establishment. For example, consider a strip of roadway where a Red Lobster is followed by a Bugaboo Creek, an Olive Garden, and a regional seafood restaurant. Each has roughly the same check average and style of service; the distinctions are in menu offerings and design. In the case of Red Lobster, the seafood theme is played down and the decor is simple and unobtrusive. Olive Garden plays up its Italian theme with grapes on the menu and colors of the Italian flag. Bugaboo Creek's heavy wood elements, rough edges, and animatronics appeal to families with young children. To stand out from Red Lobster, the regional chain restaurant has a lavish seafood display in its entryway, cueing customers that they will be eating fresh fish. The display also supports retail seafood sales for at-home preparation. In this case, additional thematic elements, like wallpaper imprinted with nautical images, can further differentiate this seafood restaurant from Red Lobster.

LOCATION

"Location, location, location," the adage coined decades ago to express the key to business success, remains as true as ever. The ability to recognize a location that is suited to a particular type of restaurant is a crucial market factor. Location is typically defined as a geographic place. The close proximity of that place to a targeted customer base makes it desirable.

Location also gives clues to customer demographics and, in some cases, customer psychographics. For example, the sleekly designed fusion cuisine restaurant that is a big hit in San Francisco would likely fail miserably if transplanted to a small Nebraska town because rural Midwesterners look for different kinds of dining and design experiences than trendy city folk in California.

> The chain-restaurant row adjacent to suburban malls is one example of where clustering restaurants tends to work well. The challenge is to create a unique identity for each establishment.

FIGURE 1.4 *At the Mercer Kitchen in New York City's SoHo district, an oversized streetside window in a cast-iron building respects the architecture yet provides patrons some privacy with a view-filtering screen.* (Photo by Joseph Durocher.)

Architecture is influenced by location as well. Freestanding restaurants in the middle of Manhattan or Chicago are rare, for instance. Moreover, different regions call for different architectural styles. The pitched roofs found in New England are there to keep snow from collecting on the roof. Typical southwestern architecture uses adobe—an indigenous material—to insulate the building from the hot summer sun. The point is to avoid grafting architectural style onto an unsympathetic environment. Successful restaurant architecture works in context with its location (Figure 1.4).

The geographic location also affects kitchen design decisions. In many urban settings, for instance, food can be purchased daily, but in more remote areas, storage facilities are needed to hold food for a week or more, and plenty of storage space must be factored into the floorplan.

Location also affects the availability of utilities. For example, urban restaurants typically have access to natural gas for cooking. However, in rural areas, a restaurateur may have access only to bottled gas—which puts out 25 percent less heat than natural gas. Electric equipment that runs on 110-volt or 220-volt single phase should pose no problems in any location, but a 3-phase 220-volt power supply is not available everywhere; upgrading that service can be costly.

Traffic patterns should be taken into consideration when picking a location for a new restaurant. For example, a restaurant that targets breakfast customers is best located on the inbound side of the road heading into a city or other concentrated employment area, such as an industrial park. Conversely, a restaurant that targets dinner guests or people looking to pick up a home meal replacement after work can benefit from a location on the outbound side of the roadway. The ease with which drivers can exit and return to limited-access highways is also important.

ECONOMIC CONDITIONS

Finally, a market analysis should consider regional, national, and, in some cases, international economic conditions. The economic climate tends to influence restaurant longevity. In volatile times, planned obsolescence can be the key to a restaurant's success. In the late 1980s, for example, the whims of fashion influenced the economic picture to such an extent that many restaurants were designed for a short but popular lifespan. In these cases, front-of-the-house design elements were chosen primarily for their up-to-the-minute look, not for their enduring value. But by the mid-1990s, economic stability and prosperity encouraged more durable designs whose high style did not eclipse comfort.

Market indicators such as housing starts can help pinpoint the economic strength of a given area. Traffic counts maintained by state transportation departments are valuable for rural and suburban restaurants. Because most customers use their cars to reach restaurants in nonurban locations, increases in traffic count tend to foretell increases in restaurant sales. The trends of the bond market should also be considered. As the cost of capital increases, the prudent restaurateur looks for architecture and design that helps minimize capital costs. Another point to keep in mind is that the market is cyclical. A drop in interest rates can be a great time to upgrade equipment or undertake a renovation.

Communities that rely heavily on a single employer can pose problematic economic challenges. When the main employer downsizes, less discretionary money is available for dining out, and those who are still employed tend to tighten their belts to save for the time when they might be laid off. Urban restaurateurs should be similarly concerned if their operation appeals to a single business segment, like Wall Street brokers or advertising agency personnel.

Concept Development

With a clear understanding of the market, one can begin to develop the restaurant concept. The answers to four initial questions yield vital background information:

1. *What experience does ownership have in the restaurant business?*

Owners with a great deal of experience are better able to work with a complex menu, service, and design concept. Those with little experience are better suited to a small operation with a limited menu and simple decor.

2. *For a restaurant renovation, is the goal to freshen the look of an ongoing business or create an entirely new personality?*

A renovation can be as simple as adding a coat of paint, changing ceiling tiles, and installing new wall sconces. More significant design alterations are required to change the personality of an existing restaurant into an entirely new concept.

3. *For a new restaurant, is the building freestanding or part of an existing structure?*

When building from the ground up, both exterior and interior architecture can be easily planned to support the concept. Creating a concept for a restaurant built within an existing structure can be more challenging because the space limits the designer's flexibility. In this case, it often makes sense to develop a concept that is compatible with the existing architecture. For example, it would be difficult to create a 1950s diner theme in a cavernous loft space punctuated by columns.

4. *If ownership has not established a firm concept, then who will develop the concept—interior designer, architect, restaurant manager, or foodservice consultant—or will many parties collaborate?*

Questions to ask before developing the concept:

- *What experience does ownership have in the restaurant business?*
- *For a restaurant renovation, is the goal to freshen the look of an ongoing business or to create an entirely new personality?*
- *If a new restaurant, is the building freestanding or part of an existing structure?*
- *If ownership has not established a firm concept, then who will develop the concept—interior designer, architect, restaurant manager, or foodservice consultant—or will many parties collaborate?*

FIGURE 1.5 *Theme is critical to the Tara Thai restaurant in Rockville, MD; it is expressed in terms of architecture, interior finishes, and lighting rather than cliché Asian images.* (Photo by Joseph Durocher.)

While input from many players can be valuable, it can also lead to confusion or a loosely defined concept. For example, the chef may want to focus on the table-top, with dramatic lighting that highlights platters of food in the center of each table. The manager, seeing a greater contribution margin coming from the bar, may want to downplay the food end of the business and position the bar as the heart of the concept. The interior designer may seek to create a strong visual impact by spending the budget on dramatic architectural elements like a soaring staircase or dramatic entry.

A concept is multifaceted and involves every aspect of the operation. It can revolve around a theme that has easily identified visual elements—a seafood theme with hanging lobster traps or a Mexican theme with cacti and oversized sombreros, for instance. However, other theme restaurants reflect a subtler approach—suggestions of a theme that give diners a feel for what they are about to get but leave a bit to their imagination. A display of fresh seafood coupled with architectural elements reminiscent of a cruise ship hints of the meal to come. The adobe walls, pottery, tiles, and courtyard fountain of a Mexican villa-style building prepare the diner for a south-of-the-border experience without screaming the message. Oversized Japanese Suiboku paintings on the wall clearly suggest an Asian food experience. These kinds of thematic references often engender a sense of realism. In many cases, theme is expressed both in the interior and on the exterior of a restaurant (Figure 1.5).

In other instances, historic recreations evoke an authentic sense of place. Period design can range from a turn-of-the-century hotel dining room to an Art Deco cruise ship motif to a 1950s diner. Ingenious use of design can help an unadorned modern building take on the character of another era, and genuine restoration or renovation can transform the restaurant into a kind of living museum. For example, in the restaurants at Williamsburg, Virginia, and Sturbridge Village, Massachusetts, the costumed waitstaff, original eighteenth- and early nineteenth-century architecture, and authentic cuisine transport customers back to colonial times.

Strong themes have become the core concept for many chain restaurants. Hard Rock Café depends heavily on celebrity memorabilia to create its sense of theme. The eatertainment concept of the Rainforest Café is supported with "boulder"-lined walkways, tropical flora, and periodic visits by animatronic creatures from the wild.

Concept can also revolve around a nontheme—an idea, an image, a shape, a pattern, an architectural style, or a central element that pulls together the concept. In Manhattan's classic Four Seasons restaurant, designed by Philip Johnson in 1959, the modern architectural backdrop of the Seagram building, designed by Mies van der Rohe, influenced every aspect of Johnson's cool, clean interior design scheme.

In many popular restaurants, the concept combines a food idea with a design idea. Pick a patriotic name and theme, and it makes good sense to roll out a menu that incorporates regional American cuisine. Similarly, a restaurant called Catch of the Day creates the expectation of a seafood restaurant—although if it sits next to Fenway Park in Boston, the name could imply an after-the-game menu.

Sometimes the food concept is dominant, and design functions as a backdrop for the chef's art. These establishments utilize such devices as partially open kitchens to allow patrons a view of the cooking process. Dining rooms are often designed in neutral palettes that permit the plate presentation to be the main attraction.

In other situations, the design bears no direct relationship to the food concept. For example, a Brazilian barbecue restaurant need not incorporate thematic elements in its design. Rather, the design can work to create an upscale feeling— even though buffet service is employed throughout most of the meal—by incorporating comfortable padded seating, high-quality tableware, and clean architectural elements.

Exterior architecture often becomes an integral component of the concept itself. Historically, elements such as Dairy Queen's gambrel roof, Howard Johnson's orange roof, and the ubiquitous golden arches of McDonald's exemplify architecture as a symbol of the restaurant. Vernacular roadside architecture literally portrays the concept (Figure 1.6).

> Exterior architecture often becomes an integral component of the concept itself. Historically, elements such as Dairy Queen's gambrel roof, Howard Johnson's orange roof, and the ubiquitous golden arches of McDonald's exemplify architecture as a symbol of the restaurant.

THE MENU

Menu planning is integral to restaurant development. Depending on the type of restaurant, some chefs and owners say, the entire operation should revolve around the menu.

FIGURE 1.6 *The giant doughnut that sits atop Randy's drive-in in Los Angeles is an iconic symbol that clearly prompts people as they drive past.* (Photo by Regina Baraban.)

However, all too often the menu is not planned in advance of the concept and the design. In fact, the chef is frequently brought on board long after construction is underway. This decision helps limit pre-opening expenses but can cause greater expenditures in the long term because the chef's input can improve both front- and back-of-the-house design; likewise, its absence can lead to subsequent problems.

It also helps if various members of the design team learn something about menu planning. The first fact to consider is that, ultimately, diners mandate what stays on the menu, regardless of restaurant type. Owners, chefs, and foodservice consultants may have a penchant for certain types of foods, but if they do not tailor their preferences to customer demand, the restaurant may soon be out of business. Restaurateurs who believe that they are in the business of educating customers about cuisine will find themselves fighting a long uphill battle. This is why operators often change at least 50 percent of the menu within the first six months of operation and why selecting equipment that affords flexibility in menu planning is important.

Unquestionably, menu offerings affect consumer behavior and affect the decision whether or not to eat at or return to a particular restaurant. Menu changes, albeit costly, can become necessary for many reasons. The menu may not conform to the production or service capabilities of the facility. The restaurateur offering flambé service, for example, may find the ventilation system cannot handle the increased smoke created by tableside preparation. A health-conscious clientele might place an overwhelming demand on the one overworked steamer that cooks seafood and vegetables. Regardless of the reason, a change of menu—and, hence, of kitchen or front-of-the-house design—should always be factored in as a possibility during the planning process.

Food may not be what brings people to a restaurant the first time. The lure might be an eye-catching exterior design, a great media review, or a word-of-mouth recommendation. However, food is, in large measure, what keeps people coming back—and anything that can be done to improve the customer's perception of that food is important. Diners want hot food hot and cold food cold, for example. Anything that gets in the way of this basic goal will lose customers. Servers prancing through the room with uncovered plates of artfully arranged foods may be a great merchandising technique, but it will backfire if the food isn't hot when it arrives at the table.

THE STYLE OF SERVICE

How will the customers be served? Will guests help themselves at buffet tables, queue up in a fast-food line, or be served at the table? Will a combination of service styles be offered such that guests help themselves to some items while servers deliver others? Will full table service be offered? The answers to these questions dictate specific spatial considerations on the design plan.

Tableservice restaurants can have many styles of service: plate, platter, cart, or any combination of the three. Plate service, in which food is plated in the kitchen and then passed over to a waitperson, who serves finished plates to the guest, requires the least amount of tabletop and dining room floor space. Platter service, in which food is assembled on platters and frenched (served onto a waiting dinner plate in front of the diner) requires larger tables and more floor space so that the server can manipulate the platter between the guests. Cart service requires the most space, as the gueridons (service carts) must be moved around the dining room and kept at a safe distance from tables when flambé cooking takes place. When food displays or self-serve stations are incorporated, even more space must be set aside for these elements in the front of the house.

THE SPEED OF SERVICE

Speed of service and turnover rate are closely allied. Fast-food operations, in which customers get their food within a few minutes, have the highest turnover rate—that is, guests occupy a seat for the shortest time. Tables should turn over every fifteen to twenty minutes in fast-food restaurants. In cafeteria operations, customers take more time to get their food and the turnover rate is a bit slower: 15 to 30 minutes. The tableservice dining experience, especially at a fine restaurant where dishes cooked to order, is the lengthiest; customers wait the longest for their food and spend the most time eating it. Turnover can range from about thirty minutes in a roadside diner to four hours in a gourmet establishment.

The amount of time a customer spends in a restaurant—both in getting food and in eating it—has design implications for both the front and back of the house. If customers are expected to dine on gourmet fare for an hour or more, then comfortable seating, such as upholstered armchairs, and an à la carte kitchen are in order. Conversely, if faster turnover is desired, then hard-surfaced chairs will help move guests out of the dining space as quickly as possible. Furthermore, the kitchen must be laid out and fitted with equipment that speeds the preparation and service of food to the guests.

The type of point-of-sale (POS) system can markedly affect a restaurant's turnover rate. For many years, servers scribbled customer orders on an order pad. They then walked to the kitchen to place the order and periodically checked back to see if their items were ready for service. At the end of the meal, settling the account was often left to a single cashier who added the value of the foods served, then handled the closing transaction.

With today's POS systems, the process is significantly streamlined. Order-entry stations located throughout the dining area enable servers to place an order without traveling to the kitchen (Figure 1.7). The entries are significantly easier

FIGURE 1.7 *Order-entry stations can be an eyesore, but here the system is integrated with the design so that it does not detract from the rest of the decor.* (Photo by Joseph Durocher.)

for the kitchen staff to read—which, in turn, shortens the time it takes to prepare an order and decreases the chances of mistakes. With the most sophisticated POS systems, pop-up menus mandate servers to include all the information needed to complete an order, like the degree of doneness, choice of accompanying side dishes, or the type of salad dressing.

To speed order entry even more, the automated process can be brought to tableside. The most popular system includes a server-operated order-entry pad that transmits the order directly to the kitchen. Some restaurateurs have even placed order-entry units in the hands of guests. As the cost of these decentralized systems drops, more restaurateurs will incorporate them into their restaurants when high turnover rates are desired, thus increasing space in the front of the house.

Speed of service is too often overlooked in the planning process. In one case, a group of owners, new to the restaurant business, approached the development of their pro forma statement without considering speed of service. They began with the following information:

Menu: continental
Style of service: leisurely plate and cart service
Number of seats: 235
Lunch turns: two per day
Dinner turns: five per day

Based on their projected fixed expenses, the owners determined that they would need $74,000 per day in revenues. To achieve this, they calculated a per-check average by dividing the total daily sales by the total number of customers served:

$$\frac{\$74,000 \text{ required daily revenues}}{\# \text{ of lunch covers} + \# \text{ of dinner covers}}$$

The resulting $45 check average was considered appropriate for this type of operation, and thus the project proceeded.

Neglecting to consider speed of service caused grave problems, however, because the restaurant could not meet the projected turnover rates and provide the leisurely dining experience expected with a $45 check average. In other words, to meet the projected turnover rates, either the tables would have to be turned in less than an hour, or the total serving time for lunches would have to stretch over 4 hours and for dinners, over 10 hours. Management had failed to recognize the amount of dining time necessary in this type of establishment.

THE PER-CUSTOMER CHECK AVERAGE

It is essential to consider the check average in concert with the other elements that contribute to the design concept. Here are two questions that need to be addressed:

1. *Will a low check average dictate more turnover and thus a sturdy, low-maintenance design?*

Low-priced menus usually lead to higher customer counts, creating the need for fast turnover. However, this must be considered in the context of the market. For example, an inexpensive fast-food operation might work nicely when located next to an industrial park where employees from various companies take half-hour lunch breaks that stretch over a two and a half hours. But if the fast-food operation sits next to a single manufacturing plant where the production line shuts down completely and everyone gets one hour for lunch, the chance of realizing multiple turns is minimal.

Where multiple turns are forecasted, durable, low-maintenance design makes sense because of the potentially high volume of business. Where only one turn is projected, a low-cost design package is critical because the revenue stream cannot support a high-capital budget.

2. *Is the cost of capital low enough to cost justify the high design costs associated with high check averages?*

When the cost of capital is low, it is easier to cost justify building a large, upscale restaurant with more expensive menu items. Low capital costs also make it possible to upgrade the design without having to increase check averages.

The cost of the meal carries with it design expectations in the mind of the customer. People don't expect a $4.50 meal tab in a luxurious environment replete with rich materials, nor do they expect to pay dearly for fine cuisine in a room that looks like a 1950s diner. Check average and speed of service must be carefully monitored and matched for successful results.

THE GENERAL AMBIENCE

Before arriving at specific design solutions, define the type of atmosphere desired for a given restaurant. How should the customer *feel* in the space? Energized, ebullient, ready to eat and move on? Relaxed, at ease, comfortable enough to linger for hours? Stimulated? Cheerful? Nostalgic? Serene? Pampered? Protected? On display?

Obviously, different types of restaurants evoke different types of feelings. The feeling of dining in a homey neighborhood coffee shop differs from the feeling of dining in a highly contemporary corporate cafeteria, a gourmet establishment, or a theatrical grand café. These feelings are a function not only of food and service but also of interior design and architecture.

THE MANAGEMENT PHILOSOPHY

Management philosophy helps dictate design philosophy. In the case of the fast-food chain restaurant, for instance, the philosophy of corporate-level management is to maximize profits for the shareholders, who are looking forward to the next quarterly report. Here, design often represents a minimal investment. It tends to be pragmatic, derivative, and safe. On the other hand, the entrepreneur looking to attract a young, sophisticated clientele may take a chance on innovative design and architecture. The restaurateur looking for the long-term growth of business may invest most of all in the hope of creating a classic design statement.

For some owners, the throwaway restaurant is appealing. These are people looking to get into the business for a minimal investment, reap the revenues that often accompany a newly opened restaurant, then get out before the bottom line crashes. They then take their money and invest it in a continuing series of new, short-term restaurants.

THE BUDGET

The budget is nearly always a limiting factor in the design of a restaurant. A big design budget is only as big as the market will bear, and not even the best-financed project can afford wasted design dollars. However, adherence to a tight budget means little if the dining room looks ruined after two weeks of operation or if management can't afford proper maintenance procedures.

Budgetary planning has inherent contradictions. Every owner wants to stretch design dollars as far as possible and not go broke before opening day. A restaurant is, after all, a business. However, modern consumers, many with a mindset hungry for new visual sensations, increasingly view design as part of the value equation that they expect from their restaurant experience.

Market demographics and psychographics influence how best to allocate design dollars. For example, the huge generation of baby boomers spends lots of discretionary dollars dining out. They want stylish design but are dealing with decreased vision and other physical limitations of the aging process. The high-ceilinged, hard-surfaced rooms that created energy and excitement in the 1980s annoyed boomers in the 1990s because they had difficulty hearing conversations at their table over the din of the room. Similarly, dimly lit restaurants are annoying for people over forty because it is hard, if not impossible, to read the menu—particularly if vanity prevents them from donning a pair of glasses. What this means for the budget is that restaurateurs who target baby boomers have to allocate enough money for proper lighting and acoustics.

The main problem with budgeting is that design is expensive. Further, good architecture takes time, and time is money. Of course, design is a relatively unimportant backdrop for food and service in some successful restaurants, and the charm of other totally undesigned bistros stems from their visual chaos. Such successes, however, are rare. Even simple interiors and rooms that appear to reflect timeworn patinas have often been designed—for a fee. Likewise, kitchen design is no free lunch, but back-of-the-house design dollars can buy a back-of-the-house layout that increases productivity and efficiency.

The costs of front- and back-of-the-house design vary wildly with location, type of restaurant, intended lifespan, and other factors. Basically, the owner pays for both goods and for services. Goods translate into furniture, fixtures, and equipment (FF&E). Services include fees for the schematic design concept, as presented in floorplans, elevations, renderings, and other architectural plans. Services also include the writing of FF&E specifications but not necessarily purchasing. Some design firms prefer to remain purely service oriented and leave the procurement and installation process to purchasing agents.

> There is no uniform method of charging for design services. The design firm's fee may be based on square-foot costs, a percentage of total project costs, a consulting fee at hourly rates, or other methods.

There is no uniform method of charging for design services. The design firm's fee may be based on square-foot costs, a percentage of total project costs, a consulting fee at hourly rates, or other methods. Many variables influence fee structures but, as a rule of thumb, most firms charge a fixed fee based on the scope of the job and on the total project cost.

Some firms that provide purchasing services charge a percentage markup based on FF&E prices. Owners should beware of design thrown in "free" by equipment or purchasing houses whose profit comes from markups. The motivation may be to overequip the space in an effort to increase the markup profits.

Budget planning must begin in the early stages of the design process. The owner should develop an initial budget as a guide and agree on a final budget before any design contract is finalized. As the project progresses, the budget must be carefully monitored. Projects always have hidden costs, and renovation often presents more expensive surprises than new construction. In truth, any number of factors may drive up the costs of one or more elements of the construction budget, so contingency dollars should be built in.

A crucial aspect of budgetary control is how design dollars are allocated. Adding one dramatic design treatment in an otherwise simple room, for example, can elevate an ordinary interior to something special. However, other design elements may hike the design budget considerably but have little impact on customers.

The best practice is to invest money where one gets the biggest bang for the buck and to spend the most on items that customers come in contact with. Good design doesn't always mean expensive design, but fine furniture and finishes cost money. Applications like faux finishes can help control costs but, in an upscale restaurant, it is advisable to mix faux with fine finishes to create a balance. Sometimes it costs less to hire a muralist or furniture maker to create custom applications than it does to purchase fine art or furniture.

A good designer knows how to prioritize and how to take from one area and give to another in order to adhere to the total FF&E budget. If surprises raise costs so high that the budget needs to be adjusted, the designer should inform the owner immediately. There's no excuse for running out of money midway through a project.

The Systems Approach:
Market Segments versus Service Systems

Restaurants can be classified in many ways. Historically, classifications are based on check average, theme, type of cuisine, or market segment. Segmentation by market (Table 1.1) or food category (Table 1.2) is the most frequently used means of classifying restaurants in the foodservice industry. Schools, employee feeding, hospitals, colleges and universities, military, and nursing homes are market descriptors that together are considered institutional or noncommercial foodservice. The primary mission of foodservice operations in these venues is to feed in-house diners such as students or hospital staff. Commercial foodservice includes such restaurant types as fast food, fine dining, and coffee shops. Other market references can include such categories as Mexican, sandwich, pizza, or chicken restaurants.

However, these classification methods do not really describe the type of foodservice offered in a given operation. Elementary school foodservice, for example, could consist of the standard straight-line cafeteria, a scatter system of individual food stations where students help themselves, or a fast-food system such as McDonald's. Each of these types has different design implications, and the term *elementary school foodservice* does not give a clear picture of the operation.

On the other hand, the nontraditional classification presented here—based on service systems rather than market segments—is a process-oriented approach that can lead to successful restaurant and kitchen design. (Table 1.3)

Using the service system classification, the designer can accurately identify styles of service and types of food delivery systems. If, in the above example, the school board calls in a designer and says, "We want to put a foodservice operation in our new elementary school," then the designer has little insight into the characteristics of the design. If, however, the board says, "We want a fast-food operation in our new elementary school," the designer has a well-established frame of reference to help determine which type of food delivery system is optimal. Similarly, the designer doesn't have much to go on if a restaurateur says, "I want to open a steakhouse." The designer knows more if the restaurateur says, "I want to open an à la carte service restaurant with a steakhouse menu, salads prepared at tableside, and a buffet-style dessert bar."

TABLE 1.1

Market Segments

- Full-service restaurants
- Fast-food restaurants
- Elementary and secondary schools
- Employee feeding
- Hospitals
- Hotels and motels
- Colleges and universities
- Military
- Recreation facilities
- Convenience and grocery stores
- Nursing homes
- Transportation
- Retail stores

TABLE 1.2

Food Categories

- Asian
- Chicken
- French
- Italian
- Latin American
- Mexican
- Middle Eastern
- Pizza
- Sandwich
- Seafood
- Steakhouse
- All other food categories

TABLE 1.3

Service Systems

- À la carte
- Tableside
- Fast food
- Banquet
- Family style
- Buffet
- Take-out
- Delivery
- Cafeteria
- Tray
- Machine
- Satellite system
- All other service systems

The term *service system* is loosely defined as the means by which food is prepared and delivered to the customer. At times, a foodservice operation combines more than one service system. A hotel, for example, may have à la carte service in a gourmet restaurant, banquet service in a ballroom, and cafeteria service in an employee cafeteria. This is called a *complex service system*. Each of these service systems needs its own set of subsystems to back it up. Subsystems include such functions as purchasing, fabrication, preparation, and assembly, to name a few. The functions performed and the layout of the subsystems vary with the type of service system or systems in a particular operation.

An understanding of each of the service systems is important because subsystem design flows from them.

À LA CARTE

In à la carte service, a waitperson takes orders from individual customers and presents them to the chef for preparation. For the most part, the preparation is done to order and, in every case, the food is plated specifically for a particular customer. À la carte service is frequently found in upscale restaurants, executive dining rooms, hotels, coffee shops, and other full-service operations. (It is sometimes referred to as *table service*, which does not convey information adequate to developing an effective design scheme.)

In à la carte service restaurants, POS systems positioned throughout the front of the house speed the order-entry process, and kitchen and bar printers enable servers to place their orders without leaving the dining room. In the kitchen, high heat and quick cooking equipment—like charbroilers and flattop ranges—are needed to support the cooking of sautéed, broiled, or fried individual portions of food. In addition, a steam table is needed to hold foods and sauces prepared in bulk.

BANQUET

Banquet-style service involves a predetermined menu that is usually prepared and plated en masse. Payment for the meal is arranged in advance. Tangential activities, such as speeches or entertainment, often occur during the banquet service period, and these activities may necessitate modifying the service time of various courses. In some instances, the starter course may be preset on the tables. Service of subsequent courses does not usually proceed until all customers have finished the previous course. Banquet service is offered through the catering departments of full-service restaurants, noncommercial feeders, and hotels as well as in catering facilities.

Bulk food production equipment is typically found in a banquet kitchen. This type of kitchen can benefit from mechanized food prepreparation equipment. Walk-in refrigeration is important to hold raw foods and cold plated foods that are ready for service. Heated holding equipment is required for holding plated hot foods. In large banquet operations, heated carts are positioned around the banquet serving area before the course is served in order to speed service. Warewashing equipment dedicated solely to banquet operations is frequently incorporated into complex food service operations.

BUFFET

In buffet service, customers typically serve themselves unlimited portions of a number of items. In some cases, servers may assist in the portioning for control reasons. Buffets can be either in a straight line or in a scramble configuration. In the straight line, customers proceed in a logical flow from the beginning to the end of the line. In the scramble system, customers approach the buffet at random points. Buffet service is typically used for complete meal service in hotel restaurants, especially for Sunday brunch. It is often found in the form of a salad bar in full-service restaurants and noncommercial dining facilities.

Some buffets incorporate stations where foods are prepared to order or in small batches. This approach usually requires special cooking equipment—for example, a gas- or alcohol-fired rechaud. A growing number of restaurateurs use induction cooktops for safety and convenience.

CAFETERIA

Cafeteria service differs from buffet service in that customers select premeasured portions. In some cases, the foods are portioned and displayed for pickup;

in others, such as with hot foods, the items are portioned by a server as requested. Diners assemble food and utensils on a tray. Cafeteria flow is generally cold items first, hot food items second, and beverages last. Whether the layout is a straight line or a scramble system, this type of service is the backbone of noncommercial foodservice and is often combined with a buffet-style salad bar.

Cafeterias work most effectively with a high volume of traffic. In the kitchen, volume production and holding equipment is necessary. Cafeteria operations frequently feature lower-priced food items in sauces, so equipment such as tilting fry kettles, steam-jacketed kettles, and deck ovens are often found in cafeteria kitchens. In the front of the house, the steam table and warming cabinets are essential design elements.

FAMILY STYLE

Family-style service occurs when food is brought to the table on platters, which are placed directly on the table for self-service. This style is seen in full-service establishments. Chinese restaurants, in particular, favor family-style service. Designers find that extra tabletop space is needed to hold the multiple dishes involved.

Another example of family-style service is a shared platter of nachos or fajita fixings in a Mexican restaurant. These platters also need additional heated holding space in the kitchen. In some instances, their sizzling creates a great deal of noise as they are brought to the table. The theater and aroma can be a great merchandiser, but smell and grease must be considered when planning the ventilation system. For safety reasons, a sufficiently large base to hold the sizzle platter must be chosen, and extra space on the tabletop is essential.

DELIVERY

Delivery service relies heavily on telephone orders, with an increasing number of restaurateurs accepting delivery orders via the Internet. Prepared food is delivered to customers via bicycle in urban areas and motor vehicle in suburban areas. The success of delivery systems depends on population density sufficient to warrant the transportation costs. Delivery service systems are typically matched with take-out systems in a chairless storefront operation and combined with tray service in hospitals, hotels, and nursing homes. Sturdy, leakproof, insulated packaging is important to delivery operations, as is heat-retention equipment that works well with the chosen delivery vehicle.

From a design perspective, the restaurant must have a comprehensive telephone ordering system that maintains customer's files. With the help of caller ID, a customer's past purchase records, address, and phone number are displayed when the order taker begins processing the order. The optimal system allows customers to charge their orders, thus eliminating the need for delivery persons to carry a large amount of cash. On the production side, menu items must be quick to prepare, and the cooking equipment must be capable of cooking foods rapidly and consistently, with little attention from the kitchen staff.

> Sturdy, leakproof, insulated packaging is important to delivery operations, as is heat-retention equipment that works well with the chosen delivery vehicle.

FAST FOOD

Think of fast food as a style of service in which customers queue up in either a number of lines or one serpentine line to place their food orders. Typically, the counter worker takes the order, assembles the food, and receives the payment. This style of service is further characterized by quick service and the use of disposables. Fast-food service can be found in chain and independent operations, elementary and secondary schools, employee feeding, hospitals, colleges and universities, the military, and recreational facilities.

Most fast feeders batch-prepare foods. Warming equipment that maintains the quality of the prepared foods plays an important role in the kitchen. Many items are partially prepared and then custom finished when ordered. Freezer storage is critical, along with oversized dry storage to hold large supplies of disposables. Dumpster space is essential to hold the large volume of trash generated.

The front of the house needs enough space for customers to queue up and place their orders. Behind the order counter, space needs vary. In some cases, the order taker must handle cash as well as assemble orders. In other restaurants, different people handle cash and order assembly.

MACHINE SERVICE

Machine service refers to coin-operated vending, in which a limited assortment of preportioned or mechanically portioned food or beverages can be obtained at any time. Staffing is required only to fill and clean the machines.

Equipment and product security are important design concerns for this type of operation. If a dining area is provided, it must incorporate low maintenance, highly durable tables and chairs, and dispensers for napkins, plasticware, and condiments.

SATELLITE SYSTEM

In a satellite system, foods are prepared in bulk at one kitchen (called a *commissary*), then transported to finishing kitchens and assembled for service at those sites. This style of service is most commonly found in schools and healthcare facilities, although such operations as Domino's Pizza prepare rounds of dough in a commissary, truck it to satellite stores, and turn it into pizza there. In addition, some full-service restaurants with many points of sale utilize satellite systems because of the economies and control available through a commissary kitchen.

Volume production equipment is required in the production areas of a satellite operation. If foods are to be transported chilled, special tumble chillers or blast chillers are needed to quickly cool cooked foods. Walk-in refrigerated space is essential for holding foods ready for distribution. Transportation equipment, whether to in-house service points or distant points, must be considered as an integral part of the overall system design.

TABLESIDE

The key element in tableside service is the preparation or assembly of foods at tableside on a gueridon (cart). Food is brought from the kitchen and placed on the gueridon, where it is finished, plated, and served or actually cooked at tableside. When foods are brought to the cart for cooking, a heating element (rechaud) must be added to the cart. Tableside service is most commonly used in gourmet establishments although, in recent years, it has declined in popularity. Most often, tableside service combines with à la carte service, with one or two special tableside menu items, such as a Caesar salad or a flaming dessert, actually being prepared at tableside.

From a design perspective, one must consider special features in both the front and back of the house. In the front, a dining room with multiple levels will not work as smoothly as one on a single level because it limits the movement of carts. The ventilation system must also be sufficiently upsized to remove the extra smoke and smells of tableside cooking.

The coordination of foods prepared à la carte and foods prepared at tableside is essential. In the kitchen, foods must be prepared quickly and held until the tableside preparations are ready for service. One of the keys to successful tableside service is to measure and assemble all of the ingredients before servers take them to the dining room. This mise en place ("everything in its place") requires additional refrigerated storage space in the kitchen.

Home meal replacement is an increasingly popular and profitable foodservice system, particularly when combined with other styles of service in full-service restaurants.

TAKE-OUT

Take-out service relies on disposable packaging that is heat stable and leakproof. Food is either batch-prepared and then packaged, or prepared to order and packaged as it comes off the fire. Food may be packaged in a partially cooked or raw state for completion at home. That usually means cooking in a microwave oven, although an increasing number of dishes are intended for heating in a conventional oven.

On the design side, seating is not required for take-out, but sufficient space is needed for customers to wait for their food. Take-out service is an integral part of many fast-food restaurants and represents most of the food sales in the convenience and grocery store market segment. Reach-in refrigerators that hold bottled and canned drinks add to the check average, as do snack items, which should be displayed for impulse purchasing near the cash register.

Home meal replacement (HMR) is an increasingly popular and profitable foodservice system, particularly when combined with other styles of service in full-service restaurants. The market research firm Salomon Smith Barney predicts that this market segment could grow at an annualized rate of 12 to 13 percent to $150 billion per year by 2005. HMR offers customers a more traditional meal than pure take-out usually does, such as an entrée, starch, and vegetable on one plate. Foods are typically batch-prepared. While some HMR consists of plated meals, many services offer customers the option to choose from an assortment of batch-prepared foods displayed in a steam table or in a glass-fronted deli display case (Figure 1.8). To maximize sales, HMR outlets may also offer desserts, beverages, and appetizers to accompany a main course.

Pure HMR outlets typically open with great flourish, garner a high customer count, and then stagnate. The most successful HMR offerings appear to be those that are integrated into tableservice restaurants. In this service system combination, one of the most important design considerations is creating a traffic flow that keeps take-out customers separate from the restaurant operation.

Food packaging design is vital for both take-out and HMR service. The packaging must be leakproof and capable of withstanding reheating temperatures. Both food packaging and carryout bags should be imprinted with the logo of the restaurant and contact information.

FIGURE 1.8 *HMR depends on visual appeal to sell food. Here, the deli display cases and soup crocks help merchandise preprepared foods. Foods in the display case are portioned by staff, while the soups are portioned by customers.* (Photo by Joseph Durocher.)

TRAY SERVICE

Tray service involves the delivery of preordered, fully assembled meals. Temperature maintenance systems are often incorporated with the tray or delivery cart in order to keep hot foods at proper serving temperatures from the time of assembly to the time of service. In other cases, hot foods are rethermalized just prior to service. This style of service is employed in hospitals, hotels, nursing homes, and airliners.

Hospitals, nursing homes, and airplanes are typically supported with tray service provided by a high-volume kitchen fitted with equipment capable of preparing foods in large batches. Tray assembly areas take up a great deal of space in such operations, and more floor space is needed to store carts and extra trayware. In hotels, much tray-service food is prepared on the hotel restaurant equipment, but a great deal of space may be needed to store room-service carts.

Subsystems

Each of the service systems just discussed are supported by numerous subsystems. One way to picture the process is to think of the service system as a wheel and the subsystems as its spokes (Figure 1.9). Every wheel (service system) encompasses some or all of the following spokes (subsystems): purchasing, receiving, storage, fabrication, prepreparation, preparation, holding, assembly, sanitation, accounting, and support stations. The layout and design of each of these subsystems relates to the chosen system or systems found in the restaurant.

PURCHASING AND RECEIVING

The nature of purchasing and receiving food affects restaurant layout. Numerous factors must be considered before arriving at spatial allocations for loading docks and receiving offices. Here are some questions to consider:

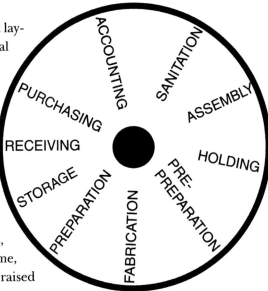

FIGURE 1.9 *The subsystem wheel depicts each of the functional areas needed to support any type of service system.*

1. *Will the food be purchased from many suppliers, all of which require time at a loading dock, or through a one-stop-shopping distributor?*

When purchases are placed with a one-stop-shopping vendor, most food items arrive on a single truck, so delivery vehicles need not vie for a spot at the delivery dock. With multiple vendors, a small loading dock can become a choke point during delivery time, when trucks queue up to deliver supplies. For large operations, a raised loading dock—ideally, fitted with a height-adjustable loading ramp—can speed the delivery of large loads if they are delivered by vehicles with high tailgates. Investigate the type of delivery trucks used by local vendors for guidance in designing the loading dock and access area. For example, if deliveries are made in a panel truck, the traffic circulation requirements are different than if deliveries are made in eighteen-wheelers.

2. *Will purchases arrive as individual cases or on a pallet?*

In some large-volume operations, pallets move directly from the receiving dock to the production areas, with no intermediate stop in the storeroom. An adjustable loading ramp or lift is essential when foods arrive on pallets. In smaller restaurants, foods arriving in single cases typically are moved to a storage area accessible to the receiving area.

3. *Will food and supplies be purchased through a company commissary?*

Many chain restaurants coordinate purchasing functions through a central purchasing office. If the "purchased" food and supplies come from a company commissary, the purchasing function—and the size of the purchasing offices—can be minimized.

4. *Will separate offices be needed for purchasing and receiving?*

Purchasing and receiving should be performed by different persons for purposes of internal control. Therefore, it often makes sense to physically separate the spaces where the functions are performed.

5. *Will purchases be made online or will distributor sales representatives (DSRs) visit the operation to take orders?*

Online purchasing requires access to the internet and a secured area for computer equipment. If DSRs drop by to take orders, the purchasing manager must have space in which to meet with them.

The amount of space required for purchasing can vary dramatically. Ideally, the purchasing area will include space to maintain records on purchases and store samples of the tableware, flatware, and glassware used in the various service areas.

STORAGE

In order to design successful storage subsystems, the designer must understand the purchasing and issuing policy of the house because these practices will affect the location, size, and type of storage spaces as well as their access requirements. The volume of business has a direct impact on the amount of space needed for storage. Equally important is the frequency of delivery. If deliveries arrive daily, the storage spaces can be significantly smaller than if deliveries arrive weekly.

Another consideration is the relative mix of dry goods, refrigerated foods, and frozen foods. Some types of operations use far more canned goods than others. Some may rely heavily on fresh foods, with little use of canned or frozen. All of these decisions have design implications. Here are additional questions to consider:

1. *Will cooks work from open storage?*

When storage areas are always accessible, cooks do not have to wait to obtain the ingredients or supplies that they need. However, from a design perspective, it is essential that the open storage adjoin the production areas so that cooks need not waste time moving between spaces. Security is a major concern with open storerooms, so entrances to storage areas should not open onto the back loading dock or be located close to employee locker rooms.

2. *Will cooks have a par stock of some ingredients issued to their work areas, with special items drawn as needed from the storage areas?*

This type of policy ensures that a par level of items like spices, salt, sugar, and other commonly used ingredients is maintained at the point of use in the kitchen. Expensive ingredients, or ingredients used for a particular preparation, are drawn from a controlled storage space. In some instances, a cage is installed in a walk-in to hold such items as alcohol, caviar, smoked salmon, and truffles.

3. *Will a storeroom manager assemble the primary ingredients for the cooks?*

This policy keeps the cooks out of the storage areas except when they pick up a cart loaded with ingredients for a particular meal. In such cases, the primary storage areas need not adjoin the preparation areas.

4. *Does the potential exist for exterior walk-in refrigeration?*

Walk-in refrigerators and freezers, when equipped with adequate locking equipment, are secure spaces that need not be located inside the restaurant building. When fitted with a weather cap, these exterior refrigerated spaces can help to minimize building costs. In some cases, a walk-in can be positioned so that its access door connects through an exterior wall of the restaurant.

5. *Will deliveries arrive at times when the restaurant is not staffed?*

If the answer is yes, a receiving space with an exterior and interior access door will allow deliveries to be made securely. This space needs to be planned at the same time as the receiving area. If an exterior walk-in is available, it can be fitted with an exterior door and a cage to allow for off-hour deliveries.

FABRICATION

Few restaurants today, unlike in the past, have fabrication areas, but gourmet establishments often incorporate seafood or bakeshop fabrication subsystems. These subsystems include those areas where food is first handled, or placed into process, prior to the preparation stage. In classical kitchens, before the advent of preportioned meats, fish, and poultry, fabrication areas were commonly used to break down primal cuts of meat; in effect, the kitchen included a butcher shop.

Fabrication areas have become particularly important for large operations located in high-rise buildings. Follow the delivery of lettuce as an example: Several cases of lettuce are delivered to a ground-floor loading dock. The lettuce is then moved to a ground-floor fabrication area, where the heads are unpacked, washed, and stored in large containers for subsequent distribution to upper-level preparation areas. Without the fabrication subsystem, the cases of lettuce would be delivered upstairs for handling, then the empty cartons and wrapper leaves sent back to the ground floor for disposal. The fabrication area helps streamline the process and cut back on vertical transportation costs. Here are some questions to ask:

1. *What items will be fabricated on site?*

In many cases, fabrication is limited to protein items like beef or fish. Cryovac and other packaging materials mean that portioned steaks and roasts are available without on-premise fabrication. However, cutting steaks or filets from whole fish close to the time of service is still one of the best ways to ensure high quality.

2. *Will a separate fabrication area be needed, or will the function be performed in the same space used for prepreparation?*

If the spaces are to be shared, most of the fabrication will have to be done during hours when the preparation crew is not working.

Cutting strip loins and other wholesale cuts into steaks in a display fabrication area is an integral part of the merchandising process in some steakhouses. In other restaurants, a glass-walled refrigerated room allows diners to view the meat-grinding and burger-forming process; passersby can view thousands of pounds of rib roasts and strip loins in an aging refrigerator through a window that opens onto the street.

PREPREPARATION

In the prepreparation subsystem, foods are made ready for the final phase of preparation. For example, prepreparation may include breaking the lettuce into salad-sized pieces and storing it in containers until ready for assembly in salad bowls. Prepreparation may be the mise-en-place work that is done for tableside flambé preparations. Prepreparation may also include mixing—and, in some cases, rolling out—piecrust that will be used to top made-to-order chicken potpies. A carefully planned prepreparation area can speed final preparation in an à la carte kitchen and improve overall productivity in any kitchen. Before this space is designed, the answers to the following questions are needed:

1. *Has enough space been allocated to prepare vegetables separately from protein foods?*

Whenever possible, the sinks used to wash lettuce and vegetables should be separate from those used to defrost meat, scale fish, or in which the ice from a crate of chicken melts. The concern is cross-contamination. Salad and vegetable ingredients that are eaten raw can easily be contaminated and cause food poisoning if prepared on improperly sanitized surfaces previously used for meat, fish, or poultry.

2. *Will prepreparation be manual or mechanical?*

Mechanized equipment can be cost-justified if it saves a sufficient amount of food and labor costs, or if it saves space. For example, a vertical cutter-mixer can produce hundreds of gallons of emulsified house salad dressings in one hour. The per-gallon cost for raw materials is far below that of brand-name dressings. Another example is a floor mixer that can quickly and evenly mix ingredients for meatloaf. A 30-pound batch of ingredients would take 10 to 15 minutes to mix by hand but only 60 seconds with a mixer. Additionally, the mixed ingredients can be put back under refrigeration or in the oven quickly, so there is less time for bacteria to develop than if they were prepared by hand.

3. *Will prepreparation for several kitchens or stations take place in a given area?*

Centralizing the prepreparation of numerous items can save time and space needs in the preparation areas. For example, the hot foods and salad stations might each need 30 pounds of peeled potatoes per shift. If the potatoes are peeled at a single station, an automated potato peeler might be justified.

PREPARATION

The preparation subsystem (also called *production*) involves the final cooking or assembly of food (Figure 1.10). Every kitchen has a cold food preparation area and a hot food preparation area, so *preparation area* may refer to the place where the preprepared salad ingredients are portioned onto the salad plates or the cooking station where the marinated ribs are broiled.

This subsystem can also extend into the dining room when foods are cooked at tableside or on a buffet table, but design may not be easy. For example, the foodservice manager who decides to offer made-to-order omelets on the breakfast buffet may encounter insurmountable limitations due to an inadequate electrical supply. Similarly, the visual appeal of an open kitchen production area may be hampered by poor ventilation systems. Here are but a few of the questions that must be asked when planning preparation areas:

FIGURE 1.1
is the step
preprepare
are assem
the hot foo
cooked for
this à la co
the equipm
cooking.
(Photo by Jos

1. *What's the menu?*

Nothing affects the design of preparation areas more than the menu.

2. *Will any of the preparation areas be in view of customers?*

The answer to this question will influence the type of equipment that should be chosen, particularly the exterior finish of the equipment. Display kitchens must also incorporate hidden garbage containers and have surfaces that are easy to clean.

3. *How many preparation areas will there be?*

A simple foodservice system typically includes only a cold food and a hot food preparation area. However, in a more complex system, one might find a bakeshop, banquet preparation, take-out preparation, and more.

HOLDING

Once cooked, food items may be held awaiting service. Some foods must be refrigerated and others heated. Holding areas are often divided into two sections: holding for food prior to plating, and holding for plated dishes. Consider a banquet for which 400 boneless Cornish game hens are roasted. A holding cart is needed to hold the hens before they are plated. The holding cart is also used to hold the dauphine potatoes and medley of vegetables that will be plated with the hens. The sauce used as a bed under the hen must also be held. This holding cabinet is positioned at one end of the assembly line, while four carts capable of holding 100 covered plates each are positioned near the other end. In this example, the holding carts are perfectly suited to a banquet-style serving system.

Each service systems requires its own custom holding configurations. These questions must be answered when planning for holding:

1. *What styles of service will be employed?*

As seen in the banquet scenario above, five large holding carts are needed to support a banquet for 400. For fast-food, à la carte, satellite, and other systems, different holding equipment are required.

2. *What is the maximum number of meal components that need to be held at one point in time?*

If the maximum number of banquet meals is 400, then five carts should be sufficient. In a fast-food burger operation, the holding areas must be sized to hold the maximum number of burgers and fries needed during peak service periods.

ASSEMBLY

Once cooked, foods need to be plated or assembled for plating. In an à la carte operation, the assembly subsystem is adjacent to the preparation and holding areas. The steaks come off the broiler and go directly onto the plate and out

to the customer (Figure 1.11). In a cafeteria or buffet operation, many foods are prepared and delivered in bulk to the assembly area located behind the serving line, then individually plated for the diner.

Here, too, it is important to identify the style of service. Banquet service requires a large area where loaded plates and pans can be laid out and foods can be plated in an assembly-line fashion. Often, mobile carts are used for banquet plating, then placed in storage during nonplating times. In à la carte service, the prime menu ingredient may come off a broiler and combined with accompaniments that were batch-prepared and held in a steam table. In this case, each meal is plated individually, so, the assembly area for an à la carte area will be much smaller than in the banquet operation.

FIGURE 1.11 *The pickup area of the kitchen shown here, next to the assembly area, is where foods are often held under heat strips awaiting pick-up by servers. The circulation in front of the pickup station affords staff the space to assemble all of the items needed to serve each course.* (Photo by Joseph Durocher.)

SANITATION AND SAFETY

Warewashing, pot- and panwashing, and interim and after-hours cleaning are part of the sanitation subsystem. Sanitation is frequently overlooked in restaurant design. Hand sinks, soap, and adequate hand drying must be easily accessible to all employees. Storage for mops, buckets, and cleaning supplies should be kept separate from food supply storage. A slop sink is essential, or floor mops will be cleaned out in the same sink used for washing greens. In addition, the decision to specify an expensive conveyor dishwasher or a more moderately priced rack machine should be based on a careful analysis of the type of operation.

Safety must be thought of in terms of food, employees, and physical structure. Food safety frequently intersects with sanitation. Employee safety addresses equipment issues and prophylactic measures that decrease the chances of physical injury. Physical structure safety includes fire detection and suppression along with ventilation. Consider these questions:

1. *How many preparation areas are planned?*

At a minimum, one hand sink is needed for each workstation. Don't forget that front-of-the-house service areas may also need a hand sink.

2. *Will protein foods arrive as preportioned frozen or fresh?*

Frozen items often need little or no handling before they are placed into preparation. However, fresh items frequently must be processed to get them ready for preparation. In such cases, equipment and supplies to sanitize an area are essential. Color-coded cutting boards help minimize the chance of cross-contamination when protein foods are fabricated on site.

3. *Will the cooking equipment be clustered in one area, or will foods be cooked in several locations throughout the restaurant?*

If the cooking equipment is grouped together, then the ventilation and fire suppression configuration is quite straightforward. If several cooking stations are physically separated, the ductwork and fire suppression connections can look like a plate of spaghetti above the ceiling tiles.

ACCOUNTING

Accounting subsystems, typically comprising cash and credit control devices, must be carefully integrated with the design of the operation. Consideration should be given to the number and placement of credit card imprinters and other credit card paraphernalia, cash registers, and order-relay devices. These should be chosen based on the needs of the particular restaurant operation. Too often, sophisticated and expensive accounting subsystems are specified for small restaurants that actually need a less elaborate scheme. Sometimes this equipment becomes an unsightly and noisy intrusion on the dining experience. Here are a few accounting questions to consider:

1. *Which stations will get order printers?*

Order printers ensure that production stations receive orders as quickly as possible. They also provide an important internal control service. Designers should ensure that cabling is run from the order-entry units to the remote printers.

FIGURE 1.12 *Mobile service stations can be moved to the back of the house for resupply, then placed conveniently in the front of the house to speed service.*
(Photo by Joseph Durocher.)

2. *How many order-entry stations will be needed?*

This information suggests the number of front-of-the-house service stations to plan for. If servers work from a cash-and-carry system, a cash drawer will be needed for the head cashier only.

SUPPORT STATIONS

Support stations are too often neglected or underdesigned, particularly in full-service restaurants and banquet spaces. This is an extremely important subsystem for both front and back of the house. In the kitchen, support stations may include all areas located near food pickup where the waitstaff obtain such items as serving trays and soupspoons. If this function is overlooked in design, waiters will run around the kitchen trying to find a tray—while the plated foods are getting cold—and then serve a teaspoon with the soup.

In the dining room, support stations are typically used to store extra silverware, glassware, and other tabletop accessories. Without them, waiters have to travel back and forth from the kitchen to set and reset the tables. In addition, if a guest drops a utensil or is served a dirty utensil, the support station provides a quick replacement (Figure 1.12).

In fast-food operations, the trash bins where customers deposit their waste are important support stations, as are the conveyor belts in cafeterias where diners leave their trays. The design of support stations closely follows the type of service.

Summary

The initial information-gathering process that must be done before the actual design phase begins is critical. A successful design begins in the planning process and integrates the front and back of the house. Careful consideration of restaurant type, the market, concept, menu, style of service, speed of service, per-customer check average, general ambience, management philosophy, and budget leads to the best design solutions.

Answers to the questions outlined here will provide the design team with important insights into critical operational elements that must be incorporated with the final design. Without an understanding of these operational components, both kitchen and interior design can negatively affect the functioning of the restaurant.

Integrative Design

The Design Team

The design of a successful restaurant does not come from the mind of one person. Rather, it reflects the efforts of a host of professionals (Figure 2.1), all of whom provide vital pieces of the picture, from kitchen equipment selection to architectural detailing to tabletop design to the integration of heating, ventilating, and air conditioning (HVAC) systems. Of course, ego is a factor to be reckoned with. Both owners and designers often view the restaurant interior as an extension of themselves. To the owner, it's the manifestation of her personality; to the designer, the manifestation of his talent. Quite often the chef (who may also be an owner) regards the kitchen as his private domain. Problems surface when individuals operate wearing blinders and so cannot make objective design decisions. Ideally, sensitive or damaged egos don't get in the way of professional collaboration.

Each professional also takes a different view of where the design process begins. Some say that it starts with the menu, others with the market, and still others with the architecture. Traditionally, however, the process of foodservice design begins with ownership. Ownership plants the initial ideas in the minds of the "design team," which, in turn, translates these ideas into a total concept and, subsequently, into a physical design.

The key team members should be involved from the beginning. Depending on the size and scope of the project, key players typically include the owner (or owner's representative), architect and/or interior designer, and foodservice consultant. As the project develops, the list of players may grow to include the chef, electrical engineers, lighting design consultants, acoustic consultants, graphic design consultants, and tabletop consultants. In the most inclusive scenario, involvement with restaurant planning extends to the employees, as they (along with the customers) are the ultimate users of the space.

Problems arise when no clear leader emerges to guide the design process. The owner should establish a team leader, someone with a balanced perspective of the

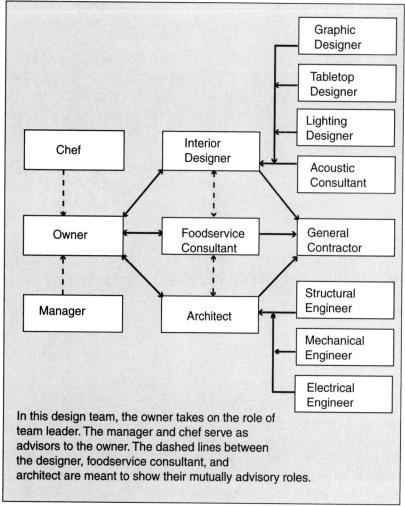

In this design team, the owner takes on the role of team leader. The manager and chef serve as advisors to the owner. The dashed lines between the designer, foodservice consultant, and architect are meant to show their mutually advisory roles.

FIGURE 2.1 *This schematic shows a sample design team for a major restaurant project.*

many factors involved in the design of the restaurant from the start of the project. This individual coordinates the planning process, disseminates ideas, and has ultimate responsibility for the execution of those ideas. The team leader should be familiar with all aspects of the operation, from menu items to actual design and construction.

Often, the owner takes on the role; after all, the owner has ultimate fiscal responsibility for the restaurant. In today's marketplace, however, many owners actually have little or no experience running a restaurant, so they often farm out the individual responsibilities during the planning phase. The owner nevertheless is responsible for integrating the various parts of the planning process into a whole. If he cannot take on this responsibility, a team leader who has that ability and understanding must be identified.

In some projects, the foodservice consultant, interior designer, or architect becomes the team leader. This can cause difficulties as the design process develops because each of these professionals has her own priorities. The head of the design team—no matter what her professional perspective—must maintain a neutral position and consider all aspects of the operation.

The nature of the project, whether the renovation of a 60-seat independently owned bistro, the new design of a 250-seat chain eatery, or the construction of a 400-seat theatrical restaurant, often dictates the choice of team leader. Many restaurant chains maintain an in-house design specialist to oversee projects, and a foodservice consultant is often the team leader for the remodeling of a kitchen. In new construction, the architect tends to become the team leader. Today, increasing numbers of design firms specialize in restaurant design, coordinating and handling every aspect of the project. In any case, without a strong team leader, the design process can become an uncoordinated and frustrating procedure that yields disappointing results.

It's important to recognize that the team does not have a set number of players or a predetermined leader. This is due to the nature of restaurant design itself. Not all projects are the same, thus not all design teams are the same. A foodservice consultant might be the only necessary resource for one project, but another might require a dozen team members.

The following descriptions of potential team members and the contributions they can make is offered as a guide to assembling the right team for a design project.

OWNER

The owner has ultimate financial responsibility for the project and frequently initiates the concept. He may or may not be experienced in restaurant operations or have training or education in foodservice management. Restaurant owners tend to have aggressive, entrepreneurial personalities and to be extremely dedicated to their work. Often, a restaurant is owned by two or more partners, each of whom has different areas of expertise. Limited partnership restaurant owners are minimally involved in day-to-day operations, yet their input during the design phase may be substantial—and potentially disruptive, if they are inexperienced in restaurant management.

Because owning a restaurant is thought to be a glamorous and profitable undertaking that does not require specialized education, it tends to attract newcomers to the foodservice industry. In the 1980s, investors flocked to restaurant partnerships in the hope of gaining tax breaks from passive investment losses. A decade later, with the stock market consistently yielding double-digit returns, investors got involved in restaurant ventures only when they felt confident about realizing true profits. Today's investors tend to rely heavily on design consultants to determine the feasibility of a concept and interpret it accordingly. They often want design creativity and allow the design firm to develop original ideas. For large-budget projects, these owners employ hospitality accounting firms with consulting branches to conduct full feasibility studies before launching a project.

At other times, owners possess skills that enable them to function in dual roles on the design team: chef-owners or architect-owners, for instance. These individuals tend to belong to the breed of owners who know exactly what they want and retain a design firm to execute their ideas. But if owners become ego-driven, the design process can falter.

CHEF

The chef (and, at times, other members of the kitchen staff) should be considered an important member of the design team. Chefs look at the layout of the kitchen from an operational perspective. They have the best understanding of what types of equipment are required to produce the menu items. The chef is responsible for efficient food production. If the selection or layout of equipment does not match the menu or the style of service that is appropriate for the restaurant, this efficiency cannot be realized. The chef (who has ultimate responsibility for the smooth operation of the kitchen) ought to be involved early in the design process, but is frequently not brought on board until the restaurant is nearly completed. At the least, a consulting chef should be hired to work with the design team while the kitchen layout is being planned.

Chef-owners are increasingly common today. These individuals often design efficient kitchens featuring simple yet durable equipment that offers quick cooking with minimal investment. Because they are also responsible for the bottom line of the restaurant, they look for equipment that serves multiple functions, thus freeing square footage for front-of-the-house seating. For example, they tend to specify equipment such as a combination oven that does the job of three pieces of equipment: convection oven, steamer, and steam-injected deck oven.

MANAGER

The manager of the restaurant can add important operational insight to the design process. Managers are frequently brought on board during the construction process and may be called on to act as the owner's representative and to interface with the project team leader on an ongoing basis. It is important for them to understand the overall design scheme and to offer input into that scheme during the planning phase. Most managers carry with them a history of restaurant layout and design experiences that can provide invaluable information to the designers. Unlike the chef, the manager looks at the design primarily from a front-of-the-house perspective. He should be knowledgeable about design issues that can improve market share, internal controls, safety, and sanitation throughout the operation.

FOODSERVICE CONSULTANT

The foodservice consultant designs the back-of-the-house operation and provides space layouts, mechanical and electrical diagrams, and equipment specifications. Firms range from a single individual to large companies with offices around the world. The scope of services may include menu planning, equipment purchasing, engineering evaluations, and management advisory services such as feasibility studies. Large firms, whose staffs include in-house architectural designers and who maintain a network of outside consultants, often provide team leadership. As leader, the foodservice consultant assists the owner in clarifying the concept for the restaurant, helps determine the feasibility of that concept within a given marketplace, and may even be involved in site selection.

Methods of charging include a flat fee based on hourly rates or a percentage of the total project cost. Some equipment supply houses have kitchen design experts on staff who provide design services, but these firms make money primarily by selling equipment.

INTERIOR DESIGNER

The interior designer is responsible for the layout and decor of the restaurant's public spaces. Like the foodservice consultant, design firms vary in size and scope of services. In general, designers develop floorplans, elevations, renderings, reflected ceiling plans, lighting plans, and furniture and accessory plans. They provide color schemes, material and decorative specifications, and all furnishing specifications. Some purchase as well as specify furnishings.

Today, increasing numbers of designers have become restaurant design specialists and take on the role of team leader. In this capacity, they may supervise a total design package from concept development to menu graphics to exterior signage to kitchen design. Other designers take on the role of team leader only for the front of the house. Most interior designers have special training or education in interior design or architecture and, in many cases, belong to the American Society of Interior Designers (ASID) or other professional organizations (Table 2.1).

Interior design fees are based on a percentage of project cost, hourly con-

TABLE 2.1. Design, Architecture, and Restaurant Organizations

Name	Web Address
American Society of Interior Designers (ASID)	asid.org
American Institute of Architects (AIA)	aiaonline.com
National Restaurant Association (NRA)	restaurant.org
Environmental Design Research Association (EDRA)	telepath.com/edra/home.html
International Interior Design Association (IIDA)	iida.com
Interior Design Educators Council, Inc. (IDEC)	idec.org
American Lighting Association (ALA)	americanlightingassoc.com
Foodservice Consultants Society International (FCSI)	fcsi.org
International Furnishings and Design Association (IFDA)	ifda.com
Color Association of the United States	colorassociation.com
Interior Designers Association (IDA)	ida.org.sg
American Institute of Graphic Artists (AIGA)	aiga.org

sulting rates, or square-foot cost. If purchasing services are provided, the design firm may charge a markup on furniture, fixtures, and equipment (FF&E) purchases.

ARCHITECT

Traditionally, the role of the architect was confined to the building structure and exterior design. Over the past few decades, however, most architectural firms have expanded their practice to include interior design as well. Construction plans must be certified by a licensed architect whenever a building permit for renovation or new construction is required. Restaurants designed from the ground up or facilities that require complex redesign of interior architecture, HVAC, or electrical systems may also require the services of an architectural firm.

Architectural input is particularly important when the interior design calls for uncommon structural elements. For example, a grand staircase that flares in two directions as it reaches a second floor is best designed by an architect. If the staircase is to be supported with wires that hang from the floor above, the plans must consider the load of the staircase on both the first and the second floor. While a designer can conceptualize such a staircase, the architect has the expertise to ensure it is safe to use.

More frequently, however, the roles of architect and interior designer are interchangeable. In these cases, which represent the majority of projects today, one individual or firm functions as restaurant designer. Architectural firms often keep interior designers on staff, and interior design firms often keep architects on staff.

The scope of services and methods of charging for an architectural firm whose practice includes restaurant design are basically the same as those of an interior design firm. The differences between the two often lie in design orientation and, at times, technical expertise in specific areas. Architects, for example, tend to deal with space, form, and volume rather than with surface decoration. Interior designers may be more knowledgeable about color and accessories.

GENERAL CONTRACTOR

General contractors (GCs) are crucial members of the design team. All too often, however, they are not properly recognized for the important role they play. It is the GC who is ultimately charged with converting the architects' and designers' drawings into bricks and mortar.

If the GC is involved with the project during the design phase, difficult or impossible structural forms can be pointed out. For example, if a restaurant design includes curved walls and ceilings, the GC can identify spots where creating such curved elements will substantially increase the cost of construction. She might also point out important timing elements during the construction phase. For example, when building a second-floor kitchen space, she might recommend that the installation of one exterior window be delayed until all of the oversized pieces of kitchen equipment are brought in. While access through a window space is not ideal, the GC might opt for this solution, having experienced the impossibility of moving a large piece of equipment up a narrow staircase. In the long run, this knowledge improves the final execution of the project and may also lead to tighter control over the construction budget.

The GC is frequently chosen by a bid process, but the same care given to the selection of other design team members should be extended. Both the quality and the cost of the GC's work greatly affect the success of the project. As with other members of the team, it's important to take a close look at the scope and quality of the GC's potential contribution before making a final selection.

The general contractor heads a team of subcontractors who together build the restaurant. In some cases, investigating the work of the subcontractors could also be important. The team leader should find out if the contractor will use union or non-union workers. For example, consider a restaurateur who rents ground-floor space in a new high-rise where building construction is done by workers from a number of unions. If the chosen subcontractor does not use union workers, work-site difficulties could lead to construction delays.

ENGINEERS

Three types of engineers are generally involved in a restaurant design: structural, mechanical, and electrical. They may be on the staff of an architectural firm but, more often, they are called in from private engineering firms as needed. Structural engineers are retained both for renovations and new construction to deal with problems involving the structural integrity of the building. For example, a structural engineer would provide input about the suspended staircase mentioned earlier. Mechanical engineers handle mechanical systems such as HVAC and work on pumping, plumbing, and elevator systems. Electrical engineers determine the amount of electricity needed for an operation and how best to distribute it. They are often called on early on a job to determine the cost of new service or expanded service.

LIGHTING DESIGNERS

Lighting designers are often retained by the restaurant designer to highlight special features of the restaurant, deal with technical lighting problems, or program a computerized illumination system. Because lighting plays such an important role in creating restaurant atmosphere, the lighting designer has become an increasingly important team member, especially for complex projects that require intricate illumination schemes. The lighting designer can also provide important insights into the quality of each light source and how it will affect the appearance of design elements, people, and food.

ACOUSTIC ENGINEERS AND ACOUSTIC CONSULTANTS

Sound, be it softening or enhancing, is best addressed by an experienced acoustic engineer or consultant who understands the sound-dampening characteristics of specific building materials. They can work to control the decibel levels within a space and help in the planning and selection of sound systems. They understand how best to deploy speakers to create either an even level of sound throughout the restaurant or to allow different areas to have varying levels of sound.

OTHER SPECIALTY DESIGNERS

Other specialty designers are usually brought on board by the team leader for big-budget projects or those that require specialized problem solving. Graphic designers, for example, may be called in to design the restaurant's logo, interior and exterior signage, and menu graphics. Art consultants are often involved with foodservice facilities that are part of much larger organizations, such as a hotel or a corporate headquarters. Tabletop designers become part of the team for gourmet restaurants or those establishments in which food presentation is key to the operational concept.

FINANCIAL CONSULTANTS

The real estate consultant becomes a team member when real estate is a critical factor in determining whether or not a project will fly. In such cases, the real estate interests in a restaurant are nearly as important as the operational interests.

The feasibility consultant conducts a marketplace study that identifies potential customers, the competition, and economic conditions of the locale in order to develop a pro forma statement.

THE FINAL TEAM

In extremely large restaurant projects, all of these specialists and others may be involved with the design process. The complexity of the project has a great impact on the complexion of the design team and the number of its members.

As the design process develops, a clear understanding of the responsibilities of each member of the team should be established. The team may move forward as a coordinated entity. In other situations, a maverick member might attempt to divert efforts from the stated goals. In still another scenario, one member has to stand up as the leader and pull the rest of the team along. These interpersonal relations are a big part of the design process, and often the most challenging. It's important to remember that every member of the team, from the team leader to the carpenter who nails and screws the pieces of the restaurant together, contributes to the overall success of a restaurant.

Space Planning: The Program

The first concrete planning for a restaurant design should begin only after the team members have thoroughly analyzed the market and have determined type of restaurant, style of service, concept, systems to be utilized, and the other factors outlined earlier. Then the data are organized into a design program that draws on the following considerations.

FLOW

An important goal of the design process is to optimize flow in terms of distance, volume, speed, and direction. Typically, flow patterns are charted for customers, employees, food, tableware, and service. Flow patterns must be considered carefully at the start of design programming.

DISTANCE

For customers, distance from a parking space to the front door of a restaurant can be critical. Where the parking lot of a large restaurant covers an acre or more of land, a drop-off area or facilities for valet parking should be considered.

Many spatial relationships are important, such as the distance from the dining tables to the rest rooms. If the rest rooms are located down a long corridor or on another floor, they will be inconvenient for customers and could lead to delays in service. In an eatertainment restaurant, the distance from the tables to the animatronic elements should be considered because the greater the distance, the less desirable the seat.

From a service staff perspective, the distance from the kitchen to each of the tables is important. When the kitchen and dining spaces are on separate floors, distance becomes a particular concern. In such cases (and in large single-floor restaurants), service stations with a full backup of supplies are essential. Distance to an order-entry station is also important to consider. For optimum efficiency in a busy restaurant, a ratio of 22 seats to a service station—fully stocked with backup dinnerware, water, and ice—is ideal.

Distance from the back to the front of the house and vice versa is a crucial component of the floorplan. For example, a display kitchen can shorten the flow of food from the range to the guest (Figure 2.2), but if the service staff is forced to return to the back of the house to pick up salads, the efficiency of the open kitchen is lost.

FIGURE 2.2 *Display kitchens can help improve the efficiency of the service staff by shortening the flow of food from kitchen to guest.* (Photo by Joseph Durocher.)

In many restaurants with display kitchens, the prepreparation for the hot foods is done in the back of the house. The food is then brought to the display kitchen, where cooking is performed within view of the customers. Artfully arranged salads and desserts are also visible to patrons and located within easy reach of the service staff. Servers need not enter the back-of-the house kitchen at all during service time. Interestingly, this setup is similar to the flow patterns in most fast-food burger operations and diners with counter service, where these functions are performed as close to the customer as possible in order to speed the flow of food. In fancier restaurants with display kitchens, cooking is kept close to the customers so they can watch the drama of food preparation.

A well-designed kitchen not only facilitates the transfer of food from the storage areas to the customer but also the return flow of dirty dishes from dining room to kitchen. Intuitively, positioning the dish return area just inside the return door to the kitchen minimizes the distance that dirty dishes must be carried. However, in some cases, the dish area is pushed deeper inside the kitchen to minimize the sound that carries from this area to the dining spaces.

VOLUME OF BUSINESS

Initially, volume projections indicate the appropriate size of a given dining area. However, looking only at the overall volume of business over the course of a day can be misleading. A corporate cafeteria, for example, must be designed to handle a large volume of traffic during a short lunch period, so seating and serving areas have to be larger than if the service were extended over three hours. Another instance of misleading volume projections is a fast-food operation on an interstate highway. Here, volume projections far exceed seating requirements because many customers take food back to their cars rather than use the restaurant's seating area. However, volume of business does dictate extra rest room space for travelers who take out food or use rest rooms without buying food.

The volume of business must also be considered when planning the parking areas of a restaurant. Local building codes frequently define the required number of spaces based on the number of seats in the restaurant. The codes may also affect the design of ingress and egress from the parking lot and mandate the installation of expensive traffic lights.

SPEED OF SERVICE

The faster the service, the more the restaurant depends on a well-designed floorplan. Fast-food operations and cafeterias should be laid out so that each area of the restaurant, all food and supplies, and every piece of equipment helps maximize speed. These fast-paced operations should have clearly defined, short lines of flow that do not cross.

Fast-food drive-through operations are similarly dependent on the speed of service. It may make sense for the design to incorporate separate ordering, cashiering, and order pickup stations. In one scenario, a guest places an order, moves forward to a second station to pay, then proceeds to a third station to pick it up. These stop-and-go steps keep customers engaged rather than thinking about how long they have to wait.

Conversely, the mannered service in a fine restaurant is an expected part of the leisurely dining experience, and placement of support equipment is not as important as in high-speed operations. For aesthetic reasons, management might even decide to eliminate service stations from the dining room. Although this lengthens the distance servers travel when resetting tables, the decision could be acceptable in establishments where diners expect a lengthy, slow-paced meal.

DIRECTION

The ideal layout creates a straight-line flow that is unidirectional, with no crossing flow patterns. Such a design may prove impossible but should be aimed for in the planning process.

Directional flow issues begin in the parking lot when guests look for a parking space. A herringbone parking space design helps define flow patterns in a way that straight-in parking does not. Once inside the restaurant, elements should flow logically so that guests need not retrace their steps (Figure 2.3). For example, the reception stand should allow people to check in and then move on to either the bar or the dining room without retracing their steps.

In the back of the house, the flow should move—as much as possible—in a straight line all the way from the receiving dock to the server pickup station. The waitstaff should be able to take the food directly to the guests and eventually bring dirty dishes and soiled table linen directly back to a cleanup area.

FIGURE 2.3 *Successful restaurants depend on flow patterns that cross each other as little as possible.*

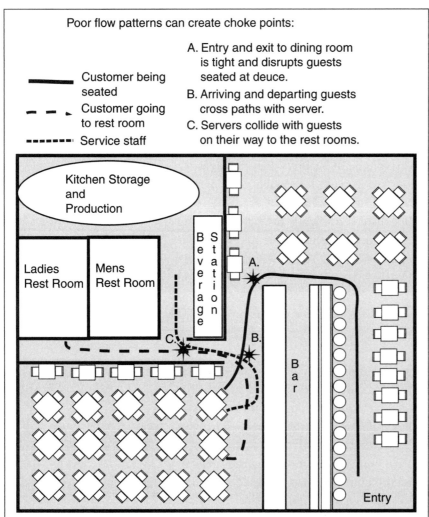

THE AMERICANS WITH DISABILITIES ACT

The Americans with Disabilities Act (ADA) of 1990 was passed to provide access for people with physical challenges to many environments. One such environment is the restaurant, which falls under Title III: Public Accommodations. The most visible result of the ADA has been the inclusion of handicapped-accessible rest room facilities. However, many other ADA design elements must be incorporated in new or modified restaurants. In 1991, the National Institute of Disability and Rehabilitation Research (NIDRR) funded ten Disability and Business Technical Assistance Centers (DBTAC) throughout the United States to offer information on ADA compliance. In addition, ADA consulting specialists can be retained to ensure that any design scheme complies with ADA requirements. As a guide, the following information was adapted from the Great Plains DBTAC, on the Web at adaproject.org/universal.htm.

TITLE III: PUBLIC ACCOMMODATIONS

Title III covers businesses and nonprofit service providers that are public accommodations. Public accommodations are private entities who own, lease, lease to, or operate facilities such as restaurants.

Public accommodations must comply with basic nondiscrimination requirements that prohibit exclusion, segregation, and unequal treatment. They also must comply with specific requirements related to architectural standards for new and altered buildings; reasonable modifications to policies, practices, and procedures; effective communication with people with hearing, vision, or speech disabilities; and other access requirements. Additionally, public accommodations must remove barriers in existing buildings where it is easy to do so without much difficulty or expense, given the public accommodation's resources.

To view the full text of the Title III Technical Assistance Manual, go to www.usdoj.gov/crt/ada/taman3.html. To view the 1994 Supplement to Title III, go to www.usdoj.gov/crt/ada/taman3up.html.

Failure to consider the needs of all physically challenged persons can lead to litigation by the Justice Department. In several instances, restaurateurs were forced to close their establishments because it was cost-prohibitive to make the facilities accessible. It is important to note that ADA regulations are frequently updated, so the design team should stay up to date on current and pending changes to the basic requirements.

Another ADA factor is the need to make changes to accommodate physically challenged employees. Fast-food restaurants that hire table cleaners who use a wheelchair will need increased space between the tables. Sight-impaired employees working in the dish area may need specially designed dish racks or audible temperature readouts. In both of these cases, minimal design modifications will enable the facility to comply with ADA.

Moving Through the Spaces

With an understanding of the importance that flow plays in a restaurant design, it is time to start the space planning process. Space planning begins with looking at the parts that make up the whole of a restaurant. These parts are not the chairs or the artwork or any of the other decor items. Rather, they consist of the spatial areas that together comprise the total front and back of the house. Each restaurant type requires its own specific design elements in these areas. The following discussion looks at spatial requirements for five major service systems.

EXTERIOR

The exterior includes every outside aspect: the parking lot, the building skin, exterior signage, landscaping, and exterior window and lighting treatments. The exterior of restaurants located in high-rise buildings consists of interior corridors. In shopping malls, public "outdoor" seating areas often comprise the exterior of a restaurant operation.

FAST-FOOD EXTERIORS Exterior signage is of utmost importance to the fast-food operation. Initial development of the design concept should include a signature ideograph or typeface that integrates with the logo. The logo helps establish a clear identity that communicates instantly to people whizzing by in their cars. Operators tend to carry elements of the logo throughout the entire fast-food environment by emblazoning appropriate surfaces with the name or ideograph as a constant reminder to their guests. Thus, signage and graphics are an important part of the total fast-food marketing plan.

Signage often works hand in hand with architecture. In the 1950s and 1960s, the sight from the highway of an orange roof heralded a Howard Johnson's. Today, the golden arches still indicate the location of a McDonald's; a black, red, and white sign shouts Pizza Hut.

Primary colors and bright lighting are commonly used on fast-food exteriors to further emphasize identity and create an upbeat, high-energy image. Gone are the days when garish fast-food signs were the accepted norm. Today, most signage, while still colorful and well lit at night, does not include flashing lights or other loud elements that are frowned upon by local zoning boards.

TABLESERVICE EXTERIORS In chain-operated tableservice restaurants, the exterior image establishes theme and identity in much the same way as it does for fast-food restaurants. The logo or ideograph displayed on the building's exterior often carries through to the inside, and architectural form becomes a recognizable icon. Pizza Hut—which is really a tableservice restaurant—relies extensively on both its signage and its building shape for identity. The Olive Garden chain is another example, with signage that hasn't changed much since the first Olive Garden opened in Orlando, Florida in 1982. The Hard Rock Café logo, which made its first appearance in London, has become a recognizable icon worldwide, although its building shape changes from location to location (Figure 2.4).

Converting existing restaurant structures that were built with recognizable architectural elements presents special problems, especially if the building in question happens to have been a known chain. In other words, to disguise a recognizable architectural form and create a new image may require extensive reconstruction. A bit of cosmetic overlay won't work.

Independent tableservice restaurants vary widely in their architectural and graphic statements. Depending on the type of establishment and the target market, exteriors range from the undesigned and unembellished concrete or brick box to innovative architectural statements. Here, too, consumers recognize exterior symbols. The aluminum-sided diner, for instance, is synonymous with a diverse, hearty, inexpensive American menu served 24 hours a day. Careful restorations or new knockoffs of this classical design have become late-night hangouts for everyone from the cross-country trucker to the urban clubgoer.

In general, suburban chain operations are situated in freestanding buildings whose architecture (like the fast-food chains) is recognizable. Independent urban restaurants frequently sport distinctive, highly individual facades with features such as floor-to-ceiling windows that afford passersby a view inside, or high-tech video displays that also hint at the electricity and excitement inside. Other places use unusual or overscaled architectural elements to create identity. At theatrical or entertainment restaurants, architecture always helps to promote the show.

An investment in architecture and graphics is an investment in image that can pay off handsomely in the long run. The challenge is to create an individual identity that nevertheless remains in context with its environment, whether a casino promenade or a rural country road (Figure 2.5).

FIGURE 2.4 The architecture of Hard Rock Cafés is different in each location, but the signage creates a recognizable image worldwide. (Photos by Joseph Durocher.)

CAFETERIA EXTERIORS The exterior of a cafeteria operation usually consists of a building shell that houses not only the cafeteria but also many other facilities (offices or hospital beds, for example). Therefore, the exterior of the cafeteria traditionally has not been integrated with the overall design program. In some operations, however, the exterior approach to the cafeteria—actually located inside the building—is designed to attract patrons. Floor treatments, artwork, and windows into the serving area can capture the attention of people as they walk by. Large businesses may dedicate an entire floor to the cafeteria, which has its own elevator or elevator access. Thoughtful design treatments, such as menu displays in the elevator or hanging banners over the escalator, can spark interest in the cafeteria and lead people into the space.

BANQUET EXTERIORS Freestanding banquet facilities benefit from landscaping that not only entices customers but also affords an excellent backdrop for photo shoots. Spaces within larger buildings are ideally located near parking areas, if the practice is to sell to customers who do not work inside the building.

FIGURE 2.5 *Distinctive restaurant signage and architecture at Universal City in Los Angeles relates to the Hollywood-themed environment.*
(Photo by Regina Baraban.)

TAKE-OUT EXTERIORS Many take-out operations are housed within an existing facility, so the exterior is not a crucial consideration. However, those that incorporate a drive-through window must consider exterior features. Traffic flow patterns change when a drive-through is added to a restaurant, and the area allocated to cars that queue up for the take-out window takes away from parking spaces. Drive-throughs are most effective when take-out foods can be quickly prepared or prepared and packaged, and pose problems when the same line is used to service customers who preorder foods and those who order on site.

ENTRY AREA

The entry area begins when customers step inside the restaurant. Its form varies greatly, depending, in part, on whether the restaurant is freestanding or incorporated in a larger building. Climatic conditions also affect the appearance of the entryway. In general, it should look inviting and should help move patrons in an orderly flow from exterior to dining. Doors usually separate the exterior from the entry, but in situations such as a shopping mall or cafeteria, patrons may walk through open portals (which are typically secured at night). Where energy efficiency is paramount, double doors, revolving doors, or air screens are important considerations. The entry area itself includes such elements as the maître d' station or reception area, coat- or bag-check area, a waiting area (often with seating), public phones, space for guests to queue up for service, and, frequently, the cash-handling systems.

FAST-FOOD ENTRY AREAS In the fast-food restaurant, the entry is the place where customers divide into queues. The two basic types of queue are: (1) several separate lines, each of which leads to a point-of-sale (POS) unit, and (2) a single, usually serpentine line. Menu selections, ordering, delivery, and cash handling all take place in this one area. The amount of space needed is determined by expected volume; it is roughly the same no matter which queue system is used.

The obvious disadvantage to the single-line system is that the customer may be faced with being the thirtieth person in line when he enters the restaurant. The alternate method breaks the queue into perhaps five lines with six persons in each line, so the customer's perception is of a much shorter queue that will take less time to get through. In actuality, the throughput (the number of customers served in a given time) is about equal in both systems. What saves time in the single line is a division of responsibilities among the servers; one person takes orders and handles cash while others assemble the order. In multiple lines, one person takes the order, assembles it, and handles money transactions. An additional advantage of the single-line queue is that it limits the number of registers and amount of front counterspace needed.

Tableservice Entry Areas On average, table-service restaurants have small entry areas that function as pass-through spaces to the dining room. In some establishments, a coatroom is tucked into a corner of the entry area. In informal restaurants, the entry space often includes a dual-purpose host and cashier station. Upscale restaurants have a maître d' station where guests check in before being led to their table, but the station does not include cash-handling functions. The check-in sta-

FIGURE 2.6 *The vestibule at Belgo Nieuw York helps transition guests from the sidewalk to interior walkways that lead to the dining areas.* (Photo by Joseph Durocher.)

tion must be close enough to the front door so that it can be easily seen, but far enough away so that waiting guests will not block the flow of other traffic in and out of the restaurant. In some international destinations, the maître d' station is located in the center of the dining area, so guests actually pass dining tables on their way to check in. This layout can confuse diners who expect to encounter the host stand in the entryway.

The entry area in chain restaurants may include everything from the waiting lines in steakhouses to newspaper vending machines in coffee shops. It is usually an unembellished area where guests wait for a table.

In an upscale tableservice restaurant, however, the entry area can set the stage for the dining experience to come. The entry is the transition zone between the outside world and the restaurant and, even in small spaces, good design can facilitate the transition with devices such as vestibules or angled entry doors (Figure 2.6). Lighting plays a crucial role in creating a smooth transition between outside and inside. Smell is also important; in the entry, customers begin to get olfactory clues about the meal to come.

In many restaurants, the entry area melds with the bar (Figure 2.7). Barriers are minimized in an effort to draw people into the space and to let them preview the experience to come. Coatrooms are set aside and, in some operations, are placed in remote locations so as not to interfere with the traffic flow or entry aesthetic.

Cafeteria Entry Areas and Serveries The cafeteria entry area is minimal in size and limited to the space where customers pick up a tray and are introduced to menu offerings. Entry areas in the traditional straight-line cafeteria, commonly used until the late 1970s, were larger and longer because they served as holding areas where guests queued up. Today's scramble designs, where patrons do not enter a line but travel to individual food stations, eliminate the need for an entry queue.

FIGURE 2.7 *The entry area at Carmine's in New York City's upper west side leads directly into the bar, which functions as a waiting area in this no-reservations restaurant.*
(Photo by Joseph Durocher.)

The servery, where patrons pick up and pay for food, is the design feature that distinguishes cafeterias from other types of foodservice. In general, it needs to be large enough to allow a smooth and continual flow of traffic during the peak lunch hour, when cafeteria customer counts swell considerably and patrons' time is limited.

The scramble-system servery was conceived to cut down queuing and to speed customers to particular food items such as hot entrées, grilled meats, sandwiches, or beverages. The marketing advantage of the traditional straight-line design was that customers were paraded past all food offerings and made impulse purchases. With the scramble system, customers choose more selectively, so attractively designed food stations are critical. Exhibition cooking and preparation, such as made-to-order grilling, stir frying, and roast carving, have proven to be popular draws.

Care must be taken to position food stations so as to maximize flow with minimal cross-traffic. Another goal is the careful placement of food and beverage stations and cashiers. Figure 2.8 is a schematic that depicts a logical flow through a cafeteria servery and into the dining space. Note that the beverage stations are adjacent to the cashiers. This placement minimizes the chance that customers will spill drinks as they move through the servery. Also note that the hot food stations are situated just before the beverage stations. This helps ensure that foods are still hot when customers reach their seats.

Efforts have been made to deinstitutionalize serveries, with less emphasis on stainless-steel surfaces and more attention to lighting, color, finishes, and textures that improve the look of the food and add warmth to the feeling of the space. Scramble systems depend on well-placed and descriptive signage to educate and direct customers. They are not as effective when serving transient guests because these guests are unfamiliar with the layout and can become confused.

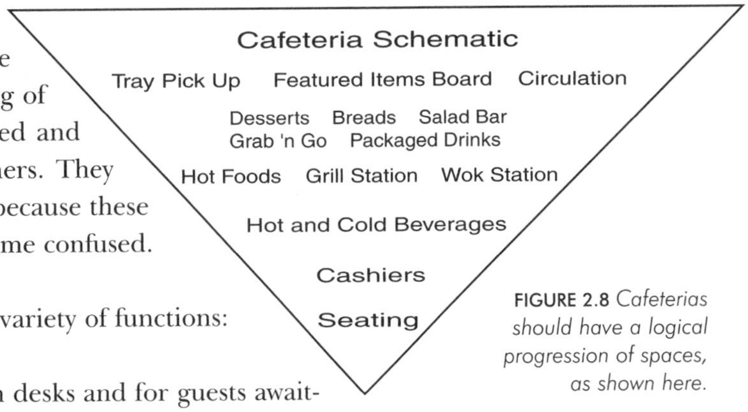

Cafeteria Schematic

Tray Pick Up   Featured Items Board   Circulation

Desserts   Breads   Salad Bar
Grab 'n Go   Packaged Drinks

Hot Foods   Grill Station   Wok Station

Hot and Cold Beverages

Cashiers

Seating

FIGURE 2.8 *Cafeterias should have a logical progression of spaces, as shown here.*

BANQUET ENTRY AREAS Banquet entry areas can serve a variety of functions:

Registration: Space is required for registration desks and for guests awaiting entry into the banquet space.

Waiting: The space must be large enough to accommodate guests waiting to be seated.

Reception: Both waiting space and circulation space is needed to enable guests to approach portable bars, or for servers to pass drinks through the crowd. In some instances, hors d'oeuvre displays or passed hors d'oeuvres must be planned for as well.

Display: Displays of program materials may also have to be planned for when designing banquet entry areas.

TAKE-OUT ENTRY AREAS The most important consideration is to provide easy access to the street. Take-out entry areas should also be planned so as to minimize the impact of the take-out business on dine-in business. This can mean a separate entryway.

DINING AREA

The dining area begins where the entry area stops, and runs to the kitchen. It frequently interfaces with a beverage service area. Typical elements include seating and server stations, ventilation, and sound and lighting systems.

Architectural treatments such as raised or lowered floor and ceiling levels often help define dining rooms. Salad bars, buffet tables, and display kitchens are frequently located in dining rooms. Nonalcoholic beverage stations, such as for coffee or espresso, may also be incorporated in this space. Because the dining space is the restaurant's revenue-producing area, it occupies the largest amount of square footage.

FAST-FOOD DINING AREAS Hard surfaces, bright lighting, and primary colors are the traditional design characteristics of fast-food dining areas because these elements facilitate easy maintenance, fast turnover, and upbeat energy. To accommodate aging baby boomers, however, these hard-edge design elements now are often softened with applications such as greenery, artwork, soft accent lighting, and toned-down or muted color schemes. Glass-enclosed greenhouse seating areas and overhead skylights are often used in fast-food architecture to mellow the ambience with natural light and plants. Play areas for children can also be found in many fast-food restaurants.

FIGURE 2.9 *The high-backed, padded booth seating at Matthew's Restaurant in Jacksonville, FL, designed by Larry Wilson, provides comfort and intimacy.*
(Photo by Joseph Lapeyra.)

Most contemporary fast-food interiors are divided into many small seating areas, with acoustic ceiling tiles or wall coverings to mute noise levels. Fixed seating made of molded plastic has given way to smart-looking café chairs with padded seats and counter seating for single diners.

Nevertheless, the design goals of easy maintenance, fast turnover, and upbeat energy remain. Today's fast-food dining areas may look more up-to-date, with lighting levels soft enough that patrons don't need to wear sunglasses, but if the interiors are too comfortable or can't withstand the spills and stains of constant turnover, the design has failed.

TABLESERVICE DINING AREAS Tableservice dining spaces continue to show great variety of size, shape, and decor. Large rooms are often broken into dining nooks with levels or barriers that create a feeling of privacy. Mirrors are used creatively to give tantalizing glimpses into other parts of the room. Comfort is paramount in upscale tableservice restaurants; the uncomfortable but high-styled seating popular in the 1980s has been replaced by padded chairs, booths, and banquettes (Figure 2.9).

The spatial plan of the dining room should always take into account the traffic flow of the waitstaff and the amount of space needed between tables. In today's restaurants, POS order-entry systems placed throughout dining spaces and remote printers located in kitchens and bars have diminished much of the waitstaff flow.

Hand-held computerized order-entry pads, which will become increasingly common, also cut back on the service flow.

In many tableservice restaurants, particularly fine dining establishments, food is the major attraction, so it is important to ensure that the dining experience, which often takes several hours, is not interrupted by distractions. Chairs should be positioned so that customers or staff don't bump into them as they move about. Temperature levels should be even throughout the meal period. Sound levels should allow for easy conversation, and lighting should enhance the overall experience.

In casual tableservice chains and independent restaurants, design is often used as a marketing tool to draw a targeted clientele. Today's theme restaurants are more about creating an experience—one that is bigger and better than the competition—than recreating a look. However, the nostalgia craze continues to draw on design elements from the 1940s and 1950s for such operations as diners and cafés.

In theatrical restaurants, barriers between dining and drinking are often lowered to create the feeling of one large space and to allow visibility between bar patrons and restaurant patrons, enabling customers to "see the show" from every seat in the house.

If the show runs on a stage, the dining space is typically one large room, perhaps tiered. Part of the entertainment might be the open kitchen, an element that became increasingly popular in the 1990s. If the show plays on video screens or incorporates animatronics, displays must be numerous enough to ensure that all seats in the house have a view. Videos and animatronic entertainment make it possible to have several dining spaces of varying size.

In theatrical or eatertainment restaurants, illumination levels can be intense, and specialty theatrical lighting is frequently used to highlight the action. High noise levels create action, excitement, and energy, and help develop the feeling of the room. However, the ear-splitting reverberation that makes conversation painful has become less common than it was in the 1990s.

CAFETERIA DINING AREAS No longer is cafeteria design typified by institutional-green masonry block walls. Today, cafeterias are often indistinguishable from full-service restaurants. Elements such as greenery, carpeting, and artwork help stylize the setting. Vaulted ceilings, exposed brick walls with soft incandescent lighting, lounge seating, indoor gardens, and water elements are more the rule than the exception.

In markets where cafeteria-style operations compete with full-service restaurants, the decor package in the servery and dining areas is upbeat and the service is often interactive (Figure 2.10). As always, acoustic control is an important design consideration, along with easy maintenance surfaces and durable furnishings.

Spatially, cafeteria dining rooms are often divided by barriers, levels, or other devices to allow customers a choice of open or intimate dining. Large cafeteria-style restaurants may have dining areas broken into several sections, some of which can be reserved for groups. Semiprivate cafeteria dining areas enable informal meetings to be conducted over a meal or a break period. Private dining rooms should also be incorporated in designs for hospitals, universities, or corporate cafeterias as optional dining/meeting space. Cafeteria dining areas are often used for special evening functions, so design flexibility should also be part of the spatial plan. Storage areas are needed for chairs and tables when the dining space is converted into a reception area or set up theater-style for a meeting.

FIGURE 2.10 *Movenpick Marche in Boston's Prudential Plaza is a popular cafeteria-style operation that attracts a diverse clientele.* (Photo by Regina Baraban.)

BANQUET DINING AREAS Banquet dining areas must be planned with flexibility in mind. A given space may be used to serve 350 people a sit-down breakfast; 300 a lavish luncheon buffet; as a plenary meeting room for 450 with full audio-visual support, and as a dinner-dance space for 275.

TAKE-OUT DINING AREAS By definition, take-out operations do not include dining spaces.

BEVERAGE AREA

The beverage area, typically serving alcoholic beverages, is found in restaurants that offer beverages outside of the dining area. It generally consists of a front bar and back bar, bar seating, and, sometimes, cocktail seating. Music and video systems are often featured. The size of the beverage area depends on the importance of beverage sales to total revenue. In some restaurants, a single beverage area services dining room customers as well as bar customers, but other restaurants include separate service bars for the dining room. Nonalcoholic beverage areas are incorporated in other types of restaurants.

Wine storage and display is an increasingly important design element in many types of restaurants. In tableservice restaurants, wine displays near the entry area can entice people to purchase wine. In theatrical restaurants, the action in the wine cellar can be part of the show when the cellar is in view of the guests. In other establishments, wine displays are used as a decorative motif in the dining room (Figure 2.11).

FAST-FOOD BEVERAGE AREAS Fast feeders don't serve alcoholic beverages, but some do install beverage bars where customers fill their own cups with whatever cold or hot beverage they desire. Such beverage bars shift the cost of labor associated with filling drinks to the customers. They tend to speed service because the cashier does not have to pour and assemble drinks along with food items.

TABLESERVICE BEVERAGE AREAS Many tableservice restaurants incorporate bars that are visually separated from the dining areas. The bar often serves multiple purposes: as a drinking spot for customers who may or may not be eating, as a service bar for the dining room, and as a waiting area for diners. It is often accompanied by a cocktail lounge, especially when food is served. Today, some restaurants serve complete meals at the bar and, increasingly, bars serve scaled-down portions for guests looking for an alternative to a full meal.

Bars can range in size from tiny to gargantuan, depending on their role in the restaurant. They play a minor role in elegant restaurants that emphasize a fine dining experience but, in many other types of restaurants, the bar has become an open, inviting area for drinking or casual dining.

It's important to integrate wine displays and wine cellars with the restaurant design. Space and equipment is needed to store white wines under refrigeration for service. Both red and backup white wines should be stored in a climate-controlled space that keeps the bottles at roughly 68 degrees Fahrenheit. If wines are to be sold by the glass, storage space for the open bottles must be provided—ideally under temperature-controlled conditions.

FIGURE 2.11 *In this seafood restaurant in New York City, a wine cellar display serves as a continuing reminder of the establishment's wine offerings.* (Photo by Joseph Durocher.)

In many tableservice restaurants, the bar can attract its own crowd as well as diners waiting for tables. In such instances, the bar should be designed and positioned to attract a customer base that will not conflict with diners.

CAFETERIA BEVERAGE AREAS As mentioned in the servery entry discussion and shown in Figure 2.8, the dispensed beverages areas of a cafeteria are typically positioned near the cashiers. However, in some retail cafeterias, the bar—which has spirited and nonspirited beverages—serves all diners along with customers who choose to sit on bar stools.

BANQUET BEVERAGE AREAS Most banquet operations use portable bar equipment. The number of bars and bartenders must be sufficient to meet the demands of the group. Generally, one bar setup should be sufficient to service 75 guests. However, if the cocktail period is short, additional bars will be needed to ensure that all guests are served in a timely fashion, even though they will take away from the waiting and circulation space available to guests.

TAKE-OUT BEVERAGE AREAS In many take-out operations, a beverage area set up for self-service is the best option. From a design perspective, this means packaged-beverage display cases that are easy to load and access are needed. For dispensed beverages, the holding capacity and type of cup dispenser is important to consider. The dispenser must be easy for staff to reload and for customers to use.

REST ROOMS

Both front- and back-of-the-house rest rooms are often included in a given restaurant. However, in some facilities, a single rest room located in the front of

the house services both staff and guests. The size of the rest rooms depends on the size of the restaurant. Larger establishments may include makeup areas for women, shoeshine stations for men, and ADA-compliant facilities.

FAST-FOOD REST ROOMS In fast-food restaurants, rest rooms must be designed to handle high-volume traffic. Fast feeders are typically used as roadside or walk-in rest stops, so the rest room volume can be greater than the diner volume. Spaces must be functional and easily cleaned with a minimum of upkeep. The rest rooms take such a heavy beating that all design applications should be durable and easy to maintain. Large-roll toilet tissue and hand towels minimize the need to service rest rooms. Blow dryers should be included as a backup when the towel dispenser is empty, particularly in employee rest rooms. Autoflush urinals and toilets help improve sanitation and minimize offensive smells.

TABLESERVICE REST ROOMS Rest rooms in the tableservice establishment should be designed with as much care as the dining spaces. Rest rooms, when artfully designed and appointed, are a welcome addition to the dining experience. They can also become marketing centers—as at Berkley Bar and Grill in Manhattan, where owner Drew Nieporent broadcasted *New York Times* reviews of his various restaurants into the spaces.

Materials and surfaces specified for the rest rooms should be durable and easy to maintain. In addition, dining room design can be extended into the rest rooms in many ways to create something special (Figure 2.12). Flowers, wallcovering, hand-painted tiles, and other design elements go a long way toward engendering customer goodwill.

Patrons of theatrical restaurants tend to be concerned with personal appearance, and their trips to the rest room often turn into lengthy visits. In eatertainment restaurants, the entertaining decor is often mirrored in the rest room design. In establishments where live shows and dancing contribute to the theatrics, rest rooms are important stops for men and women to check makeup and hair. From a design perspective, additional space must be set aside for mirrors and makeup areas.

FIGURE 2.12 *Restaurant design shouldn't end at the bathroom doors. Here are two very different rest room designs that echo their respective dining room interiors: the sleek, contemporary treatment at TrU in Chicago, designed by the Johnson Studio, and the fanciful decorative treatment at Farallon in San Francisco, designed by Pat Kuleto.* (TrU: Photo by Joseph Durocher; Farallon: Photo by Dennis Anderson, © Pat Kuleto Restaurants.)

CAFETERIA REST ROOMS Cafeteria rest rooms are usually incorporated into the design of the building that contains the cafeteria. Thus, their design is not an integral component of the interior. Like all foodservice rest rooms, however, they should be functional and easy to maintain.

BANQUET REST ROOMS Unlike restaurant rest rooms, where the flow of guests is continuous and even, banquet rest rooms must be capable of handling a large volume of periodic use. It is critical that a sufficient number of stalls and urinals be installed to ensure that banquet patrons can use the facilities quickly.

TAKE-OUT REST ROOMS As with the dining space, rest rooms are typically not needed to support take-out restaurants.

KITCHEN

Nearly every restaurant kitchen can be divided into the functional areas described in chapter 5. The kitchen is usually a third the size of the dining area, but this ratio varies greatly according to restaurant type. In many restaurants, the kitchen, once hidden behind swinging doors, sits in full view of the customers.

FAST-FOOD KITCHENS Optimal efficiency is crucial in a fast-food kitchen. Kitchen design for large chain operations has been researched, revised, researched again, and brought to a point where the placement of every element leads to the highest level of output per employee hour. Some fast feeders demand custom equipment—designed specifically for their menu—from their suppliers. As with any kitchen, the key is to keep the flow of product in as straight a line as possible and not cross it with the flow of personnel.

Expanded menus challenge the design of fast-food kitchens. The kitchen once designed to process only frozen fries and burgers now may also be the production facility for fresh produce, soup, or even home-baked breads. For new units, the design is relatively simple—plan the kitchen to incorporate the expanded menu—but adding a convection oven or a vegetable prep area can make an already tight space in an existing facility impossible.

TABLESERVICE KITCHENS Both menus and kitchens are standardized in chain operations. While the same layout may not be used in all chain kitchens, the type of equipment is always the same. The independent restaurant kitchen, however, does not follow a standard format. Frequently, batch-prepared foods are held in steam tables, where they are supplemented with foods prepared to order at a grill or fry station.

In the à la carte kitchen, where all food is prepared to order and few foods are prepared in advance, high-heat equipment capable of cooking food within minutes is most frequently included in the design. With few exceptions, kitchen space is tight because restaurateurs strive to maximize revenue-producing front-of-the-house space. Wherever possible, a single piece of equipment should be used for the production of multiple menu items.

With the exception of restaurants that have display kitchens in the front of the house, most of the food preparation and cooking in tableservice operations are performed in an all-enclosed kitchen. Pizza restaurants, whether they are chain or independent, generally have open kitchens, as do many contemporary high-design restaurants that showcase the chef's art as drama. In these cases, the back-of-the-house kitchen is even smaller. Display kitchens must be equipped with easy-to-clean equipment, typically clad with stainless steel. Cleanliness (an ongoing concern in any kitchen) is particularly important in display kitchens, so undercounter waste receptacles must be programmed into the design.

In the 1990s, an expanded emphasis on food in theatrical restaurants led to increasing numbers of display kitchen areas—from full open kitchens to large pickup windows. Some of these have seating at or adjacent to the service pickup areas, with little or no separation between the kitchen theatrics and the customers.

The display kitchen is usually split into two spaces: the finishing kitchen in the front of the house and the storage and prepreparation areas in the back of the house. Consequently, the spatial relationship between these two areas is critical. Pass-through reach-ins make it easy to back up supplies from the prepreparation area and allow finish chefs to draw from a continually replenished supply of ingredients. Theatrical lighting is frequently used to focus attention on equipment like wood-fired ovens, rotisseries, or charbroilers that are an important part of the show.

CAFETERIA KITCHENS Cafeteria kitchens traditionally have been designed with banks of steam-jacketed kettles, pressure steamers, and deck ovens, all aimed at bulk preparation of large batches of food. Recent changes in menus and servery design have changed the fare and the face of cafeteria kitchens. Foods are often cooked at the point of service, as at grill stations. Another example that moved back-of-the-house space to front-of-the-house serveries is à la carte preparation of such items as fresh vegetables, steamed off as the need arises by the counter staff in high-pressure or convection steamers located right on the serving line.

Shifting the locus of production out of the kitchen not only changes spatial allocation—requiring more servery space and less back-of-house space—but also creates different demands for cooking and refrigeration equipment in the back of the house. The introduction of tilting fry kettles, convection ovens, and multipurpose combination ovens has decreased reliance on traditional equipment. Low-pressure steamers have been replaced with faster and smaller high-pressure steamers.

The floorplan of the cafeteria kitchen depends, in large measure, on the type of organization the cafeteria is in. Hospitals, for example, require separate patient food assembly areas. Industrial kitchens may employ a satellite feeding program where foods are prepared in a central location, then served in serveries located throughout a large industrial complex. The larger and more complex the institution, the larger and more complex the kitchen. A smooth, straightforward flow from receiving to preparation to servery pass-through is always the spatial goal. Multipurpose equipment and labor-saving layouts also help achieve an efficient, successful design.

BANQUET KITCHENS Banquet kitchens require volume production equipment capable of preparing enough food in a single batch to meet the serving needs of the banquet space. Additionally, sufficient refrigerated and hot holding equipment is required to maintain foods at temperature. In the case of cold foods, refrigerated space sufficient to house carts capable of holding each of the plated courses is optimal. For hot foods, heated banquet carts used to hold and transport plated meals must be planned for. Space is also needed for plating meals in an assembly-line format.

TAKE-OUT KITCHENS Take-out kitchens can range from a nonkitchen operation supplied with foods prepared elsewhere to a limited kitchen with high-speed cooking equipment. One of the keys to a successful take-out concept is a menu that can be prepared in advance and then cooked or served quickly when ordered. Asian menus are ideal for take-out because the bite-size ingredients cook quickly in a wok. Rotisserie chicken and batch-prepared side dishes can also be suited to take-out because meals can be plated from a ready supply of cooked foods.

RESTAURANT SUPPORT AREAS

Restaurant support areas include receiving and storage areas (dry, refrigerated, and frozen), plus employee rest rooms, locker rooms, employee lounge/cafeteria, and management offices. All of these areas are located in the back of the house and are discussed in full in chapter 5.

Not every foodservice operation incorporates all these areas, and the significance of each functional area varies from restaurant to restaurant. In fact, every restaurant space has unique requirements and characteristics and should be analyzed individually in order to arrive at a successful program.

FAST-FOOD RESTAURANT SUPPORT AREAS The storage areas of fast-food restaurants are similar to those in other kitchens. Historically, limited menus placed limited demands on storage areas. As menus expanded, however, and more fresh ingredients were added, storage needs increased. For example, fast-food operators who make and bake their own biscuits must store large bags of flour, whereas they formerly received ready-to-eat rolls. A great deal of space is required to store disposables.

The offices in fast-food restaurants are usually small. Because of the sophisticated POS systems in most fast feeders, much of the paperwork ordinarily completed in a standard restaurant office is done at the registers. Frequently, these data are fed to a central data-collection office (not the on-site office), which sends reports back to the restaurant. Employee locker room spaces are limited and employees use the dining space to eat and take breaks.

TABLESERVICE RESTAURANT SUPPORT AREAS Because tableservice menus are usually more complex than fast-food operations, they require more storage for the varied types of food items. Less space is needed for dry storage, however, because most tableservice restaurants do not use paper goods.

In the tableservice restaurant, the mix of dry to refrigerated to frozen changes as a function of management policy. In some independent operations, fresh foods are used wherever possible. Others, including many chain operations, depend heavily on frozen and canned goods. The type of storage facilities needed, therefore, depends on the particular operation.

Storage areas for theatrical restaurants typically follow those of tableservice restaurants. The more varied the menu, the more storage space is needed. Fresh ingredients require more preparation space and specialty processing equipment than frozen or canned foods.

CAFETERIA SUPPORT AREAS Storage and receiving areas for cafeteria operations are frequently separated from the production areas because most cafeterias are located within a multistory building shell. One receiving dock often serves the entire building, and the storage of foodservice goods may be overseen by the storeroom manager for all departments within the building.

Offices and employee spaces are similar in size and nature to those in a commercial restaurant, although employees typically eat in the dining space (as in fast-food restaurants). Increased office space is required in complex foodservice operations such as hospitals, where multiple styles of service are supported by a single kitchen and support facility.

BANQUET SUPPORT AREAS Banquet support areas are often ignored, but they are critical to success. Space is needed to store banquet tables and chairs when they are not in use. Space is also needed to store the myriad pieces of banquet tableware that may be used only periodically. Access space to banquet areas is also important. In the case of dividable ballrooms, double-walled corridors can eliminate noise carryover while providing easy access from the kitchen area to all parts of the dining space.

TAKE-OUT SUPPORT AREAS Storage areas for packaging materials are essential. Order-taking areas and equipment must also be incorporated into the design to ensure quick and accurate communication of orders between the customer, the order taker, the food preparers, and those who assemble the orders.

Summary

Space planning for any type of foodservice enterprise incorporates common design principles. A well-designed restaurant, however, is one where the design team has carefully attended to the character of the operation and designed spaces so that they work most effectively for the customers, the staff, and management. Time must be spent developing the floorplan and considering, rejecting, and refining spatial options until arriving at the best possible solution.

The Psychology of Design

"We shape our buildings and our buildings shape us." Winston Churchill expressed this thought to the House of Commons just after World War II. He was referring to a proposed plan to change the shape of the legislators' meeting room, concerned that a change of physical environment would, in turn, effect change in the legislative process.

Churchill's point—that environment affects behavior—is a well-documented fact, but only recently has the knowledge of social scientists (environmental and behavioral psychologists) been deliberately applied to architecture and interior design. This knowledge is beginning to be applied to the field of restaurant design.

Environment and Behavior

Despite the lack of applied research, we know that customers' attitudes and behavior are influenced by their interaction with environmental elements. For example, consider the chair you are now sitting in. You might be able to read this text for hours because the design of the chair and the texture of the seat covers are conducive to reading. Conversely, you might already feel uncomfortable. The chair could be so comfortable that you want to take a nap, or the angle and hardness of the seat might cause you to adjust yourself frequently. This psychological reaction to physical features is important to the selection of seating in a restaurant, because it can influence guests either to eat quickly and move on or to linger over a meal and choose to stay for an after-dinner cordial.

Seating selection is one of many decisions made by the design team that should reflect a working knowledge of design psychology. The combination of all environmental elements affects how people feel and, consequently, how they act in a given space—how long they stay, how comfortable they feel while they are there, what they remember, and, perhaps, if they want to come back again.

How Space Is Perceived

In order to analyze the psychological impact of design elements, one must understand the many ways in which people perceive their surroundings. According to the anthropologist Edward T. Hall in his book *The Hidden Dimension* (Anchor Books, 1969), sensory apparatus falls into two general categories: distance receptors and immediate receptors. The distance receptors—the eyes, the ears, and the nose—are used to examine faraway objects and sensations. These receptors allow us to gather information without making contact with an object or person. The immediate receptors—the skin, the membranes, and the muscles—examine the world up close. The immediate receptors enable the experience of touch and the perception of such diverse sensations as temperature, texture, hardness, and shape.

Hall also defines different distance zones because distance from any given object influences the perception of that object. A classic example is the impressionist painting, which looks like blobs of color on close inspection but, from a distance, reveals a Parisian landscape. So, too, in a restaurant must the design consider the sensory impact of objects that are close to the guest along with objects that are across the dining room. Hall's distance zones, which are excellent guidelines for environmental design planning, are as follows:

1. Public distance—12 feet and beyond. The feeling of distance one gets when entering a high-ceilinged restaurant or a large open lobby. Public distance encompasses the view when walking into the dining area itself or when entering a spacious pickup area in a kitchen.

2. Social distance—4 feet to 12 feet. Customers feel social distance when they watch the television screen above a bar, entertainers in a nightclub, or the service staff bustling about the restaurant. Similarly, the kitchen staff experience social distance while working in a display kitchen, where guests walk by, or in a bakery station, where workers at other stations can be seen.

3. Personal distance—18 inches to 4 feet. The feeling of distance experienced when speaking across the table to dining companions. This is also the feeling two kitchen staff members get when working at a double-sided workstation or at a broiler station positioned next to a fry station.

4. Intimate distance—physical contact to 18 inches. The feeling of being close enough to touch a dining companion, as when seated side by side on a banquette. It is the sometimes crowded feeling when a diner's chair is bumped by passing service staff or a cook brushes past a coworker in a cramped kitchen.

Another important influence on the way people perceive space is their ethnic background and country of origin. In Europe, for example, people are comfortable in crowded dining conditions, hence the popularity of cozy cafés and beer halls where tables and people press together in a way that members of other cultures might find stifling (Figure 3.1). In contrast, the hushed atmosphere of the Japanese teahouse in downtown Tokyo, with its sense of serenity and spaciousness, reflects a totally different cultural orientation.

FIGURE 3.1 *People from some cultures are comfortable in crowded dining conditions. Customers at Belgo Zuid in London don't mind being pressed together at beer hall tables.*
(Photo by Richard Leaney, © Belgo Americas LLC.)

If management can identify the cultural characteristics of the target market, design can be geared to suit it. In this context, *cultural characteristics* could indicate ethnicity, urban versus rural preferences, the needs of bicoastal travelers, or the tastes of baby-boomers versus Generation Xers.

Distance Receptors

VISUAL SPACE

Visual perspective is affected by the structure of the eye and the angle at which objects are viewed. The retina—the light-sensitive part of the eye—is composed of three areas, each performing a different function. One important function is peripheral vision, the field of vision outside the line of direct sight.

Hall cites the following example of peripheral vision:

> A man with normal vision, sitting in a restaurant twelve to fifteen feet from a table where other people are seated, can see the following out of the corner of his eye. He can tell that the table is occupied and possibly count the people present, particularly if there is some movement.
>
> At an angle of 45 degrees he can tell the color of a woman's hair as well as the color of her clothing, though he cannot identify the material. He can tell whether the woman is looking at and talking to her partner but not whether she has a ring on her finger. He can pick up the gross movements of her escort, but he can't see the watch on his wrist. He can tell the gender of a person, his body build, and his age in very general terms but not whether he knows him or not.

(The Hidden Dimension, p. 72)

FIGURE 3.2 The field of vision from a banquette seat is wide open, while booth seating provides a feeling of intimacy. In this hybrid, diners can see into the room, but the curved design gives them more privacy than a traditional banquette.
(Photo by Joseph Durocher.)

People can perceive all specific details about an individual only when he is directly in front of the retina.

The more designers understand how vision zones work, the more effectively they can manipulate visual space. For example, a diner's field of vision is broader when sitting on a banquette than when sitting in a booth (Figure 3.2). Banquette seating also places customers within personal distance of each other, unlike when they are seated in booths, particularly high-backed booths.

Guests are more affected by surrounding elements in a banquette and more private in a booth, where the field of vision is narrower. This implies that banquette seating—which provides more visual stimulation—encourages faster turnover and is especially appropriate for a casual restaurant or one with a big open kitchen. Booth seating, because it limits visual stimulation and distractions, provides a feeling of intimacy, and leads to slower turnover of tables, works well for restaurants that want to attract business diners or romantic couples.

Personal space can be real or perceived, so using angled tables rather than banquettes can eliminate the perception that another customer is in one's personal space (Figure 3.3). In fact, freestanding angled tables can create a sense of intimacy and cut visual distraction throughout a dining room. Increasing the space between tables can also lessen visual distraction, although this is a costly technique. Lighting levels can be modified to further limit the scope of vision, and light or cool colors can help create an overall sense of spaciousness.

Designers often manipulate visual space with mirrors and reflective surfaces (Figure 3.4). Mirrors expand the sense of space as well as the field of vision. (Used incorrectly or to excess, however, they can cause visual confusion and disorientation.) Mirrored columns or mirrored horizontal or vertical planes can open up an otherwise claustrophobic room while adding sparkle and visual excitement. Here are some mirror solutions:

FIGURE 3.3 *To decrease visual distraction, designers angle tables to redirect sight lines away from other tables.*

- *Art mirrors*—These large, framed mirrors typically sit high on a wall to give an overall sense of openness to a space.
- *Mirror strips*—The strips are frequently applied above a banquette to offer the customers facing the wall a glimpse of the action behind them. Mirrored strips at eye level permit a selective (and secretive) view of the bustling waiters, sparkling tabletops, and other diners to the rear.
- *Mirrored columns*—This application allows customers seated in a middle of a room to catch a glimpse of other customers from varying angles.
- *Ceiling mirrors*—Their hard surface reflects a good deal of sound, but they tend to open up a space and offer whimsical views of activity throughout the room.

Another effective means of modifying visual space is to minimize sight lines. A frosted glass or glass brick wall, for instance, limits visual perception. Light and motion can be perceived through the glass, yet the diner maintains a feeling of intimacy. In some cases, one-way or reflective glass is used on exterior window walls. Diners can thus look out, but passers-by can't look in. However, these reflective windows can, from the outside, give the impression that the restaurant is closed, which is not good for business.

AUDITORY SPACE

Auditory space involves how the ear works and what, exactly, we hear. The ear actually picks up sound from two main zones. Primary audio space, in which one hears and is heard clearly, extends to 20 feet away. Background audio space extends from 20 to 100 feet away. In many dining areas, sounds in the primary

FIGURE 3.4 *At Ruby Foo's Dim Sum and Sushi Palace in New York City, the Rockwell Group enlivened a quiet corner with a mirrored view of the restaurant's dramatic grand staircase.* (Photo © Paul Warchol.)

audio space must be modified and turned into background noise so that diners can hear table companions and servers and can speak to them without strain. At the same time, they should be conscious of a friendly background buzz. This state has been called *convivial intimacy*. It means that guests feel secure in their privacy, yet part of a larger whole. One of the greatest challenges is to ensure that none of the seats is overpowered with background noise. Thus, the impact of ceiling speakers, wall-mounted televisions, and sound-producing equipment in the back of the house must be considered.

Control of primary and background auditory space is also important in the kitchen. Kitchens are innately noisy spaces made louder by communications between kitchen workers and the service staff. With the introduction of remote printers linked to the POS, the need for conversation between production and service staff is significantly decreased. Although background noise can add vitality and energy to the kitchen, the sound must be controlled to minimize carryover into the dining area. This carryover sound is of particular concern in display kitchens because of their proximity to dining areas.

Because the restaurant, by definition, is a noisy environment, acoustical control often involves the skillful application of sound-absorbing materials with the goal of achieving background buzz. Soft materials like carpet, upholstery, wall coverings, and curtains, as well as acoustical ceilings, panels, and banners, all help mute noise levels, but the most effective way to deaden noise is with ceiling treatments.

Designers can effectively combine acoustical materials with decorative applications. For example, a treatment composed of fabric-covered baffles that temper noise levels might serve as a unifying design statement that pulls together the entire room. Baffles, which generally are made of glass or mineral fiber bats encased in perforated metal or fabric, are especially effective in high-ceilinged spaces.

For retrofit, the acoustical panel is an efficient and cost-effective choice because installation does not involve structural work. Faced with woven fabric or perforated vinyl, the panels come in a variety of shapes and sizes and are easily attached to walls or ceilings. They can even be formed into the restaurant's logo or other graphic symbols. Similarly, plain acoustic ceiling tiles can be painted to reflect the restaurant's design theme (Figure 3.5).

Another technique that can be particularly effective in helping soften loud conversation is the use of background music. Here,

FIGURE 3.5 *Nothing is more effective for controlling noise than acoustic ceiling treatments. Here, a dragonlike design on the acoustic ceiling echoes the Asian design theme of Jae's restaurant in Boston.* (Photo by Joseph Durocher.)

the principle at work involves masking undesirable noise—voices at other tables, the clatter of dishes, etc.—with the desirable sounds of music suited to the taste of the restaurant's clientele. As noted in chapter 4, however, it is important to control the level of background music so that it does not become a distraction. Restaurants with live entertainment face a particular problem because live music often becomes foreground music. For guests who wish to listen to the music, this is a pleasing addition to the environment, but for those wishing to converse while they dine or sit at a cocktail table, foreground music can be irritating.

The obvious solution—cutting the size of the dining spaces to quiet primary audio space—is not always effective, however, because sound waves travel through floors, walls, and ceilings. Just because adjacent dining rooms are visually separate doesn't mean that they are acoustically separate. In operations that require a single dining area, careful attention to sound-catching corners, shapes, and spaces can significantly limit reverberative sound.

In some types of operations, such as the fast-food restaurant or the bar-dominated gathering place, little attention is given to controlling primary audio space because high noise levels create movement, excitement, and action—all desirable in these places. Popular new see-and-be-seen restaurants throughout the country often share remarkably high noise levels created by hard surfaces such as steel, glass, wood, and concrete. Many also have high or domed ceilings that reflect or focus sound, generating hot spots of high noise levels. It's important to consider that all of these sound-reflecting surfaces and materials can generate reverberation and cause an echo effect.

OLFACTORY SPACE

The olfactory sense is the sense of smell, which, despite its importance, is frequently overlooked in restaurant design. Smell evokes the deepest memories of all the senses, but how often does the design allow pleasant aromas to waft through the restaurant—aromas that customers will remember the next time that they think about where to eat? Given current interest in fresh, whole ingredients, perhaps their accompanying smells should be allowed to filter through the front of the house. Because an absence of smell obscures memories, the indiscriminate elimination of all olfactory sensation can have a negative psychological effect. The smell of fresh-baked breads outside a boulangerie or of slow-smoked pork shoulder at a barbecue restaurant helps stimulate the appetite. Today, aroma infusers are available for front-of-the-house ventilation systems. The infusers slowly dispense the aroma of fresh coffee, fresh bread, and dozens of other memory-provoking essences.

Another technique to enhance the guest's aromatic experience is tableside cooking. In many recipes, a dash of Worcestershire sauce is added to the heated pan. The accompanying sizzle and the aroma of the vaporizing sauce tantalizes palates and prompts others to purchase tableside preparations. This technique is used effectively in Mexican restaurants, where sizzling fajita platters are paraded to the table, in Asian restaurants, where foods are placed on a sizzle platter just before serving, and in teppanyaki restaurants, where foods are cooked on a flat griddle in front of diners.

Smells can also create negative feelings. The stale smell of beer or slightly soured mixers tells the customer that a bar lacks a good sanitation program. The smell of cigarettes where customers are trying to savor a vintage Bordeaux indicates an ineffective ventilation system. Negative smells can attach to such items as glassware; using a stale bar towel to polish clean glasses can impart an off odor that will be released when beer or other beverages are placed in the glass. Of course, the smell of garbage in the parking lot sours the stomach.

Immediate Receptors

TACTILE SPACE

Tactile space includes both what is actually perceptible by touch and what relates visually to touch. A wineglass, for example, is an item that a guest touches in a restaurant, and a nubby wall-covering is a surface whose texture engages the visual perception. Tactile space is extremely important because it can psychologically warm a room, which makes people feel comfortable.

Tactile elements involve people with their surroundings. This is particularly important in modern interiors and in large, high-ceilinged spaces, because both tend to make people feel separate from the environment. Diners often like to feel impressed by the design of a restaurant, but they don't like to feel overwhelmed. Textural architectural and decorative surfaces like fabric, brick, upholstery, and artwork can all keep the environment from feeling distant or intimidating (Figure 3.6).

The touchable items in a restaurant—seating and tabletop elements—have a lot to do with people's enjoyment of the dining experience. The degree of seating comfort, for instance, has a great deal of influence on the length of the meal and should be chosen to suit the facility. Natural materials, upholstered seats, and padded armrests maintain high comfort levels and are recommended for high-ticket establishments. Comfortable seating also helps keep customers content as they sit through the multiple courses that play a pivotal role between profit and loss in many fine restaurants.

Tactile sensations can also be negative. No one likes the sticky sensation of plastic upholstery in warm temperatures, the feeling of pitching too far forward in a hard seat, or leaning against a seat back that is uncomfortable. Yet some degree of tactile discomfort can be appropriate for a restaurant that depends on quick turnover, like a fast-food eatery. Here, the seating can be pleasing to the eye but

FIGURE 3.6 *At MC² in San Francisco designed by Mark Cavagnero Associates, the tactile quality of brick walls warms the environment.* (Photo by Joseph Durocher.)

Tactile sensations are also important in the kitchen. Well-balanced knives, solid worktables, and substantial cutting boards give kitchen workers a sense of security and comfort.

not comfortable to sit in for long. This reflects an increasingly common design technique in the fast-food environment: furniture that looks good but becomes uncomfortable to sit in after about 15 minutes.

Turnover in 30 minutes or less is not only essential to the success of fast feeders but also plays a pivotal role in customer satisfaction and the ultimate profitability of cafeteria operations. Frequently, cafeterias serve large numbers of diners in a limited period. Comfortable seats can slow table turns and lead to dissatisfied customers who wander around the dining room with trays full of food in much the same way as they hunt for parking spaces for their cars.

In any type of restaurant, the tabletop elements—table surfaces, flatware, glassware, dishware, table accoutrements—play a major role in customer satisfaction. The feel of a perfectly balanced fork, the coolness of a chilled beer mug, and the pleasant touch of a linen napkin add to the dining experience. Even in an inexpensive eatery, the choice of tabletop utensils is critical to diners' enjoyment of a meal because of the direct contact with these items. Tabletop elements, from paper plates to crystal goblets, should always be carefully chosen.

Tactile sensors are finely tuned. The fingers detect smoothness and temperature, and the muscles in the fingers, hand, and arm weigh tabletop items, calculate how well built they are, and determine imperfections in balance or form. The oenophile sipping a 1961 Château Lafite-Rothschild from an improperly balanced wineglass does not fully enjoy the experience. A five-degree rise in temperature as growing numbers of diners overload the cooling system on a hot day can make guests irritable and hasten their departure.

On the tabletop, as in the restaurant interior itself, avoiding a homogeneous textural weight is advisable. The tabletop could offer a pleasing tactile experience through the contrast of a smooth marble table surface, nubby linen-blend napkins, and cut-crystal glassware. Likewise, a casual restaurant might feature smooth polyurethane wood tabletops with woven placemats and heavy stoneware. Attention to tabletop detail helps create a strong impression of value in the minds of clients. It shows concern for the things people touch and implies a high regard for the food as well.

Tactile space is an important concern with take-out foods. A thin napkin for fried chicken tells people that they will have trouble wiping their fingers when they are through. Flimsy plastic forks and knives encourage people to take two of each and prepare for all of them to break—hardly the message that should be sent to paying customers.

Tactile sensations are also important in the kitchen. Well-balanced knives, solid worktables, and substantial cutting boards give kitchen workers a sense of security and comfort. Nonslip flooring is another crucial design element in the kitchen. The tactile sensation of secure footing is essential to a sense of safety.

Another part of the restaurant where tactile attention is important is the rest rooms. We all tend to equate a dirty bathroom with a dirty kitchen. By the same token, attention to bathroom detail causes customers to feel that management cares about the broader quality of their dining experience. Skillful use of tactile space, for instance, might mix Corian™ or marble surfaces, terra-cotta flooring, attractive dried flower arrangements, and decorative tile walls. Such textural diversity creates a pleasant effect, yet provides surfaces that are easily cleaned and maintained.

Food, of course, is the most tactile element of all (Figure 3.7). Food presentation works on many levels to impress—or distress—the diner. In addition to food's appearance, mouthfeel—its texture in the mouth and the complete organoleptic experience that includes taste, texture, and temperature—is an element of customer satisfaction.

If presented in a nondescript way, even well-prepared dishes can look unappetizing. Conversely, a carrot curl on a sandwich plate or a sprig of lemon thyme on a poached filet of ling cod go a long way toward creating the impression of good food. A delightful textural balance of foods is literally mouthwatering.

Even in the fast-food environment, tactile cues can create the impression of food value. Packaging design often plays an important part. If the standard ketchup container that spells out the word ketchup on one side and names the manufacturer on the other also shows an image of red, ripe tomatoes, the customer is more likely to perceive the value of its contents. The average fast-food container, however, has nondescript surfaces that give little indication of the contents and in no way help sell the product. Home meal replacement (HMR) offerings, on the other hand, are packaged in containers with see-through lids that allow the food to merchandise itself.

FIGURE 3.7 *This presentation of a West Indies minced turkey dish by Chef Walter Staib of Philadelphia's City Tavern contrasts the filling's soft texture with the crispness of fried plantain strips and a tortilla shell.*
(Photo courtesy of the National Turkey Federation.)

THERMAL SPACE

Thermal space relates to temperature. In the restaurant, the most important psychological effect of thermal space is its influence on one's sense of crowding: Hot rooms feel more crowded than cool rooms. Consequently, a full restaurant should be kept comfortably cool so that diners do not experience the discomfort of feeling hemmed in. Half-empty restaurants might benefit from warmer temperatures because the warmth helps create a feeling of more people in the room.

Overheated kitchens result in overheated tempers and, ultimately, have an adverse effect on productivity. "If you can't stand the heat, get out of the kitchen" does not carry the weight in a labor-short marketplace that it once did.

Temperature control is a particular problem in the design of ballrooms or restaurants with window walls. Here, the heat loads—from the occupants of the room or the rays of the sun—can periodically overload cooling systems and make the rooms feel uncomfortably warm.

KINESTHETIC SPACE

Kinesthetic space is the psychological (not physiological) perception of space. Physical conditions affect kinesthetic perception. A room that can be crossed in 1 or 2 steps creates a different sensation than a room that takes 15 steps

FIGURE 3.8 *At MC^2 in San Francisco, architect Mark Cavagnero used barriers to create intimate dining areas that allow patrons a glimpse of the activity around them. The barriers also help direct traffic flow.*
(Photo by Sharon Risedorph.)

to traverse. A 20- by 40-foot room with a 7-foot ceiling feels a lot smaller than the same room with an 11-foot ceiling.

Designers can manipulate kinesthetic space in the restaurant by a variety of techniques—mirrors, barriers, and furniture arrangements—that help achieve a desired psychological effect. A lowered ceiling over perimeter seating, for instance, affords a more intimate dining experience than a high-ceilinged central area in the same restaurant.

Another aspect of kinesthetic space is that the fewer restrictions to movement, the larger the space feels. When comparing two identical rooms with different furniture arrangements, the one that permits the greater variety of free movement is perceived as larger. This principle can be effectively applied in compact urban storefronts, where a wall-hugging seating arrangement keeps the space from feeling cramped.

The vocabulary of the social scientist can now be applied to the process of restaurant design. We examine next the psychological effects of three crucial design applications: spatial arrangements, lighting, and color.

Spatial Arrangements

Spatial arrangements should always be orderly, guiding customers and employees in a logical progression from space to space: from exterior to entry zone to dining room, from kitchen to dining room to bar and back to dining room. The restaurant exterior, including signage, parking lot, and landscaping (when applicable), is important because it creates the first impression and gives visual cues about the type of facility within. Spatial features such as large parking lots, the location of doorways, and covered walks between the valet and the entryway can draw diners in or prompt them to go elsewhere.

As for the interior, social scientists divide space into two main areas: barriers and fields. Barriers include walls, screens, symbols, and objects. Fields include shapes, size, orientation, and environmental conditions. In the restaurant, both serve functional and psychological purposes.

Barriers often act as space dividers to create feelings of privacy. For example, a dividing wall can separate the functions of entry and dining, and potted palms can help delineate small, intimate dining areas in a large room (Figure 3.8).

Fields can be thought of as the complete architectural plan: the overall layout of space with its accompanying environmental conditions of climate and lighting. These elements substantially influence how people feel in a space. A small room helps create a cozy feeling for a gourmet restaurant, and a large room helps engage diners in the see-and-be seen atmosphere of a theatrical restaurant. The mixed sensation of barrier and field of the open kitchen, and the proximity of work and dining areas, affects both the kitchen staff and the diners.

Shape also has psychological impact. Because people tend to be attracted to curved forms, architects often build large, curved walls. The upward sweep of these curved lines can be uplifting. Restaurateur Drew Nieporent suggests that restaurants "need curves, round tables, and banquettes. People like corner tables but designers don't know that. By curving the banquette, you end up with a corner."

FIGURE 3.9 *At Norma's in New York's Le Parker Meridien Hotel, Brennan Beer Gorman Monk/Interiors designed an S-curved banquette to soften the space.*
(Photo © Andrew Bordwin, NYC.)

Many recent restaurant designs use curved banquettes and other curvaceous shapes to great advantage (Figure 3.9).

Lastly, the interaction between spaces—between the outside and the inside, between the front of the house and the back of the house—can help communicate information about the quality of the dining experience and about the food itself. A display kitchen or more subtle kitchen references, like wood-burning pizza ovens or pickup windows, not only signal messages about the food but also allow diners a privileged glimpse of the back of the house. Psychologists maintain that people like seeing what goes on behind the scenes and that those staged regions that bridge the front and back of the house can generate a lot of customer interest. In this context, service staff uniforms also link kitchen and dining rooms and send messages about both the food and the type of establishment. Black jeans and a T-shirt, for example, carry a completely different set of associations from a full-skirted, blue-and-white-checked gingham uniform, the former belonging to a hip, expensive inner-city bistro and the latter to a popular, moderately priced pancake house.

Within the dining area, designers can manipulate spatial arrangements for a variety of psychological effects. A really bad table is never necessary. Terraced floor levels rising back from windows, for example, can provide each table with a view. In a large room, terracing from side to side defines spatial areas and creates islands of intimacy. Other techniques that facilitate comfortable dining and camouflage room size include lowering parts of the ceiling (mentioned previously in respect to kinesthetic space) and enclosing an area with architectural or decorative dividers. The larger the room, the greater the need for such enclosures.

Furniture arrangements can facilitate or retard interaction among people and should be chosen to suit the type of facility. For example, a restaurant that functions as a gathering and meeting place wants to encourage interaction among guests. Here, face-to-face seating and an asymmetrical bar shape can help draw people together. Other facilitators include uncluttered lounge seating and casual-looking furniture. Conversely, when privacy is desired, widely spaced tables can be arranged at angles to each other to restrict views of other diners. Chairs in a row, barriers between chairs, and linear bars act to retard conversation.

Rooms with a regular layout of tables all neatly lined up in rows seem formal. Tables that are randomly spaced throughout the room, with different sizes of tables mixed together, and rooms divided with barriers lead to feelings of informality and even intimacy.

In the back of the house, equipment arrangements can retard or improve interaction among employees. The equipment itself, or divider walls, serves as barriers. However, half-high divider walls can help interaction among workers because they allow people to talk to each other. Limiting barriers can also improve supervision. Managers who can easily see every corner of the front and back of the house can more readily supervise employees.

FENG SHUI

Feng shui is the Chinese art of geomancy: the belief that the placement and location of buildings and objects can harmonize or conflict with the natural environment and cause good or bad fortune. Principles of feng shui can be used in site selection and the placement of buildings on the land as well as the placement of elements within a building and even the naming of a business.

A restaurant with good feng shui is said to be a good place in which to conduct business, and it affords a sense of well-being and equilibrium, while a restaurant with bad feng shui will be uncomfortable for diners and bad for business. For example, a restaurant built on a *T*-shaped lot across from a triangular pond surrounded by oddly shaped trees is said to have bad feng shui that will cause the restaurant to fail.

Many feng shui principles relate to sound design principles in general use. It would be prudent to consider the positive psychological impact of integrating good feng shui wherever possible.

Lighting

Lighting is arguably the single most important element in restaurant design because incorrect lighting can obviate the effectiveness of all the other elements. Lighting is a critical psychological component as well; more than any other design application, illumination creates mood (Figure 3.10). Lighting can make a room feel intimate or expansive, subdued or exciting, friendly or hostile, quiet or full of electrifying energy. Not only is the intensity of the lighting important but also the light source, the quality of the lighting, and the contrast of light levels in different areas. In the kitchen, lighting intensity must be maintained at a level that does not lead to eyestrain.

Ideally, a lighting design consultant is retained to handle the complexities of designing an effective illumination scheme. If the budget prohibits the hiring of a lighting designer, the architect or interior designer must be well versed in lighting psychology and sensitive to the specific demands of the facility. A bustling cafeteria calls for a bright ambient light level and brightly lit architectural surfaces to

FIGURE 3.10 *The jellyfish lights at Farallon in San Francisco, designed by Pat Kuleto, create the mood of a Jules Verne fantasy at this seafood restaurant.* (Photo by Dennis Anderson, © Pat Kuleto Restaurants.)

help move people through the space. An elegant à la carte French restaurant should have a more subdued illumination scheme to encourage leisurely dining. A source of illumination between diners, like candles or reflected light bounced off the tabletop, draws them together while providing a complementary glow that helps overcome the negative aspects of downlighting.

Although the lighting scheme should always respond to the type of facility, the following guidelines for psychologically effective illumination apply to any restaurant. Remember that restaurant lighting is similar to theatrical lighting; both set the stage for a dramatic production that relies heavily on setting and atmosphere to carry it off.

A dimming control system that can modify illumination levels for optimum psychological effectiveness is important to any lighting scheme. The system should be changed in response to the time of day and to create different moods for different occasions. The same room can feel bright and cheerful for breakfast, restful for lunch, animated for cocktails, and romantic for dinner—all due to carefully planned light programming. If the budget permits, an automated system can be programmed to react to external light conditions and deliver the desired light levels for any time of day or type of function. Dimming systems should never be adjusted during dining hours, as this can be distracting to the clientele. Nevertheless, control systems should be clearly marked to facilitate manual lighting level changes, should the need arise.

Light transition zones are important so that customers don't feel blinded when they enter from bright sunlight or disoriented when they leave at night. When people step into a dimly lit restaurant from the sunlit outdoors, for example, their eyes need time to adjust before they can see clearly. Light transition zones help eyes adjust before people move on to the dining area and impart a logical psychological procession from outdoors to indoors.

Sparkle is said to enhance and encourage conversation. Sparkle comes from light fixtures such as chandeliers and multiple small pin lights. It is also produced from certain reflected light, such as light bounced off glassware, mirrored surfaces, and shiny tableware. Especially appropriate for leisurely dining, sparkle seems to create an almost magical effect that makes people feel animated but not restless.

For environmental comfort, and to avoid a homogeneous, boring effect, direct lighting (light cast directly onto an object, without reflections from other surfaces such as walls or ceilings) should be counteracted with indirect lighting. The juxtaposition of direct and indirect lighting can create an interesting yet comfortable effect. Indirect lighting can create small shadow patterns that feel friendly; however, large, dark shadows can appear hostile and should be avoided.

One of the most important aspects of psychologically effective restaurant lighting—and the most overlooked—involves making people look their best. When people feel attractive, they not only enjoy the environment more but also tend to return for repeat visits. If flesh tones look good, food also tends to look good. Both look best under incandescent lamps, but a careful mix of warm (or tinted) fluorescent and incandescent lighting can also provide a rosy, flattering glow. Strong downlighting, however, is extremely unbecoming to people because it highlights every imperfection, and light sources improperly angled can throw unflattering shadows over faces. Guests also tend to feel uncomfortable when their table is lit more brightly than the environment around them; the effect is

Light and cool colors recede. This principle can be used in restaurant design to expand a sense of space.

something like looking into a black hole. Therefore, people should not be spotlighted as if they were on stage but rather surrounded with soft light. Although strong downlighting centered on the tabletop can be used effectively, designers must install easy-to-aim lamps that can be adjusted when tables are moved.

Perhaps the most crucial element of psychologically effective restaurant lighting is balance. If a room is too bright, too dim, too deeply shadowed, or too homogeneously lit, it won't feel comfortable. Achieving the right balance involves not only the correct selection of light sources but also light programming that is sensitive to overall brightness, daylight, and the color spectrum.

Color

Color should always be chosen in concert with lighting because the two are so closely associated. Together they communicate a variety of psychological messages on both obvious and subliminal levels. Their relationship stems from color perception being a function of the type of light source and the reflective surface itself. In other words, the same color takes on different hues or appears to be a different color when seen under different light sources (fluorescent or incandescent, for example) or when viewed in direct or indirect light. Light is color itself, whether the source is a tinted bulb, a neon tube, sunlight, or a candle.

Another consideration is that the source of light affects the perception of color. Some of the light is absorbed, but the light that is reflected is highly charged with the color of the surface material or, in other words, its hue. In addition to hue, brilliance and saturation affect the perception of color. Combined, the Munsell color system gives a graphic depiction of how these three elements interact. The higher the value of the color, the greater its reflectance. The saturation of each value level can be thought of as the purity of the color. Pure yellow has a higher saturation level than a shade of yellow produced by mixing yellow with black or some other less reflective color.

Light and cool colors recede. This principle can be used in restaurant design to expand a sense of space. Conversely, dark and warm colors advance and can be used in large rooms to keep the space from feeling vast and impersonal and to instill a sense of intimacy. Warm colors become excellent highlights as points of color on a tabletop and add to a feeling of elegance.

Bold, primary colors and bright lighting encourage turnover and are appropriate for fast-food and casual restaurants that depend on fast turnover. Extremely high illumination, however, washes out the effects of colors (as well as the effects of texture), leads to eyestrain, and lessens the impact of design detailing.

Muted, subtle colors create a restful, leisurely effect. Pastel color schemes, in addition to making a small room appear larger, evoke a calm atmosphere.

Light colors can also make a room look brighter because the brightness of a color is a function of its hue. Light colors such as yellow appear brighter than dark colors such as navy blue, even when measured brightness is the same. Measured brightness is expressed in lumens, which are absorbed into dark-hued surfaces and reflected from bright surfaces. As mentioned earlier, brightness is also affected by the light source.

Because they carry various associations, colors can evoke a theme, a style, a culture, or a country. Purple, for example, is the color of royalty; green is the color of nature; and red and gold suggest a Chinese influence.

Color schemes should relate to climatic conditions. Simply put, warm colors feel right in colder climates and cool colors feel right in warmer climates. On their own, however, cool colors are generally unappetizing (maybe this is partly why food is never blue). Therefore, even in a tropical climate, cool color schemes should also employ warm accents.

Stylish color schemes reflect trends in the consumer marketplace. In the early 1980s, restaurant color palettes began to coincide with the shift toward cool hues like seafoam green, deep blue, and aqua, often combined with burgundy, peach, or rosy terra cotta. In the late 1980s, bright, clear colors became the leading fashion statement and found their way into the color palettes of the restaurant designer. In the late 1990s, warmer full-saturation colors were used to create accents against subtle background colors. Color cycles literally move around the color wheel, gradually shifting from the cool colors to the warm colors and back again, with each trend enjoying a lifespan of about eight years.

An analysis of colors themselves must be tempered by at least three facts. First, the effect of any color depends on its hue and intensity. Sky blue, aqua, and navy are all blue, but each carries a different association. Second, the perception of color changes with distance. When choosing colors, designers must compensate for the public distance from which customers view a restaurant when they enter. Third, ongoing research by experts and associations has yet to quantify scientifically the effects of colors. On the contrary, color psychology engenders much disagreement. Nonetheless, it can be helpful to consider individual colors and their psychological effects.

Red

Historically, reds suggest aggression, hostility, and passion. A limited number of colors harmonize with red because it is so intense, but the edge can be tempered with gold, wood, brass, crystal, or mirrors. Red and black are a classic combination, with an upscale, stylish association. Some say that red enhances the appetite.

Green

Green is associated with nature and general well-being. Because of its link to the outdoors and, therefore, to good health, it has become a trademark of natural and salad bar restaurants. Green is also linked with "lite" and good foods. Live plants and light-colored woods can complement green. Although it can be refreshing in moderate doses, green should not be overused because its reflective nature negatively affects the appearance of skin tones and some foods.

Yellow

Yellow suggests radiant sunlight, expansiveness, and high spirits. In small doses, it can evoke cheerful, exuberant feelings, and it is particularly appropriate in breakfast areas. Yellow commands attention and can be used effectively as a color accent or an architectural symbol, as in the McDonald's arch. Green-cast yellows, however, have a disturbing effect.

GOLD

Like yellow, gold has a warming influence. It can help offset cold materials (like stone) and brighten dark materials (like dark wood). Gold is associated with wealth and power, and it tends to invoke a timeless feeling because of its historical overtones.

BLUE

Blue is stark, cool, and refreshing. It can visually expand a room, but it does not complement most foods and so should be avoided on the tabletop. Blue goes particularly well with warm colors and materials and is complemented by bleached or light woods. It is said to have a calming effect.

NEUTRALS

Darker browns suggest masculinity, and lighter terra cottas suggest warmth and femininity. A rosy hue complements food and people. Neutrals are excellent for the tabletop because they tend to enhance the colors of food. Another advantage of neutrals is that they provide an excellent backdrop and an effective canvas for a variety of color effects. A neutral backdrop also allows for flexibility, because the mood of a room can be changed just by changing the color accents.

WHITE

White is extremely effective when it is harmonized with other colors. It works well as a background or as a statement in its own right, but it is not ideal for walls because its brightness produces glare that can lead to eyestrain. However, in a fast-food environment, where contact time is minimal, white walls can encourage turnover and are in keeping with the bright, clean atmosphere. Although white is traditionally associated with tabletops, it is not always the best choice because white tends to neutralize the color of the food and the tabletop pieces. White tabletops can also contribute to glare in sun-filled restaurants.

BLACK

Black has negative sociological connotations. It is associated with depression and mourning, but it can be stylish and it works well as an accent with all other colors. Black goes especially well with white—its opposite—creating a classic statement. It does not usually work well as a background color, with the exception of nightclub environments or in conjunction with colored lighting.

Summary

All design applications in the restaurant engage and manipulate the senses. Today, design elements are looked at separately and analyzed for their psychological contribution to the whole. Whether or not intentionally, almost every design element and environmental condition in the restaurant works as a psychological tool. From lighting to color to texture to temperature, the nuances that influence people's feelings and behavior number in the hundreds. Design choices, therefore, should reflect careful consideration of their psychological impact. Customers can be encouraged to leave or to linger, feel exuberant or mellow, feel like part of the action or secure in an intimate enclave, all as a result of design applications. Such attention to the psychological impact of design can have a marked effect on the diner and, hence, on the operation's profitability.

Notes

Aureole Las Vegas, facade
Adam D. Tihany International Ltd.
(Photo © Mark Ballogg, Steinkamp/Ballogg
Photography, Chicago)

Aureole Las Vegas, interior
Adam D. Tihany International Ltd.
(Photo © Mark Ballogg,
Steinkamp/Ballogg
Photography, Chicago)

Le Cirque 2000, Madison dining room, New York
Adam D. Tihany International Ltd.
(Photo © Peter Paige Assoc., Inc.)

Le Cirque Las Vegas, dining room
Adam D. Tihany International Ltd.
(Photo © Mark Ballogg, Steinkamp/Ballogg
Photography, Chicago)

China Grill, entry, Las Vegas
Jeffrey Beers International
(Photo © Paul Warchol)

*China Grill, rest room
garden, Las Vegas*
Jeffrey Beers International
(Photo © Paul Warchol)

*Rock Lobster conveyor
sushi bar, Las Vegas*
Jeffrey Beers International
(Photo © Paul Warchol)

Calle Ocho, dining room, New York
Jeffrey Beers International
(Photo by David M. Joseph)

Border Grill, facade, Las Vegas
Schweitzer BIM, Inc.
(Photo by Jeffrey Green Photography)

*Border Grill, dining
room, Las Vegas*
Schweitzer BIM, Inc.
(Photo by Jeffrey Green
Photography)

Farallon, pool room, San Francisco
Pat Kuleto
(Photo by Dennis Anderson, © Pat Kuleto Restaurants)

Farallon, dining room, San Francisco
Pat Kuleto
(Photo by Dennis Anderson, © Pat Kuleto Restaurants)

City Hall, Granite Room, New York
Bogdanow Partners Architects, PC
(Photo © Peter Aaron/Esto)

City Hall, facade, New York
Bogdanow Partners Architects, PC
(Photo © Peter Aaron/Esto)

Legal Sea Foods, foyer, Boston
Bogdanow Partners Architects, PC
(Photo © Warren Jagger Photography, Inc.)

Matthew's Restaurant, dining room,
Jacksonville, Florida
Larry Wilson Design Associates, Inc.
(Photo © Joseph Lapeyra)

MC², bar, San Francisco
Mark Cavagnero Associates
(Photo by Sharon Risedorph)

Next Door Nobu, sushi bar and service bar, New York
Rockwell Group
(Photo © Paul Warchol)

Next Door Nobu, dining room, New York
Rockwell Group
(Photo © Paul Warchol)

Ruby Foo's Dim Sum and
Sushi Palace, grand staircase,
New York
Rockwell Group
(Photo © Paul Warchol)

Union Pacific, waiting area, New York
Bogdanow Partners Architects, PC
(Photo © Paul Warchol)

Design Implementation: Front to Back Through the Customers' Eyes

Successful restaurant design is based, in part, on its operational effectiveness. Yet to an even greater extent, its success depends on the customer's perception of the restaurant. A customer's perception is based on a complex set of factors unique to each individual. One person may hear about the restaurant from a friend, read an advertisement, see a newspaper article, or watch the construction of the building that will house the restaurant. Another person may develop perceptions based on the fact that the restaurant parking lot is nearly full every evening when she drives past. For each of these potential customers, the data that makes up his perception comes together as a "go" or "no go" decision to visit the restaurant for the first time. Many customers decide whether or not they wish to return during the course of their initial meal.

This chapter addresses the ways in which front-of-the-house design affects the customer, from her first glimpse of the signage and facade to the end of the meal. It follows the progression of spaces as the patron perceives them, starting with the exterior and moving on to the entryway area, the dining room, the bar/lounge, and the rest room. It covers the basic principles of design decision making for such areas as signage and graphics; seating; tabletop elements; lighting; color; floor, wall, window, and ceiling treatments; and acoustics.

The act of dining out, regardless of restaurant type, involves the sequence of destination, progression, and arrival discussed herein. In an effective design, this sequence is a harmonious flow, a spatial organization that helps create a memorable restaurant experience. Once the customer enters the doors of the restaurant, the design should continue as an integrated sensory and operational experience that reinforces the decision to visit and compels the decision to return.

Exterior Image

The exterior image of a restaurant influences the customer in many ways (Figure 4.1). Obviously, location plays an important role in determining an appropriate architectural style. A restaurant nestled in the backcountry of Alaska might

FIGURE 4.1 *The inviting, contemporary facades of the Brew Moon restaurants in Massachusetts tell patrons that the brewpub is not stereotypical.*
(Photo © Warren Jagger Photography, Inc.)

be an A-frame structure supported by lodge-pole pine logs that reflect the wooded environment. A restaurant sitting off the atrium of a late 1990s high-rise in New York might be decorated with marble and stainless-steel accents that relate to the slick architectural style of the building. In these cases, the customer is conditioned by the restaurant's surroundings to expect a certain type of establishment.

Similarly, the restaurant architecture found along the miracle miles located on the outskirts of many cities and towns portends a certain type of restaurant image. People are conditioned to expect greasy-spoon diners, fast-food restaurants, and chain family restaurants on these stretches of highway, and other types of restaurants might seem incongruous.

Sometimes, conditioned expectations can be overcome by exterior design. For example, the image of noncommercial cafeterias suffers from expectations of sterile, uncomfortable, noisy environments. Today, many institutions have upgraded their exterior, signage, and entry areas to beckon patrons inside the cafeteria—where guests find that their recollections of the boring, straight-line cafeterias of yesteryear do not match the restaurant-style atmosphere.

FIGURE 4.2 *A distinctive facade, as seen here at Noodles at the Bellagio Resort & Casino, attracts customers and differentiates the restaurant from its neighbors.*
(Photo courtesy of Girvin Designs, Inc.)

FACADE

To succeed in a cluttered visual environment, a restaurant's facade must stand out from the rest of the pack. This is particularly important for restaurants on roadways, but the facade should be considered even when there is little competition. The same problem faces advertisers in magazines and on television. Today, with so many color ads, some advertisers have moved back to black and white images in an effort to stand out. The key is to be distinctive. With respect to restaurant design, the facade of the building itself can help differentiate it from the competition and create memorable images in the minds of the customers (Figure 4.2).

The exteriors of chain restaurants are sometimes quite imaginative. The facade of Bugaboo Creek, for example, with its rough wood exterior, front porch, and other backwoods elements, clearly sets the restaurant apart. Eatertainment chains engage potential diners with interactive or highly dramatic exterior elements (Figure 4.3). In other chain designs, recognizable architectural elements, such as the

FIGURE 4.3 *The thematic exteriors of the Kahunaville restaurants, a Delaware-based chain, are attention grabbers for all who pass.*
(Photo courtesy of Rodento Management, Inc.)

red roof of Pizza Hut and the golden arches of McDonald's, communicate instantly to the customer. Historically, fast-food exteriors relied on vernacular imagery to impart the idea of the restaurant. A gigantic doughnut or hot dog on the building's facade left no questions about the type of food being sold. However, reliance on architectural imagery can restrict the flexibility of the building for future occupants. It can also, if not properly protected, be easily copied. Many copycat chains have used the gambrel roof developed as a Dairy Queen symbol, for example.

Other building types can communicate to potential customers the type of experience they can expect inside the doors. Such is the case with the whimsical facade at the Wolfgang Puck Café at Universal Studios in Los Angeles, which foretells a casual, fun-filled time (Figure 4.4).

On the other hand, big storefront windows that allow views inside signal a more informal, convivial type of restaurant. The facades of bistros and large gathering places, for instance, often have windowed walls totally open to the street.

Restaurateur Michael Weinstein pioneered the wide-open gathering place in New York back in the early 1980s with places like The Saloon, Ernie's, and America, all of which allowed pedestrians unobstructed views of the lively scenes inside, and vice versa. Today, we still see this treatment in urban restaurants across the country, often with a view of a dynamic open kitchen.

Customers may browse for a restaurant in much the same way they look for a book. If they like the cover, chances are good that they will look inside.

SIGNAGE

Signage is such an important component of exterior building design that it merits its own discussion. Often, it is the most recognizable element of the facade, one that arrests people's attention and remains in their minds as a symbol of the restaurant. Especially in a shopping mall or on a highway, signage can be an extremely effective attention grabber. Different feelings are created by a big, comfortable logo versus an understated sign whose only identification is a street address.

Easy-to-read signs are essential when potential customers have but a few seconds to notice and react as they speed by. The ubiquitous roadside sign with McDonald's golden arches or the burger bun filled with the words Burger King are examples of signs that have almost become ideographs in today's culture.

Less well known but still well recognized in its venue is the seven-story-high cactus emblazoned with

FIGURE 4.4 *The facade of Wolfgang Puck's Café at Universal City in Los Angeles communicates to would-be diners that the restaurant experience is a fun one featuring open-fire cooked foods.*
(Photo by Joseph Durocher.)

the name of the Hilltop Steak House in Saugus, Massachusetts. The name, in red neon, can be seen from both sides of the highway—a mile away (Figure 4.5). Add to this a herd of inanimate cattle grazing on the front, and passing motorists know for sure that Texas-style steaks are being cooked inside the barnlike structure.

Today, graphic designers create effective signage—with type, color, form, and light—that carries strong and clear visual messages. The typeface should echo the style of the restaurant, thus giving people another cue about what they're going to encounter inside. No matter what type of establishment, a readable typeface is essential.

At times, signage becomes an integral component of the architectural design; in other instances, it is a separate element. Even when it is freestanding, however, sign design should mesh with architectural design.

Whether mounted on signposts high above the highway or integrated into

FIGURE 4.5 *The seven-story Hilltop Steakhouse sign in Saugus, MA, is a well-recognized symbol for this landmark restaurant.* (Photo by Joseph Durocher.)

facades, a well-conceived and -designed sign can become a recognizable ideograph (Figure 4.6) that symbolizes the restaurant. Used as a logo throughout the space, such a sign often creates a lasting impression.

Ideograph signs can also be integrated with advertising programs, which play an important part in developing the first impression of a restaurant. While advertising is not an integral part of the design program, it should work in conjunction with the design to express a coordinated message. Care should be given to how the colors, shape, and typeface of the sign will read in any form of advertising medium. For example, a color rendering in print media will show more accurately than the color on a Web page when viewed from a computer. Depending on the resolution setting of the computer screen, some elements—lines, for example—in the image may be illegible.

LANDSCAPING

Patrons driving or walking past a freestanding restaurant notice not only the building itself but also the natural surroundings. In fact, landscaping helps form people's first impression of the restaurant. Like the facade and the signage, landscaping gives cues about what type of dining experience awaits inside. Formal landscaping, such as an 8-foot manicured hedge flanking an iron gate driveway entrance, prepares the customer for a formal dining experience in which multiple courses are served by a large service staff.

Informal landscaping, such as nonordered gardens or free-flowing bushes and trees, prepares the customer for a more casual experience. This type of landscaping is appropriate for moderately priced restaurants with friendly interior settings that don't impose a suit-and-tie-only feeling.

Sometimes landscape design works in concert with architectural design to create a dramatic first impression. The obvious example is the restaurant located on the edge of a national forest that uses log cabin architecture. Alternatively, a restaurant's architecture could relate to the rock formations found in a desert mesa area. In both cases, the relationship between the surroundings and the architecture feels appropriate.

Landscaping is a critical concern when parking areas are situated on the restaurant property. A sea of asphalt can be hidden from the view of diners with artfully placed trees or shrubs. Landscaping can be used to conceal unsightly neighboring buildings or dumpsters as well.

FIGURE 4.6 *The tilting cups and neon signage of the Daily Grill in Universal City, Los Angeles, catch the eyes of pedestrians strolling the promenade of this popular California attraction. The steelworker hoisting an oversized Whopper on the facade of a Chicago Burger King (left) is ideally suited to the urban setting.* (Photos by Joseph Durocher.)

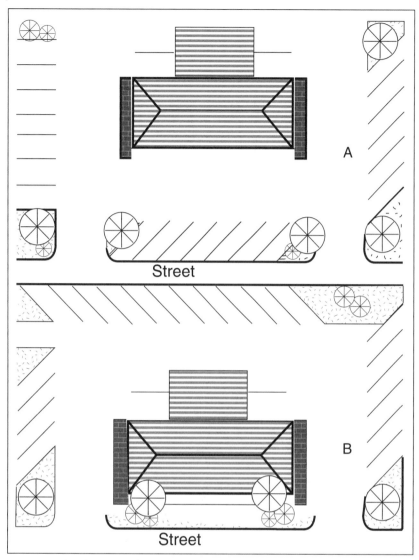

The placement of the restaurant on the property can affect its streetside appearance. For example, consider a three-acre lot comprising two acres of parking and one acre of restaurant and gardens. If the restaurant sits at the back of the lot with parking in the front, its streetside appearance will be quite different from the same restaurant placed at the front end of the lot with parking in the back (Figure 4.7).

Entry

As noted above, the exterior image creates first impressions and heightens people's expectations about what they will find inside the restaurant. The next impression is created at the arrival area, where guests step through the front door and into the entry area (Figure 4.8).

It's important that the arrival experience flows smoothly and creates an appropriate aesthetic impact. Spatial progression comes into play here as well, especially in upscale restaurants, where the design team wants to provide guests time to shift gears from

FIGURE 4.7 *The placement of a restaurant on a lot will have a marked impact on customers. In an urban setting, a restaurant set back from the road (A) can get lost between buildings that are built at the front property line.*

the outside world. In these situations, small vestibules between door and reception give patrons a brief pause before they enter the restaurant proper.

The means by which the outside is separated from the inside must be matched both to the type of restaurant and its location. In Hawaii, the problem is easily resolved; the weather allows restaurant entrances to be without physical doors. In most places, however, a door is necessary, and its form affects the customer's perception of the restaurant. A glass door allows customers to see into the restaurant, while a solid wood door creates a feeling of anticipation. In some instances, the anticipation may be deliberate and desired, but in others, it may be intimidating enough to turn a potential guest away. The shape, size, and weight of the door, along with the handle, send subtle messages.

As a general guideline, the portal to a restaurant should be as unencumbered as possible. In addition to evoking the theme of the restaurant, it should be easy to use. A heavy oak door with a cast-iron ring handle may give the feeling of entering a castle but, if not carefully balanced, it may be too hard for people to open. Glass doors or doors with windows invite guests to preview the interior and, in some cases, allow diners to look out on the show outside. Particularly in cold cli-

FIGURES 4.8 *Each of these exterior entries incorporates the name of the restaurant and sends a distinct message to customers. Some afford a glimpse of the interior.* (Photos by Joseph Durocher.)

FIGURE 4.9 *Air curtains mounted over the open windows of a restaurant allow an al fresco feel while excluding pesky insects. Such air curtains also form a barrier that helps keep down air-conditioning costs.* (Photo by Joseph Durocher.)

mates, double sets of doors minimize the blast of cold air that enters when the outer doors are opened. In some settings, energy-efficient revolving doors may be appropriate. Air curtains are used in some locations, but never in formal settings where they might disturb a guest's hair. Air curtains help with climate control and prevent flying insects from entering a restaurant (Figure 4.9).

RECEPTION

The reception area or landing area serves as a conduit from the exterior to one of the destination spaces. In a fast-food operation, the landing area should lead directly to the order counter. If the pickup counter is not immediately visible, customers can become disoriented because they expect to find it as soon as they enter the restaurant. A similar phenomenon exists in tableservice restaurants. In France, people are often drawn well into a restaurant before they are guided by the maître d' to their destination. However, in most other countries, customers expect to be greeted and guided to the dining room as soon as they step through the door.

The reception area of a cafeteria plays an important role, because it is here that customers stop to think about their options (Figure 4.10). It should include a tray dispenser, information about specials, and a vantage point for customers to view the servery. Customers gain an overview of the servery food stations and begin to develop a sense of where they will be going and what they will buy. The

FIGURE 4.10 *Webb Foodservice Design Consultants created a display column for the reception area of Beckman Instruments cafeteria in Brea, CA, that functions as a great merchandising tool. In lieu of a sign, daily specials are showcased on the column, so customers can see the actual dishes before entering the servery.*
(Photo by Don Romero.)

design of this space is particularly important in a cafeteria because, unlike the tableservice restaurant, with a maître d', or the fast-food operation, with its pickup counter, customers must make decisions about which areas of the servery they should approach, and in which order. Utensils and napkins should be dispensed near the cashier at the other end of the servery.

If people can clearly see each of the stations in the servery, even as they stop to pick up their tray, they can calculate whether or not they want to wait in line for hot entrées, grilled burgers, individually prepared sandwiches, or perhaps to make their own salad at the salad bar. Further, they must figure how many stations they will approach. Customers must be moved quickly through this reception area. Any delay can cause them to decide to skip lunch, jump in a car for a trip to the local fast-food eatery, or bring a brown-bag meal in the future.

COATROOM

The coatroom should be included in the entry area so guests can store items they do not wish to carry to the table. Coatrooms are typically found in tableservice restaurants and may have an attendant or be self-service. If a member of the staff does not control them, they should be designed so that several guests can use the space at one time. Further, some effort should be made to ensure that the maître d' can watch the space to limit the potential for theft. In upscale restaurants, care must be taken when guests arrive in furs and other expensive coats. A separate storage space for this outerwear should be considered.

Although coatrooms are common in tableservice restaurants, they are frequently overlooked in other types of establishments. In a university cafeteria, a coatroom or lockers at the entryway is a welcome design addition for storing books and coats. Students may make additional purchases when their trays are not crowded with books—purchases that otherwise might not be made. The number of students that can be seated at one time will increase because chairs will not be filled with backpacks and coats.

In malls, shoppers are frequently burdened with packages when they drop into the food court; this may limit their food purchases because their arms are full. Again, a coatroom or even a set of keyed self-service lockers could alleviate their burden and increase sales.

Without coat and package storage space, problems can arise in any type of dining area. In casual restaurants that do not have coatrooms, hat- and coatracks should be provided in the dining area—although this does not solve the problem of people setting their belongings on empty chairs at neighboring tables. If no provision is made for garments, people will drape their coats over the backs of chairs or over the drink rails in bars, thus destroying the look of even the most carefully developed design and creating a hazard for both servers and guests.

WAITING AREA

Often, people enter a restaurant only to be told that they have to wait before being seated. Waiting patrons should be able to sit down. All too frequently, however, waiting areas are eliminated from the design because they are non-revenue-producing space. However, a thoughtful design can provide needed waiting space *plus* potential for sales.

An example is the seafood restaurant where guests mill around looking at the tanks filled with lobsters or iced seafood that can be purchased for take-out at the end of the meal. The appearance of the fresh seafood tells people about the experience to come. The same is true of a steakhouse, such as the landmark Gallagher's in New York (Figure 4.11), where tons of aging strip loins are visible through the glass sidewall of a walkway that flanks the exterior and entryway.

MERCHANDISING In some types of restaurants, waiting areas have the potential of becoming incremental sales areas. For example, on Sunday mornings in most chain coffee shops, the inadequate waiting areas force guests to stand in a cramped entryway. With just a little additional space, a self-service coffee bar and take-out station could be added to the waiting area. This would provide a carryout continental breakfast for diners who would rather not wait and a welcome cup of coffee for guests who do choose to wait. The additional business generated through coffee and take-out sales, as well as customer goodwill, would justify the bit of extra footage.

Merchandising opportunities in the waiting area are unlimited. Operators can display and sell fresh-baked goods, house salad dressings or sauces, custom-printed clothing that will boost sales, etc. Such chains as the Rainforest Café and the Hard Rock Café take full advantage of nonfood sales areas. In independent restaurants as well as chains, a retail store is sometimes part of the waiting area (Figure 4.12).

In tableservice restaurants, the waiting area can incorporate design elements that serve as menu merchandising devices. Posting a menu or menu board with the specials of the evening markets the meal before the guest arrives at the table. This may speed up the ordering process because guests previewed the menu during the waiting period, thus leading to faster turnover at the tables.

New technology makes it possible for guests to make menu selections while waiting. The orders are sent automatically to the kitchen and are ready to be filled as soon as the guest is seated. One of these systems is mounted on a kiosk that stands in the

FIGURE 4.11 *The meat aging refrigerator that lines the reception area of Gallagher's in New York City merchandises the aged wholesale cuts that are fabricated into steaks for diners.*
(Photo by Joseph Durocher.)

FIGURE 4.12 *Retail stores are integrated into the entry area of many restaurants, as seen here at the Stinking Rose in San Francisco. Sales of soft goods and specialty foods related to the restaurant can significantly bolster overall revenue.*
(Photo by Joseph Durocher.)

FIGURE 4.13 *An open kitchen brings life and excitement to the dining room. At the Catahoula restaurant in Calistoga, CA, the clever addition of a mirror over the work counter gives customers a view of plates being assembled.* (Photo by Joseph Durocher.)

reception area. Another is a portable device that can be used to preview menu offerings, print out discount coupons for future visits, order meals, and play games. Such high-tech devices can keep patrons occupied while they are waiting, ensure speedy service when they are seated, and help increase table turns.

Another menu merchandising technique that depends on design is the addition of a dessert cart or espresso station adjacent to the waiting area. Both of these elements condition guests to make purchases after the meal. While a dessert cart or wine rack can be added to the waiting area as an afterthought, they are most effective as merchandising tools when incorporated with the original design. Similarly, a view of an antipasto station in an Italian restaurant predisposes waiting guests to put in an appetizer order as soon as they are seated.

The vision of an open kitchen is an excellent means of merchandising food to waiting guests. The open kitchen may be positioned so that it is at the back of the dining room, yet visible to people elsewhere in the restaurant (Figure 4.13). In more complex layouts, the open kitchen can be placed adjacent to the waiting area so that customers can, literally, focus on the meal to come, plus enjoy an entertaining view of chefs at work.

A successful waiting area previews the design as well as the menu. Glimpses into the dining area hints at the type of service, customers, food, and decor to come. However, the design should respect already seated diners to ensure that they are not distracted by the movement invariably associated with the waiting area.

ENVIRONMENTAL CONCERNS Three environmental conditions make an enormous difference to customer comfort in the waiting area: light, temperature, and sound levels. Lighting levels must be controlled to provide a painless transition from outside space to interior space. Entering the waiting area of a restaurant with an entrance facing west can be an ocular assault, for example, because going from bright daylight into a dim room is temporarily blinding. This is a particular problem for older people, whose eyes take longer to adjust to changing light levels. In all circumstances, both entry and waiting area lighting should be dimmer-controlled to relate and react to exterior lighting levels.

Temperature control in entry and waiting areas is a vital matter. In freestanding buildings located in northern climates, customers will feel chilly on cold days unless the building is properly insulated. As mentioned earlier, double sets of entry doors can help. HVAC systems should be designed so that an extra blast of heat warms guests coming in from the cold. In southern locations, an air screen can be used to limit the mixing of outside and inside air. In general, the design team must always be aware of the infiltration of outside air and program the space for maximum temperature comfort.

Sound levels must also be controlled in the waiting area, which often holds more people per square foot than any other part of the restaurant. The most effective place for sound-absorbing materials is ceilings and walls.

Both the exterior image and all of the entry areas should work together to preview the restaurant. Together, they help create an image of things to come. If carefully designed, they support the functions of the destination spaces.

Paging Systems Picture this: A couple arrives at a restaurant only to be faced with a waiting area filled with customers. The question: "Should we fight our way through the crowd to find out how long we'll have to wait, or should we go somewhere else?"

If they choose the latter, the design has cost the operation important revenue potential. One reason waiting areas are frequently overcrowded is that customers fear they will not hear the page for their table when it is called, so they do not move into the bar, where the restaurateur could accrue additional revenues.

An important solution, and one that must be considered during the design phase, is to integrate a paging system that works with the overall layout of the restaurant. Prior to the mid-1990s, paging systems consisted of loudspeakers or hostesses who yelled out the name of the next party. Today, vibrating pocket pagers or lighted pagers do the job. These high-tech pagers allow people to shop in the restaurant store, stand outside, sit comfortably in the bar, or even head for the rest room, knowing that they will not miss their page.

Destination Drinking

Customers progress to the bar for many reasons, depending on their needs and on the type of restaurant. The bar may be the patron's sole destination, a place for socializing. At other times, it acts as the waiting area, and customers sip a drink there while waiting for their tables. In still other situations, people drift to the bar for an after-dinner drink. When foodservice is offered at the bar, single diners, in particular, may prefer to eat there rather than at a table.

In gathering places or theatrical restaurants, the bar is an important operational component that serves large numbers of people and generates a high profit margin. In serious gourmet restaurants, where food is the raison d'être, the bar may consist of no more than a few token stools. Bars are most often located at the front of restaurants, so that customers don't have to wend their way past diners to get there. However, in some see-and-be-seen gathering places, guests are paraded through the dining room before reaching the bar (Figure 4.14).

Often, a view of the bar, with its throngs of patrons and bustling conviviality, helps merchandise the restau-

FIGURE 4.14 *At America, one of the earliest see-and-be-seen theatrical restaurants in New York City, a two-level raised bar sits at the back of the dining room. This design treatment draws people visiting for a drink as well as diners waiting for a table.* (Photo by Joseph Durocher.)

Drinking spaces can be divided into three distinct areas:

1. *beverage production and storage areas*
2. *the service area immediately in front of the bar*
3. *cocktail seating*

rant to passers-by. This technique works especially well on urban streets and inside hotels, where the most successful bars are open to the street or lobbies and corridors of a hotel. But every rule has exceptions and, in some restaurants, unusual bar placement—at the back of the room or up a flight of stairs—works to the operation's advantage. Such is the case at the Four Seasons hotel in New York. The Lobby Lounge bar sits up a flight of steps adjacent to the registration area. The Fifty Seven Fifty Seven Bar is located over 200 feet from the front of the hotel and up yet another flight of steps. However, this space, with its high ceilings and stylish clientele, is a destination bar for patrons from around the city. The bar location decision depends on many factors, but circulation paths should always be considered.

The placement of a cigar bar bears careful attention. Cigar bars became popular in many types of restaurants in the mid-1990s, but they were often placed in former private dining rooms or adjacent to an existing bar. It's important to consider airflow whenever a smoking area is incorporated into a restaurant. (A more detailed discussion about airflow and smoke control is presented below under "Destination Dining.")

Designing a bar operation is every bit as complex as designing a restaurant. The same ten factors outlined on page 2 should be considered. When a bar is affiliated with a restaurant, it must meld with the restaurant design concept to make the spaces mutually supportive. The selection of equipment and decor items should begin only after the nature of the bar and a managerial philosophy is established.

In the past, many operators aimed at a sales mix of 60 percent food sales and 40 percent liquor sales. The high profitability of liquor led to many promotions— happy hours, two-for-one specials, etc.—that increased beverage traffic. Today, however, there's a lot of pressure to reduce excessive alcohol consumption and concern about the legal issues of liquor liability. Even gathering places and theatrical restaurants with deliberately big bar scenes have shifted the sales mix. As long ago as the mid-1980s, New York's America, for example, reduced an initial sales mix of 40 percent beverage sales to 30 percent because management did not want to promote the establishment as a drinking place. America maintained its profitability—and its reputation as a restaurant—while decreasing many of the headaches that excessive drinking can cause.

A well-designed bar can help to control beverage consumption *and* increase beverage sales. The design of the bar's backside and service side can add to the bottom line through increased customer counts and decreased operating costs. Properly displayed call brands can increase the sale of these higher-priced beverages.

Drinking spaces can be divided into three areas (Figure 4.15):

1. *beverage production and storage areas*
2. *the service area located in front of the bar, including bar stools*
3. *cocktail seating*

BEVERAGE PRODUCTION AND STORAGE

As mentioned above, the type of equipment installed at a bar is a function of the type of operation. The low-volume neighborhood tavern may elect to serve bottled beer because the volume of draws does not warrant installing a draft system. A large-volume gathering place, where the potential for selling draft beer is apparent, may opt to sell both draft and bottled beer to increase the number of offerings. In operations where a large volume of beer sales is expected, dozens of beers can be served from a draft system.

Here are the most important questions to ask when considering bar equipment:

1. *Will wine be served by the glass?*

The least expensive solution is to place open bottles in a reach-in refrigerator. The optimal solution is to place reds and whites in temperature-controlled, glass-fronted dispenser cabinets where customers can clearly view the bottles from the front of the bar. The system automatically injects inert nitrogen gas to maximize the shelf life of the open bottle.

2. *Will frozen drinks be prepared individually or in bulk?*

Blender-prepared frozen drinks require that the bartender prepare them one or two at a time. However, the bartender can use the same piece of equipment to prepare any type of frozen drink, from margaritas to frozen daiquiris. This dispenser enables the bartender to serve a frozen drink in a matter of seconds because the drink ingredients are mixed in advance of serving times. However, the dispenser can hold and dispense only one type of drink at a time.

3. *How will liquor be poured?*

If liquors are poured directly from the bottle, each bottle needs to be within reaching distance of each bartender workstation. If liquors are dispensed with a gun or dispenser tower, less display space for bottles is needed on the back bar and in the well. However, a separate storage space where the open bottles are stored and linked into the dispenser system is required.

4. *Will a point of sale (POS) system be integrated with the beverage dispensing process?*

When a POS is integrated with a beverage dispensing system, only those drinks that have been ordered through a POS should be made by the bartender. In some setups, servers enter the drink orders at a remote order-entry station; the order is printed out at the bar, indicating to the bartender that the drink has been charged to a guest check. In automated dispensing systems, the beverages can only be delivered after the drinks are entered into a POS.

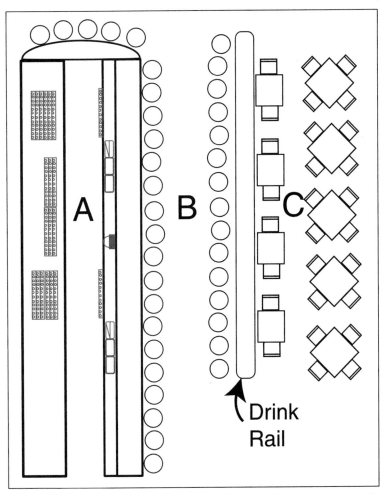

FIGURE 4.15 *A bar is typically divided into three areas: (A) production and storage, (B) service area, and (C) cocktail seating. Drink rails help divide the scene into a more active service area on one side of the rail, and a quieter cocktail area filled with tables and chairs on the other side.*

5. Will draft beer kegs be tapped centrally or undercounter?

When kegs are stored in a central refrigerated space, the brew can be directed to draft towers located on separate floors or at separate stations in a large bar. If, however, kegs are to be held in undercounter refrigeration at the bar, sufficient space is needed to manipulate the kegs to and from the bar.

Central storage doesn't disrupt customers as much as undercounter keg storage. However, the relationship of the refrigerated walk-in to the dispenser heads is important. The lines must not run too long and must be refrigerated along their entire length.

6. How will the glassware be washed?

A three-compartment sink with brushes is the least expensive glass-cleaning option. However, the time that bartenders spend washing glasses takes away from the time they spend mixing drinks and serving customers. An alternative is to install a glasswasher at the bar, allowing bartenders to load the glasses at one end and remove them at the other. A third option is to place bus buckets at the bar for dirty glasses, which are transferred to the kitchen for washing. Obviously, each of these options affects bar design and layout.

7. Will glasses be chilled?

While not essential, chilled glassware can have a special appeal. Will all glassware be chilled, or only the beer mugs? Will a clean, chilled glass be used for refills? Answers to these questions will determine the size, number, and placement of the chillers.

8. Will mixers be held in containers or dispensed from a gun?

Mixers poured from bottles of other containers typically need refrigerated or iced storage to remain chilled. Gun dispensers require a separate storage area to hold the bulk syrup that is pumped to and mixed with chilled water in the head of the gun or dispenser tower.

Because these functional aspects of bar design are usually far less successfully realized than the aesthetic aspects, a detailed discussion follows.

A typical double-sided bar workstation includes the back bar, where bottled beer, call liquors, and specialty glasses are stored, and the front workstation, where most of the mixing action takes place (Figure 4.16). At the center of all workstations is the ice bin, and every other piece of equipment should be placed around this focal point. Following the assumption that most bartenders are right-handed, the undercounter glass storage is usually placed to the left of the ice bin and the mixers to the right. Fre-

FIGURE 4.16 This sectional drawing shows the various components of a sample bar work station (A) specialty glass storage, (B) call liquors on display, (C) bottled beer cooler, (D) underbar where common glassware is stored along with utensils and mixing equipment, (E) ice bin, waste, and wash sink, (F) speed rails where inexpensive commonly used liquor is stored.

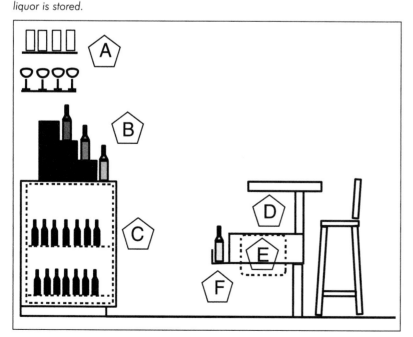

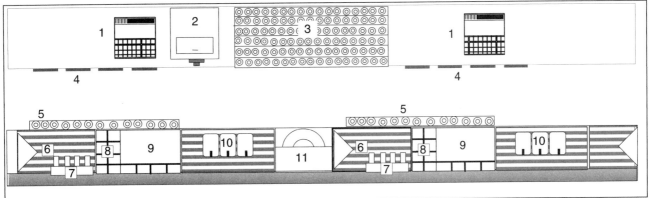

quently used liquors should go in the speed rail that fits between the ice bin and the bartender.

A bar layout involving more than one station (and more than one bartender) (Figure 4.17) is a bit more complex. As can be seen, the glasswasher is often placed between the two stations. The placement is more convenient for the bartender located to its right because she can easily take clean glasses from the washer and set them on the drainboard to await service. The other bartender has a harder time because the glasses must be carried several steps to be set on a drainboard. As an alternative, a manual washing system, with separate sinks in each station, could be installed. This two-sink system costs less than a glasswashing machine, but it doesn't really save time in the long run because it takes bartenders away from their primary business of selling drinks.

Sales control systems must be part of every beverage station. These can be simple cash drawers but, increasingly, they are POS systems integrated with beverage dispensing equipment. In one of the most elaborate systems, the bartender need only enter into the POS the desired drink and place the appropriately iced glass under the beverage head; in seconds, the glass is filled with the requested beverage. Such a system requires only three running feet of bar space and contains the POS plus a beverage service head that can dispense 71 different products.

Fully integrated cash and beverage dispensing systems are usually installed in large-volume restaurants or operations where management is not available constantly to supervise the bartenders. The liquor and mixes are frequently stored in a central location and piped to the workstations. One storage area can be used to supply several workstations at a single bar or at multiple bars. An advantage of such centralization is that pilferage is minimized because no bottles are issued to the bartenders and all drinks come out of the beverage dispensing head. No drinks can be ordered unless they are rung into the POS. Further savings accrue because liquors can be purchased in half-gallon containers rather than liter bottles. Draft beer can also be tied into the POS system. In general, one of the greatest advantages of a centralized storage and control system is that the amount of space required on the back bar is significantly decreased. Of course, the overriding question is whether or not the cost of the control system is less than the potential losses due to lack of controls.

Storage procedures for alcoholic beverages must be even more stringent than for food products. Alcoholic beverages are common targets for theft and therefore must be secured, both before and after issuing, to limit stealing and

FIGURE 4.17 *A typical double bar incorporates: (1) POS unit, (2) frozen drink machine, (3) back-bar liquor display, (4) undercounter refrigeration, (5) speed rail, (6) glass drainage and storage, (7) beer- and soda-dispensing heads, (8) mixer storage, (9) ice bin, (10) wash sink and dump station, (11) glasswasher.*

unauthorized consumption. In storerooms, this is accomplished via locked spaces kept separate from food storage areas. At the bar itself, a means of securing the liquor and dispensing equipment is imperative.

In bars where bottles are stored at the bar, well brands—the liquors used for most mixed drinks—are stored in speed rails, which run along the face of the underbar. For call brands—brands that are specifically requested—storage is generally on top of the back bar, with backup storage in cabinets. Tiered shelving, sometimes with bottom lighting, helps merchandise call brands while making them more accessible to the bartender. In some restaurants, call brands are stored in Plexiglas cabinetry above the front bar, which is another way to merchandise these higher-priced spirits.

Bottles of beer can be stored in back bar refrigeration, in ice-filled Plexiglas™ bins set on the front bar, or in undercounter bottle coolers, which are convenient for high-volume operations because they give more storage capacity than back bar refrigeration in the same amount of floor space.

Glass frosters and chillers, designed to lower the temperature of glasses before a drink is poured into them, are also included in many bar workstations. At draft beer stations, glass chillers bring the temperature of mugs and other glassware down to as low as 0 degrees Fahrenheit, which helps keep drawn beer cold. However, the cold limits the head that forms in the glass, thus decreasing profits. Outside the United States, beer is consumed at higher temperatures, which is important to consider if the bar is to appeal to an international crowd.

Workboards are important elements of any bartender's workstation. The workboard should include a counter with a sink and a waste disposal area. The sink is used for cleaning hands, drawing water, and draining glassware. A dump station for straws, napkins, and waste fruit is also needed to keep the workstation clean.

FIGURE 4.18 *Perlick's modular bar configuration speeds installation. Workstation units are held above the floor to facilitate cleaning behind the bar.* (Photo courtesy of Perlick Corp.)

OPERATIONAL LAYOUT CONCERNS

Straight-line bars are the most common and economical type to build and service. However, free-form bars have become popular in many new restaurants. While equipment manufacturers will gladly construct high-priced customized bars, modular units can generally be installed at a much lower price and still function well. A recent development from the Perlick Corporation, the largest manufacturer of bar equipment, is a prefabricated cantilevered bar unit that hangs workstation equipment from the front frame of the bar. To speed installation, the bartop and front panels slide out of place to enable plumbers, electricians, and other installers to hook up each piece of equipment easily (Figure 4.18).

One of the most important visual concerns when laying out a bar is the appearance of the underbar area. The clean lines of the back bar liquor and refrigeration systems in a straight-line bar are aesthetically acceptable. However, *L*-shaped or curved bars give customers a view of the underside of the front bar, an area that is often a jumble of ingredients, glassware, and cleaning materials.

In this situation, a glasswashing machine is a good choice because glasses are taken from the bartop and placed directly in the glasswasher, where they are out of sight of the guests. As glasses emerge from the clean side of the machine, they can be loaded into a glass froster or chiller, where again they are out of sight. Pipes, wires, and tubing must be carefully concealed where the underbar is exposed so that their appearance does not detract from the aesthetic of the bar. Other equipment needed in most bars includes blenders, frozen drink dispensers, and bottled wine or bulk wine dispensers, depending on the expected clientele and drinks to be offered.

BAR SERVICE AREA

The bar service area includes the bar stools and the standing area immediately behind the stools. Typically, one stool can be added for each 18 inches of bar length. At a bar 20 feet long, 11 guests can be comfortably seated at stools. While seating is important at a bar, the real profits come from the guests who are standing behind the bar stools. The standing area usually holds enough guests to triple the total number of clients at the bar. When a large number of standees is expected, additional workstations may be needed. The profitability of the bar will be adversely affected if the standees—or, for that matter, any bar customer—must wait while bartenders mix drinks for other guests.

If standees are expected at a bar, drink rails should be installed to separate standees from guests seated at cocktail or dining tables (Figure 4.15). Too often, this separation is omitted, and dinner guests end up being bumped against while dining.

Careful thought must be given to the section of the bar that services the dining room. Several operational decisions have a marked impact on the layout of this important space. Consider the following questions:

- Will a POS unit be incorporated with the station?
- Will the servers set up the glasses from glass storage on their side of the service bar?
- Will the servers ice, add mixers to, and garnish their own drinks?
- Will soiled glassware be returned to the kitchen or the bar for washing?

When bartenders need only portion liquor, draw drafts, and hand out bottles of beer, they have more time to attend to customers at the bar. If the service bar serves a large dining room, then sufficient space should be provided to allow several servers to access the bar at one time.

Hard, smooth-surfaced floors should be installed under bar stools and in standing areas. The smooth surfaces make it easier for people to get off and on bar stools and are not easily damaged, even when smokers snuff out cigarettes on the floor. Hard materials such as wood, brass, and tile are typically specified in bar areas. These materials are usually easy to maintain, and their sound reflecting qualities are assets if operators want to create a high-energy atmosphere.

Ventilation is vital in bar areas; in restaurants that allow smoking, people

> **Important questions to ask when considering what bar equipment to choose include:**
>
> - *Will wine be served by the glass?*
> - *Will frozen drinks be prepared individually or in bulk?*
> - *How will liquor be poured?*
> - *Will a POS be integrated in the beverage dispensing process?*
> - *Will draft beer kegs be tapped centrally or undercounter?*
> - *How will the glassware be washed?*
> - *Will glasses be prechilled?*
> - *Will mixers be held in containers or be dispensed from a gun?*

light up cigarettes more frequently here than in dining rooms. While custom ventilation systems are optimal, several ceiling-mounted smoke-filtering units can keep the air in a bar surprisingly smoke-free. As in the dining area, a well-designed ventilation system ensures that both smokers and nonsmokers can be accommodated.

Illumination sets the mood in the bar just as it does in the dining areas and, in recent years, the typical bar atmosphere has gone from dim to bright. Bar lighting has played an important role in transforming a dark hideaway into an animated meeting place.

Music and video systems have become increasingly important components of bars because they contribute to the kind of entertainment milieu that today's patrons look for when they go out to socialize. Like other design elements, these systems should be integrated with the bar design from the start of the project, taking into account such issues as speaker quality and placement, and choice and placement of video projection screens or TV monitors.

Equipment like pool tables, dartboards, and video games must be planned for early in the design process. When equipment is added as an afterthought, it can have a negative impact on nonplaying customers if the placement intrudes into their space.

In sports bars, TV monitors or video projection systems play an important role. Designers should ensure that every customer can see at least one screen. In many sports bars, diners are separated from drinkers by balconies or raised seating areas.

LOUNGE AREAS

Table seating in lounge areas plays an important role in many restaurants, especially when the lounge serves as a waiting area for diners. Table seating requires more floor space per drink served, but it creates a mood and draws a crowd that might not be captured with bar seating alone.

Lounge areas are popular before meals, but they can also encourage diners to linger after they eat, particularly if after-dinner drinks and coffees are promoted on the menu. Low cocktail seating is most commonly found in quiet lounge areas, while highboy tables and stools tend to be used in higher-energy bars. A growing number of restaurants are adding dance floors or areas for entertainers to perform in cocktail lounges. Dancing or entertainment can entice diners who might otherwise leave the restaurant to stay for an after-dinner drink.

FOODSERVICE IN BARS

Foodservice in bars has become an increasingly popular option for many types of restaurants, particularly for single diners. Because many customers have cut back on the numbers of drinks they consume, the sale of appetizers and hors d'oeuvres is increasingly important to the restaurant's bottom line. In addition to increasing bar revenues, appetizer sales in the bar area can decrease the time guests spend at dinner tables, increasing table turns.

In restaurants such as tapas bars, food and beverage sales at the bar go hand in hand (Figure 4.19). In this situation, it is advisable to locate the bar close to the kitchen. Bar-friendly food production equipment should be considered when the kitchen is distant from the bar or when food is offered after the kitchen is closed. Compact automated fryers that can be installed without ventilation hoods enable bartenders to offer items like poppers and chicken wings at any time. High-speed compact ovens that use microwaves, light, impingement air, or a combination of these cooking methods can produce pizzas, quesadillas, and other snack foods in minutes. In addition, a reach-in or chest-style freezer is usually needed to support cooking equipment at a bar.

DESIGN DECISIONS

In closing, the following points should always be taken into consideration when planning a bar design:

- A high-visibility bar can help draw patrons into the restaurant.
- The choice of partial, full, or no barriers between bar and dining room depends on the type of restaurant

FIGURE 4.19 *Foodservice options at the bar have become increasingly popular, such as at the Ciento restaurant in Portsmouth, NH, which features a tapas bar.* (Photo by Joseph Durocher.)

and the desired ambience. Some form of sound control from bar to restaurant is almost always desirable.
- If offering foodservice, the bar should be located near the kitchen unless cooking equipment will be installed at the bar itself.
- In restaurants where the bar provides beverage service to the dining room, the servers' pathway between the two areas should be short and simple. In large operations where a separate service bar is located in the kitchen, the bar can be located farther from the dining areas.
- Sound and video systems should be integrated with the design scheme and not slapped on as an afterthought.
- If live entertainment or dancing is planned for a lounge area, extra floor space must be allocated.
- Light, noise, and hard materials help create the animated, high-energy environments typical of today's gathering places.
- The type of restaurant should dictate the type of bar it contains.

Destination Dining

The elements of design must come together seamlessly in the front of the house. It is here that customers react to the environment and form opinions that will lead them to return or to avoid the restaurant in the future. The front of the house is the milieu in which guests fulfill the main purpose of going out to dine: the food. They are also influenced by service, which can be facilitated or compromised by the layout and design. It is thus important to consider how design elements work together to form the dining experience for the guest.

Numerous questions must be resolved before the design process begins:

- What is the demographic and psychographic profile of the intended market?
- How should the restaurant stand out from the competition?
- What type of cuisine will be featured?
- What style(s) of service will be employed?
- How long will the average party spend at the table?
- What type of seating (booth, banquette, freestanding) is optimal?
- What feeling should the design elements evoke in the space?

With answers to these questions as a starting point, it is time to consider the individual elements.

SEATING

When patrons progress to the table, the first element that they come into direct body contact with is their chair, banquette, or booth. Seating immediately affects how people perceive a space and how long they stay in the space. The surface and shape of the seat, its height and width, its position relative to the table (both distance from the table and the level of the occupied seat in relationship to the top of the table), its spatial relationship to other seats, and its visual relationship to other parts of the room design all influence the customer's perception (Figure 4.20).

Obviously, different types of seating make different types of impressions. The ubiquitous bentwood café chair often signals casual dining, an upholstered armchair tells patrons that the food will be serious, and booth seating signals an intimate dining experience.

TYPE OF CHAIR The hard surface and relatively small seat of a bentwood chair speeds diners along. It can be a comfortable seat for people with a small to average physique, but not for larger folks. Other wooden chairs are made more comfortable by increasing the size of the seat itself and by contouring its shape.

Armchairs are the most comfortable type of seating; they especially appeal to older diners, who use the arms to push themselves up and out of the chair. However, if the fill and webbing in the chair is not high quality, the seat height may drop to an uncomfortable point.

Banquettes on one side of a table typically are paired with freestanding chairs on the other side. Banquettes afford flexible seating, particularly in a room that also has deuce and four-top tables. Multiple banquette tables can be moved together to accommodate larger parties. As with cushioned seating, the construction of the seat padding is important. Lower-quality foam filling will quickly compress and change the relationship between the diner and the tabletop: The padding can compress to a point where diners feel the top edge of the banquette seat-face under their legs.

Booths offer an intimate experience, particularly when the backs prevent diners from seeing the action at the next booth. The spatial relationship between the booth seat and the table edge is crucial because booths cannot be pushed back to accommodate stout diners. The same cautions associated with the construction of banquette seating apply to booth seats (Figure 4.21). For any type of seating, designers can specify extra layers of upholstery material or padding to ensure comfort.

Seating can also be chosen to evoke a theme. Office chairs, for example, are ideally suited to holding business discussions over a meal (Figure 4.22). High-styled chairs evoke a hip, chic setting.

SEATING MATERIAL Wood chairs are easy to maintain and are usually lightweight so that they can be moved easily. They have a clean, attractive look and, as noted earlier, can help turn tables because they typically don't remain comfortable for long. However, that discomfort is often not appropriate. To elicit a feeling similar to that of an all-wood chair, consider a wooden chair with thin seat and back pads.

Upholstery offers an opportunity to match the colors, textures, and patterns of the overall design with the seating. Nylon upholstery holds up extremely well and, for a more luxurious look, can be blended with wool or wool and silk. Even in high-ticket establishments, maintenance is a key consideration when choosing upholstery because the finest silk won't impress a customer if it is stained or worn. In general, it makes sense to use delicate materials on seat backs rather than on seat bottoms. Choose commercial-grade upholstery that has been treated with spot-resisting chemicals to maximize the useful life of the seating. Wherever possible, avoid crevasses and button tufting, where crumbs tend to lodge.

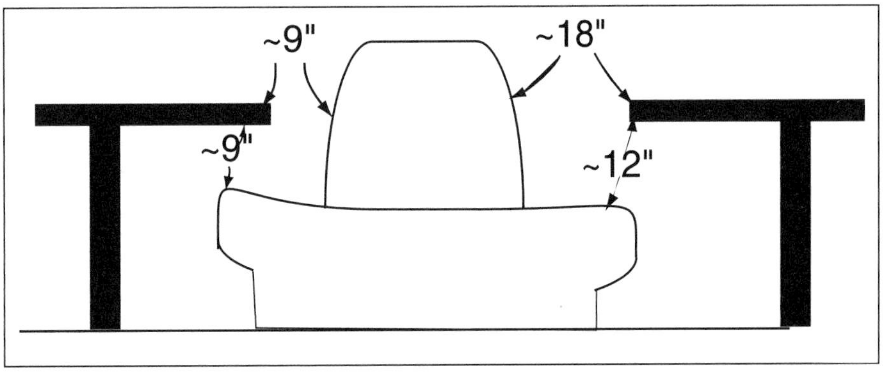

Vinyl seat coverings come in a variety of colors and patterns, and can have a leatherlike texture. Commercial-grade vinyl seat coverings are highly durable, spill resistant, easy to clean, and will not crack when fitted over high-quality padding that does not cause the coverings to bend and stretch excessively. But vinyl becomes hot and uncomfortable when sat on for extended periods, so it is

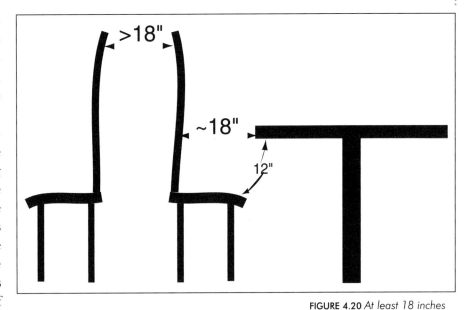

FIGURE 4.20 *At least 18 inches of space should be planned between chairs to prevent customers from getting bumped as servers and guests pass by. The same distance from the chair back to the table edge serves as a guideline. The seat cushion should sit 12 inches below the tabletop. The same rules apply to booth and banquette seating.*

FIGURE 4.21 *When the distance between the booth back and the tabletop is too narrow (left), customers feel cramped. Inexpensive construction used in booth seats means the back edge of the seat compresses while the front edge rises to make an uncomfortable seating arrangement.*

FIGURE 4.22 *These comfortable office chairs offer ideal seating for guests who conduct business over their meal.*
(Photo by Joseph Durocher.)

best suited for short- to medium-length dining experiences. Leather gives a feeling of elegance and is both highly durable and easy to clean.

Resin chairs and tables are most often used in outdoor dining spaces. Look for commercial resin furniture that has been certified for nonresidential outdoor use. Such seating is more rigid than less expensive seating and has extra material in stress areas where hairline fractures can develop. Most important, look for tables and chairs that are ultraviolet (UV) resistant. UV light can weaken some resin chairs to a point where they bend easily or break under the weight of a guest.

Wrought-iron furniture was once the only choice for outdoor seating and tables, and it is still a good choice. Wrought-iron furniture is highly durable and, because it is available in a wide variety of painted colors, it can blend in with any decor. With the addition of seat and back pads, wrought-iron seating can be quite comfortable.

STRUCTURE In addition to the covering of the seat, its size and pitch (both back and seat) affect the guest's comfort. A slight forward pitch on a molded plastic seat in a fast-food restaurant makes customers feel like they are slipping out. Such seating can speed turnover rates. Conversely, deeply padded armchairs cause diners to linger at their table.

For optimal comfort levels, seats must be matched to their intended use. In cocktail lounges, seating is typically lower and deeper than at dining tables. Dining chairs, on the other hand, must be matched closely to the height of the dining table. Although tables and chairs come in standard sizes (tables from 26 to 30 inches high and chairs from 16 to 18 inches high), the designer should always double-check that the table and seat height are matched for comfort. All too often, chairs are too low or too high. This problem seems especially prevalent with custom-designed banquettes, where seats sometimes sink so low that not only is eating difficult, but getting in and out of the seat requires a dancer's flexibility. Adding casters to the legs of a chair can make it too high to match a table.

The structural integrity of the chair is a crucial consideration. A good chair should be able to withstand the weight of even the most portly individual. In the restaurant environment, wear and tear take their toll so quickly that seating made for residential use generally won't hold up more than a few months. Antique seating should be avoided. If antique styling is needed, custom chairs can be produced based on an antique sample.

Commercial seating is built with extra structural reinforcements in order to withstand heavy use (Figure 4.23). A retail version would look exactly the same to the customer—but not for long, because it would soon begin falling apart at the stress points.

SPECIAL FEATURES The weight of movable seating contributes to the overall image of a restaurant but also has operational implications. Lightweight chairs are easy for customers to move toward and away from a table. More substantial chairs are harder to move and, as they are scooted in and out from the table, they can damage the floor surface. On the other hand, heavy seating gives an elegant or regal feeling that is appropriate in some settings.

Casters aid in moving chairs to and from the table; the type of caster must be matched to the type of flooring. Casters are particularly appropriate when installed on heavy chairs. However, they can cause a chair to slip out from under diners as they sit down or stand up, particularly when set on a hard-surfaced floor.

Booster seats and high chairs are essential for restaurants that cater to families. Space should be set aside to store these seats when not in use.

In fast feeders, cafeterias, and other restaurants that depend on high turnover, the seat itself can play an integral part in moving people through the space. For the past 25 years, molded plastic, fixed seating was the standard in high-turnover restaurants. Recently, however, in an effort to expand market share and make the space more conducive to dining, the variety of seating has greatly expanded to include wooden benches or café chairs, fashionably styled metal chairs in a spectrum of colors, and even upholstered chairs. Such seating choices create a totally different impression from the old institutional-looking furniture, but consideration must always be given to the desired turnover time. When a restaurant depends on thirty-minute turnover, chair design should not encourage patrons to linger for two hours.

FIGURE 4.23 *The elegant, woven-back Jean Georges café chair was designed by Adam Tihany to withstand the rigors of the restaurant environment.* (Photo courtesy of Colber International.)

SEATING LAYOUT Seating can create a feeling of intimacy. Booth seating, curved banquette seating, and high-backed chairs engender a private feeling, for example, because they restrict sight lines and the seating wraps around the guests.

The atmosphere is also affected by the relative position of seats and tables. The crowded feeling of a French bistro depends on tightly packed seating at small tables; in a fine dining operation, generous spacing between tables—usually in excess of 15 square feet of floor space per seat—gives a feeling of elegance. While square foot guidelines exist, they should be viewed solely as guidelines (Table 4.1).

Although part of the goal of good design is to carefully match the mix of deuces, four-tops, etc., with the size of parties that frequent the restaurant, it should be noted that a mix of table sizes and seating configurations creates more visual interest than

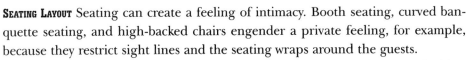

TABLE 4.1. FRONT-OF-THE-HOUSE SQUARE FOOTAGE ESTIMATES

Type of Service	Square Footage per Seat
À la carte	8-16
Tableside	16-20
Fast Food	10-14
Banquet	10-16
Family Style	13-16
Buffet	12-18
Cafeteria	12-15

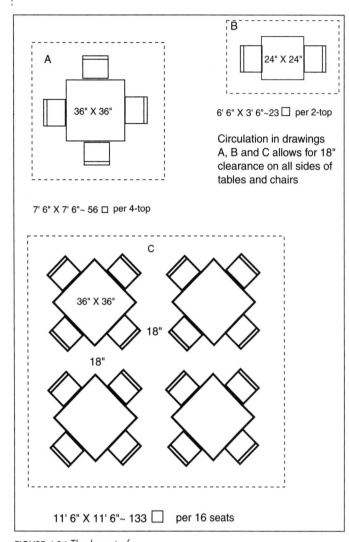

A

36" X 36"

7' 6" X 7' 6" ~ 56 ☐ per 4-top

B

24" X 24"

6' 6" X 3' 6" ~23 ☐ per 2-top

Circulation in drawings A, B and C allows for 18" clearance on all sides of tables and chairs

C

36" X 36"

18"

18"

11' 6" X 11' 6" ~ 133 ☐ per 16 seats

FIGURE 4.24 *The layout of seating and tables affects the square footage requirement per seat. In (A), 14 square feet are required per seat. (B) requires 11½ square feet per seat. In (C), the most efficient layout, only 8⅔ square feet are required per seat.*

a single type of table. Seating variety offers patrons the choice of more intimate or more open seating, depending on their mood. In addition, the table and seating selection also affects the numbers of seats that can be accommodated in a given space (Figure 4.24).

TABLES AND TABLETOPS

Every guest wants the best table in the house. Ideally, every table should be perceived as "the best table." Every seat, of course, isn't a window seat, and there is only one natural prime spot—a table that is the visual focal point of the restaurant, one from which the entire dining room can be viewed.

Designers can employ a variety of techniques to ensure that every table is indeed desirable. Terracing backward and upward from a wall of windows, for example, allows patrons in the back of the room a view similar to that seen by guests in the front of the room.

Sight lines and flow patterns of both guests and employees are crucial considerations when laying out the tables in a restaurant. Customers disdain a view of the bathroom, the smell of the garbage room, and the clanging of the pot sink. In the past, they shunned a view of the kitchen, and still do if it is seen through a set of swinging doors. But well-designed display kitchens can turn the table closest to the kitchen into a prime table. The secret is to take what could be a bad situation and make it something special. A nook adjacent to the wine cellar can become a special party space because it overlooks the wine display. A large antique table positioned in the center of the dining room can become a captain's table for single diners. Deuces elevated on a sidewall highlight those seats and put the diners on display.

The shapes of tables and the number of seats at tables are important considerations, again depending on the type of restaurant as well as the dining habits of typical customers. Theatrical restaurants, for example, feature more large tables than do small tableservice establishments where the emphasis is on food. This is because more families and groups tend to frequent theatrical restaurants, while more single couples tend to frequent traditional restaurants that emphasize the food.

The tabletop provides the guest's most immediate and personal experience in the restaurant because diners come in direct contact with their plates, food, glasses, flatware, and so on. The texture, temperature, color, and balance of each element—separately and in concert—should all be taken into consideration during the design process. An entire book could be written on the selection of tabletop elements, but basic principles can guide the development of an effective tabletop design.

THE TABLE ITSELF Size, shape, position, and surface materials are critical components to consider when selecting tables for a restaurant. For example, a series of deuces along a banquette can be moved together to accommodate larger parties. A 36-inch square table can accommodate four diners, whereas a 36-inch round table can accommodate five, although they will be somewhat crowded.

In most cases, a mix of table sizes makes it possible to deal with any number of guests in a party. Tables with swing-up wings that convert a square into a round increase flexibility, as do deuces that can be joined to make a long table. Size should also relate to the amount of hardware that will be placed on the table and the size of the plates that will come from the kitchen.

A mix of table shapes also adds visual interest to the room and helps the operation accommodate a range of diners. Restaurants typically incorporate at least round and square tables. Oval tables work well with curved banquet seating. Long rectangular tables have become fashionable for group dining or for single diners who wish not to dine alone.

The base must relate to the tabletop, how the table will be used, and the type of flooring on which the table will be set. The basic choice is between a pedestal base and four legs. The pedestal is handy because it does not get in the way of chairs when they are pushed under the table, nor do guests hit against it when they are seated. On the other hand, if large-diameter tables are used, a guest pushing down on one side of the table could cause water glasses on the other side to spill.

When tables are covered with a cloth, little thought is given to the appearance of the pedestals or legs, but when there is no cloth, the base should either add to the appeal of the room or be innocuous.

When matching the tabletop with seating, consider the following:

- *Will the table look overcrowded with a full assortment of plates, flatware, and glassware?*
- *Should four-tops be square or rectangular?*
- *Will there be a need to convert a four-top into a round that seats six?*
- *Will there be a need to convert a six-top into an eight-top?*
- *Will space be needed on the tabletop to accommodate a laptop along with tableware?*

Tabletop. The actual tabletop material itself is most important when it is visible to the guest. Tabletop materials of marble, glass, Formica™, and other hard materials give a different feeling than the warmth of wood tabletops and the fine dining image of linen. In any case, the choice should be visually compatible with the overall design. Today, resin-coated fabric tabletops, or hard materials such as marblelike compressed stone, granite, or marble are often specified for non-table-linen tabletops.

Both durability and cleaning should be considered when selecting a tabletop material. For tops that will not be covered with a cloth, surfaces that can be wiped clean with a few strokes are essential. Stone tabletops, for example, are highly durable but not easy to clean; they can stain or discolor when grease is spilled on them.

The actual size of the tabletop depends on the restaurant's style of service. An average place setting is 24 inches wide, but more room is needed to serve a formal meal and space can be tightened for banquet-style service. In cafeterias, the size and shape of the trays must be considered when specifying table size.

It's important to match the size of the tabletop with the overall dining experience. Consider the following:

- Will the table look overcrowded with a full assortment of plates, flatware, and glassware?
- Should the four-top be square or rectangular?

- Will there be a need to convert a four-top into a round that seats six?
- Will there be a need to convert a six-top into an eight-top?
- Will space be needed on the tabletop to accommodate a laptop computer along with tableware?

When dealing with cloth-covered tables, remember that while the tabletop material is invisible to the guest 90 percent of the time, it flashes into view when the linen is changed. In some casual operations, an inexpensive plywood top may be acceptable, but elegant, high-ticket establishments should carry through the high-end aesthetic, even though guests may view the tabletop for only a few seconds.

Table Support. Table bases should always be substantial enough to support the table's size and weight and to convey a secure and stable feeling to the customer. When tables are set on uneven floors, the bases must be equipped with levelers that keep the table from wobbling. Wobbling is also a problem when the table supports are not well constructed. Inexpensive bases are fashioned from lightweight materials not intended for the rigors of a restaurant environment.

NAPERY The color and design of tablecloths and napkins should be integrated with the overall design scheme. Napery design forms such a strong image in the restaurant that, at times, a change of tablecloths and napkins can create a fresh new look for the interior. Yellow-accented napery at breakfast, rose colors at lunch, and burgundy tones in the evening evoke entirely different feelings.

When specifying linen, attention should be given to flame retardancy, stainability, and texture. Polyester, cotton, or cotton-polyester blend napkins each have their own feel and usability characteristics. Generally speaking, the following should be considered when purchasing linens:

- absorbency
- color availability and fastness
- folding and starchability
- wearability
- shrinkage
- stain resistance

From a design perspective, the most important issues are color availability and fastness. Polyester fabrics come in a wider variety of colors than do pure cotton fabrics, and they do not fade as quickly.

It may be advisable to select one type of material for the tablecloth and another material for the napkin. A blended tablecloth can work quite well with cotton napkins. In any event, it is important to remember that guests touch table linens, and the feel leaves a lasting impression.

Banquet chair slipcovers and table skirts round out the linens found in most restaurants. Both of these types of linen should be fashioned from highly durable and stain-resistant material. Table skirts come in a variety of colors and patterns. Chair drapes can be permanently affixed to chairs, or they can be added to create a luxurious feeling for special events.

FLATWARE Guests handle flatware more than any other item on the tabletop; its pattern, heft, shape, cleanliness, and material all affect their perception of the meal. Stainless steel is the most common material for restaurant flatware, but a wide spectrum of grades of stainless give varying appearances after even limited use. Some inexpensive flatware shows scratches and a dull finish after only a month. Better (more expensive) grades take on a shine that lights up the tabletop. A stainless steel mix with 18 percent chrome and 8 percent nickel—referred to as 18/8 stainless—yields the best results in terms of both corrosion resistance and luster.

Silver-plated flatware is appropriate for high-ticket establishments, but it places additional responsibility on the operator. Several grades—which reflect the quality of the silver, the number of platings, and the weight of the blanks that form the individual pieces—determine the durability of silver-plated flatware. Some manufacturers plate more silver on the back of the pieces because the touch points—those areas that come in contact with the table or dishware—are thus better protected.

One popular choice is silver-plated flatware made from a stainless-steel base. However, the silver coating tarnishes quickly and needs to be burnished or polished periodically. This can be done with a machine, in soaking bins, or by hand; the polishing need must be recognized and incorporated with the overall design of the warewashing area. Sterling silver is rarely used in restaurants, not only because of its expense but also because it requires even more care than silver plate.

When considering shape, heft, and balance, it is important to beware of forks that are thin near the shank (the part of the handle that attaches to the top of the tines). When too thin, it is difficult to hold the fork without having it roll in the hand and all but impossible to use for cutting. Forks with a thin base are also prone to bending (Figure 4.25).

Knives pose a special problem because the blade, if not made of high-quality stainless steel, will show scratches and mar the appearance of even the most beautiful tabletop. Adequate metal at stress and touch points, and proper grading or thickness, yields a sturdy and well-balanced piece of flatware.

For those operations specializing in steaks and chops, serrated knives should be a part of the tabletop hardware. When seafood is served, fish knives should be included as an added tabletop feature and, in some operations, a flat sauce spoon adds an air of elegance.

Obviously, the flatware pattern must work with the other tabletop items and the overall design. Several other issues must also be considered:

Pattern lifespan—How long will the pattern be available? While a new pattern may seem like an exciting design opportunity, it may be discontinued by the manufacturer if it does not sell well.

Variety of pieces—How many different pieces are needed? Some patterns are produced with two dozen or more different pieces of flatware from which to choose for a tabletop. Others are available with a knife, fork, teaspoon, and soupspoon only. It's important to determine the variety of pieces needed for the menu (Figure 4.26).

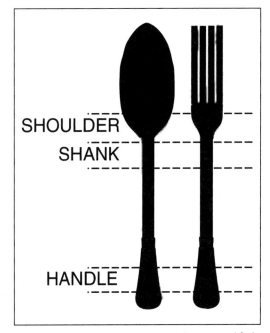

SHOULDER

SHANK

HANDLE

FIGURE 4.25 *Spoons and forks are particularly prone to bending where the shoulder joins the shank. Some manufacturers add reinforcements to prevent bending.*

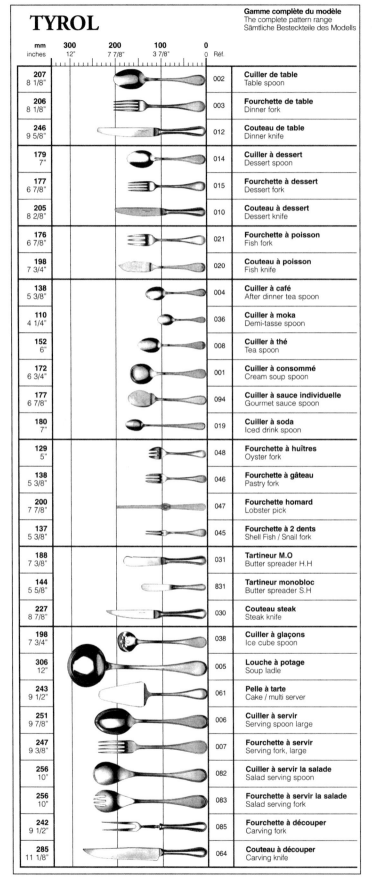

TYROL							Gamme complète du modèle The complete pattern range Sämtliche Besteckteile des Modells
mm inches	300 12"	200 7 7/8"	100 3 7/8"	0 0	Réf.		
207 8 1/8"					002	Cuiller de table	Table spoon
206 8 1/8"					003	Fourchette de table	Dinner fork
246 9 5/8"					012	Couteau de table	Dinner knife
179 7"					014	Cuiller à dessert	Dessert spoon
177 6 7/8"					015	Fourchette à dessert	Dessert fork
205 8 2/8"					010	Couteau à dessert	Dessert knife
176 6 7/8"					021	Fourchette à poisson	Fish fork
198 7 3/4"					020	Couteau à poisson	Fish knife
138 5 3/8"					004	Cuiller à café	After dinner tea spoon
110 4 1/4"					036	Cuiller à moka	Demi-tasse spoon
152 6"					008	Cuiller à thé	Tea spoon
172 6 3/4"					001	Cuiller à consommé	Cream soup spoon
177 6 7/8"					094	Cuiller à sauce individuelle	Gourmet sauce spoon
180 7"					019	Cuiller à soda	Iced drink spoon
129 5"					048	Fourchette à huîtres	Oyster fork
138 5 3/8"					046	Fourchette à gâteau	Pastry fork
200 7 7/8"					047	Fourchette homard	Lobster pick
137 5 3/8"					045	Fourchette à 2 dents	Shell Fish / Snail fork
188 7 3/8"					031	Tartineur M.O	Butter spreader H.H
144 5 5/8"					831	Tartineur monobloc	Butter spreader S.H
227 8 7/8"					030	Couteau steak	Steak knife
198 7 3/4"					038	Cuiller à glaçons	Ice cube spoon
306 12"					005	Louche à potage	Soup ladle
243 9 1/2"					061	Pelle à tarte	Cake / multi server
251 9 7/8"					006	Cuiller à servir	Serving spoon large
247 9 3/8"					007	Fourchette à servir	Serving fork, large
256 10"					082	Cuiller à servir la salade	Salad serving spoon
256 10"					083	Fourchette à servir la salade	Salad serving fork
242 9 1/2"					085	Fourchette à découper	Carving fork
285 11 1/8"					064	Couteau à découper	Carving knife

Availability—Are replacements readily available? Some patterns may not be in stock at all times, so purchasing a resupply may be problematic. Check the lead time for delivery of any flatware pattern before making a final choice.

Special care—Will the flatware need special maintenance? A burnisher not only removes discolorations but also smooths out scratches that appear on flatware; it can actually help extend the usable life of silver-plated flatware if used twice monthly.

Flatware sorters—Does automated flatware sorting make sense? The volume of flatware used in some facilities justifies the space and expense of an automated flatware sorter. The sorters minimize hand contact with flatware and the amount of labor needed to sort it.

CHINAWARE Along with the flatware and holloware, chinaware plays an important role in the customer's perception of the food. The plate's size and heft should reflect the foods being served on it. Chinaware can also anchor the aesthetics of the tabletop design.

Many restaurateurs use heavy plates that give the perception of holding a lot of food. (Bar operators have used this technique for years when they serve beers in sham pilsners or heavy-bottomed beer mugs.) Other restaurateurs choose oversized plates to create a canvas on which to arrange food artfully. While these plates help showcase and frame the food presentation, they must be carefully matched to the tabletop so as not to overwhelm the space. Oversize plates can make portions look small, which, in the long run, could lead to customer dissatisfaction. Heavy, oversized plates may not fit in standard-size plate storage cabinets and require more storage space than conventional serving vessels.

Restaurant plates decorated with or fired with color are the most commonly found chinaware in the restaurant industry. Heavily patterned plates that make strong design statements

FIGURE 4.26 *Quality flatware manufacturers like Christofle offer a wide variety of patterns, and pieces within those patterns, designed for commercial use.*
(Courtesy of Christofle Hotel Division.)

can serve as excellent base plates—those plates already set on the table when guests arrive—but they should never be chosen for serving food.

While some patterns look attractive on their own, they can actually detract from the appearance of foods. Other base plate designs, such as one with a band of color one to two inches wide around the rim of the dish, can make a striking statement in the dining room and also be suitable for serving food. All too often, however, the colored rims are marred with fingerprints from careless service personnel. Plate selection must always recognize the visual limitations and operational considerations involved with the choice.

Equal care should be taken with the selection of other chinaware items. Consider the handle design of cups, for instance. Some handles will withstand the wear and tear of brutish bus staff, while others break with a simple tap. Then there is the actual feeling of the handle. The heavy, large handle of a commercial coffee mug, while not suited to a fine dining operation, is easy to grasp. In contrast, the dainty handle of a bone chinaware teacup is fine for sipping afternoon tea in a leisurely fashion but impossible for all but the most slender individuals to easily put a finger through.

Shape, size, material, design, and the manufacturing process affect the lifespan of chinaware. The thickness of a piece of chinaware does not necessarily foretell its lifespan. Commercial-grade chinaware, produced to withstand the rigors of the restaurant market, is designed with strength and resistance to breaking and chipping as important characteristics. In addition, commercial chinaware manufacturers tend to recognize the importance of a design suitable for storage and commercial warewashing.

The following are important considerations for china specifications:

Shape. Nine-inch plates are not all created equal. The size of the well—that is, the actual area on which food is set—varies. The shoulder and rim of each style has a different width, and the angle of the rim also changes from plate to plate. The shape of chinaware affects its durability. Specialty shapes like fish and octagons, and plates with dividers can be used to create a whimsical presentation or to keep entrée items separated. The shape of a plate can relate to the products that will be served on it. For example, an oval plate is a better choice than a round plate for serving baked burritos.

Size. Size is important because it impacts portion size. A 12-ounce steak served on a 9-inch plate appears much larger than if it is served on a 12-inch plate. When selecting a chinaware pattern, it's important to review the sizes available for each plate style. If, at a later time, it becomes necessary to choose a smaller size dish, the change can be made without having to purchase plates that do not match.

Material. Chinaware is fashioned from clay containing additives that improve its hardness or porosity. An alumina body increases the strength of a piece of chinaware, makes it lighter, helps keep foods warm longer, and can be placed under a broiler.

Design. The means by which designs are applied to chinaware affects its price. The least costly method is a printed design. Decals are a bit more expensive but can give greater detail than printed designs. Hand-painted chinaware is the most expensive and adding gold or silver rim lines further increases the cost.

Manufacturing Process. The process begins with the choice of the basic clay. Chinaware that is not lead-free can pose a health risk if the glazing is cracked. Some manufacturers use a pure white base clay, while others use an off-white clay. The vitrification process fuses the components of the clay body into a glasslike substance in high-heat kilns. Some chinaware is fired in a kiln to form a bisque; then the decoration and glaze is applied and the chinaware fired a second time. Once-fired chinaware—chinaware that is fired only one time—has the decorations and glaze added prior to firing. The quality of the glaze and the temperature at which it is fired affect the durability of chinaware. Gold-rimmed plates, while they look good, are prone to premature wear because they are fired at relatively low temperatures that leave a less resilient finish than high-temperature firing. Once-fired chinaware has a dry foot, which means no glaze is applied to the bottom. The exposed base of such chinaware can abrade the surface of any glazed plate on which it is set.

Residential chinaware, like residential furniture, won't last long in the restaurant environment. Another advantage of commercial chinaware is that stock patterns are maintained for quick delivery from the manufacturer. For a minimal additional investment, custom-designed plates can be created to coordinate with a restaurant's graphics program. These signature plates can create a sense of identity for a restaurant. However, it is important to verify the number of pieces that must be purchased when reordering. As a rule of thumb, expect to order at least fifteen dozen of each item for each reorder.

The lead time needed to order and reorder is important when considering custom-designed chinaware. Producing chinaware with a simple line treatment can take a month and a half, with a crest and line up to two months, and with a more complex pattern up to three months. Developing a custom design can take the manufacturer up to four additional weeks.

In recent years, increasing attention has being paid to the aesthetics of the tabletop (Figure 4.27). No longer do ornately designed plates compete with the chef's art. Today, the shape and form of the plate serve to highlight cuisine.

FIGURE 4.27 *The simplicity of these glass base plates at TrU in Chicago creates a strong visual image in keeping with the room's modern design.* (Photo by Joseph Durocher.)

In the case of tableservice restaurants, the design team should remember that there are numerous courses to each meal and many variables to each course. Traditionally, a meal includes an appetizer, main course, salad, dessert, and beverages. But the appetizer selection alone might include a dozen or more items, each of which comes with its own garnish, serving plate, underliner, eating utensils, and condiments. The same is true for all the courses.

According to experts, the average piece of dinnerware will be used about seven thousand times and will last approximately three years of typical restaurant use, if handled properly. Some chinaware manufacturers estimate that 25 percent of a restaurant's chinaware will be broken each year. Needless to say, replacement costs can be astronomical. It is essential, therefore, that the design team not only specify well-constructed items but also make sure that all of the back- and front-of-the-house support stations be adequately designed for storage (Figure 4.28). The greater variety of tabletop elements, the greater the need for storage in the kitchen dishroom and at the front-of-the-house server stations. Replacement schedules and price are also important considerations when selecting chinaware.

FIGURE 4.28 *Service stations must be designed to hold the full variety of table elements in backup storage space, along with order-entry equipment. Built-in units can be designed to blend into the overall decor.*
(Photo by Joseph Durocher.)

GLASSWARE A fine Bordeaux is best appreciated in a high-quality, thin-walled, clear stemware wineglass. Sherry should be served in a stem sherry glass and champagne should be served in a champagne flute or tulip. However, if a different glass is selected for each type of drink, the bartender may have to stock 25 or more types of glasses. The use of a single glass goblet for all beverages—wine, beer, soda, champagne, and mixed drinks—is not the most aesthetic approach but, from an operational perspective, it is certainly the easiest.

The size and shape of glassware, along with the manufacturing process, will affect its breakability. For example, heat-tempered glassware helps protect the lip of the glass from breakage. So, too, will the shape of the glassware, as shown in Figure 4.29.

While the variety of glasses used for beverage service is usually determined by management, the designers—both back and front of the house—must be cognizant of this decision because it affects the amount of storage space needed. With more types of glassware, additional storage

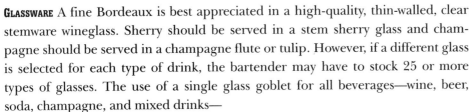

FIGURE 4.29 *Stemware is particularly prone to breakage. One option is to choose a glass with a short stem. Breakage at the lip of a glass is another problem. While tempering or building up the lip helps, a bowl that is wider than the lip also minimizes breakage when a glass falls over.*

Lighting that is too uniform makes the atmosphere seem dull. Lighting that is too harsh can cause food to look unappetizing.

space is needed in the clean dish storage areas as well as at the bar itself. A variety of glassware may also affect the requirements for storage at the server stations.

HOLLOWARE The selection of holloware—tabletop elements such as salt and pepper shakers, candlesticks, and sugar and creamer sets—must be coordinated with flatware, chinaware, glassware, and the overall design of the restaurant. In simple terms, a restaurant where fine linen and silver-plated flatware are used needs holloware that is either silver plated or high-quality stainless steel. By the same token, the 1950s diner calls for pour-top sugar dispensers, plastic water pitchers, and squeeze bottles for ketchup and mustard.

In addition, the designer must consider all flatware and holloware items necessary for each menu item to ensure that the overall look is integrated. Manufacturers don't always offer a total set of holloware in the same design pattern as flatware, so it is important to select visually compatible patterns.

In addition to matching the overall decor, holloware should be chosen to support the operation. For example, hinge-top holloware takes a great deal of abuse and, if the hinge is not strong enough, the tops will soon fall off. Holloware fitted with tops that swing back 180 degrees are easy to clean in a dish machine and are less likely to have their hinges broken.

Coffee servers are an example of holloware that must be considered in any tableservice restaurant. Glass pots work well when there is a warming plate on which to maintain the temperature because the pots are not insulated. However, servers are required to refill cups. The alternative is to place an insulated pot of coffee on the table so that customers can serve themselves. The convenience to the guest and server is obvious, but more coffee is thrown away than when glass pots are used—and self-service is not appropriate for elegant restaurants.

Silver-plated flatware, holloware, and items like chafing dishes should be stored in a secured area when not in use. Such storage areas should be planned for during the design phase of the project and not as an afterthought. Burnishing equipment and polishing supplies are often kept in these areas as well.

LIGHTING

As noted in chapter 3, lighting influences diners in many ways, from the rosy glow it can impart to people's complexions to the mysterious patterns it can throw on wall surfaces. Lighting that is too bright, or too dim, may lead to serious eyestrain. Lighting that is too uniform makes the atmosphere seem dull. Lighting that is too harsh can cause food to look unappetizing. Light can totally change the perception of colored surfaces.

The design team of Aumiller Youngquist stress the importance of choosing lighting to enhance every phase of a customer's experience. "Some designers only think about the wow factor when customers arrive and fail to consider the impact of the lighting in the parking lot when customers leave," they say. Lighting the variety of spaces in a restaurant is an art in itself, and in complex or big-budget projects, a lighting designer is often enlisted to help develop an illumination scheme.

In other instances, well-informed architects or interior designers implement the lighting program, which defines the type of fixtures and bulbs (lamps) along with any control equipment. Both operational and aesthetic issues must be considered when selecting light sources and control equipment. The operator should be educated about the basic elements and the control equipment so that he can communicate the right information to operational staff about day-to-day operation and to maintenance people about relamping and focus adjustment.

One of the reasons that restaurant lighting is so complicated is that it involves not only the selection of light sources but also the programming of light levels that respond both to various time periods and various places in the room. In order to be effective, light levels, light sources, and quality of light must all interact consistently with other design elements in the restaurant.

When establishing lighting plans for interiors, the design team should consider the following lighting classifications.

Mood/decor/art lighting. This category of lighting often creates the most dramatic illumination in a restaurant. It really begins outside with signage and architectural lighting, and carries forward to the interior, where objects or surfaces are spotlighted with overlays of direct or indirect lighting. Artwork is frequently lit with carefully focused track lights manipulated to avoid glare yet allow the images to be clearly viewed. Plantings and wall surfaces are often uplit so that they glow. Generally, objects can be spotlit with direct light for the most powerful effect, but some lighting designers caution against juxtaposing brightly spotlit objects with a dark backdrop because the contrast can cause discomfort.

People/food lighting. Effectively illuminating people and food involves delicate manipulation of light sources and light levels. The color temperature of the lamp (CCT) and the color rendering index (CRI) should both be considered when selecting lamps for restaurants. Lamps with a low CCT—2000-3000K—are referred to as *warm light* because they produce light high in the red, orange, and yellow range of the spectrum. Lamps with high CCT—>4000K—produce more blue and are referred to as *cool light*. Lamps with a high CRI rating make colors look natural and vibrant. Lamps with a low CRI rating make colors look washed out or of a different hue. For reference, conventional incandescent bulbs have a 2700 CCT rating and a CRI of 95, and halogen lamps have a 3000 CCT rating and a 95 CRI. The best fluorescent bulb produces a CCT of ~5000K and a CRI of 90. In simple terms, these three bulbs will give relatively the same color rendition, but the fluorescent will make blue colors stand out more.

Obviously, the goal is for both people and food to look as attractive as possible. Designers have different theories about the best way to achieve this goal. Without question, people and food look best under incandescent or halogen light, but improvements in some fluorescent lamps make them acceptable in certain restaurant settings. Some experts say that the space should be lit in such a way that the tables and diners become the focus of the room. However, highly focused spotlights directed at the center of a table can create glare, detract from the appearance of guests, and cause uncomfortable

> **Some experts say that the space should be lit in such a way that the tables and diners become the focus of the room.**

dark shadows. Indirect light that softly illuminates people's faces is ideal. Tabletop candle lamps can provide soft illumination when general indirect lighting is not appropriate.

Increasingly, designers must react to an aging baby-boomer population when designing a lighting plan. Gone are the days when boomers could read 9-point brown type on a rough-textured, cream-colored menu card. Higher light levels are needed to create the contrast necessary for aging eyes to read menus. Greater contrast between the print ink and the paper stock, along with an increase in type size and typeface, can also help.

Motivational/task lighting. This type of lighting is most important for the employees of a restaurant. Correct light levels—bright, but not blinding—will help them perform their assigned tasks and, in some instances, can drastically affect productivity. Task lighting is all too often overlooked in the front of the house. The bartender needs good task lighting when mixing drinks, the service staff when filling out guest checks, and the flambé chef while preparing duck à l'orange. Task lighting is essential at POS stations, particularly those that use a keyboard or touchpad for input or include a cash drawer. When touchscreens are used, light levels should be low enough to prevent glare on the screen.

Safety and security lighting are essential for the well-being of guests, employees, and management. This includes exit lights inside the restaurant, emergency lighting in case of power outages, parking lot and other exterior lighting, and lighting bright enough in the back of the house so employees can work safely. With strategic planning, none of these light sources need be offensive to look at. Emergency lights, for example, can be totally recessed into the ceiling, although emergency exit signs must always be in clear view.

THE LIGHTING PLAN All of the issues noted above, and much more, go into a good restaurant lighting plan. Most experts recommend that a variety of concealed and decorative fixtures are desirable to achieve successful results. To recap, the following factors must be considered before final decisions are made:

Location and orientation. Precisely which space will be lit affects all other factors. Exterior light, be it natural or artificial, can affect the interior lighting plan if there is an expanse of exterior glass. The angle of light fixtures must be incorporated into the plan. The direction of the lighting (up or down) should also be noted. Most restaurant lighting plans incorporate a mix of uplighting, downlighting, and direct and indirect lighting.

Types of lighting. Will a single type of lamp (bulb) be used or a mix of lamps? Will a single luminaire (fixture) or a mix be used? Each luminaire coupled with a given lamp outputs a given amount of light. Change the structure of the luminaire and the light output changes.

Distance. The distance of each luminaire from objects that are to be lit affects the plan. A room with a 10-foot high ceiling needs far fewer luminaires and lamps than does a room with a 20-foot high ceiling. Beam spread should also be considered when planning the distance between a luminaire and a surface to be lighted.

Light quality. What are the spectral characteristics of the light and how will they affect the people using the space and the appearance of colors in the space? If more than one light source is used, how will the quality of light be affected by the mix, both overall and in specific areas?

Quantity of light. How much light is needed? What is the optimal foot-candle level for each space? Must some points be lighted more than other points? The type of luminaire, lamp, distance, and number of fixtures all affect the quantity of light. Lighting guidelines for restaurants appear in Table 4.2.

TABLE 4.2. LIGHTING LEVELS IN FOOT-CANDLES BY AREA

Restaurant Area	Minimum Foot-Candles
Receiving	25-45
Storage	15-20
Pre-preparation	20-30
Preparation/Production	30-50
Warewashing	70-100
POS/Cashier	35-50
Intimate dining	5-15
Fast-food dining	75-100
Dining room cleaning	30-50

Energy utilization. Total energy consumption, total energy cost, and the coefficient of utilization (CU) of the luminaires must be considered. Incandescent lamps, while producing a high quality of light, use much of the wattage they consume to generate heat rather than light. Fluorescents are far more energy efficient and sodium and mercury vapor lamps even more so (Table.4.3).

TABLE 4.3. TYPICAL LIFE AND LUMENS/WATT FOR SAMPLE LAMPS

Lamp Type	Life in Hours	Lumens/Watt
Incandescent	750-2,500	5-15
Halogen	3,000	15-20
Linear fluorescent	10,000-20,000	80-90
Low-watt compact fluorescent	10,000	30
High-watt compact fluorescent	10,000	70
High-intensity discharge (mercury vapor, metal halide, sodium)	10,000-20,000	30-140

Maintenance. How often must the lamps be replaced? Can the luminaires be cleaned, and how? The relamping program is an important consideration that influences maintenance, luminaire, and lamp selection. Must a lamp be replaced whenever it burns out? Will lamps be replaced when a certain percentage of the lamps burn out? Will all of the lamps be replaced when the first or a percentage of the lamps burn out? Obviously, the relamping plan will affect operating costs and light levels. Some lamps are designed for a specific installation orientation—that is, some are designed for straight-down installation and others for horizontal installation. Misinstalling the fixture and lamp can significantly decrease the lifespan of the lamp.

Today, few restaurants use the 2- by 4-foot fluorescent luminaires commonly used in office buildings, with the exception of some corporate and other noncommercial cafeterias. Instead, many restaurant designers specify recessed lighting, track lighting, or indirect lighting coves as part of the ceiling design. These treatments increase the complexity of the ceiling structure but also improve the quality of lighting in the space. In some cases, skylights, either real or simulated, become a light source and a ceiling element. When cove lighting is used, the ceiling reflects light into the dining space and conceals the luminaires.

NATURAL VERSUS ARTIFICIAL LIGHT When a restaurant is entirely interior (with no outside source of light), controlling lighting levels throughout the day is relatively easy. However, when sunlight (natural) or other external lighting sources (hallways, streetlamps, etc.) enter the restaurant, establishing a lighting scheme is more difficult. The location of windows can influence the impact of sunlight because indirect light entering a restaurant is different than the glaring direct rays of the sun.

In new construction, the architect can plan north-facing windows or windows that do not face the sun during service hours, roof overhangs, or tinted glass to help alleviate the problems associated with glare. In existing buildings, exterior plantings and window-shading elements such as curtains, drapes, and blinds can minimize the impact of the sun on interior lighting levels.

The main dining room of New York's Tavern on the Green is a classic example of good natural light control. The room has a long wall of windows that, during the summer, is partially shaded by trees, with just enough light filtering into the room to create a bright and cheery atmosphere. In the winter, the leafless trees allow the sun, low on the horizon, to pour all of its warming rays into the room. During evenings throughout the year, thousands of miniature lights (Figure 4.30)

FIGURE 4.30 *The dining experience at Tavern on the Green in New York City is enhanced at night by the thousands of miniature lights on the branches of surrounding trees, creating an urban starlight.*
(Photo courtesy of Tavern on the Green.)

festooned on tree branches outside the windows allow guests to dine by sparkling urban starlight.

The use of greenhouse units in fast-food and family dining restaurants should be approached with caution because of the challenges they present. While natural light enlivens the dining areas, the glare and heat load in greenhouse units can be excessive. At night, lighting from mercury or sodium vapor parking lot fixtures will make complexions and food look pasty and unappealing if allowed to pour in through uncovered greenhouse windows.

LIGHTING LEVELS As noted earlier, lighting levels should be carefully monitored throughout the restaurant, and a light transition zone at the entry area is essential. A dimly lit dining alcove can help create an intimate milieu, but lighting levels that are too low cause problems for diners. Even the most artful plate presentation cannot be appreciated in the dark. Further, a single light level in the restaurant can cause the environment to feel monotonous.

A typical programmed dimmer system has set lighting levels for different times of day keyed to the various rooms. The restaurant manager simply pushes a number that relates to an outside brightness condition ranging from intense sunlight to total darkness, and the light level dims accordingly. Albeit more expensive than a manual system, such automatic dimming control is the superior choice because once the levels have been worked out and set into the circuit, they remain in the unit's memory forever. Management doesn't have to fool around trying to find the right light levels, and patrons don't have to experience the discomfort of a room going from bright to dim to dark to bright, as operators fiddle around for the right level.

DIRECT VERSUS INDIRECT LIGHTING As discussed briefly in chapter 3, a mix of direct and indirect lighting is usually the best choice for the restaurant environment (Figure 4.31). Indirect lighting—where the lamps cannot be seen—minimizes shadows that make people look unattractive and gives an overall glow to the space. These concealed sources can create what is called the *ambient light level*, filling the nooks and crannies with even, diffuse illumination. They can also help achieve different light levels and, as is often the case with wall sconces, cast soft patterns of light on the walls. Some designers like to use indirect lighting almost exclusively in a restaurant.

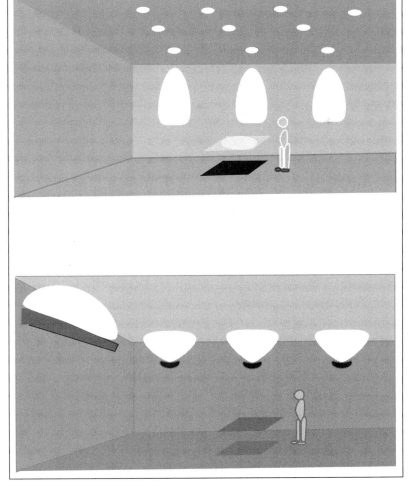

FIGURE 4.31 *Direct downlighting (top) can create glare and harsh shadows. Indirect lighting, on the other hand, creates soft overall light and soft shadows. The optimal design exploits these and other lighting techniques.*

FIGURE 4.32 *At Jardinière in San Francisco, Pat Kuleto used a mix of direct and indirect light sources, including torchères, downlights, art lighting—even an illumination element on the bar front—to create shadow and sparkle.*
(Photo by Donna Kempner, © Pat Kuleto Restaurants.)

To add the sparkle that enlivens a space, direct lighting should be applied in a controlled manner. Direct lighting usually involves some sort of visible bulb, such as exposed bare-filament lamps or chandeliers. The direction of the light path, the spread of the beam emitted from the lamp or luminaire, and the glare from the lamp must always be considered. Another direct lighting application frequently used in restaurants involves high-intensity lamps that provide a pinpoint of light on tabletops. As mentioned earlier, these lights can be used to highlight the tabletop and the food placed on it, but the effect can backfire if the light is too bright or improperly angled. In any scenario, direct and indirect illumination must work in concert to create a lighting mix that matches the overall design image of the restaurant (Figure 4.32).

SPECIAL EFFECTS Special-effects lighting is used not so much to illuminate the room as to dramatize it. Neon, in many colors and configurations, is one light source to consider. Most effective when used in moderation, it is often specified for signage—as restaurant logo outside and inside, or to identify a space in the restaurant, such as a raw bar or salad bar. Neon can also be an effective directional signal. However, the impact of the neon light must be considered. On an elaborate scale, the red, white, and blue neon tubes that form a stylized flag on the ceiling of New York's America help guide guests down a central runway leading to tables on either side and a monumental bar in the back. The light output of these lamps is low enough so that the quality of the light reaching the tabletops is not affected.

Often, theatrical fixtures are used in much the same fashion as they are on stage—to highlight interesting details. Theatrical framing projectors can be used to cast varied patterns on floors, walls, or ceiling. These devices use a template to give a variety of effects. A good alternative to the more expensive fixtures made for theaters are scaled-down versions offered by commercial lighting manufacturers, which are better suited to the restaurant environment. In either case, light can transform a monochromatic backdrop into a fascinating design of color and pattern, depending on the template design. Theatrical light projections can communicate virtually any image, including corporate logos, directional arrows, and starbursts.

The direct light of chandeliers, especially sparkling off glass and crystal, is a staple of banquet lighting. Typically used in large, open spaces, chandeliers also find their way—in highly stylized formats—into restaurants. These ceiling luminaires can provide both direct and indirect lighting to a restaurant interior. The chandelier can also be used as a focal point in a stairwell that connects multifloor restaurants.

OPERATIONAL CONCERNS From an operational perspective, the design team should be aware of several lighting concerns. As mentioned earlier, relamping policies must be considered when selecting light sources. In some high-ceilinged restaurants, the only way to change ceiling lamps is to hire a lift scaffolding. In other restaurants, ceiling lights are so difficult and expensive to replace that they are not replaced at all.

Easy relamping should be a goal of every restaurant lighting scheme, but the job can become difficult when many lamp types are used. One trick that can make the operator's life easier is to specify higher-wattage lamps than the space requires, then keep them dimmed down. A 150-watt lamp run at full capacity burns out quickly, but if it is never turned up to more than 50 percent of capacity, its life increases substantially.

Another concern is the need for additional light during cleaning periods. A separate set of lights or a dimming system that can be turned up helps with this issue. A dimming system not only allows light levels to be turned up enough for the cleaning crew but also, on slow nights in large restaurants, it enables management to leave unused sections darkened.

ENERGY EFFICIENCY Energy-efficient lighting is important in any type of restaurant operation. Fast-food operations use a little more than a quarter of their total energy consumption and tableservice restaurants use less than a tenth of their total for lighting but, in both types of operations, energy conservation plays an important role. Energy conservation pertains both to the energy used by lamps for illumination and the energy that lamps convert to heat. Certain lighting plans may actually necessitate increased ventilation capacity to prevent the dining areas from overheating.

Energy efficiency will be affected by the choice of luminaire and lamp. One option might include a low initial installation cost for the luminaire, moderate energy consumption, and high replacement frequency. Another option might entail high initial installation costs, low energy consumption, and low replacement frequency. The second option seems to be the obvious choice, yet with lighting packages costing $8-10 per square foot, a financially strapped restaurateur may choose the first option, hoping to retrofit the lighting scheme after the restaurant becomes profitable.

These and other factors must be considered when planning an illumination

A peach-colored tabletop that looks good under indirect sunlight may look washed out under direct sunlight.

scheme. In the end, it all comes together as a subliminal experience for patrons. The better the lighting plan, the less aware the customer that there is such a plan. Instead, diners bask in an atmosphere both comfortable and exciting, bathed in flattering light.

COLOR

Color is linked closely with light because, without light, there is no perception of color. With certain types of light, colors can appear more vibrant, but other types of light make the same colors look dull and gray. This is the basic principle of light reflection and is essential to the selection of color and lighting in restaurants.

When white light—light that is composed of equal color components (violet, indigo, blue, green, yellow, orange, and red)—strikes a surface that is painted red, more red is reflected from the surface than any other components of the light and the surface appears red. The same is true when light passes through a red glass or gel; the red component of the light is transmitted while the other components are filtered out of the resulting beam.

There are many classifications of color. The Munsell system, as illustrated in chapter 3, includes three important means of classifying a given color: hue (shade of a given color), value (brilliance of the color), and chroma (the saturation or purity of the color). Colors appearing on opposing sides of the color wheel are complementary colors. If a wall painted red is illuminated with a blue-green light source, it appears gray. In effect, the light reduces the apparent chroma level of the wall. Chroma levels are also affected by intensity of lighting. A peach-colored tabletop that looks good under indirect sunlight may look washed out under direct sunlight. Thus, it is important to use paints that are heavily saturated (with high chroma levels) in operations with high light levels. Pastels in brightly lit rooms can appear faded.

FLOORS

Restaurant flooring means more to patrons than just a surface to walk on. Flooring can act as a directional signal, yield a soft, cushy feeling of elegance, and either absorb or reflect sound. Selecting a floor material seems easy; it should last forever, be easy to clean, be available in colors that complement other colors in the space, deaden or heighten noise as needed, and be priced to match other design elements. As with lighting systems, a careful analysis of the advantages and disadvantages of floor covering plans is important.

By most standards, vinyl is the least expensive floor covering to purchase and install, and terrazzo is among the most expensive. In fact, the installed cost of terrazzo is approximately six times greater than vinyl. Again, the owner short on cash may opt for the inexpensive floor solution—but added to the installation cost should be the expense of maintaining the floor, its usable lifespan, and its replacement cost. These additional factors yield a total cost per square foot of flooring over time.

Vinyl flooring, for example, must be replaced after 8 to 15 years, whereas terrazzo has a much longer usable life span (over 40 years, the total cost per square foot of terrazzo is only 12 percent higher than vinyl). Unglazed ceramic tiles, if properly maintained by mopping and occasional sealing, can hold up almost indefinitely, but the finish on glazed ceramic tile wears out quickly. Marble can take a great deal of abuse, but alcohol spills will soak in and leave stains. Granite, a less porous material, withstands abuse even better than marble. Composite stone flooring, made of small, compressed bits, has become a popular, easy-maintenance option. Poured resin floors are easy to install, are impervious to moisture, clean up quickly, and are slip-resistant. Wood floors, often chosen for their warmth and eye appeal, have to be refinished approximately every nine months. Laminated wood flooring is easy to install and holds up well in abusive restaurant environments. Carpeting is the floor covering of choice for acoustic control. The thicker the carpet and padding, the more noise it absorbs. Nylon, or a nylon-wool blend, is a practical choice because it is flame retardant and stain resistant. Note that a solid color shows dirt, stains, and spills far more than a patterned carpet.

Building codes and safety issues must always be considered when choosing floor materials for a restaurant. Certain types of flooring may be excluded because of local building or health codes.

In the front of the house, it is appropriate for the designers to specify flooring for its aesthetic appeal. A mix of floor surfaces can give various sensations to the customers. For example, people can promenade down a marble runner and then settle in at their seats with warm carpeting below their feet. However, different floorings require different cleaning techniques, which means various cleaning chemicals (and polishes, where necessary), equipment, and staff training for cleaning each surface.

Flooring materials perform various functional roles. In one restaurant, for example, the bar floor might be covered with gray ground concrete that is well suited to the beating taken from spilled drinks, snuffed-out cigarettes, and dripping umbrellas as people wait for a dinner table. When guests reach the dining room, they might encounter an island of sound-absorbing carpet surrounded by a boardwalk of wood flooring for visual interest.

In the fast-food environment, just one practical flooring material can take on new meaning if cleverly applied. For instance, unglazed ceramic tile in a custom-designed pattern resembling a needlepoint rug was used in one fast-food restaurant. Here, the floor took on an aesthetic in keeping with the restaurant's postmodern/Victorian motif, but remained eminently practical.

Entry floors, because of the high wear and tear resulting from off-street dirt, should be covered in highly resilient materials. The designer should be aware that polished stone flooring becomes slippery when wet, so if specified in entry areas where rain and snow could be tracked in, they should be covered with runners. As mentioned above, relaxed dining settings benefit from carpeting, which deadens noise and gives a warm feeling to the space. However, restaurant dining areas that depend on high noise levels to generate excitement often rely on hard flooring surfaces that reflect noise, can take abuse, and are easy to clean.

For any floor material subject to the rigors of restaurant traffic, the following points should be considered in concert with the aesthetics of the materials:

Flammability. This is particularly important in display kitchens or dining rooms where tableside cooking is offered.

Entry floors, because of the high wear and tear resulting from off-street dirt, should be covered in highly resilient materials.

Color/light fastness. An important consideration with carpeting, fading can also be a problem with wood flooring.

Flooring adhesive. For conventional wood flooring, nails may be a sufficient adhesive, but in some cases box-coated nails will reduce squeaking. Box-coated nails plus glue ensure a squeak-free wooden floor. Some manufactured wood floors require a glue-down installation. For carpeting, proper adhesion prevents carpet slippage and premature wear and wrinkling. Adhesives for vinyl, rubber sheeting, and tiles (along with the subfloor) play an important role in the lifespan of the surface. While the best adhesives are significantly more expensive, they usually pay back the investment in extended trouble-free usage.

Subflooring. The wearability of the finished floor depends a great deal on the subfloor. If the subfloor cracks and splits or does not take well to an adhesive, the finished floor won't last long under normal restaurant conditions.

WALLS

Walls enclose patrons, provide surfaces for points of interest such as artwork and lighting sconces, and open vistas to the outside world. Windows are important parts of walls in many establishments, particularly in freestanding restaurants and large urban gathering places, and should be selected with energy conservation and lighting concerns in mind. The glazing itself has great impact on energy conservation. Single-pane windows are the least and thermopane units are the most efficient insulators. Window coverings such as shades, blinds, screens, and exterior awnings can improve energy usage. To minimize thermal loading, select low-E glass or triple-pane glass.

Walls and their coverings play an important role in the overall design of a restaurant. The shapes of walls, the materials they are made of, and the finishes placed on them can range from simple painted sheetrock on flat walls to elaborately curved walls trimmed with rare wood and marble. Wall treatments perform a number of aesthetic and practical roles. Hard-surfaced walls tend to increase sound levels, which can be countered by applying sound-absorbing panels.

The intricacy of the design and the quality of the wall coverings can drastically influence the cost and durability of a wall. Like floors, walls take a great deal of beating in the restaurant environment. Painted surfaces are the least resilient and should be used only in areas not prone to wear. Longer-lasting, wear-resistant materials such as vinyl wallcovering in medium-impact areas can keep maintenance costs low and wall surfaces looking like new. Installing chair rails, a wooden wainscoting, or even more resilient stone or metal material on a wall can eliminate scuffmarks made by the backs of chairs.

Much artistry can be used in the selection and application of wall materials. The rough brick, plaster, and concrete of the patched-up walls at some restaurants create a fascinating textural milieu (Figure 4.33). In fashionable and formal restaurants, cherry, bird's-eye maple, or other rare wood panels are reminiscent of high-powered boardrooms and add to the upscale atmosphere of a space. In some designs—most notably fast-food environments—wall elements are fashioned from plastic materials and slapped on as an overlay. Such treatments don't trick customers for long. Walls offer one of the most accepting pallets for interior design and art elements, but these should always be thoughtfully applied. Just because a wall exists doesn't mean it must be decoratively covered.

From an operational perspective, walls and their coverings should be easy to clean and resistant to wear and tear. In high-impact areas, special attention should be given to wall finishes. While some finishes may detract from an otherwise seamless design, a scuff mark or hole punched through a wall can be even more distracting to the customer.

CEILINGS

Too often neglected in the restaurant design scheme, the ceiling is always noticed by clientele. As with walls, hard sheetrock surfaces tend to reflect sound and light. The designer Sarah Tomerlin Lee once said that in an otherwise simple room, a special ceiling treatment could work like a woman's hat; the ceiling can dress a plain room in the same way that the hat can transform a simple sheath into a fashionable outfit. Imagine, for example, a vaulted ceiling covered with stretched Lycra sails. To accentuate the ceiling even more, ceiling lights set above the sails result in a warm overall glow in the space.

FIGURE 4.33 *A textured wall surface creates visual interest in a restaurant. Light fixtures, such as the wall sconce shown here, can accentuate the texture.* (Photo by Regina Baraban.)

Technically, the ceiling usually consists of several elements: the basic ceiling structure, luminaires, acoustical treatments, and ventilation grillwork. The basic ceiling structure may be the framework to which the other elements are attached. Painted sheetrock is often the material of choice on fixed ceilings. Structural elements are sometimes deliberately left exposed, along with the lighting, plumbing, and HVAC mechanicals, to achieve a high-tech look.

Acoustic ceiling treatments are the most effective way to control sound in a restaurant. Acoustic ceiling tiles, insulation, and other sound-absorbing materials applied to ceilings minimize reverberation and absorb sound. Ceiling alcoves, such as lighting alcoves or simply dead airspace above a perforated ceiling, also serve to trap and limit reverberation. Fiberglass panels wrapped with fabric; banners; and color-coordinated, vinyl-coated acoustical drywall panels are also popular choices for ceiling treatments. Many good designs combine a number of these treatments.

The distribution of fresh and removal of stale air is usually integrated with the ceiling treatment. Care must be taken to ensure that adequate air is supplied to all areas of the dining room without creating a draft in any one spot. This is best accomplished by installing oversized ventilation grills, but the appearance of the grills usually detracts from the appearance of the ceiling. In some cases, makeup air can be piped into the dining room via coffered ceiling spaces, thus providing indirect ventilation that limits the chance of drafts. In any case, exhaust air must be carefully balanced with the kitchen exhaust system; positive pressure must be maintained in the dining room to ensure that smoke and airborne grease does not enter from the kitchen. What this often translates into is a system where all air sweeps across the dining room, through the kitchen doors, and out the exhaust hood in the kitchen.

AIR CONTROL

One of the goals of air control in dining spaces is to deliver heating and cooling unobtrusively—meaning no drafts and no hot and cool spots. It also means controlling smoke and preventing other smells from carrying into the dining room.

HEATING AND COOLING Air-handling units are the most efficient way to control temperature and air quality in a restaurant. Such units, when properly chosen, installed, and balanced, can address all of the heating and cooling needs in the dining spaces.

However, are mechanical means of heating and cooling necessary in all restaurants? Clearly, the answer is no. Anyone who has ever sat in an open-air oceanfront dining space in Hawaii or the Caribbean knows that tropical breezes can eliminate the need for mechanical cooling. In northern climates, heat can be effectively supplied via baseboard hot water units, fresh air via open windows, and cooling via through-wall air conditioners. No matter the setting, the goal is the same: temperature and air quality should not detract from the dining experience.

For restaurants without operable windows or where dining spaces are 50 feet or more from an outside wall, air-handling units are probably the optimal means of controlling air quality. Oftentimes, air-handling units are tied into a single thermostat but, at times, some areas in the dining room are hotter or colder than others. If the air handlers have a single zone, they cannot react to such temperature variances.

The solution is a HVAC unit that delivers cool air to one area and heated air to another. These units rely on boilers for heating and chilled-water units for cooling. If, however, the system allows only heating or cooling to operate at one time, its usefulness is limited.

SMOKE CONTROL Negative air pressure in the kitchen ensures that the smoke and grease-laden air produced is exhausted to outdoors rather than flowing into the dining room. Smoke control is more complex in the front of the house, as seen in Figure 4.34. The challenge facing restaurateurs in jurisdictions that still allow smoking in public spaces is how to accommodate both smokers and nonsmokers.

The secrets are containment and filtration. As mentioned earlier, that means maintaining a negative air pressure in those rooms where smoking is allowed. It also means fully exhausting the air from those spaces rather than mixing an

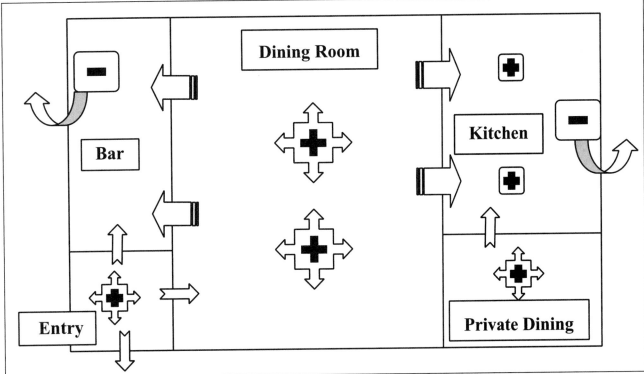

amount of the air with fresh makeup air. Wherever smoking is allowed, air-filtration units should be installed. The air filters improve the environment for smokers, nonsmokers, and servers alike. They also help ensure that the dining spaces will not take on a stale, smoky smell.

FIGURE 4.34 *Controlling smoke and dust is no easy task in a restaurant. Here, a positive pressure is maintained in the entry to prevent street dust from entering. A negative pressure is maintained in the bar to contain smoke within that area. A positive pressure is maintained in the dining room to keep cigarette smoke in the bar and kitchen smoke in the kitchen. While makeup air is added to the kitchen, the overall design promotes a negative pressure that keeps kitchen air pollution from reaching the dining room.*

Destination Rest Rooms

A visit to the rest room is a common part of the restaurant experience for most patrons, yet bathroom design is all too often neglected. When faced with budget overruns, ownership tends to pull back funding for bathroom decor. In the worst scenario, impractical design contributes to a messy, dirty environment—which may lead customers to believe that the kitchen is dirty, too. On the other hand, an attractive, clean rest room—one that carries through the design scheme of the restaurant—speaks volumes about the caring attitude of management. Bathrooms are frequently used by smokers and should contain wall-mounted ashtrays to keep the floor clean and prevent the disposal of cigarettes in a way that may lead to a fire.

Architectural reference books and local building and sanitation codes mandate the size and number of water closets required in restaurant bathrooms. As mentioned earlier, care must be taken to ensure that rest rooms comply with the Americans with Disabilities Act (ADA). However, the architectural manuals do not emphasize the importance of bathrooms to the overall success of the restaurant, nor do they discuss the ramifications of design and decor.

Privacy of both sight and sound is an important consideration for any restau-

Tiles, vinyl wall coverings, and other practical materials can help the restaurateur maintain a spotless bathroom with minimal effort.

rant bathroom. Vanity screens or some sort of labyrinth must be installed to ensure that sight lines into the bathrooms are limited from exterior view. Mirrors must be carefully placed so as not to interfere with people's privacy.

Adequate ventilation is another absolute requirement. Exhaust fans in bathrooms should be strong enough to create a negative pressure that will draw air in from the dining room, through the bathroom, and out the vent. Some restaurateurs may opt for air-freshening units, but these can't surpass the effectiveness of plain old fresh air.

In any bathroom, a sufficient number of water closets (and urinals, in men's bathrooms) are needed, with latching mechanisms that are easy to use and maintain. Easily cleaned sinks and counters are also essential, along with soap dispensers that are easy to fill and keep clean. All too often, the spout of a soap dispenser rests over the counter and leaves trailings of soap that must be wiped up frequently if a clean appearance is to be maintained. Also, trash cans are frequently undersized and end up overfilled with crumpled towels hours before the next scheduled bathroom cleaning. Air dryers should always be installed as a backup (or alternative) to paper towels.

Lighting plays an important role in bathroom design. In fast-food and other foodservice environments that use fluorescent lighting in the front of the house, fluorescent lighting is acceptable. However, in a softly lit tableservice restaurant, where incandescent lighting provides a flattering glow, the blue-hued glare of fluorescent tubes in the bathroom can be shocking and potentially ruin an evening.

Spotless bathrooms are comforting to restaurant guests, as they imply that the rest of the restaurant is also clean. Nonporous, easily cleanable materials are an excellent way of ensuring that a trip to the bathroom is not a turnoff. Tiles, vinyl wall coverings, and other practical materials can help the restaurateur maintain a spotless bathroom with minimal effort. These applications don't have to look institutional, either; manufacturers offer textures, colors, and designs that carry through a fashionable look.

WOMEN'S REST ROOMS

As reported by the National Restaurant Association, the average woman takes 8 to 10 minutes on a trip to the bathroom. Men take an average of 4 minutes. The time difference points to some important design considerations. Men generally use bathrooms for totally utilitarian purposes. Women, on the other hand, use bathrooms to perform many activities that include retouching makeup, fixing hair, perfuming, adjusting clothes, and talking with friends. All these activities require extra space and specialized elements. A makeup table or cosmetics shelf across from the sinks is an inexpensive yet helpful addition to the women's room. Mirrors over the sink and over the makeup area should be high quality, distortion-free, and polished. Wherever possible, a full-length mirror placed by the exit door is a welcome addition.

A final inclusion, particularly important in restaurants that cater to singles, is a place for women to talk within the bathroom. This may be one and the same with the makeup area or separate from it. Regardless, it should be large enough so that several conversations can be conducted. When separated from the water closet and sink areas, these spaces can have a much more residential feeling, with touches such as a carpeted floor to diminish sound levels.

MEN'S REST ROOMS

As mentioned above, men take a more utilitarian approach to bathrooms. However, such added amenities as a shoeshine are appropriate in certain settings. A hanger in the water closets is appreciated for hanging suit jackets. In fast-food restaurants or diners where laborers often lunch, two soap dispensers—one with mild soap and one with abrasive soap for deep cleaning—is an added benefit.

Vanity screens are sometimes placed between urinals. If they are to be wall mounted, they must be firmly secured or else, within a short time, they will loosen, fall from their place, and leave unsightly holes in the wall. All too often, when urinals are separated with vanity screens, they are placed too closely together and oversized men inadvertently loosen the screens as they push past them. Another disadvantage of the screens is that they are frequently splashed and rust quickly.

CUSTOMIZED REST ROOMS

The same attention to design detailing in the dining room can be carried into the bathroom for a pleasing effect. In a seafood restaurant, faux portholes can filter light into the space. In upscale restaurants with contemporary design, the standard vitrified chinaware sinks can be replaced with stainless steel. In some restaurants, a floral display in the bathroom adds a residential touch that can downplay institutional elements.

This customization can go beyond the standard applications to little elements that are peculiar to a specific type of restaurant. Consider a barbecue ribs restaurant. A toothpick dispenser and hot towel dispenser in the bathrooms become conversation pieces and are helpful to guests. An area map and distance chart on the rest room walls in roadside restaurants is useful to travelers. In many bathrooms, pay phones and vending machines can generate revenues for the owners and are helpful to the guests.

As mentioned earlier, bathrooms should be seen as an integral part of the design scheme. When well designed, they are a positive addition. When dealt with as an afterthought, they can appear incongruous and may be a reason not to return to the restaurant.

Summary

Front-of-the-house design involves a delicate orchestration of spaces that works to create a total experience. From the moment the customer first sets sight on the building to the moment when she steps back outside after a meal, design should be part of an integrated plan. Each design decision should reflect thoughtful problem solving that is sensitive both to the needs of the operation and to the design concept. Once the design team understands the basic principles discussed above, they can begin to make specific decisions.

Notes

Design Implementation: Back to Front Through Management's Eyes

In the process-oriented approach to restaurant design, solutions come from analyzing the functional needs of a given operation. To understand the principles of kitchen design, therefore, we systematically move through the back of the house from an operational point of view; starting with the receiving of unprocessed food and ending with the plating of prepared food for service. This technique enables the designer to fill in the floorplan with appropriate workstations and equipment, because each space or functional area in the back of the house has certain operating characteristics that translate into design features. While these areas are discussed individually, it is important to remember that, in the final design, they must be integrated as a whole.

Kitchen Support Areas

Kitchen support areas are those spaces not primarily designated for food preparation or service—that is, office and storage space. All too often, the back-of-the-house design process centers on the production area but overlooks the importance of support spaces. For example, if office space is insufficient, managers may not be able to secure important documents or may be hard pressed to find a space to interview new employees. If storage space is inadequate, more frequent deliveries—with an attendant upcharge from the supplier—will be required. These areas are not glamorous, but they are the backbone of the kitchen.

RECEIVING

The receiving area should be accessible to the loading dock and the storerooms wherever possible to facilitate a smooth flow of food from delivery to receiving to storage. Ideally, the loading dock leads directly to the receiving area, which is adjacent to the various storage areas. In some restaurants, the purchasing agent's office is located near the receiving area, but for reasons of internal control, the purchasing function is frequently handled from an office separate from the receiving area.

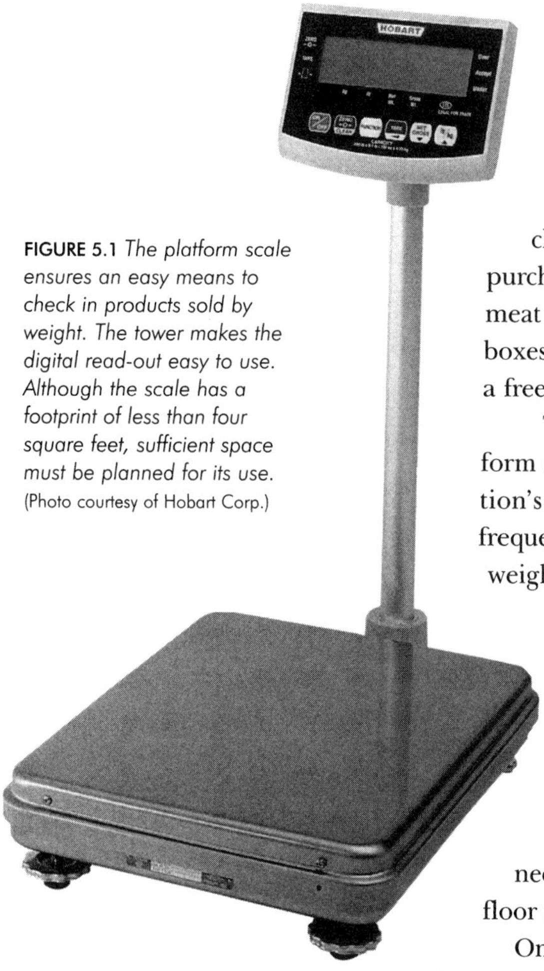

FIGURE 5.1 *The platform scale ensures an easy means to check in products sold by weight. The tower makes the digital read-out easy to use. Although the scale has a footprint of less than four square feet, sufficient space must be planned for its use.* (Photo courtesy of Hobart Corp.)

Receiving area floors must be smooth so that hand trucks and flatbed trucks can be moved about easily. All foods must be carefully inspected when they arrive, so the area should be well lit. The optimum light scheme supplies overall lighting with fluorescent tubes and task lighting with incandescent bulbs.

Scales are most important in this area, as many foods are purchased by weight. In operations where large quantities of meats are purchased, built-in floor scales are ideal; pallets loaded with boxes of meat can be rolled onto the floor scale and easily weighed. Individual boxes of meat or other items purchased by weight can be weighed with a freestanding floor scale or table scale.

The two most commonly chosen scales for this area are the platform scale and the floor scale. The chosen scale must match the operation's receiving needs. Large hotels and institutional operations frequently have a built-in floor scale capable of holding pallets of food weighing a ton or more.

However, the majority of operations purchase foods in batches smaller than 300 pounds, so a portable platform scale is called for. For ease of use, nothing beats a scale with a digital read-out (Figure 5.1). Portable platform scales are frequently fashioned from stainless steel and have a platform that can hold the largest cases. Some come with a display powered by a long-life battery that allows the scale to be placed wherever needed. A display pad that extends two and one half feet above the floor makes for easy reading.

One vital aspect of platform scales is the tare feature, which enables the receiving clerk to program in the tare weight of the packaging and automatically subtract it from the gross weight to yield the net weight of the case contents. This feature makes it faster and more accurate to weigh in a large delivery. Some platform scales can be programmed for over-under checks; this is particularly useful for weighing in portion-controlled foods. A helpful addition to a platform scale is a thermal printer that delivers a permanent record of delivery weights. This information can be attached to receiving invoices.

While trash is frequently removed through the receiving area, the building and health codes of many locales mandate a separate area to handle trash. Ideally, fresh foods should not travel through the same spaces as trash, nor should they be stored in the same area. A refrigerated space may be needed to store wet garbage from the kitchen. Refrigerating garbage, particularly in hot climates, eliminates the chance of unpleasant smells greeting guests as they arrive.

STORAGE

The storage areas should be located so that they are easily accessible from both the loading dock and the production areas. If they cannot be placed conveniently between these two areas, it makes sense to place them closer to production, because this proximity will save more labor time. Generally, food is received in large quantities and placed on rolling stock for transport to the storage areas. On a given day, a typical restaurant may receive 3 to 10 deliveries. The production personnel, however, may have to draw goods from the dry, refrigerated, or frozen foods storage areas as many as 100 to 300 times each day. In a complex food operation involving more than one kitchen, the storage areas should be placed near the most active kitchen.

Proper shelving systems are needed in every storage area to make them effective. Fixed shelving units are the industry standard, along with dunnage racks for storing large or bulky items. Good shelving should be flexible, which means that the height of each shelf should be alterable. Under ideal conditions, shelving minimizes the need for costly aisle space. This is accomplished by placing the shelves on wheels—an especially useful feature in refrigerated or frozen food storage areas. Shelf depth and overall height should match the products to be stored and the height of the people who will be drawing goods from the shelves.

The amount of shelving in dry or refrigerated space is a function of the menu, the frequency of delivery, the state of the foods as they are purchased, and the number of meals to be served. Frozen foods that are ready for cooking require the least amount of storage per customer served. Fresh food requires greater storage space. Total storage per cover can range anywhere from one to two and one half cubic feet, with the mix between dry and refrigerated/frozen storage being a function of the menu and management policy.

Lighting and ventilation in storage areas is typically poor. However, high temperatures can shorten the shelf life of certain foods and poor lighting levels can lead to inadequate cleaning and poor management. Incandescent lights, which can be turned on and off without decreasing bulb life, should be used in all storage areas. To ensure that lights are extinguished, a motion sensor that automatically turns the lights off can pay for itself in a matter of months.

As indicated earlier, storage is generally divided into three major areas: dry goods, refrigerated, and frozen. The size and location of each area are greatly affected by the menu, limitations of the architecture, and purchasing and receiving procedures. Following is a discussion of the design principles for each.

DRY GOODS

Dry goods are frequently broken into four categories:

1. *dry and canned foods*
2. *disposable paper goods and other nonchemical supplies*
3. *cleaning and chemical supplies*
4. *spirited beverages*

Ideally, each of these categories of dry goods will be stored in a its own storage space. Dry and canned foods need shelving and dunnage racks. Paper supplies arrive in large cases, so the shelves that hold them are often far apart. Styrofoam containers take up the most amount of space, but their light weight makes it possible to store them in taller piles than other dry goods. While paper goods can be stored with dry and canned goods, a separate space is essential for cleaning and chemical supplies. Many cleaning agents outgas odors that can be absorbed by dry goods like flour and pasta. For security reasons, spirited beverages must also be stored in their own space. At times, spirits are kept in a locked cage within the confines of the dry foods storage area but, most frequently, they are kept in their own area under the supervision of the beverage department. Special humidity and temperature-controlled spaces are needed to store fine wines, and draft beer requires refrigerated storage.

In addition to these long-term storage spaces, break-out pantry closets adjacent to production areas are frequently stocked with par inventory of commonly used foods. The well-designed kitchen has par stock areas of dry goods and paper goods for each production section. To ensure maximum efficiency in a bar operation, the par stock of spirits should be enough to supply a busy evening of drinks.

REFRIGERATION

Refrigerated storage units come in differing sizes and must be matched carefully to the operation. Generally, a mix of walk-in, reach-in, and undercounter refrigeration is used in restaurant kitchens. Three overriding issues must be considered when deciding on the placement of refrigerated equipment: labor costs, food costs, and food safety.

Labor Costs. One of the most effective ways to control labor costs is to design self-sufficient workstations in the kitchen. That means that each employee has work and storage space that's immediately accessible. In the cold food station, for example, reach-in refrigeration is effective. One section of the reach-in is used to hold unprocessed foods, while prepared or plated foods are held in another.

The placement of the reach-in can improve or inhibit efficiency. For example, if plated salads are stored in a back line reach-in, the production staff must physically transfer a salad to servers each time a request is made. Alternatively, reach-ins, whether floor units or overcounter units, could be placed between the preparation and pickup sides of the cold food station. This practice saves time for production personnel and ensures that servers get back on the floor as quickly as possible. Alternatively, storing mixed greens in an overcounter bulk salad refrigerator puts hundreds of portions of salad in reach of servers for quick plating.

In the hot food section, it's important to consider how far each of the chefs must travel to reach refrigerated space. Traditionally, a pair of reach-ins was installed near each end of a hot food cooking battery. Today, those reach-ins are often replaced with undercounter refrigerated drawers below each cooking station to give cooks all the refrigerated or frozen food they need within arms reach (Figure 5.2).

Food Costs. Well-chosen and well-positioned refrigeration can help prevent food spoilage. If too much heat is added to the inside of a refrigerator—due to excessive door openings or the addition of a large pot of steaming hot soup, for example—the mechanical system cannot remove the heat effectively and foods can spoil.

Lettuce will grow limp and milk will sour prematurely if stored under refrigeration where the temperature is not maintained consistently below 40 degrees Fahrenheit. Reach-ins can maintain milk at serving temperature for a couple of days, but if a milk delivery is intended for use over four to five days, it should be stored in a walk-in, where there is less temperature fluctuation.

Food Safety. Refrigeration plays a central role in a Hazard Analysis Critical Control Point (HACCP) program (see sidebar on page 139). If refrigerated spaces are not within easy reach of kitchen workers, they often allow foods to sit out on a counter for too long. If foods sit too long on a loading dock before being placed under refrigeration, the potential for food poisoning is also increased.

Walk-Ins. Walk-in refrigerators should be utilized for extended-term storage of bulk foods and for short-term storage of batch-prepared foods. Such refrigeration systems are expensive and take up a great deal of space in the operation. Walk-ins, with a weather cap, can be installed outdoors to save space inside a restaurant. In some instances, the walk-in is separated from the building but can be positioned so that its access door opens through an exterior wall of the restaurant. This practice gains valuable space inside a kitchen and eliminates the weather problem that occurs when employees have to go outside to access a walk-in. Also, with an interior door, there's little chance that an employee can steal.

FIGURE 5.2 *Garland's Arctic Fire range puts handy refrigerated and freezer drawers below the cooktop instead of the more traditional cavity oven.* (Photo displayed with permission of Garland Commercial Ranges, Inc.)

Today's walk-ins are highly engineered units that come in myriad sizes and configurations. The walls, floor, and ceilings are fashioned from sandwiched insulated panels that can be snapped together on site. To maximize the efficiency of a walk-in, it is advisable to insulate its floor. In new construction, insulation can be installed under the tile floor; in a retrofit, insulation can be installed over the existing floor. However, a ramp, whether inside or outside the walk-in, must be provided so that staff can easily roll carts in and out of the refrigerator.

Here are questions that must be addressed before choosing a walk-in:

1. *How many walk-ins are needed?*

As with dry goods, it often makes sense to put refrigerated items in separate spaces. Beer in kegs must be kept under refrigeration at all times. While canned and bottled beer can be stored in ambient temperatures, chilling them before they head for the bar ensures correct temperatures. Dairy products frequently have their own storage space, particularly when strong-smelling cheeses are on the menu. Vegetables and fruits that easily pick up odors should be stored away from dairy products or other foods that give off strong smells. In some cases, a walk-in is needed to age wholesale cuts of beef or to keep beef and other protein items separate from produce and dairy. In high-volume restaurants, fresh seafood can be kept in a separate walk-in but most often is stored in a fish file that is restocked daily.

2. *Is a remote compressor possible?*

Walk-ins require a good deal of mechanical refrigeration to keep their contents cool. The refrigeration system releases a lot of heat and the condensor fan can be noisy, so a remote compressor is often advisable. The remote compressor ensures that waste heat from the refrigeration cycle is dumped outside the restaurant rather than in the kitchen.

3. *Where will the walk-ins be located?*

Walk-ins are frequently ganged together into one space. However, a walk-in used to store kegs of beer should be as close to the dispensing point as possible. The longer the run from the walk-in to the draft head, the higher the cost of refrigerating and maintaining the supply line.

Reach-Ins. Reach-in refrigerators are available in many configurations. They can be cooled by built-in or remote compressors. Single- or multiple-section units equipped with half or full doors, solid or see-through doors, locking doors, interior lights, and externally displayed temperature readouts are among the configuration options. As with walk-ins, several questions must be addressed before a purchasing decision is made:

1. *On which side of the door will the hinges be installed?*

The directional flow of materials to and from the workstation should influence this decision. Some manufacturers offer walk-ins with door swings that can be adjusted in the field.

2. *Will each section of the reach-in have a single door, or will there be half-doors?*

This usually comes down to choosing between convenience and energy savings. Single doors support roll-in shelving and allow the user to view the contents of the entire refrigerator by opening just one door. However, while that door is held open, more heat infiltrates the unit than with a half-door reach-in.

3. *Should the reach-in have solid or see-through doors?*

Solid doors provide the best insulation, but they must be opened in order to see the contents. With see-through doors, the kitchen staff can view the refrigerator stock without opening the door.

4. *Are pass-through reach-ins appropriate?*

The extra cost is warranted only when the reach-ins will be accessed from both sides. In a layout where salad greens are washed adjacent to the back of the walk-in and salads are plated in front of the walk-in, reach-throughs are called for. They are also appropriate for cafeteria lines where foods are loaded on the kitchen side and removed by counter staff on the service side.

Specialty Refrigeration. Refrigerated drawers are often used near grill areas for holding meats and toppings, or installed near a broiler station for holding fresh seafood. They are either integrated with a typical reach-in unit or specified as freestanding units.

Undercounter refrigerators are typically part of sandwich stations or are placed under grill or broiler units. For installation under a countertop broiler or fryer, refrigerated drawers are the best configuration. When placed under a sandwich unit where tall containers of condiments and backup pans of fillings are held, reach-in units are a better choice.

FROZEN STORAGE

The configurations of frozen food storage units are similar to refrigerated units, except for the addition of chest storage, which is generally reserved for ice cream. Unlike walk-in refrigerators, walk-in freezers must have insulated floors. In addition, unless insulation is inlaid in the floor slab, a ramp must also be provided. Wherever possible, the door of the walk-in freezer should open into a walk-in refrigerator. This will improve operating efficiency of both the refrigerator and the freezer. A heater strip is an excellent addition around the doors of any type of freezer, as it prevents the buildup of frozen condensate around the door. Undercounter freezers equipped with drawers are well suited to fast-food operations where French fries and pre-breaded foods need to be in close proximity to the fryers. Chest-type freezers are perfectly suited to ice cream storage because their minimal temperature variations lengthen shelf life.

ADDITIONAL CONSIDERATIONS

Locking systems are imperative for refrigeration in complex operations. Doors that accommodate hasp locks make it possible to change locks periodically for security reasons. However, doors with built-in locks offer enough security in most restaurant settings.

The refrigerator's exterior finish must also be considered. A stainless-steel surface looks great when first installed, but cleaning and maintaining that high sheen can become problematic. An alternative is to choose refrigeration with a wood-grain or enamel surface that is easier to clean.

As an integral part of a HACCP program, a recording thermometer provides a permanent log of the refrigerator's internal temperature. The log helps monitor temperatures overnight when the kitchen is unattended. The thermometer can be linked to an automated calling system that sends out an alert message when the temperature of a refrigerator exceeds a safe limit.

Roll-in freezers and refrigerators are particularly helpful in banquet preparation areas, where roll-in carts containing pre-portioned desserts or salads can be held for service.

Office and Employee Support Areas

Restaurant offices are more functional than decorative. Space and equipment are needed to complete paperwork and to store records, product information, and reference books. Sufficient lighting, along with an adequate supply of electrical outlets, is necessary. To accommodate com-

---

Hazard Analysis Critical Control Point

Hazard Analysis Critical Control Point (HACCP) is a system of controls and documentation designed to minimize the potential for foodborne illness due to pathogens or physical or chemical contamination. HACCP programs are used worldwide because they identify unsafe links in the food chain. Once identified, the links can be eliminated.

Restaurant design and the choice of equipment play an important role in an HACCP program. Proper refrigeration helps keep foods at temperatures where bacterial growth is minimized. Easy-to-clean food processing equipment helps to ensure that employees clean such equipment as slicers, soft-serve machines, and hand tools to minimize the chances of bacterial growth or cross contamination. Open kitchens in full view of customers also decrease the chances that personnel will employ practices that could lead to contamination.

Hand sinks play an important role in an HACCP program. Foot- or elbow-operated faucets ensure that employees do not cross contaminate their hands when they shut the water off. Another option is an automated handwasher, which directs cleaning solution and rinsewater onto an employee's hands when they are slipped into the two tubes on top of the device. Paper towels and hand soap need to be accessible at each hand sink, and every work station should ideally have its own hand sink.

puters, a separate electrical supply—including an uninterrupted power supply (UPS)—and an Internet connection should be provided.

LOCKER ROOMS

Rest rooms and locker rooms are typically underdesigned and poorly maintained. Employee morale can be positively affected if the locker rooms are well ventilated and lighted and the lockers are large enough to hold clothes and other personal belongings.

An appropriate number of urinals and toilets should be provided, with enough toilet facilities for women. (Wherever possible, employees should not use the same rest rooms as guests.) In addition, space should be provided adjacent to the hand sinks for staff members to place toiletry items. For a clean, efficient operation, it helps to provide air dryers as a backup to paper towels.

Tile flooring with a floor drain is ideal for rest rooms. This treatment facilitates easy cleanup if a backup occurs or if the area needs to be sanitized. Glazed tile or vinyl wallcovering are the preferred covering for walls because they hold up better than painted, metal, and sheetrock surfaces. Adequate ventilation and lighting are essential.

EMPLOYEE DINING

Some restaurants provide an employee dining area. In such cases, durability is a key factor in the design. Tables and chairs will take a greater beating than in the customer dining rooms and, therefore, should be constructed to withstand the extra abuse. But this area should also receive aesthetic attention because employee morale will be greatly boosted by a comfortable, attractive dining room that reflects caring management. Ventilation should be adequate to handle heavy smoke loads, as often employees are allowed to smoke in the employee dining areas only. In some locations, a separate smoking section may be required.

KITCHEN

A well-designed kitchen integrates several spaces. Fabrication, preparation, preparation (hot foods, bakeshop, dessert, and salad), holding, assembly/service, and sanitation are all commonly incorporated in a kitchen design. Each of the spaces is driven by the menu and designed for the preparation and service of different items. Each must function individually, yet work in concert with other kitchen spaces.

DESIGN ESSENTIALS

Kitchen design begins with an analysis of the individual tasks that must be performed in the space. This task analysis becomes the basis for designing the kitchen and for developing training programs for employees. In some cases, for example, two people who perform similar tasks will share a given piece of equipment, so the equipment must be positioned centrally to both employees.

The next step is to develop workstations that are combined into work sections and, eventually, into the areas that make up the kitchen.

A useful step, at this point, is to create a bubble diagram (Figure 5.3) that depicts the major areas in the back of the house. In most cases, this diagram will include:

- hot foods
- cold foods
- beverage
- service
- warewashing
- storage and receiving
- offices

The size and relative position of each bubble is a function of the type of restaurant. For example, in a fast-food restaurant that relies on disposables, the warewashing bubble will be quite small (Figure 5.4) because warewashing is limited to cleaning kitchen utensils and equipment. It can be positioned at any point in the kitchen. However, the placement of the warewashing area is more important in a banquet kitchen (Figure 5.5), and the cooking areas are much larger.

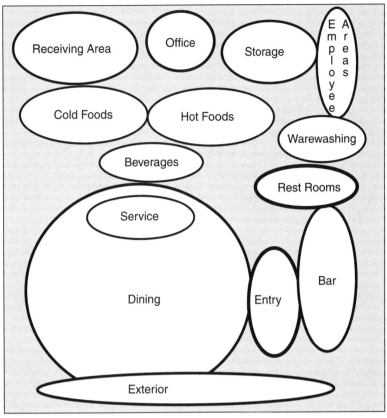

FIGURE 5.3 *A bubble diagram quickly shows the spatial relationships between major areas of the restaurant.*

WORKSTATIONS

Workstations are the building blocks of a kitchen design. A workstation is the space—flooring, work counters, production equipment, storage equipment, utilities—where a particular set of tasks is completed. Generally, the station is designed for one worker.

To understand the process of designing a successful workstation, first identify the task or tasks that need to be performed in the station. Figure 5.6A diagrams a single-sided workstation where a sauté cook stands at the range and sautés food to order. In real life, however, no workstation is as simple as this design. One essential component, for example, is refrigeration to hold the uncooked portions of meat. To resolve this, as shown in Figure 5.6B, a mobile refrigerator was added to the station.

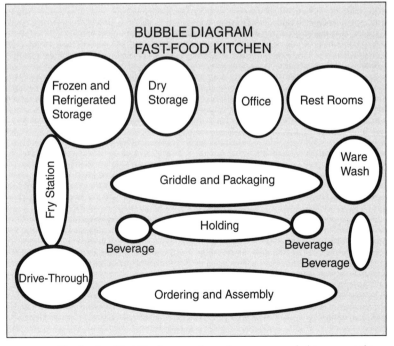

FIGURE 5.4 *The fast-food bubble diagram shows the spaces needed to support this type of service system, such as multiple beverage areas.*

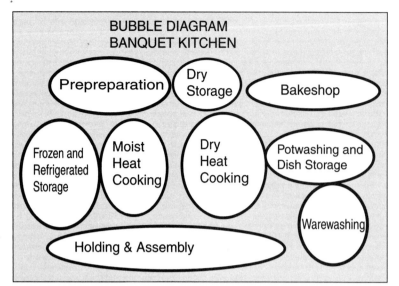

**BUBBLE DIAGRAM
BANQUET KITCHEN**

- Prepreparation
- Dry Storage
- Bakeshop
- Frozen and Refrigerated Storage
- Moist Heat Cooking
- Dry Heat Cooking
- Potwashing and Dish Storage
- Warewashing
- Holding & Assembly

FIGURE 5.5 *A banquet kitchen bubble diagram shows how this type of service system depends on warewashing and on volume production equipment.*

But the station is still inadequate. Go further and think of it as a circle, with multidirectional characteristics (Figure 5.6C). The cook sautés meat on the range, reaches around to pick up a serving plate, places the portion on the plate, then turns to finish off the plate with vegetables and a garnish from the steam table.

In Figure 5.6D, the complete workstation appears in elevation from the worker's perspective, showing the range with an overshelf where plates can be held, plus an undercounter refrigerator. Note that the overshelf eliminates the cook's need to turn around for plates and the undercounter refrigerator does not block the aisle.

The complete station is most easily understood when it is thought of in three dimensions. The sauté cook can easily reach the meat in the undercounter refrigerator. After the meat is prepared, the plates are within easy reach on the overshelf and the vegetables are ready for service on the steam table. This is not to say that this is the ideal sauté station for every restaurant. Rather, it is a station designed for a specific purpose at a specific location. The key is that the station design is based on a single worker performing a defined set of tasks.

FIGURE 5.6 *Building a workstation begins with a basic piece of equipment to which other pieces are added. For example, start with the basic range (A) and add a rolling refrigerator to the left of the station (B). Next, a steam table and plate lowerator (C) are added to make use of the full circle around the worker. In (D), the elevation shows how the refrigerator could actually be placed under a countertop range to save floor space and improve flow.*

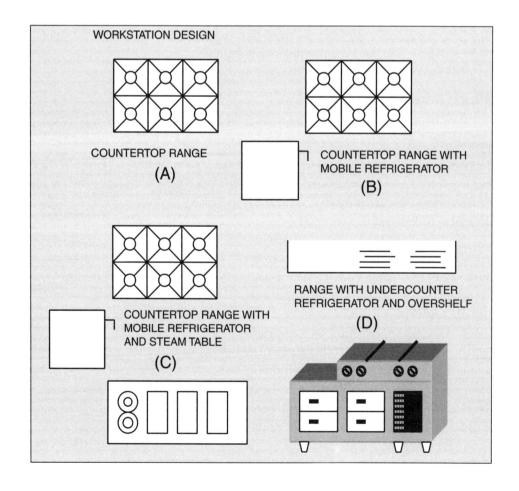

WORKSTATION DESIGN

COUNTERTOP RANGE
(A)

COUNTERTOP RANGE WITH MOBILE REFRIGERATOR
(B)

COUNTERTOP RANGE WITH MOBILE REFRIGERATOR AND STEAM TABLE
(C)

RANGE WITH UNDERCOUNTER REFRIGERATOR AND OVERSHELF
(D)

SECTIONS

Continuing with a hypothetical kitchen design, imagine that a broiler station will be installed to the right of the sauté station, with an open-grate gas broiler for broiling steaks and chops.

A fry station will be installed to the right of the broiler station. Two deep-fat fryers will be specified, for frying breaded seafood and French fries. Storage space for plates, a steam table to hold vegetables, and a freezer to hold the seafood and fries are all necessary components for these stations.

Together, these three workstations comprise the cooking side of a hot food à la carte section. However, were they not grouped together, each would have to have its own steam table and refrigerator, and the end design would be unwieldy and costly. One solution, as seen in Figure 5.7, is to place the refrigeration unit so that it is accessible to the range and the broiler stations, and to place a freezer under the fryers. The drawers of the undercounter refrigerator and freezer make them easier for the cooks to use than if they were equipped with hinged doors. On the front side of the section, a single steam table with plate lowerators on either end is added. Between the range and the fry station, a spreader plate is installed for safety; it also functions as a work surface.

Of course, compromises are always necessary. The cooks have to lean over to take food out of the refrigerated and frozen drawers—but the section can be easily worked by three people or, during slower periods, by one or two people. Task-oriented designs like this are wise financial investments because they contribute to efficient job performance.

FIGURE 5.7 *This hot food à la carte section is composed of three workstations. The position of each station depends on the menu, the type of equipment in the station, the interaction of each of the stations, and safety requirements.*

AREAS

As kitchen design progresses, sections are melded together to form areas of the kitchen. For example, the hot foods area may include an à la carte section, a long-term roasting section, and a steam cooking section.

Relative positioning of the various sections will affect the efficiency of the kitchen. Designers need to study the overall plan to determine the best location for the various sections in relation to each other within each area. In turn, the relationship between areas in terms of production and their interaction with the front of the house, must be considered.

The bubble diagram shown in Figure 5.8A, an à la carte kitchen where the servers must make several trips to the kitchen to service each table, has three glaring errors in its design:

1. *The dish machine should be placed where the bakeshop is located.*
2. *The beverage station should be located where the walk-in refrigerator is located.*
3. *The cold food station should be located where the dry goods storage area is located.*

The corrected design appears in Figure 5.8B. While the solutions may seem obvious, inefficient designs are often developed because care is not taken to think through the floorplan from an operational perspective.

The placement of workstations, sections, and areas becomes even more important in complex food-service systems where many dining areas are serviced from a single kitchen. Careful attention must be paid to the service systems in each dining area. If a table-service dining room and banquet room are to be serviced out of one kitchen, for instance, it generally makes sense to place the dish machine closer to the dining room than to the banquet space. This is because the service staff will take more individual trips to the dish machine from the dining room than from the banquet space. Similarly, the hot foods station is usually situated closer to the dining room because staff travels back and forth from the hot food station to the dining room more often than they do to the banquet space.

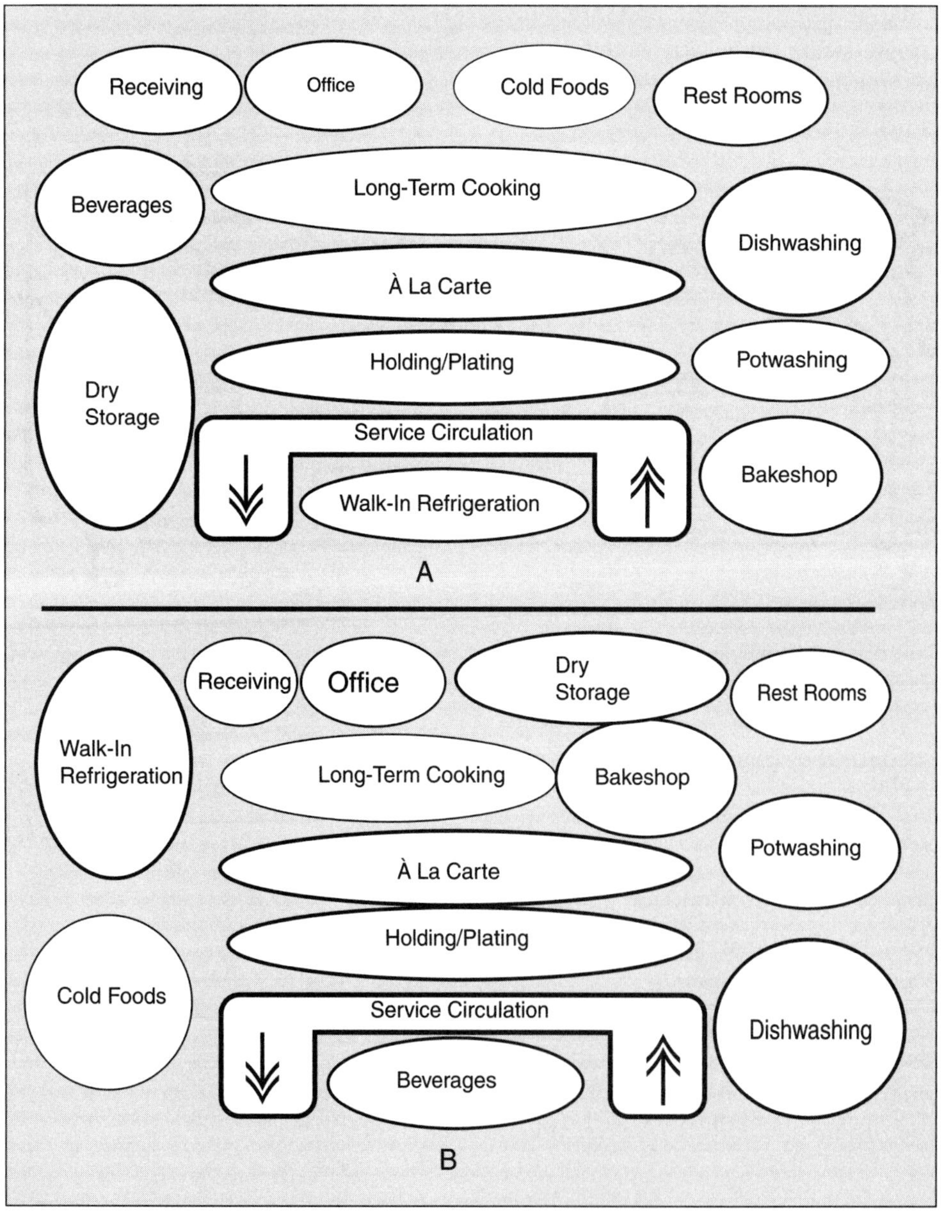

Careful thought must be given to each station and section that will make up the final design. In the worst scenario, a station is completely

FIGURE 5.8 *A detailed bubble diagram offers the design team a quick way to look at the interaction of various areas in a kitchen. In these bubble diagrams of an à la carte restaurant, layout A puts the cold food, beverage, and warewashing areas too far away from the service staff. The rearranged spaces in layout B make the flow convenient for both the production and service staff.*

forgotten. This can lead to a costly kitchen renovation long before it should be necessary.

All too often, kitchen designers go halfway. They think through functions performed in the kitchen and pull them together into well-integrated sections, but then fail to properly relate these sections to each other. A typical example occurs when a separate bakeshop is set up, requiring its own ovens, in a restaurant where the roasting ovens are only used for a portion of each day. If the bakeshop were located close to the roasting ovens, the baking and roasting could be done in one set of ovens rather than two.

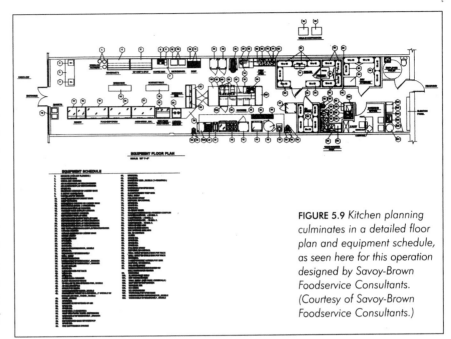

FIGURE 5.9 *Kitchen planning culminates in a detailed floor plan and equipment schedule, as seen here for this operation designed by Savoy-Brown Foodservice Consultants. (Courtesy of Savoy-Brown Foodservice Consultants.)*

Of course, bake ovens are different from roasting ovens. To cook crisp French bread, for example, a steam-injected oven is needed. However, roasts, pies, and cakes can all be cooked in a steam-injected oven if the steam is turned off. In fact, meats roasted in an oven into which steam is injected shrink less.

Flexibility is the key to planning both equipment and workstations. What serves as a sandwich station for lunch can double as a dessert station for dinner if the space is properly designed. The final outcome of planning stations, sections, and areas is the overall kitchen floorplan and equipment schedule (Figure 5.9).

KITCHEN AREA GUIDELINES

Remembering the basic equipment needed for each workstation is easy: a broiler in a broiler station, a range in a sauté station, and so on. General design requirements also must be integrated into each station if it is to function effectively. Here are some of the requirements:

- *Ambient and task lighting.* Task lighting prevents eyestrain and injuries in areas where detail work such as cake decorating and meat fabrication are performed. Task lighting is also useful when a portion-control scale is used to weigh a large number of individual portions.

- *Refrigerated, frozen, and ambient temperature storage for unprepared food.* A supply of spices centrally located in a kitchen ensures that all stations can draw from one supply. However, if spices are used frequently, space is needed to store them within a workstation.

- *Disposal or trash cans.* Space to store a trash can is frequently overlooked in kitchen design. A cutout under a work counter that might otherwise contain shelves can situate a trash can within easy reach of two workstations.

TABLE 5.1. COMMON SECTIONS WITH TYPICAL STATION CONFIGURATION

Hot Foods

À la carte range

Broiler station

Fry station

Griddle station

Sauté station

Holding

Salad and Dessert Station

Salad preparation

Dessert preparation

Frozen dessert preparation

Bakery

Mixer station

Dough holding/proofing

Dough rolling/forming

Baking

Banquet

Steam cooking

Dry heat cooking

Banquet holding and service

Short-Order Station

Griddle station

Fry station

Broiler station

Steam Cooking

Pressure steamers

Convection steaming

Floor-mounted steam kettles

Tilting braising pans

Countertop trunnion kettles

This simple feature saves labor and keeps workstations cleaner.

- *Ventilation.* Exhaust and makeup air must be provided in areas where heat and steam are produced.

- *Special floor elements.* Tile floors are commonly found in kitchens, and they are an efficient choice. But floor drains or recessed floor areas under cooking sections are often overlooked.

- *Hand sanitation.* Sinks, soap, and toweling must be accessible to every station.

- *Water supply for cooking and cleaning.* A metered water faucet saves labor when filling a large steam kettle. A hose equipped with a high-pressure spray head speeds cleanup beneath the kettle.

While no two sections are exactly alike, Table 5.1 lists five common sections with the stations commonly incorporated in them. In some high-volume operations, two or more of the same type of station may be needed in a given section.

The following discussion of each section can serve as a guide to kitchen planning.

HOT FOODS SECTION

The hot foods section can be thought of in terms of a matrix (Figure 5.10). On one axis, the station can be divided into à la carte cooking and long-term cooking; on the second axis, it can be divided into moist-heat cooking and dry-heat cooking.

Dry-heat cooking areas contain ovens, ranges, griddles, broilers, tilting fry kettles, and deep fryers. Moist-heat cooking areas include steamers, steam-jacketed and trunnion kettles, and, occasionally, ranges. As can be seen in Figure 5.10, hot food stations can also be broken down into à la carte cooking (short-term cooking) and long-term cooking.

The matrix shows that the hot food section of a restaurant can easily be divided into four sections, each of which relates to dry- or moist-heat cooking and long- or short-term preparation. In some cases, a single piece of equipment will satisfy the needs of multiple modes of cooking.

From a design perspective, grouping equipment so that it supports different cooking methods makes good sense. Long-term dry-heat cooking equipment usually needs little maintenance save for periodic checks. Conversely, dry-heat à la carte cooking requires continuous attention. The logical layout places à la carte equipment on the action side of the hot food section and the long-term equipment in a more remote location on the back side of the section.

The ovens, kettles, and tilting braising pans seen on the back side are used to cook large batches of food over long periods of time (Figure 5.11). A cook can place a roast in the oven and leave it unattended for an hour or more, depending on the mass of the roast. A cook can brown meat and leave it to simmer for a stew in a

FIGURE 5.10 *The kitchen's hot food section resembles a matrix, with equipment divided by speed of cooking and type of heat.*

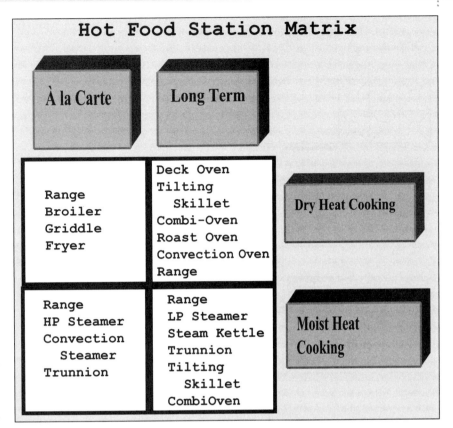

Hot Food Station Matrix

À la Carte

Long Term

Dry Heat Cooking

Moist Heat Cooking

Range Broiler Griddle Fryer	Deck Oven Tilting Skillet Combi-Oven Roast Oven Convection Oven Range

Range
HP Steamer
Convection
  Steamer
Trunnion
	Range
	LP Steamer
	Steam Kettle
	Trunnion
	Tilting
	  Skillet
	CombiOven

steam-jacketed kettle, or braise veal shanks in a tilting braising pan. An advantage to extended cooking is flexibility; a beef stew can simmer for 60 or 80 minutes with little discernible difference in the final product.

However, the equipment on the front action side of the line is designed for quick cooking of food, often made to order. Unlike extended cooking, quick cooking requires precision timing. If deep-fried scallops cook just 60 seconds too long, they will be overdone. A broiled strip steak cannot be left alone. It must be turned and cared for not only because of flare-ups when fat drips

FIGURE 5.11 *Kettles, ovens, and steamers are used for large-volume, slow cooking. They are well suited for banquet and cafeteria service systems.*
(Photo by Joseph Durocher.)

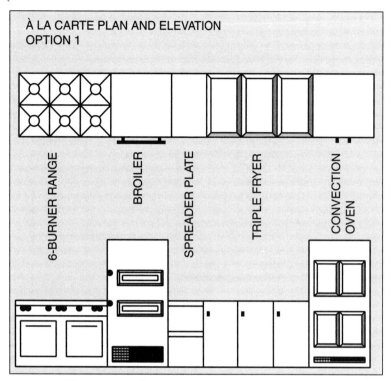

À LA CARTE PLAN AND ELEVATION
OPTION 1

6-BURNER RANGE · BROILER · SPREADER PLATE · TRIPLE FRYER · CONVECTION OVEN

FIGURE 5.12 *The plan view of these four pieces of equipment for an à la carte kitchen appears to be functional. However, the elevation drawing shows a problem with the placement of the broiler.*

into the broiler but also because the windows of time in which steak cooks to rare, medium, or well done are narrow.

A combination convection oven/steamer has recently found its way onto the front line of many restaurant kitchens. This multipurpose piece of equipment can be used as a convection steamer, a convection oven, and a high-humidity convection oven suitable for baking crusty rolls. The speed with which this versatile oven cooks makes it suitable for placement on the action side of the line.

Practical as well as aesthetic considerations pertain to the relative positioning of each of these pieces of equipment. In Figure 5.12, the layout looks logical in the plan view. The rangetop is on the left and the broiler and fryers are grouped together (separated by a spreader plate that functions as a work surface) because fried and broiled foods often go together. However, the elevation drawing reveals that the placement of the upright broiler visually separates the range from the fryers and, when the broiler racks are in the out position, the range cook is blocked from the rest of the station.

Figure 5.13, on the other hand, places the two high-rise pieces of equipment at the ends of the workstation. The broiler and fry stations are still close, but the sight lines along the entire station are not interrupted. Placing the high-rise equipment on the outside ends of the station also improves the efficiency of the exhaust equipment.

STATION OPTIONS

The selection of hot food equipment depends heavily on the menu items and their style of preparation. Flexibility is important, but a completely flexible kitchen will be problematic for the production staff. Following is a brief guide to the generic needs of each hot food station:

Broiler Station Options. In this category, several pieces of equipment are all referred to as *broilers*. Each yields a different product, so it is important to understand the advantages of a particular broiler. Gas, electric, and charcoal are the major heat sources from which to choose;

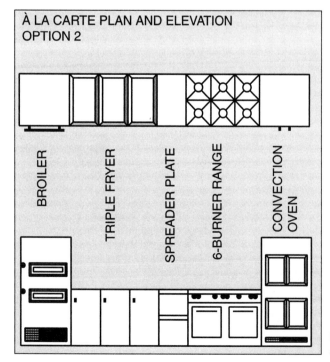

À LA CARTE PLAN AND ELEVATION
OPTION 2

BROILER · TRIPLE FRYER · SPREADER PLATE · 6-BURNER RANGE · CONVECTION OVEN

FIGURE 5.13 *These drawings are of the same pieces of equipment shown in Figure 5.12, but with improved sight lines and flow patterns.*

hardwood is used in some instances. Each heat source and broiler configuration has specific cooking characteristics.

A major differentiating characteristic of broilers is the location of the heat source. Top-heat broilers can broil steaks and vegetables, and color the tops of casseroles. These broilers are heated with gas or electricity. Charcoal broilers—specifically mesquite—are high-heat, high-smoke broilers that need careful attention during the cooking process and create so much smoke that the ventilation system may require modification. Gas and electric broilers are available with two cooking levels, which can save floor space.

Rotisserie Options. In rotisserie cooking, the heat source is usually vertical rather than horizontal. Gas, electric, or charcoal is used to heat a rotisserie. An important design concern is the amount of radiated heat that emanates from a rotisserie, particularly when it is not fully loaded.

Rotisseries cook with dry heat, but the continual rotation of foods as they cook helps maintain their natural juices. Chickens are the most frequently cooked rotisserie items; lamb, pork, and beef dishes can also be prepared on this equipment. Some rotisseries can be fitted with baskets so whole fish or whole onions can be cooked.

Rotisseries are often placed in display kitchens, where the rotating motion of foods is a merchandising tool. Cooking with hardwood charcoal adds merchandising appeal, but without careful attention, the benefits can outweigh the costs of maintaining the fire.

Fry Station Options. Both gas and electric fry units are available. The major differentiating feature is the size of the fat bin, rated in pounds of fry medium. The amount of fry medium and the amount of food that can be cooked in a single batch are directly correlated. Generally, a 1:5 ratio of food to fry medium is used as a guide. If more food is placed in the fryer at one time, the temperature of the fry medium will drop excessively and the cooking time will be extended. During the extended cooking time, more fry medium is absorbed in the food. Not only does that result in a grease-laden product but also it increases the cost of replacing the fry medium.

The heat source and distribution of heat to the fat kettle affect recovery time. Operating practices also affect the efficiency of a fryer. For example, some countertop fryers use a ribbon element that snakes across the entire bottom of the fry bin. The large surface area and full coverage of the bottom of the fry bin ensures that these fryers recover quickly and provide even cooking. However, if freshly breaded foods are cooked in this fryer, the breading that falls off during cooking can collect around the elements. This leads to slower recovery time, premature browning of the fry medium, and increased fat breakdown. An alternative electric fryer places the heating elements around the inside wall of the fry bin, so breading that flakes off foods does not fall directly onto the heating elements. The point here is that the kitchen designer must think about how each piece of equipment will be used (and abused), then select it in the context of the overall operation.

Floor-model fryers generally have large kettles and, therefore, the highest cooking capacity. Tabletop models that can sit on top of an undercounter refrigerator are space savers, but their smaller fat kettles translate into smaller batches.

The appropriate number of fryers rests, in part, on the number of fried foods that appear on the menu. Potatoes should be cooked in a fryer that is used for nothing else. Seafood should also be cooked in its own fryer. Items like onion rings, jalapeño poppers, and breaded mushrooms should be cooking in a third fryer.

In high-volume operations, multiple fryers are needed to cook a single food item. For extremely high-volume cooking of a single item, a convection fryer affords the highest output, continuous filtering, and a smaller footprint than conventional fryers. A pressure fryer is often used to cook fried chicken, which is difficult to cook in a conventional fryer.

A convection air "fryer" that produces fried foods without using fat as the heat transfer medium is suited to operations where customers are concerned about fat content. Another alternative is a robot fryer. A batch of frozen foods is placed in the load chute and, after a set time, the fully cooked foods emerge out the side of the fryer. A final type of fryer is a floor model that comes with its own hood, air filter, and fire suppression system. These are designed for seasonal operations, home meal replacement (HMR), and take-out kiosk operations, where installing an exhaust hood would be cost-prohibitive.

At the end of each shift (or day of cooking, at most), the fry medium in each fryer needs to be filtered. If several fryers are ganged together, the optimal design solution is to purchase a built-in filter beneath one of the units. Where only countertop fryers are used, or several fryers in separate locations, a portable filter offers the best solution. Failure to filter the fry medium frequently leads to premature breakdown of the fat, lowered smoke point, rapid darkening of the fry medium, and increased potential for fires.

If freshly breaded foods are on the menu, adequate space and equipment must be built into the design to accommodate the breading process. For low-volume restaurants, a manual three-step breading process is appropriate. This requires enough space to hold the food to be breaded, a pan of flour, a pan of egg wash, a pan of breadcrumbs, and a pan to hold the breaded foods. The amount of space is reduced if a batter-style breading is used. An alternative to hand breading is a partially or fully automated breading system.

A dump station used to receive foods after frying is needed in medium- to high-volume operation (Figure 5.14).

FIGURE 5.14 *These double gas fryers from Frymaster are mated to a dump station with heat lamp, optional computer cooking controls, and auto-lift baskets. The built-in filter makes it easy to maintain fat quality.* (Photo courtesy of Frymaster.)

For fast-food operations where fries are bagged, a heated area for holding the filled bags should also be planned.

Griddle Station Options. The choice of surface materials on the griddle affects heat-up time and the evenness of cooking as well as ease of cleaning. Chrome surfaces clean to a high gloss and thus are appropriate in areas where guests can see the griddle surface. The downside to this cooking surface is that foods shrink more than when cooked on other griddle surfaces. As with the chrome griddle, rolled steel has excellent heat transfer capabilities yet foods shrink minimally.

The size of the cooking surface, the number of cooking zones, and the British thermal unit/kilowatt (Btu/kW) rating must all be considered as part of the design process. The overall size determines the total number of items that can be cooked at a given time. Griddle surfaces are particularly important in restaurants where breakfast foods, like pancakes, make up an important part of the menu. When several types of foods will be cooked on the griddle simultaneously, it is important to have a number of temperature controls that can vary the temperature across the surface of the griddle. The recovery time—the time for the surface of the griddle to heat back up to the set temperature—will vary depending on the Btu/kW input, the thickness of the griddle surface, and the material in the griddle surface.

Sauté Station Options. Three types of ranges or cooktops, using gas or electricity, are generally used in this station:

1. *The flattop sectional range usually has three sections, each of which can be heated individually. The ringtop range is a variation.*
2. *The open-top range includes from two to eight open burners or elements, with grates over them in gas ranges.*
3. *The induction range or cooktop uses an inverter coil to create heat in ferrous pans.*

- *Flattop ranges.* Flattop and ringtop ranges offer a large cooking surface on which a variety of cooking vessels can be placed. However, these solid-top ranges need heat-up time no matter what the heat source.

  A nice feature of the ring-top range is that the center rings can be removed, thus allowing the range to give immediate heat through a central burner while the rest of the flat surface heats up. The sectional flattop allows the greatest flexibility in that sections can be turned on as needed. Flattop and ringtop ranges are the equipment of choice in restaurants where substantial sautéing is mandated by the menu. The real advantage to flat-surface ranges is that cooks have greater flexibility in the selection of pots and sauté pans.

  A flattop range is ideal for breakfast operations where egg pans are used to cook eggs or omelets. The entire surface of the range can be loaded with pans—in contrast to an open-top range, where pans can only be placed on a burner or element. Flattop ranges radiate a good bit of

Kitchen designers should keep in mind that rangetops are subject to considerable wear and tear.

heat, and because they are not typically turned on and off during a shift, they tend to make the work environment less comfortable for chefs.

- *Open-top ranges.* Open-top ranges have individual controls for each burner or element. In the case of gas, heat is immediate and, depending on the configuration, electric burners come up to temperature in a matter of seconds. The disadvantage to this type of range is that a pan must be placed directly over the heat source.

  Wok ranges are a variant on the open-top gas range. The burners on these ranges have high Btu ratings—up to 80,000 Btu. Wok cooking is similar to sautéing and plays an important role in restaurants that offer Asian or fusion cooking.

  It should be noted that the efficiency of gas burners in both open- and flattop ranges is diminished roughly 25 percent when propane, rather than natural gas, is used as a fuel. From a design perspective, this means that foods will take longer to cook, which could translate to a need for a larger number of flattops or more burners to meet the demands of the restaurant.

- *Induction range.* Induction cooktops use an inverter coil that generates instant heat when a ferrous cooking container is placed on top of it. In effect, the cooking container itself becomes the heating element, so little heat is lost from the cooktop. When the container is removed from the cooktop, the inverter coil immediately reverts to standby mode to save electricity.

  Because induction cooktops don't get hot, they are safer than other cooking surfaces, particularly when used in guest contact areas. Induction cooktops are suited to both back-of-the-house and front-of-the-house applications. Consider them for cooking omelets at brunch, tossing pasta at a buffet, and for primary cooking in remote catering locations. They are available with flat surfaces or with indented surfaces designed to hold a wok.

  Look carefully at the kW ratings for the induction models under consideration. For most restaurant applications, the extra expense of a 5 kW versus a 3 kW cooktop is a wise investment. Another point to consider is that these cooktops operate only with ferrous-based pans, like a rolled-steel egg pan.

Kitchen designers should keep in mind that rangetops are subject to considerable wear and tear. The materials used for sectional or ringtops are usually heavy gauge and can withstand a beating. However, in some open-top ranges, the burner spiders are so lightweight that they will bend or bounce out of place when a heavy pot is set on the range.

Not all ranges are created equal. A light- or medium-duty range is all that is needed to cook individual orders of eggs or pan fry a few chicken breasts, but if large, heavy sautoirs are used to cook multiple portions, a light-duty restaurant range can't stand up to the beating. Slide a full pot across the grates of an open-top range. If the grates move, a heavier-duty range is probably called for. On the electric side, a flat cooking surface is essential if heavy sautoirs or pots will be placed on the cooktop.

Several equipment options are available for the sauté station range. Frequently, the range comes with an oven situated under the rangetop, but because of its placement, it is difficult to reach and can restrict flow behind a busy à la carte range. However, numerous design modifications over the years have significantly improved the roasting and baking capabilities of the ovens found under most rangetops. Gone are the days when hot spots, slow heat-up, and uneven cooking temperatures caused most chefs to use their range ovens as storage cabinets.

Some manufacturers offer optional convection ovens or a combination of one conventional and one convection oven. Most oven interiors are lined with porcelain walls, although some are equipped with continuous clean surfaces.

Still other ranges come with refrigerated drawers under their cooktops. These refrigeration units are integral to the range and put foods within close reach of cooks.

Another range option, the salamander, is a top-mounted minibroiler that is best used for browning the tops of casseroles and sandwiches. It is a useful choice if the kitchen has no other way to top-brown food, but it does not do the job of a full broiler. Perhaps the most useful (and inexpensive) option is a simple overshelf that can preheat plates, hold sauté pans, and so on.

Sauce Station and Steam Kettle Station Options. In some kitchens, the sauce and sauté station are one and the same, with chefs preparing stocks and sauces in pots and pans on a flattop range. Other kitchens, however, add a separate station to prepare such items as soups, stewed foods, and stocks in addition to sauces.

One of the most frequently used alternatives to making sauces on the rangetop is the steam-jacketed kettle. This piece of equipment ranges from a 32-ounce oyster cooker for individual portions to huge 150-gallon units. The steam jacketing envelops a half to all of the kettle interior. Fully jacketed kettles heat faster, but they also bake sauces onto the sides of a half-filled kettle, wasting product and making cleanup difficult.

Kettles can be heated with a built-in electric element, steam from a central supply, or steam from an undercounter steam generator typically heated with gas or electricity. A properly sized steam generator can heat several pieces of steam equipment at one time. Today, stainless steel is the preferred material for steam kettles because it never reacts negatively with food products.

For large-capacity steam kettles, a swing-up electric mixing arm ensures that the contents cook evenly. With the addition of a pump and bagging station, a cook-chill program can be implemented. After cooking, most sauces and stocks are transferred to large pots and placed in a hot water bath (bain marie) or steam table for service. A cold water bath should be considered for chilling stocks and sauces if they are to go into refrigerated storage. Cook-chill foods packaged in a flexible bag are chilled in a tumble chiller, while foods stored in steam table inserts are chilled in a blast chiller.

The size and number of kettles, along with the steam source, are important design concerns. Sauce stations where kettles are used should be placed over a recessed portion of the floor or positioned so that the drain water from the kettle flows into a drain trough in the floor. A water-metering faucet saves time filling the kettles. For cleaning purposes, a flexible spray hose should be installed.

A properly sized steam generator can heat several pieces of steam equipment at one time.

Compartment steamers use steam as a medium to transfer heat. Low-pressure steamers are capable of producing hundreds of portions per batch, so they are typically used in banquet, catering, and institutional settings. High-pressure steamers are suited to cooking roughly 40 portions per batch and are a good choice for the à la carte line. Convection steamers are also fast cooking and can be purchased with a built-in steam generator. Unlike pressurized steamers, convection steamers can be opened at any time during the steaming cycle. Single-portion steamers are small countertop units that cook or reheat portions using a built-in steam generator. When steam kettles, trunnions, and compartment steamers are included in an à la carte layout, a single steam generator that heats all of the equipment should be considered.

Holding Options. Any of the previously mentioned pieces of equipment in the hot foods section can be used to hold foods. A steam table, whether dry or wet, is frequently utilized. A single steam table with room for 6 to 12 inserts is usually sufficient, but the size of the steam table should always be closely matched to the menu and the expected volume of the operation. The only other specialized pieces of equipment that can be included for holding food are a heated holding/warming cabinet and a roll warmer.

SALAD AND DESSERT

In most restaurants, the salad and dessert stations are grouped into one section and must function as both preparation and service areas. However, the dessert station may be backed up with a bakery where the major production work occurs.

Salad and dessert sections vary greatly depending on the menu offerings and styles of service in the restaurant. In an à la carte restaurant, salads and desserts may be prepared and plated as ordered. In large-volume operations, the preparation and plating will likely be accomplished prior to the serving period and stored for waiter pickup. In restaurants offering banquet service, additional preparation equipment, rolling stock, and storage space are required for both the salad and the dessert station. However, some general requirements and considerations are worth noting.

Salad Station Options. Salad greens must always be carefully washed for service. A two-compartment sink with sideboards is well suited for this job. One of the compartments can be used for cleaning greens and the second for draining washed greens. Sideboards are necessary for holding unprocessed greens and washed greens. Salad spinners, typically equipped with an electric motor, remove more of the water from greens than if they merely drain while sitting in a colander, allowing salad dressings to adhere properly.

In many restaurant operations, reach-in refrigerators are used for holding washed salad ingredients. (For banquet service, a walk-in refrigerator is helpful.) The reach-in refrigerator must have tray slides to hold the sheet pans that most often become the shelves in a refrigerator. Sheet pans are also used to rack up portioned salads when salads are plated in advance of service. If the service staff is responsible for plating salads as needed, an overshelf salad green refrigerator puts an evening's worth of greens within easy reach.

When the salad station does double duty as a sandwich station, slicers (Figure 5.15) are frequently incorporated to slice salad and sandwich ingredients. A vertical cutter mixer is also useful in this station when large amounts of tossed or chopped salads are prepared. Perhaps the most commonly used and versatile piece of equipment for cutting, chopping, and mixing in the salad station is the tabletop chopper with assorted attachments.

Dessert Station Options. Desserts, including frozen concoctions, are often prepared in the salad and dessert section of the kitchen. In other kitchens, dessert preparation—making, mixing, and other preparatory steps—takes place in the bakeshop, with only the plating coming from the dessert station.

As with salads, desserts need plenty of refrigeration. Frozen desserts require an ice cream chest and, if preportioned, a reach-in freezer. Soft-serve machines are required where soft ice cream is served. Space to hold toppings must also be considered. A countertop mixer is needed in the dessert station, where cream or other toppings are whipped from scratch.

Work counters, shelving, and other storage areas are vital to dessert sections. Rolling stock is helpful for moving trays, clean dishes, and raw materials about the kitchen. In general, flexible equipment capable of preparing a wide range of products is the key to success in salad and dessert sections, as they are often used to prepare an assortment of ever-changing offerings.

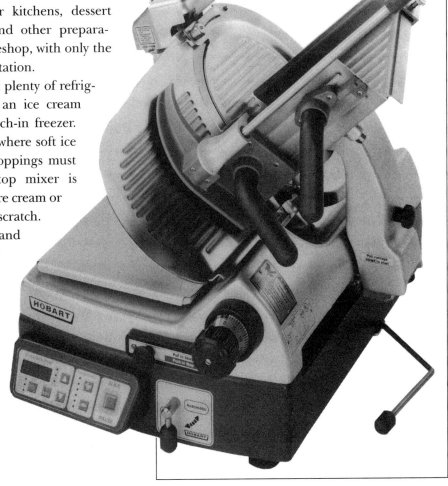

FIGURE 5.15 *Hobart's ergonomically designed slicer incorporates numerous safety features not found in its predecessors. The easy-to-clean features of this slicer make it especially desirable for salad prep and display cooking areas.* (Photo courtesy of Hobart Corp.)

BAKERY

The bakery section may be a stand-alone section of the kitchen or shared at certain times of day with other production areas. In most kitchens, the bakery comprises six primary stations:

1. Storage and weighing. Bulk ingredients such as flours and sugar, along with frequently used spices, toppings, and tools, need to be within easy reach. Because baking is a science, scales are needed to closely measure the ingredients.

2. Mixing. The mixing station includes the mixing and support equipment needed for the preparation of batters, doughs, and toppings. Support equipment includes racks to hold extra bowls, hand tools that support the mixing, and extra mixer attachments.

3. Dough holding/proofing. This is a passive station where doughs are held, generally under controlled temperatures, while they await the rolling/forming process.

4. Dough rolling/forming station. Bread or pastry is rolled or formed as needed, sometimes by mechanized devices and sometimes manually. Racks to hold pans and trays used in baking should be stored in this station.

5. Baking. The type and amount of items to be baked often determines the type of oven used for this step (Figure 5.16). For example, crusty breads require steam-injected ovens, whereas cookies do not.

6. Finishing/decorating. Most bread products need little more than a cooling rack after they emerge from the oven, but other baked goods need equipment for decorating, including trays, racks, mixers, and, in some cases, cooktops.

Storage and Weighing Station Options. Storage of and ready access to raw materials is essential to efficient bakeshop design. At the heart of many bakeshops is a baker's table with overhead drawers for holding spices and sufficient clearance under the countertop to store bulk material containers. Refrigerated storage is also needed in this area to chill shortening and butter used in cooking and to hold fillings.

FIGURE 5.16 *Conveyor ovens are appropriate for extremely high volume bakeries and commissary operations.* (Photo by Joseph Durocher.)

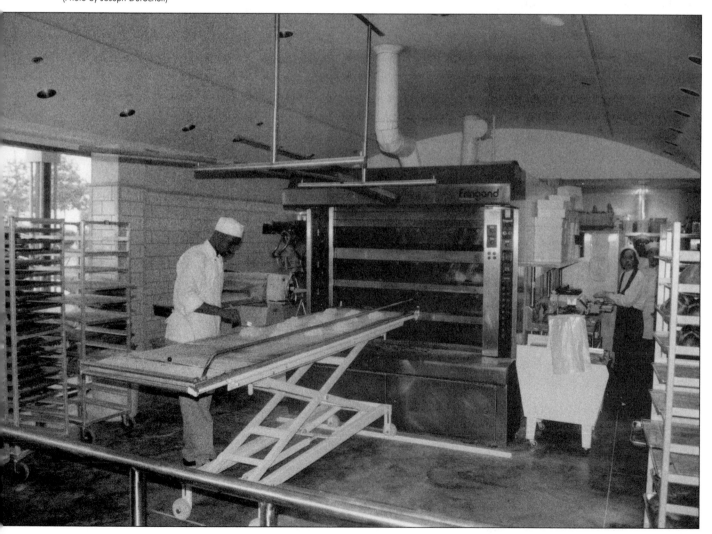

Weighing equipment must also be considered for this part of the bakeshop. Balance-beam scales are frequently used by bakers in midsize restaurants, but for large-volume production, a mobile platform scale is called for.

Mixing Station Options. Mixing is usually done mechanically. Floor-model mixers are appropriate for heavy dough products, and table-model mixers are appropriate for pastry and batter products and for small batches of bread dough. In some cases, a vertical cutter/mixer can even be used for mixing yeast-raised doughs and for making pastry crust. For mixing high-gluten dough for bagels, pizza, and French bread, a spiral mixer should be considered.

Dough Holding/Proofing Station Options. Yeast-raised products generally go through two proofing steps. The first step is a bulk proofing of dough as it comes from the mixing station. A second proofing is required after the dough goes through the forming station. While dough can rise at ambient room temperatures, the additional heat and moisture in a proof box will speed and improve the process. After pie pastry or puff pastry are mixed, they are usually held in refrigerated storage to improve their workability. Holding and proofing is not necessary for batter products.

Dough Rolling/Forming Station Options. Puff pastry dough goes through several rolling and folding steps, which are separated by time in a refrigerator. While rolling can be done with a rolling pin, a mechanical dough sheeter is much faster. Rolls can be portioned and shaped with the help of a dough cutter; numerous other specialty pieces of forming equipment can produce products ranging from bagels to croissants.

Baking Station Options. Designers should consider the various uses of the bakeshop ovens before deciding on equipment specifications. If the bakeshop will be used in the early hours of the day for the preparation and baking of breads and pastries, and during the afternoon and evening for banquet preparation, then multipurpose ovens are needed. Their placement must be convenient to users in the bakery, banquet, and hot food areas.

The most common oven classification is the deck oven. Deck ovens can be stacked three high for increased output per square foot of floor space and are available as roasting or baking ovens. Roasting ovens, which have greater height in the oven cavity, are similar to baking ovens but can hold large top rounds and other wholesale cuts of meat with ease. Deck ovens can be fitted with steam injectors, which help create the crusty surface on French and Italian breads.

Another option is the convection oven, which is quite effective for baking. Convection ovens can also be used for roasting, but misuse can lead to excessive meat shrinkage. Convection ovens can be double stacked for maximum output.

Combination ovens are the newest class of oven used for baking. These ovens are capable of functioning as convection ovens, convection steamers, and steam injected ovens (Figure 5.17). Their flexibility makes them best suited as a multipurpose oven used by many stations.

Cavity ovens are designed for small- or large-volume baking and roasting. The

standard cavity oven—one that is placed under a rangetop—is acceptable for roasting but generally is not ideal for baking. However, the rotary oven, which holds foods on arms that rotate like a Ferris wheel inside the oven cavity, is effective as a bake or roast oven in large-volume operations. Another type of cavity oven accepts an entire proofing cart without the need to transfer product from the cart to oven shelves.

For a dedicated bakeshop, deck ovens are the best choice, with steam injection capabilities for times when crusty breads are baked. No matter what oven type is selected, sufficient rack space is needed to cool baked goods and to hold them for service.

Finishing/Decorating Station Options. In bakeshops where special confections and toppings are made, additional stations are required. A candy station, for example, will need a rangetop and, in some cases, a trunnion kettle. Cakes and pastries need to be decorated, and mixers and ranges are sometimes used to make the frosting or fillings used during this phase.

BANQUET

A banquet section is required only in a restaurant where banquet service cannot be accomplished from other production stations. Meal preparation for small private parties, for instance, will not require a separate banquet station. However, when banquet business typically exceeds by 25 percent or more the ongoing volume of the restaurant, then it makes sense to design a separate banquet section in the kitchen.

Banquet Steam Cooking. Steam equipment for banquets consists of large steam-jacketed kettles—over 10 gallons—for soup, sauces, and stewed items, plus large-volume low-pressure steamers. As with the à la carte section, the steam equipment can use central steam or be self-contained. Due to the large volume of food cooked in this area, floor drainage is necessary for the disposal of wastewater. This can be accomplished through the installation of a floor grate and drain that runs the entire length of the section, or by a recessed floor with drain holes.

Dry Heat Banquet Cooking. One or more tilting braising pans can be helpful in large banquet operations. The flexibility of these pieces of equipment makes them ideally suited for numerous types of food preparations, a requirement often placed on the banquet production department. As with steam equipment, floor drainage is necessary for cleaning. It makes sense, therefore, to locate braising pans close to the steam equipment.

As mentioned above, the roasting station, will also be one and the same with the bakeshop, so the ovens selected for most banquet operations should be capable of roasting or baking a wide range of product. Often a mix of ovens—deck and convection—is chosen to increase flexibility.

Banquet Holding and Plating. Banquet food can often be held in the same equipment that is used for proofing breads or in the equipment used for its preparation. For example, soup for a banquet frequently stays in the steam kettle in which it was made until service time.

A plating station or area is essential for quick service to a large banquet. This can consist of a simple countertop or, in operations where many banquets are served, a special banquet plating cart. In cases where plating and holding equipment is purchased for banquet service, the pieces should be as portable as possible. Portability will allow the equipment to be removed from the plating area when not needed, thus improving traffic flow in the kitchen.

Holding equipment for plated foods is essential for large banquets and catered events. The plated dishes are covered and placed in carts that can be wheeled to the point of service. Banquet carts should be capable of holding food for at least 45 minutes without affecting quality.

SHORT ORDER/QUICK-SERVICE SECTION

Short-order/quick-service sections in compact kitchens consist of several stations, all of which are handled by one person. Such is the case in small diners around the world. The cook has every piece of equipment within reach at all times. In larger restaurant kitchens, several individuals may handle short-order sections. For any short-order section to work, the following design elements must be considered.

Griddle Station. The griddle station design covered in the à la carte section discussion also pertains to short-order/quick-service sections. However, in short-order restaurants, where items such as burgers are prepared in batches, a clamshell top speeds the cooking process. Clamshells can be heated platens that swing down and sit atop the food on the griddle, heated hoods fitted with radiant heaters that cook from the top, or a clamshell under which steam builds up to speed cooking. The platens work best when foods are the same thickness throughout. If foods vary in thickness, the radiant hood works best.

Fry Station. High-volume short-order/quick-service restaurants frequently employ more fryers than à la carte restaurants. In many quick-service fast-food restaurants, the fryer is one of the two primary pieces of cooking equipment. Often, fryers are ganged together to form a bank of equipment. In such cases, a built-in filter system should be chosen. The fry medium from each fryer can be filtered and pumped back into the fryer with the help of a single filter.

For extremely high-volume quick-service restaurants, a convection fryer can increase output and provide continuous fat filtration while using less energy per pound of food cooked. Automated breading equipment should be used when freshly breaded foods are sold. Mechanized systems for cutting potatoes should be used when freshly cut fries are featured.

Broiler Station. Pull-out broilers are found in some short-order restaurants, but frequently the broiler is actually integrated with the underside of the griddle. The alternative is the conveyor broiler, which is typically used to cook burgers.

Toasters are often integrated with the broiler station. Pop-up toasters are intended for low to medium volume, while conveyor toasters are designed for medium to high volume. Conveyor toasters offer the advantage of being able to toast items of varying thickness.

SPECIALTY SECTIONS

Specialty sections sometimes must be incorporated with the design of a kitchen. Fabrication sections for meat, poultry, or seafood preparation may be required in some designs. Stations that use specialty equipment, like a tandoori or wood-fired pizza oven, will also require special design consideration.

Dining Room Support Areas

This discussion addresses three support areas that bridge the gap between the back and front of the house:

1. *Display kitchens.* While the display kitchen is actually an extension of the back of the house, its design has a considerable impact on the ambience and operation of the front of the house.
2. *Service stations.* Service stations, situated in the dining areas, enable the waitstaff to take care of tabletop needs without traveling back and forth from the kitchen.
3. *Warewashing areas.* Warewashing—which, in a loose definition, embraces all dish- and potwashing—is physically placed in the back of the house, but it greatly influences the efficient operation of the front of the house.

DISPLAY KITCHENS

Today, the display kitchen has become the hallmark of many types of restaurants, from fine dining to neighborhood bistros. The significance of display kitchens is that the functioning of the kitchen is within view of the customer. In some cases, all of the preparation is done in view of the customer. At the other extreme, all of the prepreparation and par cooking is done in the back kitchen and the display kitchen is nothing more than a finishing station.

The designers of any type of display kitchen must consider the sight lines from the customers' vantage point. In restaurants where the guests have a full view of the entire display kitchen, every item must be well placed and kept well ordered.

In restaurants where diners have a partial view of the display kitchen, the hidden areas, such as the undercounter spaces on the front line, need not be kept in perfect order. From a design perspective, the full-view kitchen should use undercounter shelving with cabinet doors, while open shelving is fine for the partial-view kitchen.

All display kitchens benefit from a clean and well-organized appearance. In an enclosed kitchen, many indiscretions can be overlooked, but when a guest sees a messy work station in a display kitchen, she won't be inclined to eat the food. The area needs an adequate supply of hand- and tool-washing sinks to keep it spotless. While much of the preparatory work is accomplished in the back of the house, last-minute manipulations always require cleaning, be it a roast tenderloin that is carved and sauced as ordered, or the occasional spill from an overfilled soup bowl.

PRIMARY PRODUCTION DISPLAY KITCHEN

Traditional American diners and the primary production display kitchen go together like ice cream and pie. The short-order cook stands with his back to a counter, flipping eggs and flapjacks, toasting bread, frying potatoes, and making sandwiches, all while watching over the meatloaf baking in the oven below the rangetop that holds a pot of boiling potatoes. At breakfast and other meals, customers sit on counter stools to order and eat their food and to chat with the short-order cook.

With the advent of fast-food operations, the production display kitchen expanded into another type of restaurant. Display kitchens are well suited to the quality, service, cleanliness (QSC) mandate of fast-food restaurants: When the kitchen is in full view of the customers, production and service workers are compelled to keep it clean and to properly handle food products.

Until the 1980s, however, when consumer concern and awareness of food mushroomed into a national obsession, production display kitchens were not deemed appropriate for serious restaurants. Not long ago, the worst seat in the house was next to the swinging doors that led to the kitchen. A view inside was considered less than elegant. Today, the production display kitchen is integral to many types of restaurants. Guests are willing to pay a premium for the privilege of sitting at the chef's table, which actually sits inside some kitchens. In cafeteria-style steakhouses, diners order their steak and watch it cook while they select the accompaniments for their meal. In many pizza parlors, customers are entertained by the dough-twirling pizza cook as he "creates" their pizza. In numerous table-service restaurants, customers are paraded past the open kitchen, where they can preview the type of food they will be ordering (Figure 5.18) or catch glimpses of the ongoing cooking as they enjoy their meal.

In fact, the primary production display kitchen has become popular in all sorts of establishments, and the best seat in the house has become one that affords patrons a good view of the chefs at work. In gourmet establishments, gleaming copper pots and colorful tiled walls frame display kitchens through open or glass windows. In noncommercial cafeterias, most people would rather wait in line at the short-order station to watch their burgers and sandwiches grilled and sliced to order than save time by picking up batch-processed, preprepared food.

FIGURE 5.18 *When a display kitchen sits in the entryway of a restaurant, customers can't help but notice the action in the back of the house. Here, in the entryway of Belgo Nieuw York, people often hang out to catch the view while waiting for a table.* (Photo by Joseph Durocher.)

There is really no common formula for figuring out which food items, equipment, or even type of restaurant will benefit from a production display kitchen. In each of the above-mentioned restaurants, a feeling of involvement and intimacy with the kitchen is created. In the most successful display kitchens, a feeling of theatrical performance entertains customers and stimulates their appetite.

For display kitchens to be most effective, nearly all of the prepreparation should be completed elsewhere. Such operations as chopping, slicing, pounding, and so on should be performed out of sight of the diners. The preprepared raw materials are then assembled for cooking in view of the customer. As with any à la carte range in the back of the house, efficient prepreparation is the key to success.

For example, a well-designed pizza display kitchen will require rolling/turning the pizza, covering it with sauce and toppings, and slipping it into the oven. Thirty to 60 seconds are needed to assemble the product, then 7 to 15 minutes to bake it. In the case of a sandwich station on a cafeteria line, when all the ingredients are ready for use, it takes 30 seconds or less to assemble condiments and fillings on the chosen bread.

Backup raw materials must be close at hand for a production display kitchen to work effectively. Pass-through refrigerators that connect to the prepreparation kitchen and undercounter refrigeration will facilitate an efficient flow from the back to the front of the house. Under ideal conditions, each display kitchen has its own refrigeration and other storage areas.

Cleanliness is of vital concern in a production display kitchen. Clean-looking employees, equipment, walls, and floors are all important. Easily cleaned surfaces and convenient waste disposal areas will help maintain cleanliness, as will upgraded ventilation to minimize grease buildup and carryover of odors to the dining room.

Stainless steel has been the preferred material in back-of-the-house kitchens, but many display kitchens sport tile, plastic laminates, and other less institutional materials to create a look that fits with the front-of-the-house design.

The appearance of the cooking equipment is another concern. A stainless-steel top for the griddle gives a clean look when eggs are cooked in front of the guest. Compact tabletop automatic-lift fryers reflect a simplicity of design in keeping with display cooking, in contrast with the heavy-gauge, black-enameled surfaces of an open-top range with oven. When tabletop equipment is used, the undercounter area can be filled with refrigerated storage space.

Another type of equipment worth noting is the rotisserie. Here, cuts of meat are roasted on what is technically a vertical broiler unit. The pieces of meat revolve on a skewer in front of the heat source, thus ensuring even cooking and browning and a well-textured surface. The most elaborate rotisserie units are fitted with black iron, brass, and stainless steel, and actually become a decor element. Some units are fired by charcoal, but the gas rotisserie, made popular by the Boston Market chain, brought rotisserie chicken into the restaurant mainstream.

A consideration with all rotisserie units is the amount of heat they give off. The radiating heat can be so intense that guests cannot be seated within 15 feet of the rotisserie. A see-through barrier can help block radiant heat. This makes it possible for patrons to enjoy the view without sweating through their meals.

FINISHING DISPLAY KITCHEN

When a display kitchen is used as a finishing kitchen, it functions like a cafeteria line where the line personnel plate up previously prepared foods. This technique may be used in a tableservice restaurant, but with an extra bit of flair.

For example, imagine that the waiter orders sole Mornay through the open window of a finishing area display kitchen. What patrons see is the previously poached sole (which may also be used for other menu items) portioned into a casserole dish, covered with Mornay sauce; placed under a cheese melter for a few moments, removed, garnished with previously chopped parsley and a wedge of lemon, and set on an underliner. Total time required for assembly is less than 30 seconds. Time from placing the order to when it is ready for pickup is less than 5 minutes. Although no "real" cooking takes place in the display kitchen, guests have the perception that their food is being prepared right in front of them.

The finishing kitchen may also make use of microwave ovens, compact tabletop convection ovens, or quartz ovens. The microwave oven can be used successfully in many types of display kitchens. For example, a milk-based chowder may be held at lower than serving temperature to keep it from breaking. When ordered, it is portioned into a soup bowl and brought to serving temperature in a matter of moments in the microwave. The technique is also used successfully in Mexican restaurants, where ingredients for tacos and other items are held cold, assembled, then heated in the microwave oven for service.

However, not every item is suited to microwave heating, and attention must be given to the menu before this type of oven is specified. The tabletop convection oven or quartz oven can be used effectively for heating casserole items that are held cold for service. In some operations that have gone to a cook-chill system, the contents of sealed pouches holding the special of the day are slipped into a serving dish and rethermalized—literally, reheated—in a convection or quartz oven. Alternatively, the pouches can be reheated in a hot water bath.

SERVICE-ONLY DISPLAY KITCHEN

The service-only display kitchen is nothing more than a plating area. As with the other types of display kitchens, it assists servers in speeding food to their waiting guests.

In many instances, certain elements of the meal come from a service-only display kitchen and other elements come from a back-of-the-house kitchen. Soups and preplated appetizer items are often served from the display kitchen. An antipasto bar can be displayed for guest viewing and server access. The food setup in a tapas bar, where items are displayed and subsequently portioned by the service staff, is another example of a service display kitchen. This type does not offer quite as much drama, but guests still benefit from a feeling of involvement, and the servers are helped in the performance of their duties.

HYBRID DISPLAY KITCHEN

Some restaurants employ a hybrid of these three types of display kitchens; Movenpick's Marché concept is an example. In some areas of the Marché, servers merely dish up preprepared foods. In other areas, such as the wok station, preprepared foods are assembled, heated, and ready for the guest in a matter of minutes. In a third area, the staff actually open oysters for oysters on the half-shell, assemble raw ingredients that are cooked up into a fresh bouillabaisse, and grill off items ranging from chicken breasts to steaks.

TAKE-OUT DISPLAY KITCHEN

Today, the take-out/HMR market can generate significant incremental sales for the restaurant. Display kitchens are a tremendous merchandising aid that encourages take-out business. Seeing items prepared as well as foods on display in refrigerated cases intrigues diners. Take-out/HMR kitchens support three presentation techniques:

1. *Ready to eat.* This is the take-out format common to fast-food operations. In most cases, the foods are prepared, packaged, held, and ready to eat when the guest arrives. This format requires quick-cooking foods and equipment. By definition, the menu offerings must be limited.
2. *Ready to heat and eat.* This format presents fully cooked foods that are held in a refrigerated state. In some cases, the fully cooked foods are held in platters in refrigerated cases, from which they are sold by the pound or portion. Complete meals may be portioned and displayed in refrigerated cases in packaging that can go directly into a microwave or a regular oven.
3. *Hybrid take-out/HMR.* In this configuration, a guest might purchase a prune and walnut stuffed loin of pork for roasting at home; cooked asparagus spears ready for reheating in the microwave oven; and Cajun-style roasted Red Bliss potatoes that go into the pan with the roast for the last 15 minutes.

To effectively capture the take-out/HMR market, care must be exercised in the selection and placement of equipment in the display kitchen. Most important, the display kitchen must be placed so that take-out/HMR patrons do not track through the dining room. The ordering and waiting area for take-out/HMR should not interfere with the flow of traffic in and out of the restaurant. In particularly high-volume situations, the entrance to the take-out/HMR area should be separate from that to the regular restaurant. This separation of service is found in fast-food restaurants equipped with drive-through windows.

At a minimum, the design should include as much self-serve equipment as possible. Portioned hot foods should be held in heated display cases that can be accessed from both server and customer sides. Refrigerated deli display cases should be used when servers portion out chilled foods. If customers choose their own portioned chilled foods, an open-top meat display case is the optimal equipment choice.

Planning for carry-out service must be integrated with the initial design process to ensure that adequate storage space for take-out containers is included in the design. Payment for carry-out items should also be considered when planning the design, and the production staff should not be required to handle money.

SERVICE STATIONS

Service stations, also referred to as server stations and waiter stations, are often viewed by designers as a necessary evil in the dining room—necessary, because they enable waiters to provide efficient service, and evil, because they have no inherent aesthetic appeal; they can be an ugly blot on an otherwise pure design. The truth is that service stations need not be intrusive obstructions in the dining room if they are carefully conceived and developed in the early stages of the design process (Figure 5.19).

Service stations should be designed as functional appendages of the back of the house. No matter where they are placed, they must be well stocked with all the backup supplies that waiters will need to service the dining room. In tableservice restaurants, that may include 50 or 60 backup or reset items. In a fast-food operation, it may include nothing more than a bottle of spray cleaner, toweling, and extra trash bags.

The aesthetic design of service stations should be well integrated with the front-of-the-house design. In some restaurants, the service station is a finely crafted piece of furniture that blends well with the overall decor and helps segment the dining area. In other restaurants, the service station is integrated with an architectural element that keeps the station hidden from view. In still other restaurants, the service stations are not situated in the dining room but in the service pickup area immediately adjacent to the kitchen. All of these configurations can efficiently support waitstaff functions without detracting from the overall design scheme.

The purpose of the service station is to improve the speed and efficiency of service and to function as a backup to assist in the quick resetting of tables during peak demand periods. This is particularly important in large operations where servers must travel long distances from the kitchen, or in operations where several small dining rooms are serviced from a central kitchen. There are no set rules for what should be incorporated into a service station. The design of any station should rely on management philosophy, the menu, and the type of service. In some tableservice restaurants, it is appropriate to incorporate an ice bin, water station, coffee and tea burners, roll warmer, and all the elements required to reset tables and hold soiled tableware and linen.

If standard operating procedure, after seating a guest, is to ice a glass, fill it with water, present warm rolls, then to finish the meal with a bottomless cup of coffee, a well-equipped service station is absolutely essential. An all-important component of the service is the POS, which links the servers and the kitchen.

> The aesthetic design of service stations should be well integrated with the front-of-the-house design

FIGURE 5.19 A service station can be built to look like an integral part of the design, as it does here in the Payard Patisserie and Bistro in New York City, designed by the Rockwell Group. (Photo © Paul Warchol.)

WAREWASHING AREAS

As mentioned earlier, the placement of the warewashing equipment can significantly affect the efficiency of a restaurant. Placement is simple in a restaurant with a single dining room: just as the server enters the kitchen. When operations have multiple points of service with a central warewashing station, however, the location of warewashing equipment is trickier.

In a complex operation, the placement of warewashing will be affected by the number of trips servers take and the volume of tableware brought to the warewashing station. Consider a hotel where banquets are served from one side of the kitchen and the dining room is served from the other. Dishes are hand-carried to and from the dining room. However, service to and from banquet areas is accomplished by carrying dishes on sheet pans that are set on tray stands. After service, the sheet pans are moved to the service corridor and placed on mobile racks, which are wheeled to the dish area.

In the above example, although the greater volume of dishes comes from the banquet area, warewashing should be located closer to the dining room because the waitstaff makes more frequent trips to and from the dining room service areas. If the use of bus buckets is integrated with dining room service, however (thus limiting server time running back and forth from dining room to warewashing), the location of the warewashing system could change. It is, therefore, crucially important to consider specific operating procedures when making decisions about the location of warewashing.

Placement of warewashing in other than tableservice restaurants is also important. To be most effective, the warewashing in a cafeteria-style restaurant should be located near the cafeteria exit. This may necessitate separating the warewashing section from the kitchen. The alternative is to install a (costly) conveyor system or to use mobile carts where users deposit their trays, with filled carts transported to the warewashing facility.

The three classes of dish machines are:

1. *Single-rack machines.* The basic single-rack machine is designed to meet the needs of smaller restaurants. When set up for hot water sanitizing, these machines can clean more than 50 racks of tableware per house. Newly introduced equipment includes front-loading models that can be easier to install than the commonly used side-loading units. Rack machines are also available for installation in a corner space, with doors that open on adjacent sides. Yet another model offers a tall chamber that makes it possible to wash sheet pans and dishware in a single, compact machine.

2. *Rack conveyor machines.* When used to their full capacity, these machines can service all but the largest institutional and banquet facilities. Assuming a continuously loaded standard-size rack, a rack conveyor machine can clean about 200 racks of tableware per hour. Twin-tank rack machines are capable of cleaning up to 360 racks per hour. Useful features on this type of dish machine include a side-loading model that allows for corner installation. This can save up to 20 square feet in the dishroom layout. A power

unloader pushes racks away from the clean end, which makes it possible for just one operator to handle both ends of the machine.

3. *Flight-type machines.* The largest of all dish machines, flight-type units are capable of cleaning tens of thousands of pieces of tableware per hour. Straight flight-type machines offer the advantage of direct loading of dishes onto pegs, which speeds cleaning and minimizes the number of racks needed to support the operation. A variation on this theme is a merry-go-round dish machine that requires tableware to be loaded onto racks.

When planning a bar operation, glasswashing is particularly important. Consideration must be given to the noise and space required for an undercounter glasswasher versus a manual washing system versus transporting the glasses to and from a remote warewashing facility. A key consideration is that the bartender should spend as much time serving drinks as possible.

POTWASHING SECTION

Closely aligned with the warewashing area is the potwashing station. Although the potwashing station may be separated from the dish machine, most operations keep the two areas together because of crossover staffing. Further, in large operations where there is a sanitation supervisor, it is easier to supervise the staff when the stations are closely linked. Another reason for placing the two operations together is that, in some locales, the pots must be sterilized, and the dish machine is the best place to accomplish this.

The potwashing process may be mechanized through the installation of a motor-driven device that grinds the dirt off the pots. In operations where the volume of pots and pans is substantial, a potwashing machine similar to a single-rack machine can effectively remove food buildup from most trays, pots, pans, and utensils. An alternative to ease the potwashing chore is a wash sink that uses high-powered jets of hot water and detergent. In this case, the cleaning solution, heat, and abrasive action of the pressurized water jets loosens all but the heaviest food buildup.

Environmental Conditions

The lighting, ventilation, spacing of equipment, types of surfaces, and sound levels all have an impact on the effectiveness of production staff in the kitchen. These environmental factors can also affect employee turnover rates, which, in turn, affect the restaurant's bottom line (Figure 5.20).

LIGHTING

Direct lighting in the back of the house is desirable but must be carefully engineered. Although sufficient light is needed to differentiate between a piece of flank steak and a piece of skirt steak, too much light can create glare that ultimately leads to eyestrain. When properly angled, however, direct task lighting is practical and energy efficient.

FIGURE 5.20 *The kitchen at TrU in Chicago provides a comfortable working environment for the chefs. The space is well lighted, and acoustic ceiling tiles mute noise. Makeup air vents in the ceiling bring cooled air into the hot cooking area.* (Photo by Joseph Durocher.)

To ensure that food looks its best, using incandescent lamps in the food production area can be helpful. The result is that the cuisine is viewed under the same type of light by the chef as by the diners.

Historically, mood lighting was not important in most kitchens, but its role in display kitchens is vital. Theatrical spotlights, for example, are used to highlight the work surfaces and food arrangements in many display kitchens. Here, the lighting scheme provides adequate illumination for the cooks and a focal point for guests to view their meals in preparation.

Ventilation

The ventilation system is composed of exhaust and makeup air. Exhaust air is generally removed from those portions of the kitchen where smoke, heat, and steam are created. Building codes, in most communities, require that ventilation hoods be installed over all heat- and smoke-producing equipment. Further, the codes require that fire detection and extinguishing systems be installed as part of the ventilation system.

The comfort level of employees is determined by the amount of air removed from the kitchen. However, for every cubic foot of air removed through the hoods, makeup air must be provided. Makeup air can come from ducting that dumps treated air into the kitchen, the dining room, or both. A negative pressure should always be maintained in the kitchen (more air drawn out of the kitchen than is supplied by makeup air ducts in the kitchen) to ensure that smoke and grease are kept from the dining room.

There are two schools of thought about adding makeup air to a kitchen. The first approach is to add the air evenly throughout the kitchen; the second is to add the air where it is most needed. Fresh air is dumped near the dish machine, in the fabrication area, over the bakeshop, or in other areas where heat builds up. In certain newer hood systems, some of the makeup air is added right at the face of the hood. This limits the amount of air drawn across the vertical face of the hood. A flow of exhaust air that becomes too strong is discomforting to the cooks. To control hearing and cooking costs, a minimum of conditioned air should be drawn out of the dining room. Dining room air is filtered, heated, or cooled and, therefore, costly if too much is exhausted through the kitchen exhaust system.

ACOUSTICS

Kitchens can be noisy places to work. Too much noise can cause discomfort and create unsafe working conditions, and high noise levels may obscure communications between production and service staff. Ultimately, this process leads to guest dissatisfaction.

Noise can be controlled through the careful selection and placement of noise-producing equipment as well as the installation of acoustic treatments. If a dish machine is placed, for operational reasons, near the entry of the kitchen, acoustic controls are needed to prevent the carryover of sound into the dining room. Meat grinders and potwashing stations are frequently removed from central production areas where servers interface with the cooks because they create excessive noise.

Acoustic ceiling tiles are commonly specified in kitchens. Sound-absorbing insulation in the wall between the dish area and the dining room may also be called for. To limit the sound of the dish machine in the rest of the kitchen, a wall separating the dish area from the remaining back of the house can be helpful.

Summary

An operational and managerial understanding of all kitchen requirements is essential before a successful design can be implemented. It may be helpful for management to draw up a wish list of desired features and equipment. In any case, it behooves the kitchen designer to ask many specific questions regarding back-of-the house procedures. Will management serve frozen green beans, or will storage and processing space be needed for fresh beans? Will pies and cakes arrive from the local bakery, will frozen pies have to be baked off, or will raw ingredients have to be stored in order to bake breads and pastries from scratch? The answers to these and countless other questions all markedly affect the space and equipment requirements of a restaurant kitchen.

Mini-Case Solutions

In previous chapters, we discussed the basic principles of front- and back-of-the-house design. Once these are understood, developing individual design schemes becomes possible. This chapter presents a selection of interesting solutions found in today's restaurants.

These cases have been culled from hundreds of examples to demonstrate the diversity of problem solving involved with restaurant design. However, the design of a restaurant does not begin with the reinvention of the wheel. Good design follows basic principles, and good designers and restaurateurs learn from experience.

In each of the cases, challenges faced by the design team and an explanation of the solutions they created are presented. While each can be studied individually, it is interesting to note that a number of challenges were common to several designs.

Finally, note that each of the solutions was created for the individual restaurant at a particular time and in a particular space. Would the ice buckets built into the railings at Jardinière work elsewhere? Is the preorder board installed in new Burger Kings appropriate to other drive-through operations? Is a full-scale bread bakery, as discussed in the Beacon case, appropriate elsewhere? The answers to these questions are unknown. The solutions presented here may, however, inspire the insight that helps to solve your restaurant design challenges.

Mini-Case Solutions

Aureole

LAS VEGAS

Designer: Adam Tihany International Ltd., New York
Owner: Circus Circus Development
Year opened: 1999
Number of seats: dining room, 174; fine dining room, 68; private rooms, 84; bar/lounge, 44
FOH: ~9,000 square feet
BOH: ~3,200 square feet
Service style: tableservice
Menu: progressive American cuisine

Adam Tihany's design for Aureole is every bit as spectacular as Chef Charlie Palmer's cuisine. The homage to wine is the signature design element in this massive restaurant housed in the Mandalay Bay Resort & Casino.

The wine cellar is actually a wine tower that soars from the dining level past the entry level and toward the skylight-capped ceiling. This tower of laminated glass and steel, four stories tall and 14 feet square at the base, was designed by Tihany as an interactive sculpture with its own kinetic energy.

The design experience begins at the facade of Aureole (Color Plate 1), a white wall with offset oval tube windows that drill toward the interior of the restaurant. Uplighting washes across the cutout letters that spell *Aureole* to create a playful shadow effect. The sleek look of this exterior sharply contrasts with the garish facades of the surrounding shops and casino.

The wine tower is directly in front of the entryway. Diners get an intimate view of 10,000 bottles of wine held at 55 degrees Fahrenheit on sand-blasted Plexiglas™ wine racks as they descend stairs that wrap around the tower. The complete wine list includes roughly 2,000 selections and is backed up with a total inventory of nearly 40,000 bottles.

Flying wine angels are an integral part of the show. Tihany was inspired by a scene from the movie *Mission Impossible*, in which Tom Cruise was flown through space attached to steel cables. That's just what the wine angels do in the wine tower. Whenever a bottle of wine is ordered, they hook a set of cables to their flying harness and away they go to retrieve the requested bottle.

The wine tower dominates the entry of Aureole Las Vegas.
(Photo © Mark Ballogg, Steinkamp/Ballogg Photography, Chicago)

Surrounding the base of the tower is the bar and lounge, an ideal vantage point from which to view the action. Here, dark brown suede on the walls and beige-colored limestone flooring creates a comfortable, clubby atmosphere.

The show at Aureole changes as customers progress from the bar to one of three dining rooms. In the main dining room, the ceiling height drops precipitously and the space takes on a contemporary feeling that reflects the nature of Chef Palmer's cuisine. Tihany enlivened this elegant room with fanciful free-form sculptures created by glass artist Luciano Vistosi. Four large custom-designed light boxes mounted on the ceiling cast a warm glow. Seating includes two sets of back-to-back banquettes with bottom-lit glass partitions that separate the banquettes from each other and add privacy for diners.

At the back of the main dining room is the dramatic entrance to the Swan Court dining room, targeted to VIP clientele. Guests who enter the Swan Court feel as if they are stepping into another, even more luxurious realm. After walking through a doorway framed by water flowing between two sheets of glass, they come to a high-ceilinged, semi-oval room with an elaborate ceiling treatment and a wall of wraparound windows that overlook an outdoor pool and waterfall. Well-spaced seating includes high-backed booths and tables that face the windows. A third, L-shaped dining area can be used as overflow for the dining room or closed off for groups.

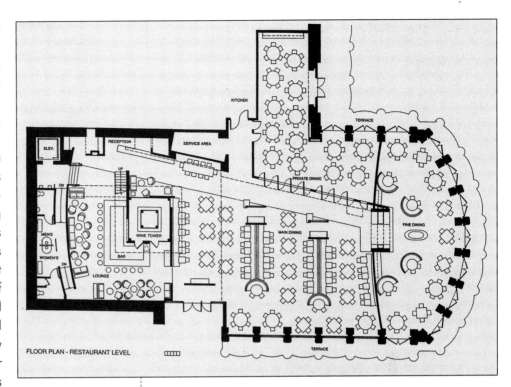

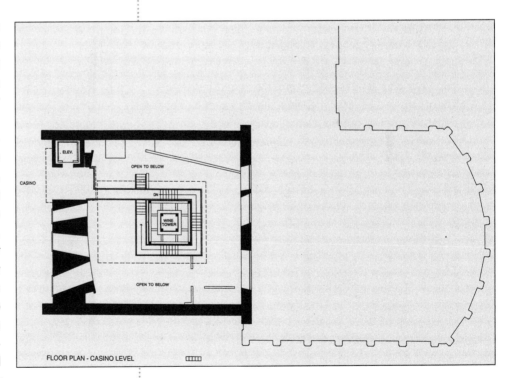

Aureole Las Vegas floorplan.
(Courtesy of Adam D. Tihany International Ltd.)

BD's Mongolian Barbeque

NAPERVILLE, ILLINOIS

Designer: Chipman-Adams Ltd., Architects, Park Ridge, Illinois
Owner: William Downs
Year opened: 1996
Number of seats: dining room, 150; private rooms, 40; bar, 30
FOH: 4,100 square feet
BOH: 2,300 square feet
Service styles: raw ingredient buffet; grill chefs cook food on exhibition flattop grill
Menu: meats and vegetables cooked on an exhibition flattop grill; salad bar

Customer participation and exhibition cooking are the hallmarks of BD's Mongolian Barbeque, a 16-unit chain of restaurants located primarily in the Midwest. BD's Mongolian's fully interactive concept engages diners in the process of selecting ingredients for their meal and overseeing the cooking on a flattop grill. The large dining room's radial floorplan focuses the view from each table on the exhibition cooking area. Adjacent to the dining room is a bar area on a raised platform. Bar-goers are clearly separated from the dining area, yet the raised platform affords them a clear view of the action on the floor.

Customer interaction with the food preparation process in this type of operation poses operational and design challenges. To increase circulation around the salad bar and buffet area where diners select vegetables, raw meats, and sauces for grilling, the architects broke the buffet into small islands that allow greater freedom of movement. This significantly reduces line buildup as guests portion raw ingredients into their bowls.

From the buffets, diners proceed a few feet to the cooking station. As they watch their food lined up and cooked on a six-foot doughnut-shaped griddle, they interact with each other and with the grill chefs. Decorative railings help separate the seating from the circulation areas around the griddle, and sufficient aisle space allows guests to flow easily to and from the buffet/cooking area and their tables. The aisles also accommodate servers, who bring bowls of rice, tortillas, and beverages to the tables.

Because the cooking area is the restaurant's focal point, the seating area wraps around it to give the greatest possible number of customers a view. From an operational perspective, the cooking and buffet areas also had to be located close to the kitchen prep area.

One of the challenges presented by the exposed grill was how to capture its heat and smoke while maintaining a balance of air temperatures in the dining spaces. The solution was an extensive hood with integrated makeup air that resembles a traditional yurt, the tentlike structure of the nomadic Mongolian people.

The Naperville, Illinois, restaurant design is the prototype for the design of all of the other BD's Mongolian restaurants. Each of them has a prep kitchen, grilling area, raw ingredient buffet, and salad bar. The bar and seating areas are adapted to each location. However, each unit incorporates the rustic

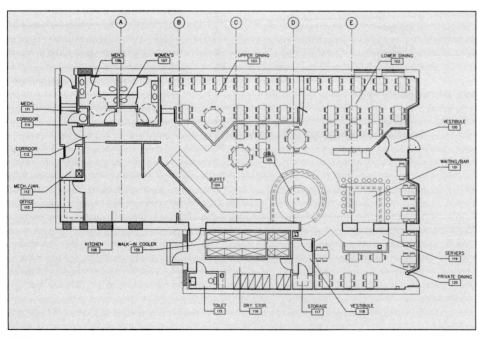

BD's Mongolian Barbeque floorplan.
(Courtesy of Chipman Adams Ltd.)

At BD's Mongolian Barbeque, customers queue up to watch their meals being grilled
(Photo by Charlie Mayer Photography)

design elements and warm earth tones of Mongolia. A large hand-painted mural is created for each facility that blends the traditional images of Mongolia with the local community flavor. The restaurants can be built in 10 to 12 weeks, with much of the equipment, casework, and furniture constructed off site and shipped ready for installation.

Heather Eppink, marketing director for BD's Mongolian, says that the design provides customers with a pleasing, comfortable atmosphere and meets the operational needs of the staff. It also helps establish and build the chain's brand identity. She predicts the chain will grow to 90 restaurants by the end of 2004.

Beacon

NEW YORK

Designer: Morris Nathanson Design, Inc.,
Pawtucket, Rhode Island
Owners: Chef Waldy Malouf, David Emil
Year opened: 1999
Number of seats: dining rooms, 142;
private dining, 76; bar, 28
FOH: 6,285 square feet
BOH: 3,900 square feet
Service style: tableservice
Menu: live-fire cooking

When partners David Emil and Waldy Malouf approached Morris Nathanson Design to plan a restaurant based on the romance of wood-fire cooking, it was a no-brainer that the center stage would be an imposing hearth. Chef Malouf explains the design brief: "We wanted a sophisticated, cosmopolitan room that felt comfortable, that evoked a spirit of generosity and hospitality. We wanted all of the spaces—kitchen to dining room, dining room to bar, bar to kitchen—to interact with each other as one space." Malouf

challenged the designers to create a tavern for the twenty-first century that discarded cliché tavern references from the twentieth century.

Chef Malouf ditched his toque and donned a hard hat to take on the role of construction supervisor—much to the chagrin of the contractors—for the entire project. It's a good thing that he was involved, because several major problems cropped up that needed his direct attention. For example, while the main kitchen was being installed, workers discov-

ered that a column was in the wrong place and the entire kitchen had to be redesigned and reinstalled.

Then there was the challenge with the flue for the wood-burning oven. When the design team researched code regulations, they learned that a separate flue was needed for each piece of wood-burning equipment and that the flue had to terminate no less than six feet above the building's roof line. What they failed to note was that the 9-story building that Beacon is located in on 56th Street in Manhattan is also part of a 15-story building that faces 57th Street. Soon after Chef Malouf fired up the wood stove, he was visited by the New York Fire Department and forced to extend the flue an additional 6 stories.

Dining spreads over two and a half floors in a layout reminiscent of a classic Broadway theater. The entry is on the street level of the restaurant. If guests have to wait, they can have drinks at the street-level bar or in a second-floor lounge area that also serves as a dining area. A private dining room upstairs seats up to 76. To meet ADA requirements, bathrooms were installed on both levels.

Downstairs tables include a dining area that Chef Malouf calls "the pit." Here, seating for roughly 40 guests is eight steps below the street level, immediately in front of the stage. "This is seen as the prime seating area," says Morris Nathanson. "There is no barrier between the diners and the hearth. It's like sitting in front of a fireplace." Chef Malouf works the pit as expediter; he coordinates the interaction between the chefs and the service staff. Often, he delivers a plate of food to guests or chats with them when they visit the expediter station.

The back of the house is also built on two levels. No behind-the-scenes kitchen equipment backs the display cooking line, so Chef Malouf chose equipment that is highly reliable and capable of standing up to the rigors of cooking hundreds of meals each day. The display kitchen incorporates an oven, a fryer, a range, grills, and a rotisserie.

Only the oven is wood-fired, although the grills use wood chips to add a tinge of smoky flavor to foods cooked over them. A tile and slate hearth surrounds the cooking equipment. The work counter is fronted with wood trim to enhance the warm feeling of the space; it is here that Malouf stands to conduct his culinary orchestra.

The basement level of Beacon is used for storage and some prepreparation. Most significant, Chef Malouf installed a full-scale bakery in this area, complete with roll-in ovens. The output of this bakery serves Beacon and up to 21 clients from surrounding businesses, making it a profit center for the restaurant.

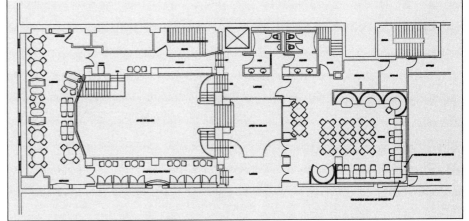

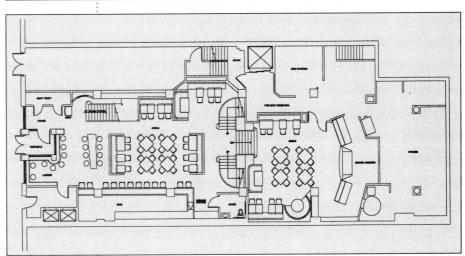

Beacon floorplan.
(Courtesy of Morris Nathanson Design, Inc.)

The view from Beacon's second floor shows first floor dining and the open-hearth cooking area.
(Photo © Warren Jagger Photography, Inc.)

Beckman Instruments Employee Cafeteria

BREA, CALIFORNIA

Designer: Webb Foodservice Design
Consultants, Inc., Tustin, California
Owner: Beckman Instruments
Year opened: 1997
Number of seats: dining room, 166
FOH: 3,013 square feet
BOH: 3,202 square feet
Service styles: scatter-system servery
Menu: hot entrées, sandwiches, salad and
fruit bar

Cafeterias often have an institutional look because they are built as big square boxes. That was the problem faced by Jim Webb of Webb Foodservice Design Consultants when he started the redesign of the Beckman Instruments employee cafeteria. His simple yet effective solution was to introduce a circular design aesthetic for the entry, servery, and dining areas. The entry (see Figure 4.10) is clearly circular in its architecture from floor to ceiling, including a novel column rising from the middle of the foyer that serves as a merchandising platform for daily specials and helps define customer traffic patterns. The recessed niches in this space form a gallery for displaying artwork and provide a convenient tray storage area located out of the flow pattern.

The servery incorporates sufficient aisle space for circulation with a centrally located, round salad bar that serves as a focal point in the center of the space. Eleven specialty food areas are on radius counters, and two beverage stations flank the cashier stands as customers head for the dining room.

The dining room continues the circular motif with curved lines on the ceiling, in the lighting effects, in the railing, and on the walls. Booths and settees border each side of the dining room and are joined with freestanding tables that accommodate from two to six seats. The use of fabrics on the settees and booths, carpeting on the floor, and an acoustic ceiling treatment help create a quiet, comfortable environment.

The facility provides a relaxed lunchtime setting for employees and serves as a meeting space. The back kitchen (also designed by Webb Foodservice Design Consultants) supports the main scatter-system servery, where roughly 300 meals are served daily. The servery also doubles as a serving area for catered events. In addition, the kitchen produces food for executive meals and meetings throughout the corporate campus. The kitchen includes a supervisor's office from which all functions in the back of the house can be viewed. Storage areas and the potwashing area flank the central production area, which has three entry points to the adjacent servery.

Clever cost-saving and creative decisions were integrated with the design. The radius coun-

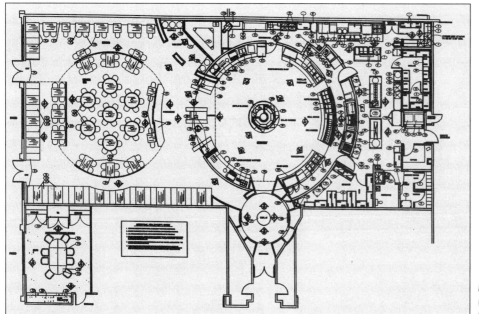

Beckman Instruments floorplan.
(Courtesy of Webb Foodservice
Design Consultants, Inc.)

The clean, modern design of the Beckman Instruments cafeteria offers employees a welcome escape from their offices.
(Photo by Don Romero)

ters in the servery were installed on rectangular bases whose standard construction helped keep the servery expenses under budget. In the kitchen, Webb created storage nooks on the radius walls that would have otherwise been wasted space. Also in the kitchen, the designers installed a water-mist fire-suppression system instead of a dry chemical, CO_2, or other chemical suppression agent system. The efficient mist system was less expensive to install and is less costly to maintain.

The redesign has led to a 50 percent increase in business and provided Beckman Instrument executives with a great place to entertain future clients and prospective employees without going off the property. It has also had a positive impact on the foodservice employees, who appreciate the modern kitchen equipment and the clean, attractive working environment.

Belgo Nieuw York

NEW YORK

Architect: Michael Zenreich
Designers: Foreign Office Architects
Owner: Belgo Group PLC, UK
Year opened: 1999
Number of seats: upstairs dining room,
   120; downstairs dining room, 150; bar, 15
Total area: 8,700 square feet
Service styles: tableservice to beer hall-style
   tables
Menu: hearty Belgian fare, including a wide
   selection of mussels and more than 100
   Belgian beers

Zoning regulations sometimes affect a restaurant design in profound ways. Such was the case at Belgo Nieuw York, which opened in a building located in a part of New York that allows no restaurant to exceed 5,000 square feet of public assembly space. This initial challenge became the driving force behind the restaurant's architectural layout. Architect Michael Zenreich, who handled the code compliance efforts for Belgo, had to work with a 8,700-square-foot building of which 3,700 square feet could not be used for dining or drinking.

The second challenge was the overall shape of the space—roughly 28 feet wide by 150 feet deep. The building was previously used as a warehouse, with a loading dock that set the first floor roughly 4 feet above street level. A third constraint, one faced by all restaurants, was compliance with ADA accessibility guidelines. Finally, two means of egress that

reached the front of the building were needed for each floor of the restaurant.

"The egress issue and the ramps—chosen rather than an elevator—determined the layout," says Zenreich, whose office provides expedited code compliance for many restaurant projects. "The idea," he comments, "was to take what was a problem and turn it into a design feature." His solution uses two ramps. One, about 150 feet long, leads from the entry to the downstairs dining room. "This ramp was done originally for ADA compliance but it creates a velocity that forces people to walk through the space and experience it," notes Zenreich. A second ramp, roughly 59 feet long, takes customers up the 4-foot rise from street level to the first-floor dining space. The ramps and the back-of-the-house elements pared down the building's footprint to meet code.

A special characteristic of the first-floor ramp is that it

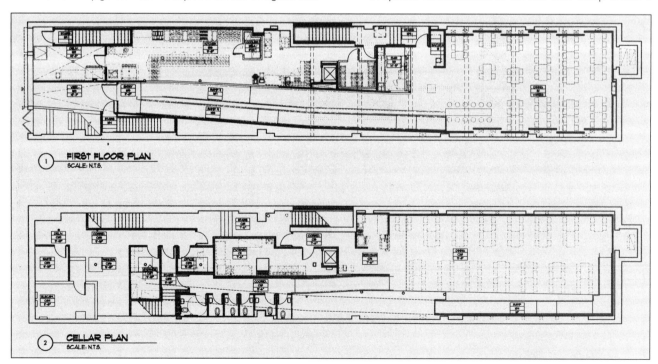

① **FIRST FLOOR PLAN**
   SCALE: N.T.S.

② **CELLAR PLAN**
   SCALE: N.T.S.

Belgo Nieuw York floorplan.
(Courtesy of Belgo Americas LLC)

passes an open kitchen where customers can catch an intimate glimpse of the kitchen action and chat with the expediter before heading for the dining room.

Belgo Nieuw York is the first U.S.-based restaurant opened by the Belgo Group PLC, headquartered in London, which had eight other units in the United Kingdom as of January 2000. The signature Belgo design elements were created by the Foreign Office Architects (FOA), also in London. The architects used computer generated three-dimensional modeling to create curved wall and ceiling sections on the top floor. Customers feel as if they are dining inside a giant mussel shell, or maybe a wine cave. Downstairs, a low ceiling creates a more intimate feeling,

and a large mural incorporates multilingual phrases on the back wall.

Both floors have the lively animation of a Belgian beer hall and a quirky, hip attitude, which are themes that run through every unit in the chain. The open kitchen and vaulted ceilings are Belgo signature elements. So are the servers' monklike uniforms, inspired by Trappist robes and brewing aprons. Long tables are arranged in the fashion of beer-hall seating, and hard-surface treatments were intentionally chosen to create a lively buzz.

The vaulted ceiling on the main floor of Belgo Nieuw York is one of the chain's signature elements.
(Photo by Mathew Mauro, © Belgo Americas LLC)

The Bellagio Hotel Casino Restaurants: Graphic Design

LAS VEGAS

Graphic Design: Stephen Pannone, Girvin Design, Inc., Seattle, Washington
Owner: Mirage Properties, Inc.
Year opened: 1998
Number of restaurants: 15
Service styles: varied, from fine dining tableservice to stand-up espresso
Menu: varied, from contemporary French to sushi

The three-thousand-room Bellagio Hotel Casino is patterned after the Italian village of Bellagio, which overlooks Lake Como. It is fronted by Lago de Bellagio, a 10-acre man-made lake. However, the mandate for the overall design program was to avoid an obvious theme, according to Stephen Pannone, senior design director of Girvin Design, Inc. Pannone was responsible for many of the hotel's graphic programs, including for all 15 restaurants. This encompassed exterior signage, menu graphics, merchandise graphics, employee uniform graphics, tableware logos, etc.

At an estimated cost of around $1 billion, Bellagio's entire graphic design program took 20 months to complete. "So much time was spent in the search for the inspiration of each of the restaurants that the owners wanted the graphics to be equally special," says Pannone. The research produced detailed design directives. For example, when speaking of one of the Asian restaurants, Bellagio executives characterized it with such phrases as "elegant Hong Kong," "turn-of-the-century," and "opulent style" rather than the simple "we want an Asian restaurant." They also wanted the design to stay away from the glitzy look that people associate with Las Vegas.

One graphic design question that had to be resolved for all the restaurants was whether or not the graphic logo—which Pannone calls the "mark"—would be used on name-brand merchandise. A second consideration was to create

The Olives logo at Bellagio Hotel Casino was redesigned with a stylized O.
(Photo courtesy of Girvin Design, Inc.)

graphics that appealed to an international clientele. A third challenge was to keep a consistent level of graphic design for each of the individual units.

Perhaps the trickiest task Pannone faced was the challenge of making the graphic identity of each restaurant distinctly different while creating a portfolio of related logos. The task was complicated by the location of most of the restaurants on a retail promenade that leads from the street directly to the casino; the restaurants are interspersed with shops and boutiques such as Tiffany & Co. and Giorgio Armani. Each of these retail stores has its own logo, which Pannone's graphics had to work with in context.

Some of the restaurants needed a whole new graphics program; others (like Le Cirque) had existing graphics that were imported to Las Vegas with few changes. One of the most challenging restaurants, says Pannone, was Olives, a branch of Todd English's casual Mediterranean restaurant of the same name in Boston. Here, an existing graphics program needed to be redesigned. Bellagio executives, English, and Pannone worked together to create a new Olives graphics program for the Bellagio setting. The hard part, says Pannone, was "trying to extrapolate the old restaurant into the new one. We did that by taking the O that looked like an olive and the black and copper colors used in the Boston restaurant." The Olives logo was applied not only on the exterior signage and menu cover but also on the hats worn by the cooking staff and on the plates. The server uniforms sport a copper-colored, embroidered O that serves as an elegant visual reference to the sophistication of the restaurant.

For each of the Bellagio restaurants, Pannone had to figure where on the facade to apply the graphics. This meant, among other things, understanding sight lines for each establishment. In some cases, space was limited; Olives, for example, is tightly sandwiched between the Giorgio Armani and Hermés boutiques. In this case, an awning was installed. The logo was applied to the awning, to the accordion doors on the front of the restaurant, and throughout the interior (see facing page).

"The restaurant I like best," says Pannone, "is Shintaro, because all of the elements—the color palette, textures, interior decor, and graphics—work together to create an overall experience." Pannone's graphic program carries through the textural design theme with black leather menu covers that have a brass plaque bearing the Shintaro logo, and rope rings that bind the back and front covers together. Attention was paid to every graphic detail in the restaurant, right down to the chopstick sleeves adorned with Japanese calligraphy.

The graphics program for Shintaro, one of the restaurants at Bellagio Hotel Casino, extends from exterior to menu to chopstick sleeves.
(Photo courtesy of Girvin Design, Inc.)

Border Grill

LAS VEGAS

Designer: Schweitzer BIM Inc., Los Angeles
Owners: Chefs Mary Sue Milliken and Susan Feniger
Year opened: 1999
Number of seats: downstairs dining room, 116; upstairs dining doom, 100; tortillaria, 20 at stand-up tables; main patio dining, 100; bar, 44
FOH: 7,000 square feet, plus patio
BOH: 3,100 square feet
Service styles: tableservice, counter service
Menu: authentic Mexican

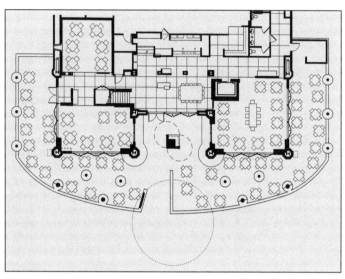

Border Grill floorplan, first floor.
(Courtesy of Schweitzer BIM, Inc.)

Border Grill floorplan, second floor.
(Courtesy of Schweitzer BIM, Inc.)

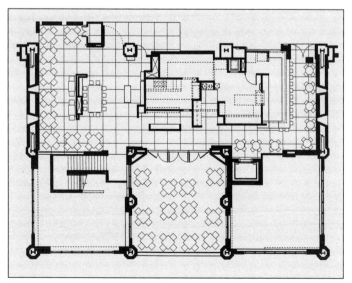

Bringing their Los Angeles Border Grill concept to Las Vegas presented interesting challenges to chef-owners Mary Sue Milliken and Susan Feniger. The restaurant is located on the property of the lavish Mandalay Bay Casino Hotel, which also houses an exclusive Four Seasons hotel on its top four floors. Two heavyweight competitors, Aureole and China Grill, are on the same property, as are a host of other restaurants. Milliken and Feniger always make food the main event in their restaurants, so architect Josh Schweitzer knew from the start that they would not want the kind of showy elements found in many Las Vegas establishments. "No water shows, no flying sommeliers. Just big bold shapes and colorful murals to complement the great food," says Schweitzer.

One aspect of the location is that Border Grill is physically separate from the other restaurants at Mandalay Bay. It overlooks an 11-acre water park and beach, and is adjacent to the hotel's convention center. Most people reach the restaurant via the ground floor, where the pools and beach are. The other access is on the second floor, past a series of restaurants, the shopping area, and a long walkway that leads to the convention center.

Border Grill's colorful, exuberant design is not inspired by its location, except that the second-floor windows were enlarged to open the view and to play up the idea of a big open space connected to the outside. The resulting space is full of natural light.

The first floor incorporates three dining rooms and an al fresco patio dining area. In the center of the first-floor entry sits the host stand. To the left of the host stand is a grand staircase that leads up to the second floor. A service bar and pastry display are also located near the host stand.

The second floor has a patio that extends to the front of the building. Other dining options include a large bar and a cantina that features a more limited menu than the restaurant below. A small kitchen and tortillaria (tortilla making station)

The tortillaria area at Border Grill Las Vegas features larger-than-life murals by Su Huntley and Donna Muir, high-boy tables, and bright red padded stools.
(Photo by Jeffrey Green Photography)

serves as a visual focal point and as a take-out station. The tortillaria, reminiscent of the street vendors found in Mexico, is a convenient place for people to grab a taco before heading back to the convention center. Seating in this area consists of high-boy tables and bright red padded stools. All the seating areas on the second floor overlook the main patio seating on the first floor. Seating on each of the floors includes a signature "mesa grande" table for large groups (up to 12 people downstairs and 18 people upstairs).

Schweitzer's design uses layers of forms, colors, and murals to unite the multilevel space. It resembles a cubist composition of geometric shapes and colors. Su Huntley and Donna Muir, the same artists whose work is seen in the chef-owners' other restaurants, created the larger-than-life modernist murals that appear throughout Border Grill. Many are pictorial abstractions of faces. Downstairs, some of the murals measure 25 by 25 feet. They extend back and up into the second-level spaces, seeming to float into the cantina and bar areas and come down the walls. "From outside," enthuses Schweitzer, "people walking by the pools or along the grand walkway can look in Border Grill's windows and see huge heads floating on the ceiling and layers of artwork adorning the walls." In fact, the wall art is a big street sign for the restaurant. "We played with the concept of layers of huge spaces and murals looming over people. This was our answer to the scale and flashiness of Las Vegas: a bigger-than-life idea," says Schweitzer.

Brew Moon Restaurant & Microbrewery

BRAINTREE, MASSACHUSETTS

Designer: Darlow/Christ Architects, Cambridge, Massachusetts
Owner: Elliot Feiner
Year opened: 1998
Number of seats: dining room, 170; bar, 105
FOH: 5,300 square feet
BOH: 2,000 square feet
Brewery: 1,200 square feet
Service style: tableservice
Menu: diversified foods drawn from 13 ethnic groups; custom beers

Notwithstanding the importance of its handcrafted beers, the design of Brew Moon, a growing restaurant chain headquartered in Massachusetts, was not intended to resemble a typical brewpub. "We view ourselves first as a restaurant, with the surprise that we make our own beer," says Elliott Feiner, president and CEO of Brew Moon Enterprises, Inc., in Needham, Massachusetts. His mandate to Darlow/Christ Architects was to create an inviting contemporary environment that supported the Brew Moon theme without screaming microbrewery. "We want customers to choose us based on a restaurant experience that includes food from 13 different ethnic groups, great beer, and a distinctive design," comments Feiner. He assembled a planning team that included the architects, graphic designers, chef, and brewmaster; they worked together from the beginning of the project.

The Brew Moon group, 5 units strong as of January 2000, is expected to grow to 12 restaurants by 2001, when a public offering is anticipated. The Braintree, Massachusetts, location shown here—the only freestanding unit in the group as of this writing—exemplifies the features that make the design of Brew Moon a cut above its competition. The overall design program for Brew Moon won the *Business Week/Architectural Record* award for design in 1997.

One difference between the Braintree Brew Moon and the first Brew Moon, which opened in Boston in 1994, is acoustic control. "Back in 1994," says Peter Darlow of Darlow/Christ Architects, "the cool thing was to make restaurants loud." By the time the Braintree unit opened in 1998, customers wanted a quieter environment. To help mute noise levels, the architects opened the ceiling to the roof deck and sprayed the underside with an inch of black, chopped paper material that absorbs sound. Iconic elements that relate to beer and the brewing process float below the coated ceiling. Sandwiched between the underside of the ceiling and the floating elements are the black-painted mechanicals, which tend to fade from view. According to Darlow, sounds that

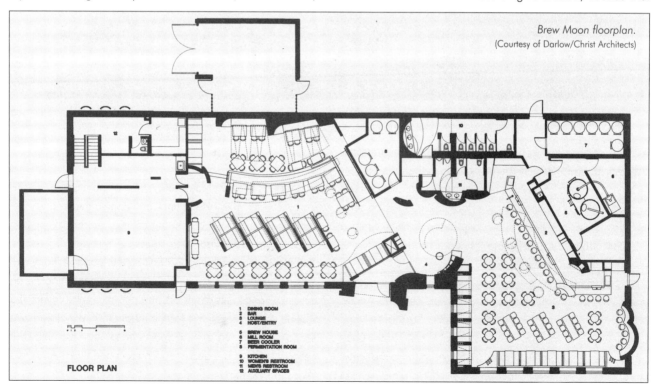

Brew Moon floorplan.
(Courtesy of Darlow/Christ Architects)

FLOOR PLAN

1 DINING ROOM
2 BAR
3 LOUNGE
4 HOST/ENTRY

5 BREW HOUSE
6 MILL ROOM
7 BEER COOLER
8 FERMENTATION ROOM

9 KITCHEN
10 WOMEN'S RESTROOM
11 MEN'S RESTROOM
12 AUXILIARY SPACES

Brew Moon's stylish interior only hints at the fact that it incorporates a microbrewery.
(Photo © Warren Jagger Photography, Inc.)

bounce up from the dining area get absorbed in the acoustic material or trapped in the ceiling elements before they can bounce back down.

Unlike at typical brewpubs, tanks and brewing equipment are not visual focal points in Brew Moon. At Braintree, the brewhouse is located in back of the bar and is only partially visible. Most of the brewing process, which takes only about ten hours per week, goes on behind the scenes. However, the design pays tribute to the brew theme with two large wall friezes, one depicting the ingredients used in brewing and the other the brewing process itself. A third frieze relates to the Braintree locale.

Subtle moon references are ubiquitous in the restaurant. The graphic design firm Plus Designs, Inc. integrated

Brew Moon logo elements throughout the space. Tall, rectangular stainless-steel wall sconces have hidden bulbs that cast the shape of a waxing moon on the wall. Round cutouts on the chair backs represent the full moon. Dyed-in colors on the concrete floor depict the moon in its many phases. These are all subtle images that diners might notice after repeated visits. "The goal," says Feiner, "is to keep people coming back. We do that by making the design like an onion. When guests return, they peel back a layer and see some new design element that they hadn't seen before."

Burger King Prototype

RENO, NEVADA

Designer: Burger King Corp.; input from
Fitch Consulting
Owner: Don White, Franchisee
Year opened: 1999
Number of seats: dining room, 100
Total area: 4,100 square feet
Service styles: counter, dine-in, take-out,
drive-through
Menu: burgers, fries, and other fast-food
items for breakfast, lunch, and dinner

The exterior of Burger King's new prototype, with blue, red,
and yellow accents, shows the new streamlined logo.
(Rendering used with permission from Burger King Brands, Inc.)

Burger King's new prototype, the first of which opened in Reno in 1999, is definitely customer driven. The old restaurant design had not been updated in 20 years. The prototype was built on the site of an existing Burger King in just 60 days.

One of the design objectives was to better reflect the essence of the Burger King brand, says corporate spokesperson Charles Nicolas. "We were built on the premise of 'have it your way,' so we incorporated a have-it-your-way design. The new dining area includes movable chairs and tables for varying size groups. We also installed new kitchen equipment, including a broiler that allows us to add more menu variety."

Traditionally, Burger King has used red and yellow in its color palette. The new design added blue on both the exterior and interior. The building keeps the same footprint as older units, but the dining room area is larger. In addition to the movable seating, there are large booths and seating for

singles. The prototype also incorporates a two-story play area with an interactive fun center.

The menu boards are the most significant change to the servery area. Customer feedback told Burger King that posting breakfast and lunch/dinner items at the same time created confusion. In the prototype, the menus are displayed on meal-specific menu boards. This not only improves the appearance of the menu boards but also speeds service.

Important changes were also made to the back of the house. The prototype includes a new broiler with a multichain conveyor belt that can cook foods at different temperatures and speeds. One of the conveyors is dedicated to cooking

Burger King's new servery incorporates
day part meal-specific menu boards.
(Photo used with permission from
Burger King Brands, Inc.)

Whopper patties, while the others can be adjusted to meet varying demands. "We can add thicker, more indulgent items to our menu with this new broiler," says Nicolas. Examples are half-pound burgers, pork chops, and fish fillets.

The conveyors are extremely efficient. Frozen patties are automatically dispensed onto the conveyors from a loader that can hold up to 30 patties at a time. At the end of the cooking cycle, the broiled patties are deposited directly into heated holding pans. This saves time on both ends of the broiler; formerly, employees placed patties one at a time on the conveyor and then picked up the cooked patties and placed them into heated wells at the cooked end.

Other back-of-the-house equipment changes include a cheese melter that replaces the microwave, heated bins that hold either the beef patties or the broiled chicken patties, and a new preparation module with a heated work plate that is ergonomically designed for assembling sandwiches. The new system also does away with the assembly-line system used in older Burger Kings. Instead, each sandwich is custom assembled by a single person.

The drive-through system (which accounts for 50 percent of Burger King's sales) also underwent a major design change. With a dedicated broiler and workstation for drive-through only, the new prototype unit is reportedly capable of shaving 20 seconds off of each order—a 12 percent reduction in time per car.

The drive-through system has two new elements. First is the preview board that (like the menu board inside) is day-part-specific. Customers drive up to the preview board to check out the menu, then drive forward to the order board. They dictate their order and view the list of ordered items on a color LCD screen built into the order station. At the end of the order cycle, the check total is displayed on the screen. When customers arrive at the pickup station, another readout again displays the check total. Clear packaging helps people see what is inside the bag, and a customer courtesy zone can be used after driving away from the pickup window to check the order. This area has a kiosk that allows customers to call in requests.

By the spring of 2000, 46 additional Burger Kings in Orlando, Florida—all corporate-owned—were renovated based on the new prototype. According to Nicolas, every new Burger King restaurant built after spring 2000 will reflect the new design.

Cal Poly Campus Market

SAN LUIS OBISPO, CALIFORNIA

Designer: Webb Foodservice Design
Consultants, Inc., Tustin, CA
Year opened: 1998
Number of seats: 22
FOH: 4,174 square feet
BOH: 2,301 square feet
Service styles: counter service and market
Menu: fresh sandwiches, pizza, baked goods,
and flavored coffees

Campus markets, particularly at schools with strong agriculture programs, have traditionally offered a showcase for the byproducts of these programs. They sold milk and ice cream from the dairy studies programs, meat products from the animal science department, and produce and fruits from the crop science department. Today, many campus markets have expanded their offerings to include other food and sundries for the grab-and-go market, and added seating areas for those who wish to eat on site.

Before its 1998 renovation, the campus market at Cal Poly (California Polytechnic Institute) at San Luis Obispo was a grocery store that offered just a few made-to-order food items. First opened in the 1950s, it didn't come close to taking advantage of the students who passed by it in droves every day. Recognizing the potential to capture more business, the University asked Webb Foodservice Design consultants to transform the existing facility into a beautiful, upgraded space for $380,000. The designers quickly proved that it would cost $800,000 to produce the project that had been described. The administration realized that the existing 3,500-square-foot space was far too small to take advantage of the Campus Market's full business potential. Eventually, after studying a pro forma submitted by Webb Design that

included all the construction and furniture, fixtures, and equipment (FF&E) costs, and a detailed business plan, they approved increasing the market's footprint to nearly 6,500 square feet—and the budget to $1.2 million.

The facility is broken into foodservice sections along the left side of the space; specialty packaged foods displayed on round display units and shelving in the center of the room; beverages, milk products, and frozen foods on the back wall; and produce and convenience items along the right side of the space (see facing page).

The foodservice side of the market includes a coffee bar, a grill station, a deli, and a pizza area. At the coffee bar, customers can either get made-to-order espresso or pour brewed coffee from glass pots. At the grill station, they can pick up sandwiches from a hot well, including a signature barbecue meat sandwich. Instead of being prepared on an al fresco grill, as in the past, the meat is cooked on a gas-fired charbroiler with a hickory wood chamber that imparts a smoky flavor to the foods cooked above it. This equipment, much easier to control than a wood-burning grill, was chosen with the transient student labor force in mind. Similarly, for pizzas, the designers installed a conveyorized Impinger oven instead of a wood-fired oven, which would require much

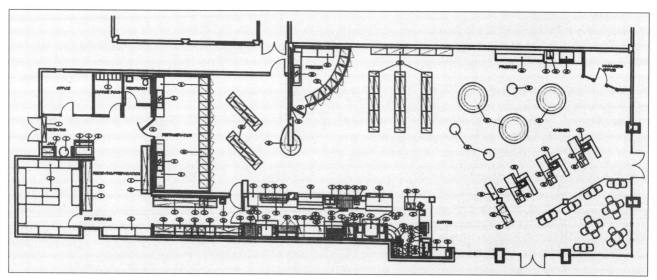

Cal Poly Campus Market floorplan.
(Courtesy of Webb Foodservice Design Consultants, Inc.)

Cal Poly's Campus Market showcases foods produced by the university's agricultural program and gives the campus community an inviting spot for a quick bite.
(Photo by Dave Cook)

more attention. With the Impinger oven, the cook simply places the raw pizza on one end of the conveyor belt; seven minutes later, the pizza emerges perfectly baked.

Much of the ambience of the space is created by the vivid food displays. In addition, the architects commissioned a 40-foot mural that depicts many of the crops and livestock raised by the students on campus.

The renovated facility has the appeal of a modern specialty food market. In late 1999, it was generating three thousand transactions daily, an increase of volume 25 percent over the business plan projection.

Calle Ocho

NEW YORK

Designer: Jeffrey Beers International, New York
Owners: Jeff Kaddish and Paul Zweben
Year opened: 1998
Number of seats: dining room, 150; private rooms, 30; bar, 35
FOH: 4,180 square feet
BOH: 1,757 square feet
Service styles: tableservice
Menu: Nuevo Latino with Cuban influence

Calle Ocho is the type of restaurant that Robert Redford's character in the 1990 movie *Havana* would have hung out in. Redford played a gambler looking for one last score before Battista fell from power. One can imagine him plotting in one of the curved booths that line the north wall of Calle Ocho's dining room.

From a design perspective, the segmented ground-floor space presented the greatest challenges to the Jeffrey Beers International design team. The designers placed the bar at the rather narrow entry and a C-shaped lounge area in a nook that rises six steps beyond the bar. The lounge is flanked with a light wall embedded with color rounds of art glass that resemble the bottoms of bottles. On an adjoining wall, a floating mirror is seemingly suspended in a field of bamboo.

Guests next pass through a narrow corridor flanked by rest rooms and emerge into a dining room with a vaulted ceiling, vibrant colors, and an oversized fireplace at the far end.

Calle Ocho was named after the bodega-lined 8th Street in Miami, but it is much more elegant. The concept involved refining typical Cuban cuisine and presenting it in a stylish, contemporary environment. "Calle Ocho is an imaginative journey to a modern, extravagant Cuba, had the revolution never occurred," says designer Jeffrey Beers. "The vast space has been divided into a series of sumptuous areas with a saturated palette of color, texture, and material, leading from the intimate bar-lounge into the soaring main dining room."

The bar area echoes Cuba's sultry Caribbean atmos-

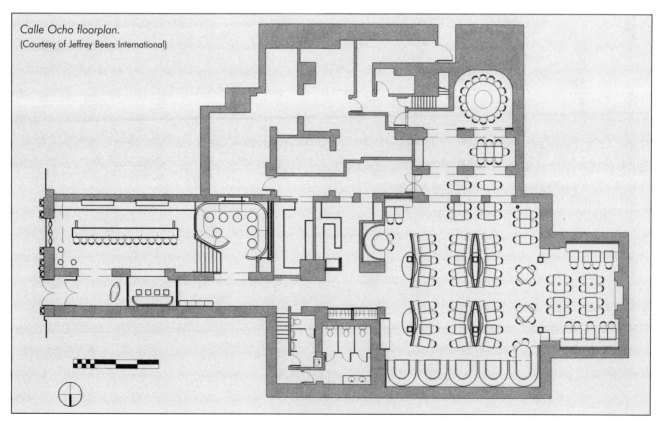

Calle Ocho floorplan.
(Courtesy of Jeffrey Beers International)

New York City's Calle Ocho evokes an imaginary Havana.
(Photo by David M. Joseph)

phere. A rich mahogany bartop, fronted with concrete and set on blackened steel legs, is placed against a whitewashed brick wall. Overhead, two oversized ceiling fans spin lazily against a vibrant, lime-colored ceiling. Two raised seating areas, a cozy nook set directly across from the bar and the C-shaped lounge, offer guests plush, comfortable seating for intimate conversation or for viewing the action at the bar.

Entering the main dining room from the sensuality of the bar and lounge feels like stepping onto a dance floor. The space gives the illusion of extending much higher than the glowing, curvaceous louvered ceiling that drives people's eyes to the far end of the room. Columns of perforated metal with underlying scrollwork support giant mambo lampshades that glow with light. Rich fruit colors on upholstered bench-style seating in the center of the room stand out against the dark cherry floor. A hand-painted mural of gigantic fruits and

oversized cigar-box labels commands the wall above rounded booths. At the far end of the dining room stands a two-story-high wall of heat-patinated copper panels that surround a century-old terra-cotta tile fireplace.

The slatted ceiling (above) serves as more than a design element. The arched slats sit below a skylight—an uncommon architectural feature on the first floor of buildings in Manhattan—that runs the length of the room. They help mitigate the glare of natural light entering the space during the day and minimize heat buildup.

China Grill/Rock Lobster

LAS VEGAS

CHINA GRILL:
Designer: Jeffrey Beers International, New York
Owner: Jeffrey Chodorow
Year opened: 1999
Number of seats: dining room, 180; private
   rooms, 45; bar, 14
FOH: ~8,000 square feet
BOH: ~3,800 square feet
Service styles: tableservice and family style
Menu: French and Southeast Asian fusion

ROCK LOBSTER:
Number of seats: dining room, 180;
   café bar, 28
FOH: 4,300 square feet
BOH: 800 square feet
Service styles: conveyor belt, robot waiters
Menu: seafood, sushi, and other café fare

This is a story of two separate yet intertwined restaurants located in the Mandalay Bay Casino in Las Vegas. One of the restaurants is China Grill, which has sister locations in New York and Miami's South Beach. The second restaurant, called Rock Lobster (initially named And Zen Sum), is a more casual café with communal tables. Both are accessed from the casino concourse, which is home to numerous other restaurants and lounges.

Rock Lobster's conveyorized sushi bar is in keeping with its brightly lit, futuristic interior.
(Photo © Paul Warchol)

From the exterior, both China Grill and Rock Lobster are fronted by a moat incorporating an abstract interior landscape. To reach them, people walk over a drawbridge. From there, the similarities between the two restaurants end.

The dramatic entrance to China Grill juxtaposes various materials, shapes, and colors. A Chinese-red porte cochere extends from the entryway. It is supported by cylindrical anodized-aluminum posts that reach down to a glass-brick walkway leading into the restaurant.

At China Grill Las Vegas, a laser projection system enlivens the ceiling above the main dining area.
(Photo © Paul Warchol)

In the foyer, a broad, three-step staircase descends from a black terrazzo-floored entry level to an oversized bar with seating upholstered in Beaujolais-colored crushed velvet. Floating above much of the bar area are large cream-colored, waferlike light elements that resemble fried shrimp chips. A delicate lamp base fashioned from antique bronze metal rods is tied into an electric box in the floor and supports clusters of these light elements. The seating is a mix of single chairs and two-person settees lined in facing rows. Between each facing row of seats are rectangular tables. More intimate seating is available at curved booths that hug two of the walls of the bar. A custom carpet lining the floor in the middle of the bar and the fabric covering on the seats themselves are the only materials that absorb sound in this high-style space. It is meant to buzz with the sights and sounds of fashionable diners.

In the center of the restaurant is a truncated conical

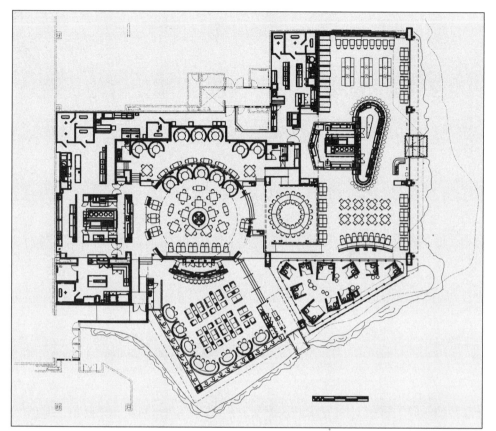

China Grill Las Vegas/
Rock Lobster floorplan.
(Courtesty of Jeffery Beers International)

Rock Lobster is made from of a series of aluminum security walls that roll up like a garage door. When the wall is open, it looks like an opening in the window wall system. This entry looks onto the casino concourse. Inside the restaurant, Rock Lobster is a study in futuristic geometry. Lemon-tinted light boxes are interspersed on a wall of off-white panels to form a random checkerboard. Most of the seating is at long common tables lined with cushioned bench seats and punctuated with boxy floor lamps with square, tangerine-colored shades. There is also some booth seating. Translucent, vinyl-coated fabric panels that rise above booth backs are stretched like awnings by a stainless-steel tubing frame.

The most futuristic design element of Rock Lobster is the sushi bar, where plates of food emerge from a sushi kitchen on a continuous conveyor belt that glides in front of seated guests. A three-sided video screen with three projectors over the bar energizes the space with a continuous play of text and video images.

Tying these restaurants together is a triangular-shaped "garden" of ten freestanding unisex toilets that designer Jeffrey Beers calls pavilions. Guests from China Grill and Rock Lobster walk through giant stainless-steel beaded curtains to get here and wait their turn sitting on round zebrawood stools. Translucent glass on parts of the pavilion exterior cause these toilet enclosures to glow when occupied.

form covered with dark mahogany paneling that defines a central seating area. Its inside walls are covered with wire-cloth panels made out of brass, creating the visual effect of an eighteenth-century gold-leaf screen. The ceiling of this area is formed with a wire-mesh and paper convex orb and lit from above to create a warm glow. Images are projected onto the bottom side of the orb from a laser hidden in the middle of a round, high-backed banquette in the center of the room, creating an ever-changing light show. A second seating section on a slightly elevated platform incorporates deuces and rounded booth seating. Diners who sit here and in the bar area can view the light show through large openings in the conical form that defines the central dining space.

China Grill and Rock Lobster have completely different design treatments, save for the perforated stainless-steel ceiling panels found throughout both restaurants. The entry wall of

City Hall

NEW YORK

Designer: Bogdanow Partners Architects, PC, New York
Owner: Chef Henry Meer
Year opened: 1998
Number of seats: dining room, 115; oyster bar, 7; bar, 50; Rose Room, 35; Granite Room, 100
FOH: ~9,000 square feet
Downstairs kitchen: 1,500 square feet
Upstairs kitchen: 1,500 square feet
Service styles: tableservice, banquet service
Menu: classic New York grilled items and raw seafood

Much of City Hall's concept is rooted in chef-owner Henry Meer's love for Manhattan, past and present. "I was born in Manhattan and I am a passionate New Yorker," says Meer. When he first saw the cast-iron building at 131 Duane Street in New York's historic Tribeca district—originally opened as manufacturing facility in 1863—it immediately conjured up images of traditional New York restaurants, places where cuisine was about "ice-cold oysters and perfectly grilled steaks." His design brief to Bogdanow Partners Architects was to create a warm, welcoming environment that helped guests leave the daily grind behind. "We wanted the restaurant to be a refuge, even it was just for an hour's lunch," says Meer.

City Hall restaurant updates the feeling of old New York with a comfortable, contemporary design.
(Photo © Peter Aaron/Esto)

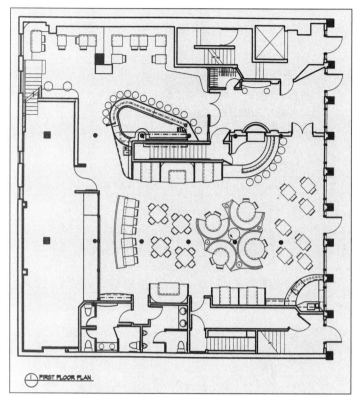

City Hall restaurant first-floor floorplan.
(Courtesy of Bogdanow Partners Architects, PC)

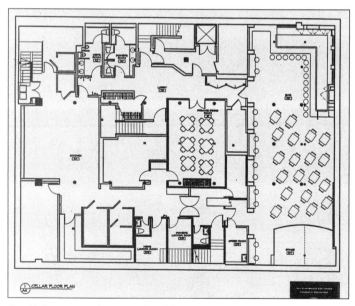

City Hall restaurant basement-level floorplan.
(Courtesy of Bogdanow Partners Architects, PC)

The outcome is a grand-scale New York restaurant that evokes the city's past while ensconcing diners in contemporary comfort.

City Hall's facade and entrance lobby are both landmark and quite traditional. The restoration of the facade is true to the neoclassical style of the 1860s, with 9 classic arches spanning a 75-foot width along the street. Each of the arches rests on stately Corinthian columns, which also appear inside the restaurant.

The spacious entry foyer, with a travertine floor, cast-iron columns, and high ceilings, resembles a historic hotel lobby. It is a welcome center and a hub of activity for arriving and departing guests. From here, people flow to one of three areas: dining room, bar (where there are tables for diners who wish to smoke), or private function spaces one floor below. Guests who are visiting the bar or public dining areas are directed to the coatroom behind the host stand, while those going to the private function rooms use a separate coatroom on the basement level. This arrangement requires staff for two coatrooms but helps achieve a smooth flow through the restaurant because function guests can move through the entry area without getting in the way of the dining and bar guests. The basement level also has separate rest rooms for function room guests. City Hall has nine rest rooms in all, which is an unaccustomed luxury.

Guests pass a fresh fish and seafood display en route to the main dining room. With its 15-foot ceilings and simple black steel chandeliers, the dining room feels expansive. Eyes are drawn to a series of backlit black and white poster-size photographs of old New York that hang high on the walls. Meer persuaded the curators at the Museum of the City of New York and the New York City New York Archives to allow him access to their archived photos, many taken by such photographers as Bernice Abbot and Walter Rosenblum in the 1930s. (The photographs are documented on the back of the menu.) Marching down the middle of the room is a row of structural cast-iron columns; clustered around one of them is a cloverleaf of circular banquettes. A mix of freestanding and booth seats round out the seating mix.

Comfort was a paramount design concern. Tables are generously spaced—"a huge luxury in New York," notes Meer. The designers specified a double layer of padding on the chairs, an acoustic ceiling treatment that mutes noise, and a black, gold, and burgundy color scheme that is an updated interpretation of the old-style steakhouse. "We wanted the restaurant to appeal to women as well as to men," says Larry Bogdanow. "We chose pearwood for the

City Hall's well-stocked coffee station
is right up front in the dining room.
(Photo by Joseph Durocher)

tabletops, which has warm, medium tones that appeal to everyone, instead of traditional dark woods like mahogany and walnut that have more of a men's club feel."

Two prominent service bars are housed in the dining room. The oyster bar, placed immediately inside the entry door, is where people can enjoy such items as a chilled platter of fresh oysters, an assortment of fruits de mer, or a steam-kettle pan roast prepared to order from a variety of seafood. While it offers stools for seven people, the oyster bar also functions as a showcase in its own right. It has a scalloped zinc face, a counter made of terrazzo and mother-of-pearl, and working chowder kettles behind the counter.

The second service bar, one that is hidden from view in most restaurants, is the coffee bar. This is not a place for guests to sit on a stool to sip a cup of coffee; rather, it is Meer's answer to the challenge of giving each diner a good cup of java at the end of the meal. "In most restaurants," he says, "preparing coffee is left up to whichever server finds the coffeepot empty. It is a chore that they take no pride in." Not so at City Hall, where a dedicated staff member is charged with making all coffees.

To help connect the kitchen and the guests, three windows give a glimpse into the back of the house. A fourth window looks directly into the meat-aging cooler, where prime wholesale cuts of beef are aged for 21 days. "New Yorkers often don't like the noise of an open kitchen," says Bogdanow. "We like to use glass to provide a view and then control that view."

City Hall's cozy bar area has three seating options: bar stools at the zinc-topped bar, a seating area of rich pearwood tables and banquettes that border an exposed brick wall opposite the bar, and a mezzanine-level lounge with upholstered couches and chairs.

Meer credits much of City Hall's success to the restaurant's banquet space, which consists of two private dining rooms and a dedicated kitchen on the basement level. The smaller Rose Room features a vaulted ceiling made of orange-red Venetian stucco, stone floors, and cherry cabinetry. The larger Granite Room was carved out of found space that sits under the sidewalk. Here, exposed brick and raw fieldstone walls, cast-iron columns, and a ceiling that opens to the granite-slab undersides of the sidewalk above reflect the original nineteenth-century architecture. In one corner of the room is an L-shaped bar fashioned from bricks saved from demolition elsewhere in the building. While it looks like Al Capone would feel at home here, the Granite Room is also outfitted with unobtrusive floor ports that hold ISDN lines and video and audiovisual hookups, and it has a small stage with a state-of-the-art sound and projection system.

Chipotle Mexican Grill, Store #4

DENVER, COLORADO

Designer: Brand Gould, Director of Design and Development, Chipotle Mexican Grill, Inc.

Owner: Steve Ells, CEO, Chipotle Mexican Grill, Inc.

Year opened: 1996 (fourth store in a chain of over 80)

Number of seats: dining room, 55

FOH: 1,119 square feet

BOH: 1,227 square feet

Service styles: quick service made to order

Menu: custom-made burritos and tacos

Chipotle Mexican Grill is a fast-growing chain of restaurants that serve fresh food fast. As of January 2000, the chain comprised 80+ restaurants; 33 of these opened in 1999 after McDonald's purchased a 40 percent minority interest in the business.

The restaurants share a clean, contemporary look created by Chipotle Director of Design and Development Brand Gould and his in-house design team. Although each is tai-lored to its location, they all sport such materials as corrugated metal, birch veneer plywood, glass, and exposed elements like steel piping and ductwork. "We use a common vocabulary of design elements that are orchestrated differently in each space we go into," says Gould. CEO Steve Ells has said that design is one of the chain's key selling points.

Asked to identify which restaurant best exemplified the Chipotle design aesthetic, Gould picked unit #4, located in

an urban neighborhood of residences and businesses. When asked about the design, he began by describing how the food is prepared and served. Customers place their orders at a tortilla station. A warm tortilla or taco is placed on the makeup counter and begins to move toward the cashier. Customers travel along with the item, indicating the types of ingredients they want added. At the cashier station, guests pick up their finished burrito or taco, select their drinks, and pay. One of the greatest design challenges was trying to keep the queue away from seated diners—no small task during peak serving periods.

The back-of-the-house design is straightforward and functional. Unlike most quick service restaurants (QSR) operations, there is no freezer (none of the Chipotle restaurants has a freezer because all food is fresh). As in all Chipotle units, the open display kitchen has three parallel components. The first level is the holding and assembly line. Immediately behind that line is the chefs' table, which they use to prep foods before cooking and to pass over foods to the serving staff. Behind this table is the production line, where chefs are continually cooking small batches of fillings as the serving line staff orders them up. "Our goal is to keep the preparation and cooking in full view of the customers," notes Gould.

This particular location was not inherently interesting. It had a long, narrow dining room measuring roughly 70 by 17 feet and an extremely low ceiling of just 9 feet. The designers used a community table, dividers, and bench seating to help break up the space. They covered the ceiling with inexpensive gypsum board, allowed ductwork to poke through, and added slightly arched canopies with built-in lighting to create architectural interest and further fragment the tunnel-like room. Along the left side of the space, they replaced small windows with large glass doors to induce a more expansive feeling.

The floor slabs are acid-stained concrete with a sealer. Acid stain produces a floor color called padre brown, which is a brownish-red burnt umber. The intensity of the color on any part of the floor depends on the lime content of the concrete and what was previously on top of the concrete flooring: The color is intentionally uneven. The tables and chairs are

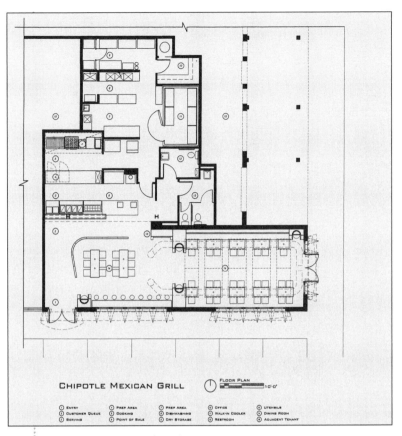

Chipotle Mexican Grill floorplan
(design © Chipotle Mexican Grill, Inc., 2000)

fashioned from metal tubing, stainless steel, and plywood. Illumination is provided by off-the-shelf lights fitted with par-20 lamps. As in all Chipotle restaurants, corrugated barn roofing is used as wainscoting, and trash receptacles, rather than being identified by signage, are identified by vertical architectural elements.

In quick-service restaurants like Chipotle, guests are not encouraged to linger. High sound levels, caused by hard surfaces and music, play an important role in helping to turn tables in less than 30 minutes. That quick turnover rate is also helped by the seating itself. There are no pads on the seats. Flat plywood chairs and booths with a back pitch of just one inch keep customers from lounging but provide enough comfort for a short meal.

Unlike other operations that serve burritos and tacos, there are no references to south of the border. "While the food has a Mexican spin," Gould comments, "we are not trying to do anything that looks Mexican or southwestern. I think this helps us roll out our design across different parts of the country, because we can easily adapt the style to different locations."

*Chipotle's contemporary interior is designed
for high traffic and low maintenance.*
(Photo © Steven Adams Photography, Denver, CO;
design © Chipotle Mexican Grill, Inc., 2000)

Le Cirque 2000

NEW YORK

Designer: Adam D. Tihany International Ltd., New York
Owner: Sirio Maccioni
Year opened: 1997
Number of seats: dining room, 108; private dining, 200; bar, 54
FOH: 4,042 square feet
BOH: 4,300 square feet
Service style: French tableservice
Menu: classic French

Reincarnation. That's what Le Cirque 2000 is all about. It's a rebirth of the long-adored Le Cirque restaurant, which first opened in New York in 1974. It is an innovative interpretation of the restaurants in the Villard Houses, built in 1882, that once housed the Archdiocese of New York in opulent splendor and are now linked with the New York Palace Hotel.

This was where Le Cirque 2000, under the watchful eyes of ringmaster Sirio Maccioni and designer Adam Tihany, pitched its tent. Tihany created a circus that floats in the space, a circus that juxtaposes the old with the new in a high-wire act that intrigues all who buy a ticket for the show.

Tihany worked with spaces plastered with gold-leaf covered ceilings, intricately carved wooden walls, and century-old chandeliers. Landmark restrictions prohibited him from piercing the walls, floors, or ceilings. "Turning this restriction into an asset, our solution was to treat this august space as if a circus had been unpacked inside of it," he says. The design juxtaposes the historic architectural backdrop with fanciful, modern furnishings, all custom-designed for the space.

"No shape, no color was too bold," says Tihany. In the bar, oversized neon rings dance overhead between giant torchères, fashioned from metal and Plexiglas, that seemingly reach for the ceiling. The base of the front bar and the back bar glow with translucent panels. Guests recline in plush three-legged armchairs.

Diners proceed to either the Hunt Room or the Madison Room. In the leather and red-hued Hunt Room, red and white striped light towers rise from the checkerboard-covered banquette backs. In the Madison Room, plush purple and blue chairs and multicolored lighting elements stand out against a glittering coffered gold ceiling. High-backed Tihany-designed chairs in both rooms feature clown button details down their backs.

The bar area at Le Cirque 2000.
(Photo © Peter Paige Photography)

Le Cirque Las Vegas

LAS VEGAS

Designer: Adam D. Tihany International Ltd.,
New York
Owner: Sirio Maccioni
Year opened: 1998
Number of seats: dining room, 75; bar, 13
FOH: 2,450 square feet
BOH: ~2,000 square feet
Service style: French tableservice
Menu: classic French

Le Cirque Las Vegas, located in the Bellagio Hotel and Casino, presented Adam Tihany with a different set of challenges from those he faced when designing Le Cirque 2000 in New York. "Although there were no landmark issues to address, this time I was designing not only once more for the world's greatest restaurateur/showman, Sirio Maccioni, but also for the world's most discerning hotelier, Steve Wynn," he says. Tihany's solution was to create the flavor of a seventeenth-century traveling circus with luxurious materials and custom murals. The resulting design is one of a kind, yet it evokes the same Le Cirque spirit found in the New York establishment.

In a city where glitz is ubiquitous, Le Cirque Las Vegas is a haven for fine dining, a kind of oasis-with-an-attitude where people can escape the larger-than-life Las Vegas aesthetic. They enter the vaultlike front doors, traverse the star-studded entry with its rich brown and gold tone accents, and arrive in a compact and hushed bar where a jacket-and-tie policy is strictly enforced.

In the bar, the decor incorporates the circus motif in the wine display case, on the floor, and in the large oval overhead fixture, built of colorful art glass and backlit to create a warm glow in the space. Seven red and gold striped armchair stools surround the half-round bar.

The dining room is the center ring of this opulent circus. Here, a billowy, multicolored tented ceiling of glowing raw silk creates a cozy feeling. Circus murals by Paulin Paris surround the room and set the stage for the theatrical food presentations that are a Maccioni hallmark. Deeply padded armchairs keep guests comfortable for five-course meals that can last all evening. Tables appear somewhat close together, but the acoustics of the room ensure a feeling of privacy. Lighting is a mix of downlights and diffused light that filters through the ceiling fabric.

The bar area at Le Cirque Las Vegas.
(Photo © Mark Ballogg, Steinkamp/Ballogg Photography, Chicago)

Ciudad

LOS ANGELES

Designer: Schweitzer BIM, Inc., Los Angeles
Owners: Chefs Susan Feniger and Mary Sue
  Milliken
Year opened: 1998
Number of seats: dining room, 84;
  patio,108; bar/cantina, 44
FOH: 5,100 square feet, plus patio
BOH: 3,100 square feet
Service style: tableservice
Menu: South American classics and creative
  Latin fusion

Historically, good restaurants are few and far between in downtown Los Angeles. But Mary Sue Milliken and Susan Feniger saw an opportunity to capitalize on a changing market and a changing cityscape when they worked with Schweitzer BIM to transform a former Southwestern-themed lunch place into a hip destination restaurant.

The site the owners chose for Ciudad is directly across from the 1,354-room Westin Bonaventure Hotel—the largest hotel in Los Angeles—and close to the Staples Center arena. It had been a lunchtime restaurant for surrounding businesses since 1968; the last restaurant tenant shuttered the doors in 1994. In the intervening years, an increasing number of young Angelinos moved much closer to the city center. "We saw the potential not only for a downtown lunch crowd but for people coming to the area to go to the theater, museums, and concerts," says architect Josh Schweitzer.

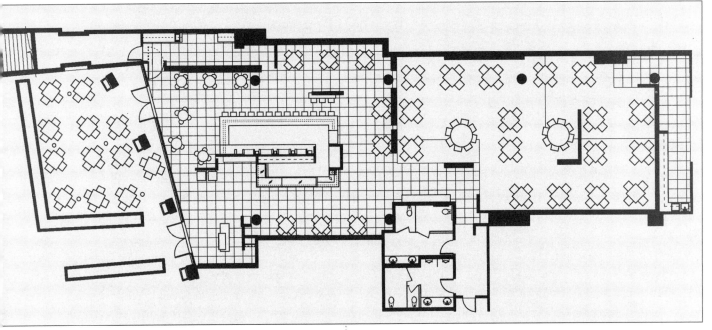

Ciudad floorplan.
(Courtesy of Schweitzer BIM, Inc.)

The space presented many challenges. It was dark and gloomy, with fake beams and adobe references. The only natural light came from a low strip of windows that overlooked a front patio area, and the main back room was underground. Nearly everything had to be gutted before construction. While this gave Schweitzer the opportunity to work from the ground up, he also had to work with a modest $650,000 budget.

Schweitzer wanted to push the design in the same way the chef-owners wanted to push the food. This is not a Mexican joint; rather, it features South American, Spanish, and Cuban cuisines, with a nod to the food's European roots. Schweitzer's design plays off the emerging modernism that transformed world architecture in the 1950s and 1960s. To that aesthetic he added playful colors and integrated mural work, an important design element in Latin countries 40 years ago. Artists Su Huntley and Donna Muir created the Miró-like murals that animate Ciudad's walls, ceilings, and room dividers.

Ciudad's low ceiling over the bar area jumps to 18 feet in the dining room, where it explodes in a variety of heights, textures, and colors. "Ceilings," notes Schweitzer, "are like free space. You don't have to worry about using them to fit in another table or more chairs. So I sculpted the ceiling to cre-

ate a skyscape." In this cavelike room, the architect created faux skylights by punching holes in the ceiling. He painted the surfaces above light blue and lit them to give the appearance of real skylights. In some places, colorful drywall backdrops contrast with raw concrete. In others, the surfaces are tied together by murals painted on the concrete.

Bright color animates the restaurant. Schweitzer chose yellow as the predominant color "because it lightens up the space and is completely different from what people would expect in an underground room." Large, boxy light fixtures play with form and color. Inside the lamps, low-wattage bulbs in red, yellow, orange, and pink add more light and warmth to the space.

Because Milliken and Feniger periodically use the space to conduct cooking classes, Schweitzer could not divide the dining area to help control sound levels. Carpeting helps, but the restaurant can be noisy. "It plays a little rough on some of the businessmen clientele, but for the young, hip crowd who come to Ciudad for an evening out, it works," Schweitzer comments. "There's a sense of exhilaration that happens with the high noise level."

*Ciudad's bold, quirky design reflects the
chef-owners' style of cooking.*
(Photo by Douglas Hill)

Credit Suisse First Boston: On Nine Employee Dining

LONDON

Foodservice design: Cini-Little International, Inc., Rockville, MD
Interior design: Parker Roberts Design Associates, London
Owner: Credit Suisse First Boston
Year opened: 1999
Number of seats: dining room, 740
FOH (including servery): 19,547 square feet
BOH: 3,700 square feet
Service styles: market concept, servery-style cafeteria
Menu: grilled items, pizza and pasta, carvery, deli

The planning, design, and installation of the On Nine Restaurant in the Credit Suisse First Boston (CSFB) bank in London was an integral part of what the owners dubbed Project New World. This effort included the total renovation of an existing 20-floor building, the construction and fitting out of an extension building, and the fitting out of a new linking building.

Throughout the project, staff workers were relocated from one area to another, with a total of 16,200 staff moves over the two-year term of the project. The foodservice operations in each of the three buildings needed to function without interruption in support of the relocation program. The On Nine Restaurant was the most important food outlet in this chess game because of its size and location in the complex.

The market-concept servery at Credit Suisse First Boston.
(Photo courtesy of Cini-Little International, Inc.)

A mandate given by CSFB to the foodservice designers, headed by Bob Plumb of Cini-Little, was that the space required a high level of design flexibility so that any catering company could operate the facilities. One of the most complex issues addressed by the design team related to the ventilation system. The challenge was to develop a system that allowed the caterer to use the full extent of the servery counters for either cooking or serving food without compromising effective ventilation to the area. The ventilation design also had to support a fully flexible servery design with removable hot plates and sneeze screens.

To make sure the ventilation design was going to work, the foodservice designers developed a full-size mock-up of the system and checked the airflow rates. During this testing phase, they adjusted the exhaust and makeup airflow rates of the system to obtain maximum exhaust.

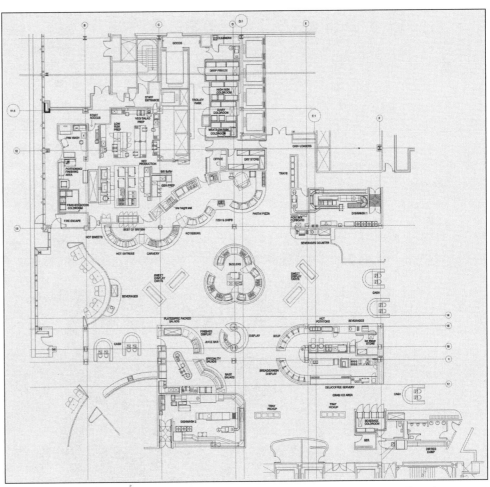

Credit Suisse First Boston floorplan.
(Courtesy of Cini-Little International, Inc.)

The ventilation layout was divided into two areas: the island servery, which is a series of service stations remote from the kitchen, and the main servery counter, which backs up to the kitchen. At this main servery counter, the ventilation system had to accommodate cooking on the servery line as well as in the back of the house.

Cini-Little divided both servery areas into cells, each of which can be controlled centrally with a shut-off damper. The damper adjusts the amount of air removed from each cell. The island servery has 17 identical cells. The control requirements were simplified because each cell has the same static pressure due to the design of the canopy (facing page). The exhaust formula is based on any mix of nine cells—management requires that only nine cells operate at any one time; when shifting between cells, one shuts down before a new one is activated.

The design of the second exhaust system was a bit more complex. The main servery has 16 cells but, because of the design, each has a different static pressure. To adjust

for this, a pressure transducer was added to monitor the pressure differential across the grease filter in each cell to ensure optimal airflow. The same types of control parameters were set up as in the island servery. All the controls for both serveries are centralized on a single panel located in the main kitchen.

The island servery is totally flexible, with no fixed service points. The same is true of the main servery, save for two areas: a fixed grill area for steaks and burgers, and the pizza/pasta station, which is built around a 4,000-pound wood-burning pizza oven. Approximately 70 percent of all hot foods are cooked to order. Additional equipment includes custom-built induction cook units that are used for stir-frying, undercounter refrigeration units to hold raw ingredients, deli makeup equipment, and equipment for beverage service.

Elvis Presley's Memphis

MEMPHIS, TENNESSEE

Designer: Aumiller Youngquist, PC, Mt. Prospect, Illinois
Owner: Elvis Presley's Memphis L.L.C.
Year opened: 1997
Number of seats: dining room, 180; private rooms, 50; bar, 90; terrace, 75
FOH: 7,500 square feet
BOH: 5,000 square feet
Service style: tableservice
Menu: contemporary Southern cuisine

How do you design a restaurant that looks like a place where a rock-and-roll icon would have hung out? How do you make the interiors memorable for those who followed his career? These were two of the most significant challenges faced by the team of Aumiller Youngquist when they were commissioned to design Elvis Presley's Memphis. "We were determined to keep the design from becoming a stereotype," says Bill Aumiller. "Another concern," notes Keith Youngquist, "is that fans saw [Elvis] in different ways depending on which part of his career they followed. So each part of his life is depicted in the design."

The restaurant is not a museum, although many of the details are priceless elements taken from "The King's" private life. For example, guests can shoot pool on the table at which Elvis played with the Beatles during their one and only meeting. Memorabilia includes such items as Elvis's leather biker jacket and Las Vegas jumpsuit (displayed in cases lit with a fiber-optic lighting system that keeps the lamp—and its accompanying heat—outside the cabinet). Several similarities to the design of Graceland—Presley's personal residence, now an attraction—such as the fabric-covered walls found in some areas of the restaurant, were incorporated as well.

The project was a renovation of an existing building on Beale Street—the former Lansky Brothers Clothing Store, where Elvis purchased the suits that he wore on the Ed Sullivan Show. Aumiller and Youngquist (both architects) kept the exterior nearly intact. They gutted the interior but kept an eye out for anything that could be salvaged and used for the new design. This they did with some of the brick arches and walls that appear in various parts of the space. To help with the challenges of operating a two-story restaurant, they added a finishing kitchen to the ground floor.

Taking a walk through Elvis Presley's Memphis is like taking a trip through the time-

Elvis Presley's Memphis is the kind of place "the King" would have liked.
(Photo by Keith Youngquist)

line of the performer's life. The design for each room relates to his tastes during a given decade. Moving through the space, guests can find the era that they enjoy or feel most comfortable with. Carpeting is used as an acoustical treatment on both levels, except on the floor in the stage area (called the Memphis Showroom). While the designers were concerned about high noise levels, performers such as Jewel and Los Lobos have commented on how well the acoustics work for their music. Volume levels are highest in the stage area, lower in the more distant carpeted spaces, where the music softens to a pleasant level each evening when the bands strike up around eight or nine o'clock.

Over the stage is a huge video screen that is joined with 20 other monitors strategically placed throughout the restaurant so that nearly all diners have a view. Throughout the day, video clips are played on the monitors. When live performers come on stage, a camera broadcasts the action to the remote monitors so that it can be seen from every seat in the house.

A tremendous amount of theatrical lighting is used in the Memphis Showroom. The restaurant's main lighting focus is here as well: a chandelier that was originally made for a Saudi prince. "We wanted to emulate the chandelier that hung over Elvis's dining room table," says Keith Youngquist. To highlight the chandelier as a visual focal point, the designers used downlighting to brighten the tabletops but kept illumination levels low elsewhere in the stage area.

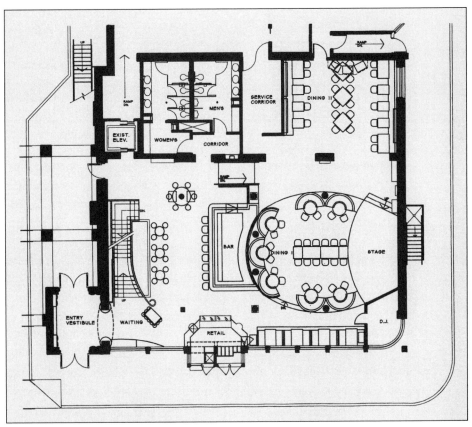

Elvis Presley's Memphis first-floor floorplan.
(Courtesy of Aumiller Youngquist)

Elvis Presley's Memphis second-floor floorplan.
(Courtesy of Aumiller Youngquist)

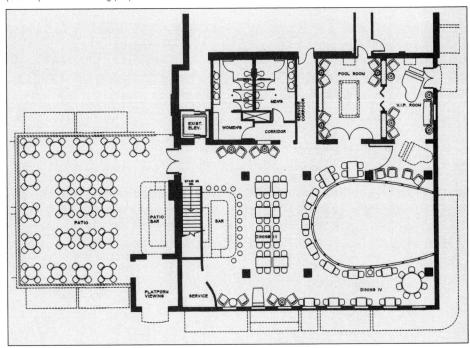

Farallon

SAN FRANCISCO

Designer: Pat Kuleto, San Francisco
Owners: Chef Mark Franz; Pat Kuleto
Year opened: 1997
Number of seats: dining room, 200; private
    dining, 222; bar, 22
FOH: 6,872 square feet
BOH: 7,203 square feet
Service style: tableservice
Menu: fresh seafood and other farm-fresh
    products, meat, and game

"I pushed the envelope at Farallon," says designer-owner Pat Kuleto, "because I thought there were no exciting seafood restaurant designs in San Francisco. Every seafood restaurant had the same old classic look." Kuleto and his chef-partner Mark Franz had 100 percent control over the project, so Kuleto was able to implement all his design ideas. Franz and Kuleto spent months discussing details of the project; for much of that time they worked without drawings, just with ideas in their heads. The outcome of their efforts is an extravagant undersea fantasy reminiscent of *Twenty-Thousand Leagues Under the Sea*. Details include suspended lights that look like jellyfish, bar stools shaped like octopi, illuminated kelp pillars, and sandy-colored flooring with inset marble-tiled fish.

Much of Farallon's design concept stems from Kuleto's and Franz's love of the ocean; they both have long histories as sailing, fishing, and diving enthusiasts. The space itself is in a building designed in 1925 by Meyer and Johnson as an Elk Club's saltwater plunge room.

"The original layout of the space was almost impossi-ble to work with," notes Kuleto. Trying to tie the 22-seat Jelly Bar, located at the front right of the space, into the rest of the restaurant posed the first challenge. The staircase leading to balcony seating posed the second problem. Yet another challenge was the installation of the jellyfish lighting fixtures, made in New York; they weigh tons. Kuleto was continually mindful of earthquake concerns and made everything super-strong. For example, all the substructures are steel. The kitchen layout also posed challenges because it had to be spread over two floors due to limited space on the main floor.

After walking through the Jelly Bar, guests continue past a curved staircase whose sweeping carriage shines with 50,000 caviarlike, iridescent indigo-blue marbles. The ceiling here is painted deep blue to evoke the sky at twilight overlooking an underwater milieu. Tucked behind the staircase is a dining area known as the Nautilus Room, fitted with six intimate booths in a space that resembles the inside of a nautilus shell. The light fixtures here are made with barnacles, some glass and some real.

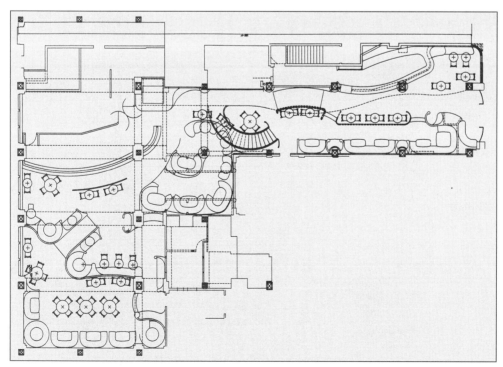

Farallon floorplan.
(Courtesy of Pat Kuleto Restaurants)

*Farallon's sea-urchin chandeliers express
the restaurant's undersea fantasy theme.*
(Photo by Dennis Anderson, © Pat Kuleto Restaurants)

The largest dining area is the Pool Room, completely accessible via ramps. Here, Kuleto designed giant light fixtures that resemble sea urchins and commissioned three paintings portraying the San Francisco wharf at the turn of the century. Curved booths and freestanding tables offer a variety of seating options. To increase seating flexibility, several tables quickly convert from a four-top to a six-top with a roll-out extension. An elaborately painted mosaic design of mermaids, circa 1925 and credited originally to Anthony Heinsberger, was fully restored and graces three Gothic arches. In the building's original incarnation, the arches capped the former two-story space above a pool that is still located in the basement of the building.

Also in the Pool Room is an open kitchen that continues the design with hammered copper and metal fish scales above the exhaust hood and hand-blown glass light fixtures that look like blue squid. A ten-seat semiprivate dining area off the Pool Room sits next to the restaurant's wine cellar.

Jardinière

SAN FRANCISCO

Designer: Pat Kuleto, San Francisco
Owners: Chef Traci Des Jardins and Pat Kuleto
Year opened: 1997
Number of seats: dining room, 150; private
  rooms, 15; bar, 40
FOH: 4,415 square feet
BOH: 3,233 square feet
Service style: tableservice
Menu: French-California with fresh, seasonal
  ingredients; daily selection of American
  and European cheeses

Jardinière, located in a corner landmark building near San Francisco's Civic Center—with the opera house on one corner and the symphony on the other—is an elegant two-story restaurant created as a celebration of food, design, and the good life. Designer-owner Pat Kuleto collaborated with chef-owner Traci Des Jardins to create a sexy, clublike interior warmed by deep red carpet, heavy aubergine velvet draperies, mahogany columns, and brick walls.

A wood and glass front door with a cocktail-glass design and an entry floor inlaid with marble lead guests immediately to the restaurant's oval mahogany and black marble-topped bar in the center of the restaurant. The celebratory cocktail motif continues here with table lights shaped like martini glasses and martini glass-shaped light sources under the lip of the bar that are reflected as black shadows inlaid in the marble flooring below.

Jardinière feels like an art-deco supper club.
(Photo by Donna Kempner, © Pat Kuleto Restaurants)

To the left of the host stand, a pewter-colored, red-car-peted curved staircase leads to a multilevel second-floor din-ing area. A cutout in the second-floor slab the size of the bar below connects the two floors; it provides a view between the two spaces and creates a buzz of energy. Railings that encir-cle this atrium area look like ribbons of pewter-colored metal interspersed with ten custom-built bottom-lit see-through wine buckets built into the posts. Kuleto says that the novelty of the wine buckets generates white wine or Champagne sales to everyone who sits at the tables around the railing.

Seating on the first floor is all on one level. On the sec-ond floor, a raised L-shaped seating area with six intimate curved booths nestled along the exterior wall is accessible by a ramp. Throughout the space, square mahogany pillars hold massive glowing torchères.

Above the second floor cutout—which is a metaphor for an inverted champagne saucer—sits a pale gold-tinted domed ceiling sparkling with fiber-optic pinlights that resem-ble champagne bubbles. "The ceiling treatment was a big challenge," recalls Kuleto. "It tends to focus sound to a point, and I figured I might end up with deaf bartenders." Adding to his concerns was a band platform that juts into the open atrium slightly lower than the second-floor level. His solution to both these challenges was to alter the size of the cutout by manipulating the railings. The result is a space where the sounds of entertainment and dining mix to create an ener-gized buzz rather than an unpleasant racket. Thick carpeting throughout both floors and heavy drapery treatments on the windows also help mute noise.

One of the restaurant's signature elements came about after a scouting trip to New York, when Des Jardins and Kuleto savored "an unbelievably perfect cheese platter" at the Gramercy Tavern. They agreed that evening to install a cheese room in Jardinière. This temperature- and humidity-controlled room, tucked under a staircase in the first-floor din-ing room, is the only one in San Francisco.

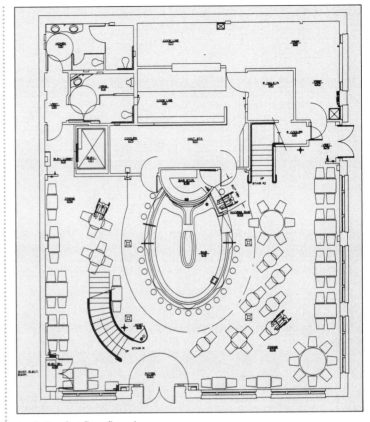

Jardinière first-floor floorplan.
(Courtesy of Pat Kuleto Restaurants)

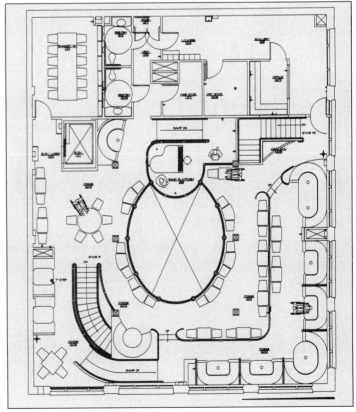

Jardinière second-floor floorplan.
(Courtesy of Pat Kuleto Restaurants)

Kahunaville

BUFFALO, NEW YORK

Owner: Rodento Management, Inc.
Designer: David Tuttleman
Architect: Mitchell Associates, Wilmington, Delaware
Year opened: 1999
Number of seats: dining room: 350, bar and lounge, 100
Game Area: 5,200 square feet with 110 machines
FOH: 14,000 square feet
BOH: 8,000 square feet
Service style: tableservice
Menu: theatrical Americana

Kahunaville is the name of an emerging eatertainment restaurant chain that is based in Delaware. "It's an island that floats around the oceans of the world collecting interesting people, found materials, and new food as it goes," says founder David Tuttleman. Working with a group of close friends, Tuttleman first opened the Big Kahuna Nightclub in 1993 in Wilmington, Delaware. Based on feedback from this operation, Tuttleman and his team developed the concept for Kahunaville.

When asked to define the concept, Tuttleman says, "It's really the new genre of eatertainment that includes great food, service, decor, and entertainment, and we're not ner-

Kahunaville's dancing waterfall is a big family attraction.
(Photo courtesy of Rodento Management, Inc.)

vous to say that." While many eatertainment chains underwent significant downsizing, Kahunaville was named one of the hottest concepts in 1999 by *Nation's Restaurant News*. Expansion plans called for the seven-unit chain to add three units in 2000 and five per year thereafter.

Sharon Banta, Kahunaville's director of marketing, portrays Tuttleman as somewhat of a risk taker when it comes to design. "In our second unit, David wanted to install a waterfall but was cautioned against it due to the high cost. He ignored the advice, went ahead and installed it, and now the waterfall, with choreographed lights and dancing waters, has become one of the focal points of a visit to Kahunaville."

The time from site selection to opening day typically takes just three months. With 350 dining seats, a total of 100 seats in the bar area, and a 5,200-square-foot game area, the Buffalo, New York, Kahunaville (facing page) is typical of units in the chain. Average weekly sales hover around $135,000, built on a $10 average check at lunch and a $15 check at dinner.

There are several design themes. "I believe in running water in a big way," says Tuttleman, who calls himself the Mayor of Kahunaville. Each restaurant has a 1,500-gallon waterfall that becomes a dancing water show backed up by rocks. "All of a sudden it gets quiet, lights change, and then a two- to-four minute choreographed water show emerges," enthuses Tuttleman.

Secondly, the use of massive "rocks" is extensive. In lieu of real rocks, fiberglass reinforced rock surfaces are custom-created for each restaurant. "Every surface that guests can touch needs to be indestructible," notes Tuttleman. He uses old, rusted tin roof material and reclaimed barnwood in various areas as trim. Preserved palm tree trunks with preserved palm fronds attached create a jungle canopy above diners. The space is decorated with salvaged marine products like buoys, block and tackle, and glass fishnet floats, along with bamboo, eucalyptus, and peeled cedar treated with linseed oil.

Mitchell Associates' John Raftery documents Kahunaville's architectural components. "We get involved with the layout, space planning, code requirements, and construction documents," says Raftery, "and David does the theming on site."

Tuttleman's philosophy is that the design need not be perfect, and he encourages the craftspeople who build the restaurant to be creative. For example, the

"rocks" incorporate dozens of faces, personal signatures, and other messages on their surfaces. The same holds true for the signs, produced in a corporate sign shop, which look like they are painted on driftwood. All the artwork, including murals, menu design, and other printed materials, is done by an in-house team.

An element especially designed for kids in this family-friendly chain is two animatronic turtles placed in a pool. Children are also drawn to the $1 million arcade that's filled with 110 games; these are rotated from store to store to keep an ever-changing selection.

Tuttleman loves lighting and incorporates lots of fiber-optic illumination in the design. He cuts large bundles of fiber-optic strands to deliver light wherever it's needed. Colored lights and spotlights are mounted around the bar, where servers periodically come together to dance on the bar top.

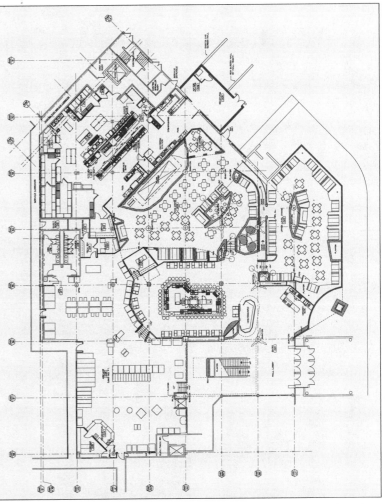

Kahunaville floorplan.
(Courtesy of Rodento Management, Inc.)

Legal Sea Foods

BOSTON

Designer: Bogdanow Partners Architects, PC, New York
Owner: Roger Berkowitz, Legal Sea Foods
Year opened: 1999
Main Floor FOH: 5,124 square feet
Main Floor BOH: 2,556 square feet
Total seating: 264
Basement Level FOH: 4,265 square feet
Basement Level BOH: 1,700 square feet
Total seating: 124
Service style: tableservice
Menu: fresh seafood and raw bar

The Boston flagship of the 19-unit Legal Sea Foods chain enticed customers for nearly 20 years to its location in the Park Plaza Hotel building. Over the years, ownership periodically improved the space but, by the late 1990s, its decor elements had become dated. When the lease on the space skyrocketed, Legal Sea Foods decided it was time to create a new flagship, which they did right across the street in a space on the ground and basement floor of a parking garage.

"They wanted something new," says architect Larry Bogdanow. His firm came up with a comfortable, appealing design suggesting the sea in innovative ways that befit the corporate mission: "If it isn't fresh, it isn't Legal."

The new space was long and narrow, with low ceilings and windows on three sides. The restaurant's location on the ground and basement levels posed additional challenges. "The greatest challenge," says Bogdanow, "was to come up with a design that made the basement space inviting." Private dining rooms were an important part of the concept but could be placed only in the basement. The results: three private rooms, each wired for audiovisual presentations, that can be opened to accommodate roughly 80 diners. Each room has its own entrance to the kitchen, so the flow patterns of guests and staff need not cross.

The design and location of the downstairs bar was also challenging. The policy of the house is not to take reservations except for large parties, so diners typically sign in at the host stand and proceed to

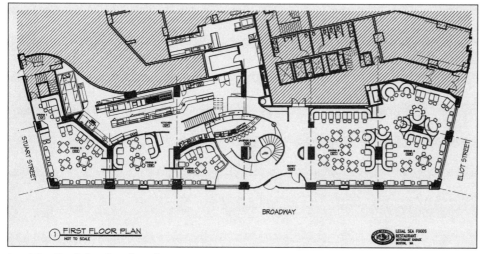

Legal Sea Foods first-floor floorplan.
(Courtesy of Bogdanow Partners Architects, PC)

Legal Sea Foods basement floorplan.
(Courtesy of Bogdanow Partners Architects, PC)

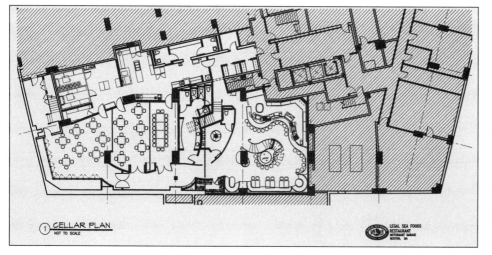

the bar, where they wait for 30 to 40 minutes. Because this is a waiting bar rather than a destination bar, placing it in the basement makes good use of space that might otherwise be perceived as Siberia. The coatroom and main rest rooms are also located in the basement, so guests can access them when they first arrive.

Special care was taken in the design of the staircase to make the trip downstairs a welcome activity. Bogdanow created a grand staircase with undulating iron railings. The staircase curves back on itself as it descends on bluestone treads and risers dotted with glass bubbles. To maximize the connection between the two floors, it sits in an extra-large cutout.

Sitting at the top of the staircase on a raised platform overlooking the kitchen is a small oyster bar that also serves as a regular bar during slow times. This is the perfect setting for single diners who wish to eat a quick bowl of chowder or a platter of fresh-shucked oysters.

In the first-floor dining rooms, the designers installed digitally blown-up underwater transparencies by David Doubilet, a frequent contributor to *National Geographic*. None of the fish, which are from the North Atlantic and Caribbean seas, appear larger than life. The backlit transparencies are large enough so that they can also be seen from the street, and some are used as dividers between the front and back of the house. Bogdanow recognized that all these blue-water shots could make the interior feel cold, so he used a warm copper mesh on the ceiling that floats below acoustic panels, Douglas fir floor-

ing, and seating fabric in muted pumpkin and other warm colors to counteract the cool blue.

Throughout the restaurant, the designers worked hard to prevent customer and staff flow patterns from crossing. The entries to the downstairs kitchen from the backs of each private dining room are one solution. Another is on the first floor, where the waitstaff flows behind both sides of the oyster bar to reach the kitchen. This keeps them from colliding with customers around the staircase or at the host stand.

At Legal Sea Foods, curvaceous architectural treatments transformed a boxy parking garage into an inviting interior.
(Photo © Warren Jagger Photography, Inc.)

Lidia's Kansas City

KANSAS CITY, MISSOURI

Design Firm: Rockwell Group, New York
Owner: Chef Lidia Bastianich
Year opened: 1998
Number of seats: dining room, 160; terrace, 240; private dining, 45; bar, 35
FOH: 7,800 square feet, including the 1,200-square-foot terrace
BOH: 2,400 square feet
Service style: tableservice
Menu: Northern Italian

Creating a prototype restaurant in a 100-year-old freight house that sits adjacent to the second-largest train station in the country presented interesting challenges to the designers. "The overall concept is a casual yet upscale environment that encourages family dining in a space with a slightly contemporary look that utilizes traditional northern Italian colors and design elements," recalls the Rockwell Group's project manager Niels Guldager.

The approach to the entryway is bordered on the right by an herb garden, where many of the herbs used in the kitchen during summer are grown, and on the left by a terraced area that seats up to 240 during warm-weather months. The entry delivers guests directly to the bar area, which incorporates the most significant architectural element added to the space: a massive floor-to-ceiling fireplace and hearth clad in warm green and gold slate that can be seen from everywhere in the restaurant as well as outside. The

hearth serves as a visual anchor for the space. The tiles were chosen because their texture, scale, and colors contrast with the traditional warm orange brick that makes up the skin of this old warehouse space. Lidia Bastianich cooks in a wood-fired hearth in her home kitchen; in essence, the restaurant's hearth became a symbol of the chef-owner and her earthy approach to cuisine. Bastianich also owns three acclaimed restaurants in New York—Felidia, Becco, and Frico—and is the host of the public television show *Lidia's Italian Table*.

As in any good Northern Italian restaurant, wine plays an important role in the design of Lidia's Kansas City. Three significant design elements help merchandise wines. First is the back bar, which is actually a wine display wall fitted with storage cubbies. The freestanding wine wall also provides space to display a variety of grappas and the call liquors. The second element is a pair of enormous wood timber wine displays that act as screens between the bar and dining room

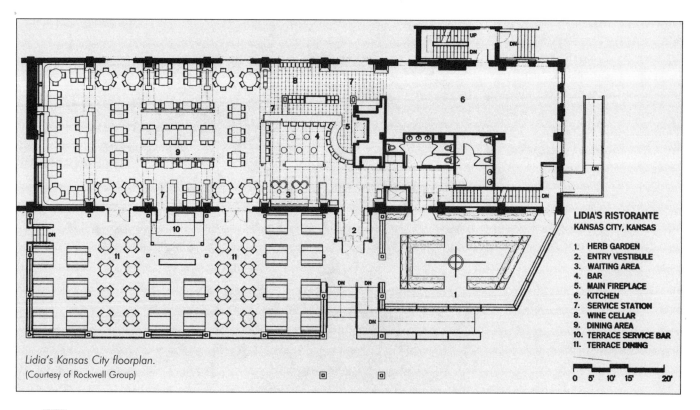

Lidia's Kansas City floorplan.
(Courtesy of Rockwell Group)

LIDIA'S RISTORANTE
KANSAS CITY, KANSAS

1. HERB GARDEN
2. ENTRY VESTIBULE
3. WAITING AREA
4. BAR
5. MAIN FIREPLACE
6. KITCHEN
7. SERVICE STATION
8. WINE CELLAR
9. DINING AREA
10. TERRACE SERVICE BAR
11. TERRACE DINING

0   5'   10'   15'   20'

Wine imagery abounds in Lidia's Kansas City.
(Photo © Paul Warchol)

area. The timbers were taken from the old warehouse and reused to frame the display. Stretched inside the frame is a sheer fabric and a set of heavy glass shelves that support wine bottles in various sizes; these are held in place with bronze-finished rods. Lighting behind the sheer creates a shadow effect. The entire frame hangs from one of the exposed trusses that support the original wood ceiling.

The third design element that supports wine sales is three pairs of interlocking rings that line the wall directly opposite the fireplace. Each of the backlit rings is six feet in diameter. Art-glass segments and wine bottles enliven the wall. Stretched across the top of one set of rings are pictures of old Kansas City, while above a second set of rings are photos of Lidia and her family.

A final element that links the spaces together is massive lighting fixtures that appear initially to be multicolored grape bunches. "Most of the design elements grew up from the ground plan," recalls Guldager, "so we felt we needed a beautiful statement that hung in the space. We were intrigued with the shapes of the grappa bottles, and the lights are abstractions of those bottles." Again, predominately Italian colors are used, and each hand-blown globe is swirled and spotted with many colors. To facilitate relamping, a pulley was installed that lowers the entire fixture.

Matthew's Restaurant

JACKSONVILLE, FLORIDA

Designer: Larry Wilson Design Associates, Inc., Jacksonville, Florida
Owner: chef-owner Matthew Medure
Year opened: 1998
Number of seats: dining room, 50; chef's table, 4; terrace, 24
FOH: 1,104 square feet; terrace, 600 square feet
BOH: 736 square feet
Service style: tableservice
Menu: continental, with Mediterranean overtones

Located in an old bank branch building in the historic San Marco district of Jacksonville, Florida, where boutiques and restaurants abound, Matthew's is a jewel box space in which designer Larry Wilson attended to the details of the environment in much the same way as chef-owner Matthew Medure attends to his cuisine. This is a small restaurant, with 50 seats inside and a seasonal terrace that can be set for 24. Chef Medure serves dinner only to customers who pay an average of $100-120 per couple.

Lighting plays an important role at Matthew's. Says Wilson, "We wanted to maintain flexibility in the seating, so we needed a lighting system that gave general illumination without blasting light. We also wanted to simulate a candlelight feel, particularly for the tables in the center of the room." So the designer avoided pinlights in the ceiling and instead installed a mix of floor-recessed halogen uplights, recessed incandescent cove lights, surface-mounted incandescent MR-16 accent lights, decorative pendants, and decorative wall sconces. All the fixtures are independently controlled and dimmable to ensure a proper illumination balance.

A hand-sanded privacy screen shields the waiter station and the back of the house from diners. The screen is supported by wax-polished rusted-steel columns and backlit with votive candles set directly behind it.

While small rooms feel intimate, they can also cause diners to feel a lack of privacy. To overcome this, Wilson created a private space within the space with high-backed, heavily padded booths. The booths allow a feeling of enclosure even next to a table of eight. Cantilevered lights set off the artwork placed on the wall in each booth to enhance the intimacy of the space and to give a warm glow as the light bounces off the ash wood paneling.

The greatest design constraint was the size of the space. Chef Medure wanted an exposed kitchen and a small office. Space was also needed for wine storage and two handicapped rest rooms. What resulted was a tightly designed back of the house and a dining space that does not feel cramped.

"Detailing is very important in a space this small," notes Wilson. He inlaid the tabletops with stainless-steel inserts to link the kitchen stainless with the rest of the space. Fronting the open

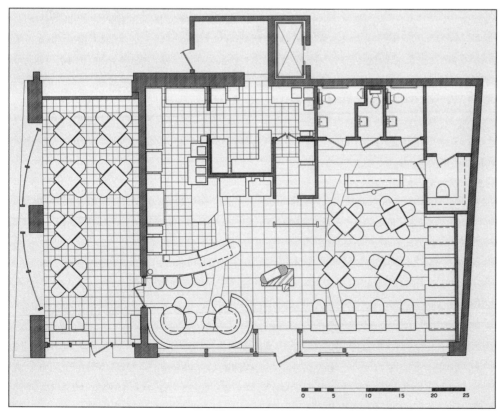

Matthew's floorplan.
(Courtesy of Larry Wilson Design Associates, Inc.)

kitchen is a chef's table, where four diners can look directly into Medure's kitchen and enjoy his personable banter while he cooks. This table also doubles as a place for customers to enjoy wine or dessert.

The most personal detail at Matthew's is a raven-topped square column at the host stand, which is a focal point in the compact room. Chef Medure's grandmother and brothers lovingly called him "little bird" during his childhood. The column's three-dimensional raven watches over the dining room and serves as a tribute to the chef's grandmother.

At Matthew's, the creative use of lighting sets the tone in this sensual, pocket-sized restaurant.
(Photo © by Joseph Lapeyra)

MC²

SAN FRANCISCO

Designer: Mark Cavagnero Associates, San Francisco
Owner: Saverne Properties
Year opened: 1998
Number of seats: dining room,114; private dining, 30; bar, 35
FOH: 4,000 square feet
BOH: 2,600 square feet
Service style: tableservice
Menu: contemporary California French

MC², a restaurant and bar that exudes stripped-down, contemporary styling, is located in a 125-year-old landmark building in the Jackson Square area of San Francisco. "Our overarching idea," comments architect Mark Cavagnero, "was to do something new and stylish in keeping with the area."

Cavagnero's design concept focused on making the original brick walls "the jewel of the whole design." He stripped away everything in the formerly chopped up space to those vintage walls, keeping only the earthquake supports in place. The brick helps warm the hard-edged space, and the open steel adds a bold, contrasting tension.

However, in their original state, the massive steel earthquake supports seemed cold. Cavagnero softened their appearance by applying a gun-blue coating that eats light and downplays the size of the elements. Other steel elements

in the restaurant, such as the back bar shelves, maître d' stand, and bar stools, are shiny stainless steel, with rounded edges that diffuse light and cut glare. No surface in the restaurant is painted. "Every element is true unto itself," says Cavagnero.

With all the hard surfaces, one would expect the decibel levels to be off the scale. That's not the case, due to a ceiling treatment of hemlock slats with black-painted, sound-absorbing acoustic treatments above them. "The goal," says the architect, who perfected his sound-controlling techniques while designing theaters, "is to reflect the upper-end sounds and absorb the low sounds." From an operational point of view, this means that four people can have dinner in the restaurant on a maxed-out Friday night and talk to each other across the table without screaming.

Because this was not a typical restoration, one of the greatest design challenges was the landmark status of the building. If the landmark commission said no to a proposed feature, Cavagnero usually had a contingency plan in mind. That helped the owners, because they never felt trapped in a losing situation. Cavagnero was well prepared for this type of challenge because of his experience designing public and civic buildings that needed far more administrative due diligence than most restaurant projects.

The licensing issues were addressed in a 30-day master planning project. Cavagnero initially looked at seating, turnover, and permit requirements. He then turned his attention to the required planning issues, such as valet parking. The design team also did due diligence to determine the site's appropriateness in the big picture. "This technical planning laid out the groundwork," notes the architect. "Without it, we wouldn't have had a restaurant that worked."

Many other challenges came into play. The space that now houses MC² (and its adjacent sister cafe, Zero Degrees) was formerly a hodgepodge of private businesses on seven levels. ADA requirements mandated that the front and back

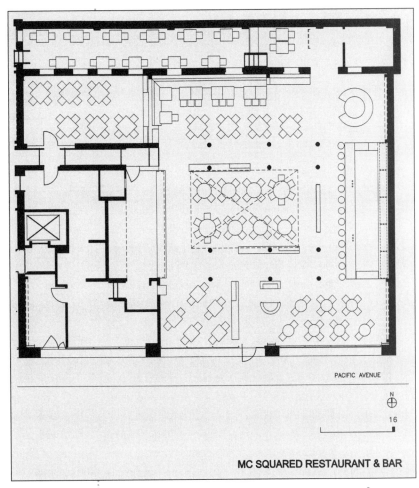

MC² floorplan.
(Courtesy of Mark Cavagnero Associates)

of the house conform to accessibility guidelines. A new exterior window wall had to replicate the landmark features of the surrounding Jackson Square architecture. The building needed upgrades to electrical, earthquake, plumbing, and mechanical systems. All told, the project took two years of planning and execution, including eight to ten months of design work, five months of permitting, and ten months of construction.

MC² is an edgy study in architectural contrasts: masses of brickwork set against finely wrought stainless steel; huge, gun-blue metal seismic supports side by side with delicate wood ceiling slats. "It's about composition," says Cavagnero. "Reflective against absorptive, glossy against matte, large against small."

MC² is a study in architectural contrasts.
(Photo by Sharon Risedorph)

Next Door Nobu

NEW YORK

Designer: Rockwell Group, New York
Owners: The Myriad Restaurant Group, Chef Nobuyaki Matsuhisa, Robert De Niro
Year opened: 1998
Number of seats: dining room, 65; sushi bar, 10
FOH: ~1,200 square feet
BOH: 800 square feet
Service style: tableservice
Menu: authentic Japanese, with an emphasis on raw shellfish and noodles

It's often tough being a younger brother, always in the shadow of your older sibling. But such is not the case with Next Door Nobu, the feisty younger brother of the venerable Nobu restaurant that has drawn diners to its trendy Tribeca street corner in New York since opening in 1994.

"One of the most important things about Next Door Nobu was that it not look like an addition to Nobu," stresses Sam Trimble, the Rockwell Group principal in charge of the restaurant's design. The concept called for a more casual restaurant, one that catered to a younger, no-reservations crowd willing to toss their coats over the backs of their Thonet chairs. The menu is similar to Nobu's innovative Japanese menu, with the addition of noodle dishes and a raw bar. Seating is limited to 75 due to building code requirements that called for two means of egress if the seating capacity went over that number—an impossibility because the building is landlocked in the back.

A design requirement set by chef-owner Nobuyaki Matsuhisa was that the sushi bar must connect with the kitchen,

which posed a challenge in this long, narrow space. The question that faced Trimble was, "How do we organize the space so that the sushi bar is connected with the kitchen, yet serves as a focal point for the restaurant?"

The Rockwell Group's solution was to create a reverse-S curved wall that runs along the south side of the restaurant from the front door to the kitchen wall. A small grouping of banquet seats is set into the streetside end of the curve, and the sushi bar is set in the other. The entry to the kitchen became nothing more than an opening in the wall. Rest rooms and storage spaces were placed in the basement.

The next challenge involved placement of the service bar. Chef Matsuhisa didn't want to have a drinking bar. The Rockwell Group resolved the problem by creating a custom piece of "furniture" that sits in the space like a sake temple. Customers don't really know what it is, except that it is beautiful and glowing. The enclosure is fronted with five rows of sake bottles with translucent backlit panels resembling rice paper behind them. Inside is the refrigeration for the bar and

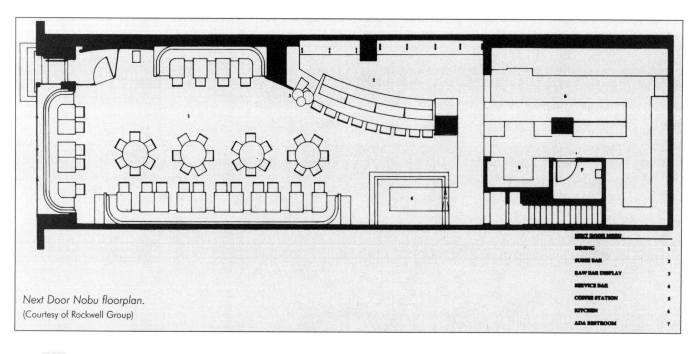

Next Door Nobu floorplan.
(Courtesy of Rockwell Group)

NEXT DOOR NOBU	
DINING	1
SUSHI BAR	2
RAW BAR DISPLAY	3
SERVICE BAR	4
COFFEE STATION	5
KITCHEN	6
ADA RESTROOM	7

At Next Door Nobu, Japanese fishing basket chandeliers and a service bar decorated with sake bottles are two examples of ordinary objects used in creative ways.
(Photo © Paul Warchol)

a work area for the bartender. "A lot of the energy in the restaurant comes from the counterpoint of the sake temple and the curved wall," notes Trimble.

While the design team didn't want next Door Nobu to look like a noodle shop, they were inspired by the Japanese film *Tampopo*, where a John Wayne-like character, who drove the Japanese equivalent of an eighteen-wheeler instead of riding a horse, was on a quest for the perfect noodle shop. With that in mind, the acoustic ceiling tiles resemble ramen noodles. On the face of the curved walls, specially treated sheets of seaweed were pasted in place over a plastic laminate, then coated with epoxy resin to create a deep green lacquered wall with a great deal of textural character.

The idea of found objects—using everyday things like sake bottles in ways that make them special—was also an important inspiration for the project. Japanese fishing baskets suspended at different levels from the ceiling became quirky light elements. A rotating, tiered display of iced seafood sits in a grouping of old woks. Four large tatami mats hang on the rubbed plaster wall behind the banquette on the north side of the room; this wall also has little inserts of mother-of-pearl laid out like calligraphy. Banquette seat backs are covered with scraps of fabric quilted together to support the found look.

Certain elements in the restaurant, such as the black Thonet chairs and scorched ash wood accents, show a family resemblance to its big brother, but Next Door Nobu has an identity all its own.

Norma's

NEW YORK

Designer: Brennan Beer Gorman
Monk/Interiors, Inc., New York
Owner: Parker Meridien Hotel
Year opened: 1998
Number of seats: dining room, ~100
FOH: 1,650 square feet
Service style: tableservice
Menu: breakfast all day

Breakfast is one of the most important meal periods in urban hotels. It captures overnight guests and, if the space catches on, can become a place for local businesspeople to meet for power breakfasts. Such was the intent for Norma's, a restaurant located in the Parker Meridian Hotel in New York. Situated on West 56th Street, the hotel is centrally located in a business and tourist section.

Named after the wife of hotel owner Jack Parker, Norma's was conceived as the hotel's equivalent of a coffee shop. It is joined in the hotel by Seppi's, an upscale bistro, and Jack's, a bar just off the lobby. Unlike most hotel coffee shops, however, Norma's offers specialty breakfast items throughout the day.

One of the design challenges was that although the center of the hotel is lit with a huge skylight, Norma's sits in a windowless room off the lobby, up a short flight of steps. "People don't have breakfast meetings in dark and dingy spaces," says Gregory Stanford, the project designer. "The room needed to be bright." To achieve this, the designers fully opened the wall between the restaurant space and the brightly lighted lobby, and installed a mix of illumination to enliven the room. On the wall facing the entrance are six large, backlit portholes, covered with translucent material and edged with shining stainless-steel rings, that are flanked by two stainless-steel columns. These bright focal points beckon people into the space. Throughout the high-ceilinged restaurant, downlights and wall washers create soft overall illumination with no hot spots.

The sleek, minimalist room, with wood, leather, stainless-steel, and aluminum accents, is virtually bare of decor. "Urban businesspeople are leading cleaner, more efficient lives and don't need all those decorative references," Stanford notes. "Instead, the restaurant environment becomes an uncluttered backdrop."

Ownership decided against the original idea of putting a classic buffet in the center of the space, but, says Stanford, "we still needed to break up the room." The solution is a two-sided, curving leather banquette that acts as a room divider while creating a sense of intimacy.

There are no tablecloths over the architectural-glass tabletops, rimmed with aluminum edging reminiscent of classic diners. The table setting, however—Sasaki china, Italian glassware, Boda Nova flatware, Nambe salt- and peppershakers, and bud vases—is more elegant than dinerlike. To accommodate power-breakfasters, the tabletops were resized up to 38 inches square (from the usual 32 or 34 inches) to hold notepads, day planners, and laptop computers.

*Norma's sleek, bright interior and oversized
tables set the scene for power breakfasts.*
(Photo © Andrew Bordwin, NYC)

Palladin

NEW YORK

Designer: Adam D. Tihany International Ltd., New York
Restaurant developer: Andrew Young and Co., Inc.
Owner: The Time Hotel
Year opened: 1999
Number of seats: dining room, 96; bar, 15
FOH: ~2,500 square feet
BOH: ~900 square feet, plus support areas
Service style: tableservice
Menu: French-inspired brasserie style

A football field away from Times Square in New York sits the Time Hotel, a hip hostelry with 164 rooms, 28 suites, the Time Bar, and Palladin restaurant. In the hotel, designer Adam Tihany used bold primary colors to create design excitement: Different-colored guest rooms are infused with scents that match the color of the room. The Time is no ordinary hotel, and its only restaurant had to live up to the cachet of its surroundings. Tihany, restaurant developer Andrew Young, and chef Jean-Louis Palladin collaborated to achieve that goal.

From a design perspective, the long, narrow space presented a challenge. To add enough space for an entry area and bar, the lobby had to be relocated to the second floor of the hotel. Elevator corridors were also moved, and the kitchen functions were split over three floors. The primary cooking section of the kitchen is on the restaurant floor, but support areas are divided between the basement and second floor of the hotel. "The only way to come up with such solutions," says Young, "is to think creatively, outside the box."

Young and Chef Palladin envisioned an upscale brasserie featuring food more casual than the chef's renowned French fare. They wanted a design that combined hard edges with soft finishes to create a sense of place and style. From an operational point of view, they needed flexible seating to accommodate parties of various sizes.

Palladin is not meant to be formal. Tihany's design walks a fine line between the bistro aesthetic and the techno-feeling of the rest of the Time Hotel. Design elements such as floor-to-ceiling glass panels backlit with neon and cubes of color are a counterpoint to the plush, deep grape seating upholstery.

The original linen order called for tablecloths, but when he saw how formal they looked, Young had the tablecloths cut into runners that criss-cross the tabletops. Simple oversized white china showcases Chef Palladin's cuisine. The waitstaff wear uniforms of different-colored shirts and the ubiquitous bistro apron. Planters in the center of each table feature greenery that is changed weekly.

With a chef of such repute, an open kitchen would seem in order, but this was restricted by fire codes. The design team was also concerned about excess noise. Instead, a glass-fronted display kitchen allows guests a view of the action without the accompanying din. Fabric-wrapped acoustic panels on the ceiling and fabric seats and banquettes also keep sound to a comfortable buzz.

*A plush, textural design treatment elevates
the brasserie atmosphere at Palladin.*
(Photo © Peter Aaron/Esto)

Pittsburgh Fish Market

PITTSBURGH, PENNSYLVANIA

Designer: Zakaspace, Fort Lauderdale, Florida
Operator: Double Tree Liberty Center
Year opened: 1998
Number of seats: dining room, 200; private dining, 20; bar, 33; sushi bar, 11
FOH: 7,000 square feet
BOH: 3,300 square feet
Service styles: tableservice, counter, take-out
Menu: seafood, steak, sushi

"Hotel food? No way." This attitude held by many travelers became one of the challenges the designers at Zakaspace took on when they created Pittsburgh Fish Market in the Double Tree Liberty Center Hotel. To reverse the negative image of a hotel restaurant, Zakaspace developed a separate identity for the space, one that appears to be owned and operated by a restaurant group not associated with the hotel.

Three separate entrances to the restaurant—from the lobby, the street entrance, and from the atrium of an adjacent office tower—each give customers a sense of arrival. The handles on the door that leads from the lobby, for example, are fashioned in the shape of King Chinook salmon. Adjacent to the atrium entrance is a café and retail area called the Market Place that incorporates oversized refrigerated cases where fresh-cut seafood for home cooking plus prepared meat, poultry, vegetables, and side dishes are displayed and sold. The seafood theme is expressed in subtle ways. For example, draperies are wrapped in thin layers of a netting fabric and lightly decorated with colorful lures and other fishing gear items.

The octagonal Fish Market Bar lies directly in front of the hotel entrance; its hanging glassware can be clearly seen from the glass wall and doors that separate the hotel lobby from the restaurant proper. The bar incorporates a mahogany-stained soffit, which helps define the space, and a tongue-and-grooved plank ceiling. Its octagonal seating arrangement provides for eye contact between all patrons, promoting the "see-and-be-seen" setting. This design resulted in an attractive social environment, with each bar stool representing thousands of dollars per week in revenues. Additional bar seating is available in a raised platform area where patrons can order food from the dining room or sushi bar menu.

Located near the Fish Market Bar is a horseshoe-shaped sushi bar. Halogen luminaires, hung from a curving stainless-steel track fitted with multicolored pendant lamps, float above the black granite bartop. Along the back wall of the sushi bar sits a 100-gallon aquarium spotlighted with halogen track lights.

The designers positioned the entire bar area to be the first restaurant space people encounter when they enter from either the hotel lobby or the separate street entrance. An open exhibition kitchen is the focal point of the restaurant's main dining room. Here, two raised platform levels hold booth and table seating. The booths are large enough to accommodate six diners but are intended to seat only four. Throughout the dining room, mahogany-covered columns connected to cream-colored stucco beams help break the long space into more intimate areas. Burlap tie-back drapery on the columns further distinguish individual areas within the dining room.

Thematic doors invite guests into Pittsburgh Fish Market, a complex hotel restaurant that incorporates dining, a bar, a sushi bar, and home meal replacement.
(Photo by Sanderson Photography, Pittsburgh, PA)

Ruby Foo's Dim Sum and Sushi Palace

NEW YORK

Designer: Rockwell Group, New York
Owner: Steve Hanson
Year opened: 1999
Number of seats: 400
Total area: 10,000 square feet
Service style: tableservice
Menu: pan-Asian dim sum, sushi, and wok specials

When restaurant guru Steve Hanson, owner of seven other notable restaurants in New York, teamed up with the Rockwell Group to create a stylish Pan-Asian megarestaurant on the trendy Upper West Side of Manhattan, the outcome was overwhelmingly embraced by locals and people around the city.

"The big challenge," explains Sam Trimble, the Rockwell Group's principal in charge and project designer, "was the need to spread the restaurant over two floors." This included integrating an area several steps up from the second floor intended for private dining (but, in reality, used as over-

flow because the restaurant is so popular) with the rest of the dining area on that floor. "The solution," says Trimble, "was to make a strong central focal point that all the different spaces make reference to." This focal point is a massive S-curve that flows from the front door up the staircase. The curve helps knit front, back, upper, and lower portions of the restaurant together.

To this, the designers added a red display wall that hugs the staircase and ties the levels together vertically. The wall is a showcase of Asian art and craft visible from everywhere in the restaurant. "People interpret it as either an enormous Bento box or a Chinese bookcase," notes Trimble. "We like that it can be seen either way."

Deciding on the individual objects that would go on display in the restaurant was somewhat of a treasure hunt for the Rockwell Group design team. They visited New York's Chinatown to get inspiration for color schemes and ideas about how to display objects together. They created storyboards with photography taken in Chinatown as well as in Asian countries to collect ideas about what kind of objects to select for display. It was important that the final design incorporate references not only to China but also to Japan and other Asian countries.

Some of the Asian references are subtle; others are bold. For example, the back bar units were inspired by Chinese apothecary cabinets. Clear glass jars filled with dried foods like shark fin and sea cucumber sit on the top shelves, just as they would in a real Chinese medicine cabinet. The massive curved drink rail that separates the bar from the entry area is faced with backlit strings of mah-jongg tiles separated by an abacus of green glass beads on metal rods.

The most striking Japanese references can be seen in the design of the two sushi bars. Behind each bar is a backlit wall that resembles a crisp white shoji screen. Stainless-steel and white Corian surfaces make the bar feel super-clean. Operationally, says Trimble, the owner wanted a sushi bar on

Ruby Foo's Dim Sum and Sushi Palace floorplan.
(Courtesy of Rockwell Group)

both levels to reassure customers that the menus were the same upstairs and downstairs. While sushi can be ordered from any table in the restaurant, only the second floor area has seating at the sushi bar itself.

The boldest references are on the red display wall. Here, cubbies of various sizes showcase objects taken from pan-Asian venues. Gold Buddhas, colorful Mongolian hats, stringed instruments, a prayer gong, and other objets d'art pop against the bright Chinese red background. The same bento-box format is used to break up the walls in the third-level dining room upstairs. Throughout the restaurant, cast-plastic tabletops in colors inspired by signs in Chinatown are decorated with large calligraphy characters that wish diners good fortune.

The first-floor sushi bar at Ruby Foo's Dim Sum and Sushi Palace is one of many focal points in this ebullient Asian restaurant.
(Photo © Paul Warchol)

Sullivan's Steakhouse

AUSTIN, TEXAS

Designer: Aumiller Youngquist, PC, Mt. Prospect, Illinois
Owner: Lone Star Steakhouse and Saloon, Inc.
Year opened: Sullivan's Steakhouse, 1996; Ringside Jazz Club and Private Dining, 1997
Number of seats: dining, 210; private dining, 116; bar, 50; Ringside Jazz Club, 83
FOH: 6,450 square feet; Ringside Jazz Club, 1,450 square feet
BOH: 3,800 square feet
Service style: tableservice
Menu: traditional steakhouse

Hotel companies have been creating brands targeted to different price points for years. The owners of Lone Star Steakhouse & Saloon, Inc. have taken a similar approach and broken down their pricing and brand names into three segments: Lone Star Steakhouse & Saloon, with a reported $20 check average, Sullivan's Steakhouse, with a $40 check average, and Del Frisco's Double Eagle Steakhouse, with a check average of more than $60.

Bill Aumiller and Keith Youngquist were familiar with the Lone Star Steakhouse & Saloon concept when they were first contacted to create a prototype in Austin, Texas, for a more upscale brand that was eventually called Sullivan's. Ownership wanted a sophisticated setting that did not include the cowboy memorabilia found in the Lone Star restaurants. The resulting design reflects a 1940s Chicago steakhouse.

The prototype is in an existing building formerly used for manufacturing, located in an area of Austin busy with nightlife. "In the beginning of the design process, we were thinking of a design that related to an adventurer's club or a gentleman's club," recalls Bill Aumiller. "As that thought took hold, we started to look at boxing around 1890, in the days of Sullivan." Boxers of that era were high-profile personalities on the social and sports scene. Some of the artwork displayed in Sullivan's relates to boxing; some shows famous boxers in situations that have nothing to do with the sport.

The Austin prototype opened in two phases. First came Sullivan's Steakhouse, with a bar, dining room, and private dining level. It was so successful that the private dining area was always used as overflow seating. The second phase was hurried along and, a year later, the Ringside Jazz Club opened. The jazz club was integrated with several other Sullivan's Steakhouses (there were 13 as of early 2000) when space was available and the market called for it.

The main dining area in Sullivan's is on one level. This includes a platformed dining room, known as the library, which can be broken into three dining spaces with movable glass partitions to provide intimacy in the space. On slow nights, management can close off the library and turn the lights down to make the main dining area look full even though the restaurant is not.

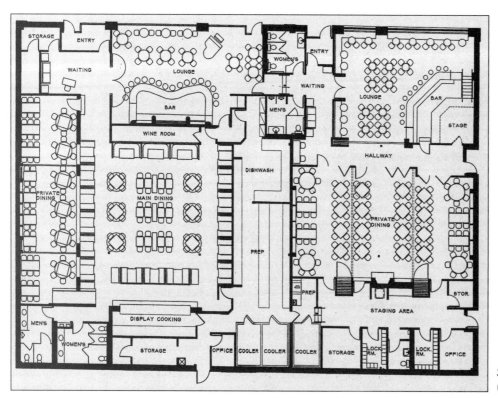

Sullivan's Steakhouse floorplan.
(Courtesy of Keith Aumiller Youngquist)

At the front end of the dining room is a wine room fronted with large windows. The red wine is held in this temperature-controlled room, complete with a library ladder to reach the top storage shelves. At the back of the dining room is an open kitchen shielded from view by a translucent screen that rises beside a bank of banquettes. Some tables were oversized in order to hold the large breadbaskets and platters of meat and side dishes the restaurant is known for.

The Ringside Jazz Club is easily accessible through the bar and via its own entrance. Local musicians welcomed the club because they were accustomed to playing in bare-bones rooms where decor was not important. Here, the space is comfortable and the sound is well controlled. The club, which seats 83 in an appropriately tightly packed area, incorporates a stage behind the back bar. The designers installed a sound blanket on the perimeter

At Sullivan's Steakhouse, levels and sliding glass partitions break up the space into discrete dining areas. (Photo © Steinkamp/Ballogg Photography, Chicago)

walls to absorb reverberation. They specified a mix of acoustic tiles and fabric-wrapped acoustic panels on the ceiling, depending on the amount of sound control needed in any given part of the space. Because the area is fairly small, there is no problem with echoing.

Throughout the restaurant and club, a comfortable ambient light level from various sources and directions enlivens the space and keeps it from looking like a dark, somber men's club. Downlights and votive candles in holders shaped like old English bulldogs illuminate the tabletops and the diner's faces.

TrU

CHICAGO

Designer: The Johnson Studio, Atlanta
Owners: Lettuce Entertain You Enterprises, Inc.; chefs Gale Gand and Rick Tramonto
Year opened: 1999
Number of seats: dining room,112; private rooms, 72; bar, 13
FOH: 4,642 square feet
BOH: 3,490 square feet
Service style: tableservice
Menu: progressive French, prix fixe

The design at TrU in Chicago, a fine dining jewel in the Lettuce Entertain You Enterprises restaurant empire, carries food as art beyond the plate. In fact, "the restaurant is intended to be a gallery, primarily for culinary art, but for visual art as well," says architect Bill Johnson, principal of The Johnson Studio. Repeat guests are greeted with changing art elements as well as changing menus to keep the experience stimulating.

The entry area incorporates a small bar, access to the second-floor function space, and access to the dining room. In the dining room, the drama unfolds with 15-foot ceilings, two walls of full-height windows, and a massive 5-foot-round

Mark Balloga ©1999 Steinkamp/Balloga Photography

anchoring column that centers the space. The windows are softened with backlit sheer curtains that run from floor to ceiling. Like an art gallery, the room is painted white. Understated deep-blue upholstery does not detract from the artwork or the cuisine.

Chef-owners Rick Tramonto and Gale Gand (the pastry chef) played an active role in the design process, particularly in the kitchen, which is a showcase unto itself. Originally, a glass window wall was going to separate the dining room from the kitchen. As the design evolved, it was decided that less was more and that an occasional glimpse into the kitchen would be sufficient to connect the guests with the back-of-the-house action. A set of four window boxes was cut into the wall. While the backs can be removed to provide a kitchen view, they usually serve as food art displays that change periodically. For example, the opening-week display featured bunches of asparagus held in a white mannequin's hand in each window box. Everyday items like tomatoes are grouped together in a way that shows how ordinary objects can become art in the hands of an artist. Displaying food as art in the restaurant continues with tabletop elements such as a curving glass "staircase" used to serve a caviar appetizer.

Guests are frequently invited to tour the immaculate kitchen. Access is through a frosted-glass door that automatically slides open when approached. The garde manger and hot food stations sit immediately to the left. Overhead shelves in the garde manger area hold serving plates. Copper pots are stored on hooks in the hot foods area. The six most privileged seats in the house are in a glassed-in room in the kitchen.

The dining room is a study in luxe minimalism. Unlike competing fine dining establishments in the neighborhood, TrU attracts a young, nontraditional clientele interested in the chefs' fresh approach to haute cuisine. Widely spaced, oversized tables and chairs add to the air of understated luxury. Fabric window treatments and plush padded carpeting help control noise throughout the space.

The Johnson Studio developed a lighting plan with two objectives: to add drama to the room and to highlight the art and culinary presentations. To achieve this, they used high-intensity, narrow-focus halogen spots throughout the space. Direct light pops out the colors and textures of the art and cui-

sine. Elsewhere, soft light and shadow animate the room.

Unlike the soaring first floor, the second-floor private dining room has a low ceiling: 7 feet, 6 inches. To add visual interest to the space, the designers created a wine display on the entire north wall.

The rest rooms reflect another interesting design element. Rather than washing their hands in a bowl-shaped sink, patrons wash over an angled piece of plate glass that drains to a trough attached to the wall. "The bathroom sink is purely for fun," says Johnson.

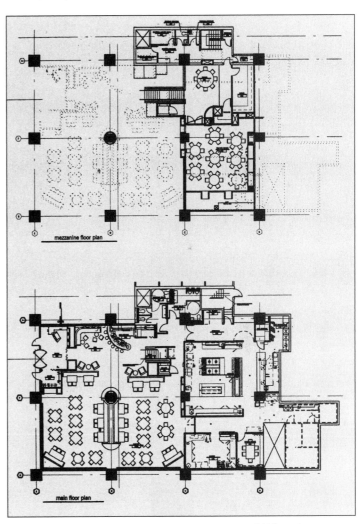

TrU floorplan.
(Courtesy of The Johnson Studio)

TrU's unembellished interior is a gallery for food and art.
(Photo © Mark Ballogg, Steinkamp/Ballogg Photography, Chicago)

Union Pacific

NEW YORK

Designer: Bogdanow Partners Architects, PC, New York
Owners: Jeff Kadish, Steve Scher, Paul Zweiben
Year opened: 1997
Number of seats: dining rooms, 119; private dining, 24; bar, 70
Total area: 10,000 square feet
Service style: tableservice
Menu: French with Asian overtones

On 16 September 1994, when the *New York Times* reviewed the restaurant housed in the space now occupied by Union Pacific, the lead lines commented negatively about being seated in "Siberia" with the quote "Oh, no! They're taking us upstairs." When former *New York Times* restaurant critic Ruth Reichl reviewed Union Pacific on 5 August 1998, she enthused about the cuisine for the first four paragraphs and lavished praise on the design in the fifth.

Union Pacific owners Jeff Kadish, Steve Scher, and Paul Zweiben knew from the start that in order to put a world-class chef in a world-class space, they needed to make significant changes to the interior of the restaurant. The existing space had a poor entry sequence; there was no greeting or waiting area. A large bar that was often crowded encroached on diners seated at tables. Only a small strip on a riser featured prime seating. A glassed-in service aisle in front of the open kitchen ate up valuable floor space. Then there was the mezzanine seating that the critic had dubbed Siberia.

The Bogdanow design team first opened the tiny entryway so that customers could see into the restaurant.

The soaring ceiling at Union Pacific creates a visual focal point that also connects the first floor to the mezzanine.
(Photo © Paul Warchol)

They designed an inviting, peaceful waiting area with comfortable seating and a wall of water trickling into a shallow pool. A Japanese garden-style bridge connects the entry area to the downstairs dining room and small bar. Additional bar seating, accessible through the restaurant, is available in a basement bar called Kashmir that has its own identity and streetside entrance.

Translucent glass windows were used to enclose the two exposed walls of the kitchen, and the service pickup area was moved into the kitchen proper. The glass allows diners to see movement in the kitchen, but the kitchen is not the focal point of the space.

With the goal of making every table a prime seating location, the designers split the main dining space into front and back zones. In the front area, half-round banquettes create privacy while allowing a view into the room. In the back area, wall-length banquettes mix with freestanding tables. Behind the back-room banquettes are square illuminated light boxes scored with a delicate Asian wave pattern. Fabric-wrapped panels behind these help with acoustic control.

The ceiling treatment in the rear dining room is the restaurant's dramatic focal point. Here, the designers accented a skylight with a series of decorative arched trusses that soar to 16 feet and tie the main floor to the mezzanine area. Two layers of fabric stretched under the skylight dampen sound.

The design team's greatest challenge involved converting "Siberia" into a desired seating area. Their first step was to line the railing of the mezzanine with deuces, all of which have views of the action below. Then, in an area with a limited view, they installed a chef's tasting room, enclosed in woven mesh, that seats six. A private dining room along the streetside edge of the mezzanine is capped with a gold-coffered ceiling that is attractive to diners within and visible to passersby outside who look up into the space.

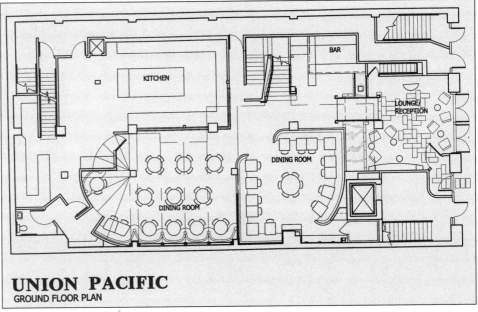

UNION PACIFIC
GROUND FLOOR PLAN

Union Pacific first-floor floorplan.
(Courtesy of Bogdanow Partners Architects, PC)

Union Pacific mezzanine floorplan.
(Courtesy of Bogdanow Partners Architects, PC)

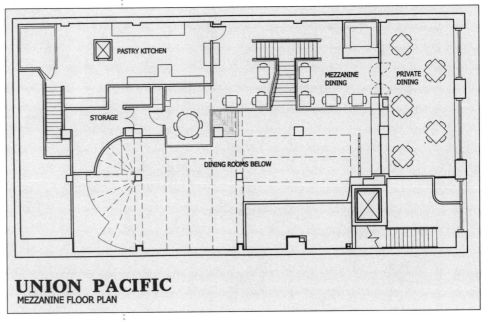

UNION PACIFIC
MEZZANINE FLOOR PLAN

In the rear of the mezzanine over the kitchen, a six-top table dubbed "the skybox" offers a commanding view of the first floor below. Warm-toned woods and color accents of wine, cream, and gold create a romantic feeling throughout the restaurant.

University of California Los Angeles (UCLA) Hedrick Hall

LOS ANGELES

Designer: Webb Foodservice Design Consultants, Inc., Tustin, California
Owner: UCLA
Year opened: 1998
Number of seats: dining room, 500; private room, 50
FOH: 13,118 square feet
BOH: 7,573 square feet
Service style: modified marketplace servery
Menu: freshly prepared foods, including grilled items, pizza and calzones, burgers and fries; salad bar and granary

Like many universities, the University of California Los Angeles has learned the benefits that accrue from upgrading its foodservice facilities. The 20,000-square-foot foodservice in Hedrick Hall—home to 1,044 students—was originally opened in 1964 with a straight-line cafeteria. The 1998 renovation by Webb Foodservice Design Consultants radically altered food, design, and service with a modified market concept that revolves around freshness. It is one of many upgrades planned for UCLA's foodservice operations. "The university has seen that it can basically self-fund these projects based on the return in labor savings, food cost reductions, and increased participation," says designer Jim Webb.

How does the design save labor? "In this market concept," explains Webb, "you have back- and front-of-the-

The cafeteria at UCLA's Hedrick's Hall brings foodservice out into the dining area.
(Photo by Dave Cook)

house staff acting as one, both cooking and serving." That means the person who cooks the salmon steak on the line also serves it to waiting students, leading to an increase in the meals served per labor hour. It's worth retraining back-of-the-house employees with guest service skills, notes Webb.

Another benefit is that each servery "platform" works like its own restaurant. "Employees are now in charge of their own area, and they help to merchandise it and take ownership of it," says Webb. Future plans call for a central commissary kitchen to preprepare foods to be sent to satellite halls on campus, further lowering labor costs.

The design team began by carefully selecting menu items, rethinking the preparation process to put labor at the point of sale rather than back in the kitchen, engineering the servery platforms, and figuring out where to place the platforms. Hedrick Hall is a board plan operation, so cash registers are not needed. This results in an intimate relationship between the servery and dining areas. Diners can clearly see all parts of the servery from their tables.

The servery incorporates exhibition cooking for omelets, wok cookery, pasta dishes, and casserettes (individual casserole dishes that are baked through an Impinger oven); a soup/salad express island; a grill for burgers and chicken breast sandwiches; a pizza and calzone area; a granary (dessert station that has fruits, breads, muffins, coffees, juices, and yogurt); and a Eurokitchen for premier entrée items. Throughout the space are several beverage stations that house both cold and hot beverages, including a self-serve espresso machine.

The exhibition style of cooking, where students get to watch their entrées being cooked and plated, has resulted in improved service time. Multiple cooking platforms also give customers more locations to queue up for their entrées, thus reducing the length of the lines. The new design can feed 100 students every six minutes without stockpiling prepared dishes. Care was taken to provide cooking equipment that is easy to operate and capable of keeping up with peak demands. Individual platforms can be

shut down during off-peak hours. Because most of the cooking is done out front, the prep kitchen was dramatically reduced in size.

Throughout the space, free-flowing soffits, hanging trellises, ceramic tile and stonework accents, and natural wood treatments warm the space and create a comfortable ambience. These elements are highlighted by strategically placed low-voltage and incandescent downlights. Dining room seating is completely portable and can be rearranged to accommodate special food events. The staff periodically repositions mobile cold food display equipment to allow employees to prepare specialty salads in the dining areas.

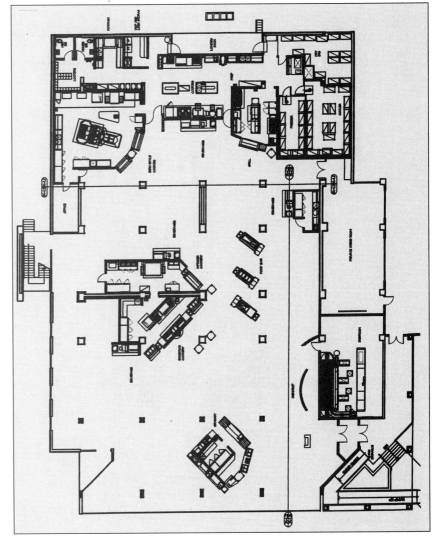

UCLA Hedrick Hall floorplan.
(Courtesy of Jim Webb Foodservice Design Consultants, Inc.)

Wildfire

OAKBROOK, ILLINOIS

Designer: Aria Group Architects, Inc., Oak Park, Illinois
Owner: Lettuce Entertain You Enterprises, Inc.
Year opened: 1998
Number of seats: dining room, 182; bar, 64
FOH: 5,426 square feet
BOH: 2,861 square feet
Service style: tableservice
Menu: open-flame cooking of chicken, ribs, steaks, etc.

Display kitchens add excitement to any restaurant, and when wood-burning equipment is featured, the entire restaurant seems to come alive. Perhaps the source is the faint aroma the burning wood imparts to an order of spit-roasted herb chicken, or the rich, sweet smell of slow-smoked baby-back ribs with tangy tamarind sauce. Add to the aromatic experience the visual kick of stacks of split logs lining the face of the pickup station. All this comes into play at the Wildfire restaurants, a multiple-location concept that is part of the Lettuce Entertain You Enterprises family.

The Oakbrook, Illinois, restaurant shown here is the second Wildfire (the first is in downtown Chicago). Nearly every item is cooked over an open flame, be it a wood-burning rotisserie, oven, or grill. The technique posed problems in this locale because the live-fire cooking equipment in a restaurant elsewhere in town had caught fire three times. Convincing town officials that the kitchen equipment was safe was an important step in the design process.

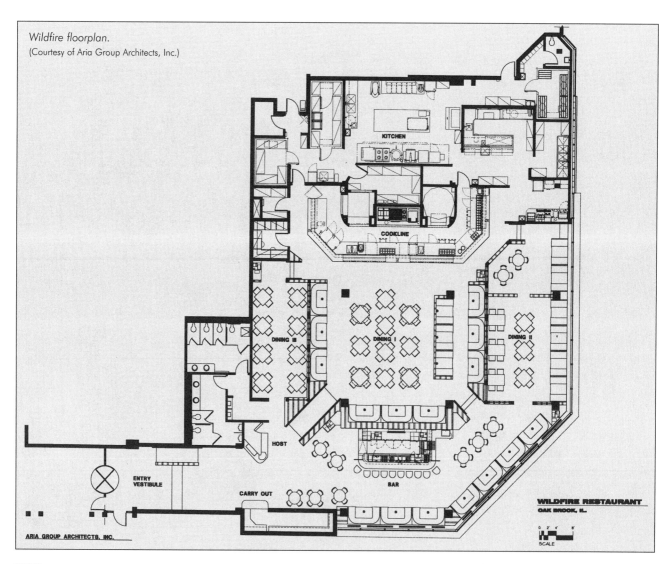

Wildfire floorplan.
(Courtesy of Aria Group Architects, Inc.)

Wildfire is located on the second floor of the Oakbrook Shopping Center, an inwardly oriented open-air mall with upscale shops and Neiman Marcus as the anchor store. "The actual entrance is from the inside mall, but the back of the restaurant faces the parking lot," notes Jim Lencioni, principal, Aria Group Architects, "so we clad the exterior back with stone and cedar siding, wrapped the windows with wood, and added an awning that shades all of the windows to make it look like we built the restaurant independently from the rest of the mall." The exterior's strong visual image gives Wildfire its own identity.

The design resembles a 1940s dinner house with Art Deco accents. "We wanted to create a clubby, comfortable space rather than a rustic, high-ceilinged space that felt cold," says Lencioni. Leather on the booths, chairs, and bar stools, and the brass-headed pins that rim the backs of seats contribute to the clubby feel. The black concrete bar floor is scored and highly polished to look like blocks of stone. The dining areas feature a lot of wood—on the floor, walls, ceilings, and the uncovered tabletops—that further warms the space. Wooden blinds along the exterior windows provide shade.

Halogen downlighting is used sparingly. Sconces, table lamps, and ceiling pendants create a comfortable glow. Green and cream-colored murals of palm leaves, oversized leaf designs on draperies, and large black and white framed photographs from the 1940s contribute to the Art Deco feel.

The designers divided Wildfire's dining space into three main seating sections. The central section sits directly in front of the display kitchen. The two side areas are slightly elevated and overlook both the central seating area and the display kitchen. Oak-stained columns and beams create areas within areas. Floral-patterned draperies also define seating nooks, or close off entire sections when the restaurant isn't busy.

The live-fire hearth at Wildfire is a signature element of this multi-unit restaurant concept.
(Photo © Mark Ballogg, Steinkamp/Ballogg Photography, Chicago)

Notes

....

....

....

....

....

....

....

....

....

....

....

....

....

....

....

....

....

....

....

....

....

....

....

....

Speak Out on Design

Much can be learned from those who are involved with restaurant design on an ongoing basis. Owners must effectively communicate their concept to designers and work closely to ensure it is correctly interpreted. Designers and architects are charged with translating the owner's concept into a layout and environment that supports the restaurant. Chef-owners not only have to be involved during the creative and construction phases of a project but they also must work with the design after the restaurant opens.

To gain insights into how various members of the design team think, we interviewed a mix of designers, architects, owners, and chef-owners about the design process. They all agreed that two elements are essential to the success of any front- and back-of-the-house design: ongoing communications during the design process, and an efficient layout.

Bill Aumiller and Keith Youngquist

Principals

Aumiller Youngquist, PC, Architecture and Interior Design

Mt. Prospect, Illinois

Number of restaurant projects: ~1,000

Aumiller Youngquist was founded in 1980 by Bill Aumiller and Keith Youngquist, two architects with the common goal of providing foodservice operators with an effective way to communicate their vision through innovative architectural design. The firm has designed restaurants ranging from Chicago's Scoozi (1986) to the first Del Frisco's Steakhouse in New York (February 2000). Their goal for all projects is to rethink the design process and create spaces with unique identities.

Bill Aumiller and Keith Youngquist.
(Photo courtesy of Aumiller Youngquist)

Q: From your firm's perspective, what constitutes good design?

A: For us, good design is concept-driven. First comes the food concept. We take it from there to develop a design statement to show what people could expect in the restaurant. We strive for one cohesive statement. We don't talk like designers, we talk like restaurateurs. We determine what the owners are trying to accomplish from a financial and design perspective.

Q: Does good design mean expensive design?

A: The concept is the driver. If you want an upscale space with fine finishes, you have to pay for it. A barbecue shack allows for an inexpensive job. For a crab shack in London, we relied on carpenters to build the tables in a ramshackle way. They weren't expensive, but they still have a hand-hewn look that is appropriate for the space.

Another technique is to limit the fine finishes. We've used faux finishes to help control costs, but there has to be a fine balance. The idea is to put the money in the places that customers have contact with and use less expensive material elsewhere. We have one client who insisted on a particular light fixture twenty-five feet above the floor that used an anodized aluminum ring at a cost of four thousand dollars. At that distance, the same effect could have been spray-painted onto a ring for a dollar and a half.

Q: How important is good design to the success of a restaurant?

A: Good restaurant design has to function well. If the restaurant doesn't integrate design and functionality, it will have problems making it. A successful design zeroes in on the market and the intention of the restaurant.

Q: How can restaurateurs best work with designers to create a successful restaurant design?

A: Most important is for the owner and designer to get on the same conceptual page and stay with it. A storyboard and project book before any drawings are started will help ensure that the designers are in step with the restaurateur. There should be periodic reality checks to match design issues, function, and the menu together.

There should be lots of time allocated for preplanning, up to two months including an all-day brainstorming session during the preplanning phase that brings the key members of the design team together.

The restaurateur should share the business plan with the designer. That gives us some idea about the budget. Owners often don't want to reveal their financials because they are afraid that we will spend too much. But they need to have enough money to realize the project. Sometimes our clients have great plans and great taste, but their financial projections are unrealistic.

Q: What's your secret to a good restaurateur-designer relationship?

A: Initially, we don't talk about design and decor, but about floorplans and the functional aspects of the restaurant. Due to the high costs of labor, flow is the major issue that we look at when considering floorplans.

We try to understand everything about the client and to help the client understand everything about the design. The only bad idea is the one that the owner does not share with the designer, or vice versa.

We must all agree on solutions. This eliminates the loop of presenting designs that do not meet owner's expectations and then having to redo them.

Q: What are the primary means of controlling sound in a restaurant setting?
A: Materials are important. The layout and relationship of spaces also has a tremendous influence on noise levels. For example, bars should be placed in a separate room to help keep the dining space quieter.

You have to start with the ceiling in term of acoustics. In some restaurants, for example, we use padded acoustic ceiling panels that are filled with an acoustic blanket and covered with fabric. Then we move on to the walls, which we sometimes cover with a spray-on acoustic material. Floors come next, and we're seeing a resurgence of carpeting and runners in restaurants to help deaden noise.

Q: What types of sound systems do you use to help balance noise in a restaurant?
A: When it gets too noisy, don't turn up the sound system to overpower the noise of people talking. Music should be muted, so that it contributes to the mood.

Q: What new and innovative lighting elements have you used recently? What cautions do you have?
A: We are still big users of low-voltage lighting with long lamp life—up to ten thousand hours when dimmed. We use fiber-optic lamps in display cases to minimize heat build-up. That's really important when you display items like chocolates that would melt under a normal lamp.

Some energy-saving fluorescents work well. Fluorescent light quality is improving and can even help make people and food look good. This is due to the temperature of the lamp and lenses that improve the quality of the light coming out of it. We stay away from cold fluorescents and use neon only in a cove situation where it is completely hidden.

We think as much about how lighting affects guests when they exit a restaurant as when are in it. This extends all the way to the lighting in the parking lot. The cold metal halide lights typically used in parking lots will change the warm feeling created by lighting inside the restaurant.

Q: How have you used lighting control systems?
A: They can be expensive. A computerized lighting system helps when there is exterior lighting interacting with interior lighting. We do recommend them, because it is difficult for managers to properly adjust sound and light levels.

Q: What are the greatest challenges that you're facing today regarding tabletop design?

A: Our biggest challenge is to ensure that the tabletop works with the concept. It should not send a different message to the customers. We look for consistency with the concept.

Q: What trends do you see in tabletop design?
A: Simplicity. We're seeing much less in terms of painted and patterned plates where the food has to battle with the plate for star billing. Decorative plates are sometimes used as base plates but then removed when the food hits the table. The impact of food presentation on the plate is the most important consideration.

Q: How would you define eatertainment restaurants? What do you think of them?
A: We don't like the word or use it. It is superficial in a lot of respects. The closest definition would be multifunctional units that provide food, entertainment, and drinking within one venue. The overall experience can be better than a poorly themed and poorly thought-out concept that throws a bunch of stuff together. But most of these eatertainment places aren't really based on food. Folks will only come back once or twice for the animatronics.

Q: What do you see as trends for the future?
A: Barriers are coming down in terms of niche market definitions. Fast-food operators are taking another look at their designs and aiming for a higher level in an effort to attract a wider clientele. The lines between upscale and casual are becoming blurry. Some casual places have an upscale look; some upscale places look more casual.

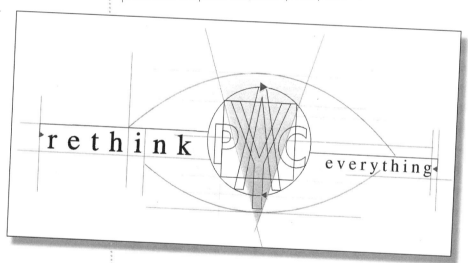

Aumiller Youngquist's new corporate logo.
(Courtesy of Aumiller Youngquist)

People have complained about noisy restaurants, so decibel levels are coming down. That leads to more carpeting. With more baby boomers wearing glasses, light levels will be raised and light sources like sconces in booth seating will help focus brighter light where it is needed. Easy-to-read graphics will also become important.

We also see an influx of technology in terms of service systems, communication systems, and entertainment, including video and audio, to create an entire package.

The bar is being raised throughout all of the dining segments, resulting in a less stereotypical approach to design.

Larry Bogdanow

Principal
Bogdanow Partners Architects, PC
New York

Number of restaurant projects: ~50

Larry Bogdanow and his partner, Warren Ashworth, lead a team of designers who use ingenuity rather than big budgets to solve design problems. Their restaurant designs, encompassing projects that range from City Hall in New York to Legal Sea Foods in Boston, are known for comfort and longevity. Bogdanow is particularly proud that his early restaurant designs, which date back to the mid 1980s, are still operating successfully.

Larry Bogdanow.
(Photo courtesy of Bogdanow Partners Architects, PC)

Q: What do you think is the single most important element of a successful restaurant design?
A: Flow. This includes how diners, service staff, and food move through the space. In terms of the front of the house, it starts when people enter the restaurant. Since they often have to wait for a table, there should be comfortable waiting areas—places to sit down other than the bar. For those who do choose to wait at the bar, there should be a walkway that offers a clear path from the maître d' station. The rest of that flow involves getting people from the bar or waiting area to the table. From an operational point of view, the flow of servers to and from the kitchen and the service stations is equally important.

Some of the most common design mistakes happen when flow patterns aren't considered. One of the worst is when the corridor to the bathroom is also the corridor to the kitchen. That's a terrible design: Guests who are going to the bathroom should not have to bump into the waitstaff hurrying back and forth from the kitchen.

Q: What are some other common design mistakes?
A: Not making every table a good table. A crowded corner table can be turned into something romantic and desirable. Seating in a wide open space doesn't have to feel like an old-fashioned cafeteria. Designers can use all kinds of techniques—color, lighting, booths, banquettes, screens, spatial orientation—to create the feeling of separate, smaller areas within one main space.

Another mistake is not paying attention to the design of the service station. It's offensive for guests to see a flashing computer screen or something that looks like it belongs in a motel kitchenette. We try to make that station into a piece of furniture that is nice to look at, like a breakfront or a china cabinet. I'll fight for a flip screen on the POS so customers won't have to stare at the screen. Things like water, coffee, bread, butter, and glassware can be displayed on beautiful glass or wood shelving that fits into the overall design of the room.

Q: Where does theme fit in?
A: The design theme should come from the building itself or from the food. There are many ways to express theme in the design. But the more that theme becomes the one overriding feature, then the harder it is to keep people coming back to the restaurant. People may try the Hard Rock Café in different locations, but they probably won't return to the same Hard Rock location again and again.

Q: Does good design mean expensive design?
A: Not always. If one of the goals is to keep the budget down, then knocking out the budget in the early days of the schematic design is helpful. It's important for operators to know when we discuss the program early on that the mechanicals are fifty to sixty percent of the overall budget and the visible part of the front-of-the-house budget is a relatively small percentage overall.

We keep track of the budget as it develops throughout all the phases of the project. If a design element comes in higher than expected, then we deal with it. We also try to follow the philosophy of value engineering all the way through.

Then we try to use simple things in a creative way—for example, simple blond masonite walls that are given a shiny lacquer finish to make the wall surface look like faux leather. Pine floors painted red and green, then waxed—there is no maintenance because when the paint chips away, a multicolored look is created.

Q: How can restaurateurs best work with designers to create a successful restaurant design?
A: Restaurant owners should realize that they need to be able to get along with their architect/designer for a couple of years. It's a long-term association, so make sure to develop the relationship and feel completely comfortable with it before signing the contract.

During the project, the owner should designate a person to be in charge of day-to-day contact with the design team. Ideally, there should be regularly scheduled meetings with all of the project consultants and weekly meetings with the architect/designer on the job site.

Q: What is the relationship of design to cuisine? To what extent does/should the menu influence the design?

A: Food is an easy theme to design around. At City Hall, for example, Henry Meer knew exactly what he wanted right from the start: a New York restaurant with traditional New York cuisine. That gave us a clear design direction.

If the owner doesn't know what the menu will be, we bring it up as part of the planning process. It has to be identified early for the front-of-the-house design to work. If a chef isn't on board at the start of a project, there should at least be a food concept.

Q: Your firm is known for creating interesting designs that are also practical for the operator. What is there about your approach to the design process that makes this happen?

A: I think it's the follow-through. We identify the issues and make sure they're addressed throughout the design. We don't compromise flow and circulation. Servers have to be able to reach the kitchen. The bus staff has to be able to clean the tables. When a noisy party comes into the restaurant, other guests still have to be able to hear their dining companions. Acoustic control is a big issue with us. I don't believe that a loud restaurant is a good restaurant. It doesn't matter how nice the space is if people can't hear each other. And what good does it do to play music if people can't distinguish what type of music it is? So we try not to compromise on acoustics either.

Q: What's your take on open kitchens?

A: These days, the open kitchen aesthetic seems to be everywhere, although it is less ubiquitous in New York because New Yorkers are more demanding about noise. The noisiest elements, like dish- and potwashing, should be in acoustically lined spaces so that guests sitting at the table on the other side of the wall don't hear the din. We like to use glass to provide a view and then control that view. It doesn't make sense to give people a view of raw protein foods or anything that shows blood.

In general, kitchen areas occupied by the waiters should be kept to a minimum, particularly in urban locales. More space should be dedicated to prep rather than to pickup. A small waiter's pantry will help keep servers on the floor rather than hanging out in the kitchen. It also makes sense to allocate activities like making stock and baking to a basement prep kitchen or other out-of-the-way location.

Q: How has restaurant design changed in the past fifteen years?

A: Back in the mid-1980s, there were a lot of clubby, disco-inspired elements in restaurants, like metallic colors and flashing lights. There was no acoustic control. Now, a lot of people are trying to be futuristic. Oranges, reds, and hot pinks are coming back, but styles and colors change quickly.

Perhaps a more lasting change is that restaurant seating has gotten more and more comfortable. We order samples for our clients to try out. One restaurant owner had one hundred sample chairs delivered and sat in them all before making a choice.

Q: What are the most important trends in restaurant design today? Any forecasts for the next ten years?

A: Bathroom design has become very important. In the future, we'll see great restaurant bathrooms with nice materials, stereo sound, hang-out space, telephones, and even television monitors. Because more people are going to restaurants and bars rather than to clubs and discos, the lounge area has become a lot more important. We're designing lounge areas for more than just drinking, with elements like hydraulic lifts that adjust a table's height so it can work for drinking or dining. In hotel restaurants, we're seeing the evolution of the 24/7 coffee shop into a stylish space where guests can get small plates of food to be shared, kind of like American tapas.

Another trend is the retail side of the restaurant business: selling merchandise and take-out. The merchandise is moving away from T-shirts and baseball caps and toward something that relates to the particular restaurant, like signature sauces, salad dressings, or baked goods. Prepared foods that put the label of the restaurant in someone's kitchen are an ongoing reminder of the place. In terms of restaurant design, take-out and retail sales require an area separate from the entryway where diners wait for their table to be ready.

In terms of materials, the two main directions are low maintenance and green. We won't use rain-forest materials in our projects any longer. Instead, we're experimenting with recycled materials such as sunflower seed husks compressed to make fiberboard.

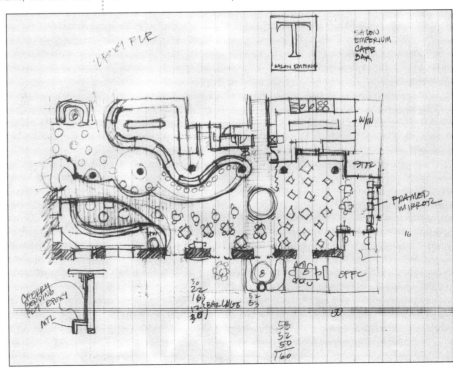

Concept sketch, T Salon Emporium.
(Courtesy of Bogdanow Partners Architects, PC)

William V. Eaton

President and COO
Cini-Little International, Inc.
Rockville, Maryland (15 offices worldwide)

Number of restaurant projects: more than 5,000

Bill Eaton heads the world's largest food facilities design and consulting firm, with hundreds of employees and 15 offices worldwide. Eaton joined the firm founded by John Cini in 1971. He is a forward thinker who believes in teamwork to create innovative back-of-the-house solutions.

William V. Eaton.
(Photo courtesy of Cini-Little
International, Inc.)

Q: What constitutes good kitchen design?
A: First, something that functions well, that allows the owner/operator to manage labor. A quality design continues to work even when it is stressed with increases in business volume. A good design also lasts over time, with equipment that continues to function well.

Q: How can good kitchen design help decrease employee stress?
A: We start by doing a great deal of workstation analysis that ensures that employees are provided with adequate workspace. We strive for shorter reaches and accessibility to the tools and equipment needed in each station. Then we consider little things, like adding color and reducing noise. We also strive for a design that allows servers and the kitchen staff to communicate effectively.

Q: How do you control noise in your kitchen designs?
A: The best way to reduce noise is to install a high-quality ventilation system. Ventilation systems typically add a lot of noise to the kitchen environment. We work with the manufacturers to ensure that the fan and ductwork is properly sized to minimize noise levels. We also work to screen and buffer some of those areas in the kitchen that produce a lot of noise, such as the potwashing and dishwashing areas.

In front-of-the-house support areas, we make sure that there is a place for everything and that everything is in its place. That reduces noise because things find their way to their designated spots more quietly than if they are merely tossed into a space.

Q: How would you describe the relationship between functional/operational efficiency and aesthetic appeal, particularly as it applies to open kitchens or servery operations visible to customers?
A: Function is paramount. At the same time, these spaces need to be attractive. We design for efficiency first and then consider what will be visible to customers. We look at what should be screened: kitchen waste and some hand activities, soiled ware, and anything else that looks disorganized. We put the preprep in back, out of view of customers. The goal is to show off the fresh foods and the theatrical activity.

Q: What specifically do you do to achieve a balance between design and function in open kitchen designs?
A: We work with the designers. Egos must be set aside to solve problems. You have to pay attention to each other's needs and then work to find the solution. You almost can't meet enough.

Q: When do you serve as the team leader in a design project?
A: Typically, from ten to fifteen percent of the time.

Q: Does good kitchen design mean expensive design?
A: Not necessarily, but quality kitchens are not inexpensive. Cini-Little designs might have a higher price tag but, in the long term, they are less expensive. What you have to consider is the capital expenditure on day one and balance that with operating expenditures. Also, good equipment lasts for a long time before needing repairs. And there are times when a costly, custom-designed piece of equipment can actually save four to eight man-hours per day. That translates to roughly twenty thousand dollars per year, which may pay for the added equipment investment in just a few months.

Q: When does it make sense to choose custom-designed equipment?
A: Particularly in today's shrinking restaurant kitchens, custom pieces of equipment may be the best way to meet specific spatial or operational requirements. We specify custom equipment more in display kitchens to create an arrangement that can't be realized with off-the-shelf equipment. But to help control the cost, we often work with standard components that we then have customized. That leads to a lower price than using completely custom equipment.

Q: How important is good kitchen design to the success of a restaurant?
A: It's paramount. Any kitchen will produce food, but at what cost to the restaurant's profitability? If a bad layout wastes labor, there are consequences. The customer might like what's coming out of the kitchen, but if more labor is needed or if there is higher staff

turnover due to the layout, it becomes an added expense to the operation.

Q: Can you offer some ideas on labor-saving equipment?
A: The majority of labor savings can be realized through efficient workstation design. Not a lot of equipment out there is labor saving. But the combination oven can be a labor saver if its programmable features are properly used. As for automation, it still has not come very far, and I don't see a move toward automation any time in the near future.

Q: How do you work with restaurateurs to create a successful kitchen design?
A: We define the goals of the restaurateur and develop a well-documented program. And we have to be able to change and flex the program as it comes together to a final point where we're almost offering a plan that describes how to operate the restaurant. Restaurateurs must be able to communicate their needs and ideas and then listen to our ideas. It is only through this exchange that success can be realized.

Q: When and how often do you interface with front-of-the-house designers or architects on a typical project?
A: We work together throughout the project. We insist on being deeply involved in the whole process due to flow patterns, access routes, and the whole service process. We frequently need to instruct designers and architects on how the front and back of the house must interrelate. We don't step on their toes, but we try to understand their needs.

Q: What trends in kitchen design do you see over the next ten years?
A: Open kitchens are certainly a trend. Almost every foodservice system we're currently designing has some aspect of an open or display kitchen. It reinforces the eatertainment mode we are in.

Kitchens are getting smaller, driven by reduced budgets. We are working very hard to make every workstation more efficient so that the labor quotient is less. In doing that, very often the station size is reduced, or two stations are combined into one that is smaller than the two individually. Then there is the constant push to "fresh" combined with just-in-time (JIT) delivery systems that reduce the amount of space needed for storage.

I also foresee improved environments for employees. This is a critical point, as the labor market has all but disappeared. In order to attract people into the foodservice industry, we must pay more, give better benefits, and develop a better work environment. Here again, a con-

stant refinement of the workstation to make it more efficient and more ergonomically comfortable will help. Colors, natural light (required for years in Europe), and better support facilities like lockers, rest rooms, break spaces, etc., all come into play.

Q: What major changes will we see in the equipment of restaurant kitchens?
A: We are already seeing faster methods of cooking that enhance quality. The Turbochef and FlashBake technology now owned by Blodgett (Maytag) and Vulcan respectively use convection and microwave or quartz and microwave to improve delivery. We will continue to see the development of equipment that can do individual portions or small batches quickly, which also improves quality. These will be smaller, more expensive pieces of equipment.

Q: How about changes to cafeteria serveries?
A: The move to display cooking, fresh presentations, more variety, and much more merchandising will continue to grow. Healthy food will be offered, but *fresh* and *variety* will be the buzzwords.

Q: How will computer programs help to create even more efficient kitchen designs?
A: We at Cini-Little, for example, are developing highly detailed three-dimensional models of individual workstations that will be used to examine the stations and to show clients exactly what they will be getting. Computer-simulated walk-throughs or fly-overs and fly-throughs will become commonplace. We are also using computer simulations of employee task movements to test efficiency of work patterns and stations. Aside from that, we will be downloading foodservice equipment brochures from manufacturers' Web pages directly to our digital laser printer. It is the beginning of the end for the equipment catalogs as we know them today.

3-D rendering of Café Centro.
(Courtesy of Restaurant Associates and Cini-Little, Inc.)

Pat Kuleto

Designer-Owner
Pat Kuleto Restaurants, Inc.
San Francisco

Number of restaurant projects: ~165

Pat Kuleto.
(Photo by Dennis Anderson)

Everything about Pat Kuleto's life has something to do with food and wine: as a builder, a designer, a restaurant owner, and a vintner. He began his career more than 25 years ago as a general contractor, started building restaurants in the 1970s, and gained fame for his design of San Francisco's Fog City Diner in 1985. In 1993, he embarked on his first partnership with a chef to open Boulevard in San Francisco. Kuleto's joie de vivre is reflected in his restaurant designs.

Q: Speaking as a restaurant owner as well as a restaurant designer, what does successful restaurant design mean to you?
A: First and foremost, a restaurant has to work. I may have a concept or idea for a location or space, but I always design it from a functional/operational standpoint first. I think of the layout from the perspective of all the key positions in the restaurant—chef, busser, waiter, dishwasher—and see how they need to do their jobs. If the place doesn't work functionally, you may be missing some of the benefits that the space can bring.

From an aesthetic perspective, design should make people feel comfortable. It also has to be an exciting, transporting, and dramatic enough experience to get people engaged. You want them to look around the space and feel thrilled to be there. After a while, however, that initial excitement settles down. To keep people coming back, a restaurant's design should keep unfolding to reveal new features and reasons to return. Design should not scream at guests, and people should not be hit with the entire design on the first visit. There should be enough design surprises and subliminal experiences to draw customers back again and again.

Anything that is successful has to last, so good design must have longevity. Today, this is more important than ever due to the high cost of opening a restaurant in the first place. Finally, good design doesn't overpower the food. It's in balance with the food.

Q: What is the single most important key to good restaurant design?
A: I don't think there is one single feature for all restaurants. All the components have to work together, but that's not easy to do. I think that lighting is probably the most powerful design element in my restaurants. Creating a space that offers intimacy and has comfortable sound levels is also key.

Q: Does good design mean expensive design?
A: I don't think so. We went through a period in the 1980s when design was very expensive. This is still true in some cases today. You have to spend enough to make a place feel comfortable. We now have many intelligent ways—from a financial point of view—to cre-

ate a successful and creative design on a tight budget. You can do nice things with lighting, spatial relationships, wall textures, and other areas that command attention. They need not be expensive, but they have to be well done. The worst possible thing you can do is to try to design a restaurant on the cheap. It's also a bad idea to try copying the design from another restaurant. Sure, you can use ideas that you see elsewhere, but if you copy ten ideas from each of ten restaurants you'll end up with a cheap reproduction.

Q: Given your background as a general contractor (GC), how would you characterize the GC's role on the restaurant design team?
A: The GC is very important. He deals with reality. A good GC can be of tremendous help in determining how a restaurant comes together. Restaurateurs have the philosophical concepts and designers have the aesthetic concepts. A good GC interprets those concepts and turns them into reality. It's one thing to produce a two-dimensional rendering, but then the GC has to create it in three dimensions. They should never be thought of solely as building tradesmen but rather as an integral part of the team.

Q: From a historical perspective, has restaurant design become more important to the overall success of the restaurant?

A: Absolutely. When you look back over the past fifteen years, you can see how design has become a critical element. In many cases, it is more important than the food, service, or location. For example, customers would rather get good food in a place with a really great design than to get great food in a place with a crummy design. I'm talking about good design in legitimate restaurants here. Inappropriate, flashy design that has nothing to do with good food is just weird stuff. We saw lots of that in the past, but now there's a trend back to traditional classic design elements.

Q: Is the importance of restaurant design a lasting trend?
A: Years ago, the availability of talented designers and good design products was limited. Today, it is easier to get better design quality and interesting products, and I believe that trend will continue.

Q: How do you use design to merchandise wine?
A: You want to get wine in front of people visually. Most people are romantically inclined to wine and designs that support wine sales are very effective.

Whenever I have an opportunity, I put wines on display, whether it's by putting a table in a wine cellar, installing wine cabinets in a dining room, or putting wine displays in the bar or over service stations. Some years ago, at Kuleto's in San Francisco, we felt something was lacking in the design. Across from the cook line was a piece of wide crown molding that already existed, so I displayed all the bottles on our wine list there. That simple addition dramatically changed the look of the place and improved our wine sales.

Q: What usually gets in the way of successful designer-restaurateur collaboration? How can they best work together?
A: The collaboration is really based on how well the restaurateur can define a concept, assuming that he has a concept. Usually, restaurateurs come with a vague idea, like they want to open a seafood place or a chop house. And they might have an idea of how the restaurant should feel, but the challenge is that they must have the ability to communicate those ideas and feelings to the designer. It's then the designer's responsibility to interpret what the restaurateur has said and combine that with his or her own talent. The result should be a design that uses the designer's skills and a design that works for the restaurateur.

Designers can't work in isolation from the chef, the kitchen, the restaurateur, or the business objectives. Designers need to communicate what they are trying to pull off as they move along with the project. They must have the ability and desire to communicate with the rest of the team to create a design that hits the exact market that the restaurateur is targeting. The worst problems arise when a restaurateur has an idea of what kind of restaurant will work in a situation and then the designer takes it in a different direction.

Q: How closely do you generally work with a kitchen design consultant? At what phases in the project?

A: What we typically do is identify the location of the kitchen and then design a typical kitchen that will work for the restaurant. We determine a geographic layout of the kitchen that functions as well as it can. We then work with the chef, if one is on board at the time, and bring in a kitchen designer to be a part of the team. We ask the kitchen designer to choose the individual pieces of equipment and the best way to fit them together. I always feel that, at a minimum, the kitchen should be roughed out by the chef before it goes to the kitchen consultant.

Q: How has restaurant design changed since you've been in the business?
A: A lot has changed over these past twenty-five years. For one thing, restaurant design has actually come into existence as a profession. Restaurant design didn't really exist until the 1980s because there were no restaurant design specialists out there. Since then, it has been legitimized and its importance recognized by the financial industries. Restaurant design has also become an art form with a signature that is as distinctive as an artist's. It's taught in university programs, and one of the first things that is talked about when a restaurant is opened is its design. Today, a designer can be as famous as a chef.

Restaurant designers are now held accountable to meet laws, codes, OSHA [Occupational Safety and Health Administration], fire safety, and even ADA requirements. We used to be able to pull a permit by submitting just a couple of sheets of paper describing what we were going to build. Now, it's a three- to six-month process with tons of documentation to get through the permitting.

Wine label from Kuleto Villa vineyard.
(Courtesy of Pat Kuleto)

Henry Meer

Chef-Owner
New York

Restaurants owned: 2

Henry Meer is a lifelong New Yorker. His love for Manhattan and the culinary traditions on which it was built are formative elements in his life and in his restaurants. After eight years of tutelage under the watchful eye of Jean-Jacques Vongerichten at Côte Basque and ten years with Andre Soltner at Lutece, three of which he served as sous chef, Meer opened the Cub Room in 1995 and City Hall Restaurant in 1998. When it comes to design, he has some special insights.

Henry Meer.
(Photo courtesy of Henry Meer)

Q: Where does restaurant design begin?
A: You begin with the end. Ask yourself, "What is the end product?" If the end product is a sushi restaurant, then you need a sushi bar. You need to define what you want to accomplish. You don't need to know the exact menu items, but you need an idea of the kind of food that will be served.

There's an evolution to the kitchen design that happens after the menu is finalized. The menu will dictate what equipment is and is not needed. At City Hall, I initially wanted a European Waldorf-style range. But after developing the menu, I realized it wasn't practical for the type of dishes we'd be preparing and gave up the idea.

Q: What are the most important elements of a successful restaurant design?
A: Flow is critical. There should be a welcoming area for guests that they come to first, no matter where they go next. In addition, the welcome center also works for those who might be going to private rooms. Plan for lots of traffic. Good flow and layout from the front directs people into other areas.

A restaurant is never finished. We're always tweaking to get the flow right, to make it work better.

Q: You have said that private dining rooms are one of the keys to a financially successful restaurant. What are your major design considerations when it comes to private dining rooms?
A: When you have private dining spaces, a separate bar, rest rooms, coatroom, and kitchen are essential so that private dining works independently from the main parts of the restaurant. If we had but one coatroom for both the dining room and the private dining areas at City Hall, we would have a bottleneck. The same would hold true for the kitchen if we were trying to use one space to serve banquet food at the same time as dining room food. And having enough bathrooms to serve the needs of guests in various areas of the restaurant, including private dining, is critical.

Q: What is most important to consider when purchasing kitchen equipment?
A: Buy top-quality equipment so that the kitchen staff and the restau-

rant can succeed. The options are to buy top-notch equipment for the long run or to buy a used piece of equipment that will break down quickly. Over time, fixing equipment can cost more.

Q: How do you design the kitchen to make it more efficient?
A: Flow is crucial. Where does the food come in and where does it go out? Mise en place is critical so the staff don't have to keep running for replenishment. This means refrigeration right at the cooking station. We use undercounter refrigerated drawers to keep foods cold before they are cooked.

Q: What advice would you give to owner-operators about working with designers and architects?
A: First, have a clear idea of what you want to accomplish. Second, surround yourself with design team members who can give you great input on front- and back-of-the house elements. Feel comfortable with those people and then delegate responsibilities to them because you can't do everything yourself. Find good people you can work with, let them bring ideas to you, and then make the decisions.

Q: Do you have any recommendations about installing utilities in the kitchen?
A: Add up all the Btus and kilowatts you think you'll need and then double those figures. Imagine the requirements with all of your burners cranking at one time and also anticipate growth.

Q: Do you have any money-saving design tips?
A: Dedicate a space to do your own laundry. We send our table linen out but wash all of our employee uniforms at a savings of one dollar and ten cents per uniform. That saves a tremendous amount of money.

Q: Cleanliness has become increasingly important. How can design help to maintain cleanliness in the kitchen?
A: Put all of your equipment on wheels; even your ranges, broilers, and ovens. Make sure that they are connected with flexible connections. Then pull them out from the wall at least one time each week and clean under and behind them.

Drew Nieporent

President
Myriad Restaurant Group
New York

Restaurant impresario Drew Nieporent has been in the business for 22 years. He has operated dozens of restaurants and partnered with such notables as Robert De Niro, Francis Ford Coppola, Robin Williams, and Japanese chef Nobuyuki Matsuhisa to develop restaurants under the Myriad Restaurant Group umbrella. Today, his cell phone rings continually during our interview and he answers it "Hello, command central." But between those calls, we were able to sneak in the following questions.

Drew Nieporent.
(Photo courtesy of Myriad Restaurant Group)

Q: What role does design play in the ultimate success of a restaurant?
A: Design is critical for a number of reasons. In this day and age, there is so much competition that it takes more than just food and beverage for a restaurant to distinguish itself. When people enter a space, it's like they're meeting a person; there's an immediate reaction. Subliminal factors including the size of the room, seating shapes, and lighting lead to a "like" or "don't-like" decision. And especially in cities like New York, design can help to bring people into the restaurant for the first time.

Q: Which of your restaurants is most successful, from a design point of view, and why?
A: Nobu is a great example of how everything works in sync. We told the designer, David Rockwell, that there should be no clichés. He came up with nontraditional yet strong artistic images of things that one would see in Japan. The overall look is new contemporary, and there's enough going on in the design to keep people visually engaged throughout the dining experience. The design fits perfectly with our goal of making the Japanese dining experience more accessible to the U.S. masses.

Q: How involved do you personally get with the design of your restaurants?
A: I am very hands-on. I work side by side with the designer and edit the work. One of my biggest jobs is to guard against overdesign. First and foremost, the restaurant must be operationally sound. Looking good comes after that.

Q: Does good design mean expensive design? How expensive?
A: It is so expensive to build a restaurant. Our designers usually get twenty percent of the overall costs. The trouble is that some designers only think about aesthetics and, shortly after the restaurant opens, the carpet looks terrible and the light fixtures don't work, even though the design cost a fortune. Good design has to incorporate good workmanship, and it has to work physically.

Q: What are the biggest mistakes designers make?
A: Sometimes the design is so powerful and so gaudy that it doesn't relate to the food at all. It can be overwhelming. High-backed banquettes may look dramatic, but they shouldn't interfere with people's sight lines and block their views, because it's important for most people to see and be seen.

Another area to watch out for is lighting. So many restaurants are too dark. When people can't see what they're eating, it negatively impacts the experience.

Q: Any other tips on what makes a comfortable restaurant environment?
A: Lots of curves and round tables. People always like corner tables, and by curving the banquette, you end up with a corner. That's a functional design solution most designers don't know about. And nothing is more important than sound control: You'll have happy customers and good reviews if you design a restaurant that isn't noisy.

Q: What are the characteristics of a good designer?
A: The best designers listen to the client and try to synthesize their needs and thoughts into the design solution. They take into account that there is another personality in the equation and recognize that the operator stays involved with the restaurant while the designer moves on.

Q: It has been said that we're in the age of the celebrity restaurant architect. Is the name more important than the design?
A: Food journalists have popularized those designers because their work has been successful. Their names have become a brand, and that does help attract people to the restaurant. But there can be a backlash: The public can say enough already with the famous name. The other thing operators should be aware of is that the celebrity designer may attach his firm name to a project but not have much to do personally with the design.

Q: What are the most important trends in restaurant design today?
A: Overall, designers are looking to do things that have never been done before. But specifically, it depends on where the restaurant is located. The look in London is minimal, with white frosted glass and hard surfaces everywhere. In San Francisco, the look is more funky. Whimsy is popular in New York, but I don't think New York is necessarily leading the way. Many designers of New York restaurants are reacting to outside influences rather than creating an original look.

Richard Melman

Chairman of the Board
Lettuce Entertain You Enterprises, Inc.
Chicago

Number of restaurants: ~70

Richard Melman.
(Photo courtesy of *Crain's Chicago Business*)

Chicago native Richard Melman grew up in the restaurant business. In 1971, he and his partner, Jerry Orzoff, raised $17,000 and opened R.J. Grunts, the first in what was to become an empire of more than 70 establishments owned and licensed by Melman and his partners. Over the years, Melman has developed about 75 restaurant concepts. Known as a charismatic and creative leader, he views himself as "part artist, part businessman."

Q: What constitutes good restaurant design, from the customer's perspective?

A: I think customers want to feel comfortable. And comfort comes not only from physical things. Comfort comes from what they sit or walk on, what they see, feel, and smell. I think customers feel good design rather than look at every little detail.

Q: How about from an operational perspective?

A: It absolutely starts with the proper space planning. Without the proper space planning, things just don't work as well. Another issue is how to make the room feel right for different functions. For example, a certain restaurant might have dancing on Friday and Saturday nights and dining-only on weeknights, so you need to create a room that looks full and festive on the nights when there is no dancing.

The space-planning challenge is affected by the number of seats needed for profitability. And the flow has to be logical, so that servers can reach whatever they need in just a few steps. If they have to walk thirty steps for water, the operation has problems.

Q: Where do you get your inspiration?

A: I'm always looking for holes in the marketplace or ways that I can do something a little better. I spend a lot of time talking with people to get ideas and checking out the competition. For example, I thought about TrU and saw that there were other four-star restaurants in its neighborhood, but none that were hip, young, and arty-feeling. We also saw the potential to serve lunch at TrU because none of the others had tapped the lunch market.

Q: How important is design to the success of restaurants today? To your restaurants?

A: When I got into this business nearly thirty years ago, the truth was that all you really needed to do was serve good food. Over time, service and design have become much more important. So has marketing and location. Today, there are so many elements in the mix that makes for success. I wouldn't put design first, but it certainly adds to a great experience—or detracts from one if a space is poorly lit, poorly laid out, or acoustically imbalanced.

Q: What is the relationship of design to food and service? To what extent does or should the menu influence the design?

A: The menu does influence the design. In most cases, the style of the food should be mirrored by the style of the design. I don't like restaurants where food and design are disconnected because there needs to be some continuity of food, service, and decor. We always think about all of the elements that make up a restaurant, from the uniforms to the food to the tabletop display. For example, I wouldn't want a Spanish restaurant to have a French look.

Q: How involved do you personally get with the design of your restaurants? How about the chef's role? Does the chef give input to or interact with the restaurant architect?

A: I get very involved with the design of our restaurants. I work with architects, designers, and artists. I'm sort of a coordinator. I don't take the credit for the design, but I clearly set a direction. We usually put a design team of nine to fifteen people together. The chef is a big part of the design team because food is the heart and soul of the restaurant. Some of our chefs get involved with the interior design, but some really only look as far as the plate.

Q: Do you get involved with kitchen design?

A: I get involved with kitchen design to a certain extent, but we have chef-partners who are more knowledgeable than I am. I get involved in the menu, which determines how the kitchen should be laid out. I don't dictate the kitchen layout or demand that it be fitted out with equipment from one manufacturer. I look for pieces of equipment that can do the proper job for what we envision. For example, different griddles are needed for pancakes and hamburgers. The same holds true for the choice of broilers. We try to develop a kitchen line with efficiency in mind.

Q: Who designs the open kitchen in your restaurants—architect, chef, foodservice consultant, or some combination?

A: It's always a combination. I might get together with a partner and talk about what we want the kitchen to feel like, starting with the basic design and moving on to the color, style, and lighting. Then we leave it to the designer, architect, and chef to plan the space.

Q: From a historical perspective, has restaurant design become more important to the overall success of the restaurant these days? If so, do you think this trend will last?

A: Yes, I think that restaurant design has become more important and that this is a lasting trend. But I'm not talking about over-the-top or over-done restaurant design. Good design can be as uncomplicated as using the right mix of colors and materials to generate a clean, sophisticated feeling.

Q: An article in *Crain's New York Business* said that the 1990s were the age of the celebrity restaurant architect. Do you agree? Has name become more important than the design?

A: Well, this was clearly a true statement. Designers like David Rockwell and Adam Tihany have become big names and put their mark on the whole field of restaurant design. I'm sure their names attract people to the restaurant for a first visit. But if they don't have clients who know how to run a good restaurant, the restaurants won't stay in existence no matter how great the design. I think it is true that the restaurant architect has come to the forefront, but the operating foundation has to be strong or these places won't be around for long.

Q: Does good design mean expensive design?

A: Not necessarily. What's expensive in restaurants is the electrical, plumbing, ventilation, and other elements that are hidden behind the walls. These will continue to rise in cost. But you can still create a great look with a ninety dollar chair and inexpensive wall treatment. Expensive does not always mean good taste, either.

Q: What usually gets in the way of successful restaurateur-designer collaboration? How can they best work together?

A: The biggest problems occur when there is no single person with vision leading a project. Projects that have three or four people who are leaders still need one designated person who says no or yes. This should be someone with taste, passion, and sensitivity. If there is a clear leader, usually the team will come together.

Q: What are the most important trends in restaurant design today? Will they last?

A: I think the open kitchen will continue to have a place because it gives the chef an opportunity to understand the customer better. Acoustic control is another trend. I, for one, like a restaurant with a little noise, but that's a fine line. I don't like loud, loud, loud restaurants. There needs to be enough acoustic control so that people feel comfortable and can hear their dining companions across the table.

Q: What's your take on eatertainment restaurants?

A: Eatertainment restaurants have begun to fall on hard times, but this business is cyclical. It's a big world and, at different times, people want different things. I think people who build these ten million dollar interactive palaces need to be careful. It's not a direction in which I would go.

The bar at TrU
(Photo © Mark Ballogg, Steinkamp/
Ballogg Photography, Chicago)

Mary Sue Milliken and Susan Feniger

Chef-Owners

Los Angeles

Restaurants owned: 3

Mary Sue Milliken and Susan Feniger each began cooking in high school, and they haven't stopped since. They opened their first restaurant together in 1981. Today, millions know them as the "Too Hot Tamales," which is the name of the Food Network television show in which they delight viewers with their playful banter and insights into world cuisine. Catching up with these world travelers is no easy feat, so their answers came via a conference call with Milliken in Las Vegas at the Border Grill and Feniger in Los Angeles at her home office.

Mary Sue Milliken and Susan Feniger.
(Photo by Gary Moss)

Q: When planning the kitchen, how do you determine how much space is needed for back versus front of the house?

A: Our rule of thumb is to allocate as little space as possible to the kitchen. Sometimes we inherit an existing restaurant, and that impacts the relationship between the spaces. Basically, we work from a formula based on the rent and projected profits. We calculate how many seats are needed to make a profit at a certain check average with a certain number of covers. If we don't have enough space left for the kitchen based on the number of seats we need, then maybe that particular real estate isn't a good choice.

Q: Do you have a preferred restaurant size?

A: The best size for us is a seventy-five-hundred-square-foot restaurant. It gives us plenty of seats and enough space in the kitchen for the kinds of food that we're doing. The goal is to have a restaurant that is always full, where you have to turn people away. We also feel there are efficiencies in a tight, well-organized kitchen—although there are some drawbacks to a compact kitchen if you do a lot of catering or if the restaurant gets swamped. We would rather feel like we are operating at close to capacity than doing more than we can handle.

Q: What are the steps you go through in designing the actual layout of the kitchen—that is, workstations, sections, etc? Do you bring in a kitchen consultant to assist with the layout and equipment selection?

A: We bring in a consultant, not to lay out stations but to update us on the newest, hottest equipment. We want to know what new kitchen design innovations might fit into our plan. When it comes to laying out stations, it's second nature to us. For example, for the grill station, we need a space to cut the skirt steaks when we take them off the grill. And the cutting board in the pantry needs to be large enough to hold plates and salad mixing bowls.

Q: What types of equipment are common to all of your kitchens?

A: The grill, for sure. At the Border Grills, we have the comal (a thick cast-iron surface) for making tortillas. One piece of equipment we'd like to have at Ciudad is a slow cooker that we could use for cooking lamb shoulders and short ribs.

Q: Have you used any equipment with built-in computer programs, such as a programmable combination oven? Do you use automated equipment?

A: We haven't used anything with computer programs. Our first thought is that it would be too costly. We really do try to open restaurants as inexpensively as possible because our goal is to maintain as much ownership as possible. We strive for functional, but not necessarily fancy, solutions. As for automated equipment, we are in the handmade food business. But automation has its place in other kinds of places.

Q: Do you do things to make the kitchen environmentally comfortable or aesthetically pleasing for the people who work there?

A: We wish we did more. At Ciudad, we painted the kitchen yellow even though the kitchen is a landlocked rathole. The kitchen is always the worst space in the building. But we air condition our kitchens and we play music. At City [a former restaurant in Los Angeles], the employee locker room was a dump. At Ciudad, it's a lot better. We have become wiser about the back-of-the-house environment over the years. People need to feel good about the space. Most important, we try to create a respectful, casual, and supportive environment; that's what our management style is.

Q: Open kitchens have become a trend. What's your take on them?
A: For us, they make no sense. We closed an open kitchen at one of our restaurants. Open kitchens are nice in some places, but we don't feel like it is our style. It's noisy and intense in the kitchen, and we don't want to put that onto the customers. The kitchen is a place to bond as a community with other hard-working people. To be put on display adds a lot of pressure.

Q: What is the relationship of design to food and service? To what extent does or should the menu influence the design?
A: We think food and design are closely related. Our goal is to create a space where the most important elements are the guest and the food. Customers should always feel comfortable in the room. Different concepts create different kinds of experiences, but the food, the space, and the service should always relate to each other.

Q: How important is front-of-the house design to the success of your restaurants? Is it more or less important than it was ten years ago?
A: It's always been important to us. We have always wanted to make a strong, bold statement and delight our customers with design. We want both the front of the house and the food to be cutting edge: familiar and comfortable yet different from what people find elsewhere. It is important that people be attracted to the front-of-the-house design. Josh [architect Josh Schweitzer designs their restaurants] is so much a part of our concept; he totally gets it as one big picture. The food ties into the murals, the murals tie into to the menus, the menus tie into the lights and the signage. It all works together.

Q: How involved do you personally get with the design of your restaurants?
A: Intimately. That's how we can keep our prices down. Knowing Josh since fifth grade, we feel an amazing trust in his sensibilities. We talk a little about what we want and the feel of what we want and then place it in Josh's hands. We have learned, as creative people, that you have to let other creative people run with their ideas. We never insert ourselves into the artistic process, except for communicating the goal of the place. From there, it is up to the architect. It is a lot like how we manage our staff: We give them room to be their own worst boss and to give the most that they can give.

Q: What do you think usually gets in the way of successful owner-designer collaboration? How can they best work together?
A: The biggest pitfall restaurant owners make is not spending enough time outlining the details. If you don't invest the time to communicate and make decisions in a timely manner up front, you end up with garbage. It's hard to prioritize the hours needed to make all of the decisions about a project. Each space is different, and it requires a lot of time for owners and designers to communicate. If you do your homework in the beginning, it's a lot easier. Rushing the planning process makes for strained relationships later in the project and ends up in a lot of finger pointing.

Q: Where would you like to take your restaurant concepts from here?
A: We want to open more restaurants, but the most important thing is to open restaurants with food that we can be really proud of. Neither one of us has any desire to open restaurants just to make money. We've worked hard for twenty years as partners to keep our reputation high. To open more restaurants, we need to carefully manage our time and develop a strong management and employee team. It involves finding the right location and taking things slowly.

Mural graphics from Border Grill.
(Courtesy of Schweitzer BIM, Inc.)

Morris Nathanson

Principal
Morris Nathanson Design, Inc.
Pawtucket, Rhode Island

Number of restaurant projects: ~500

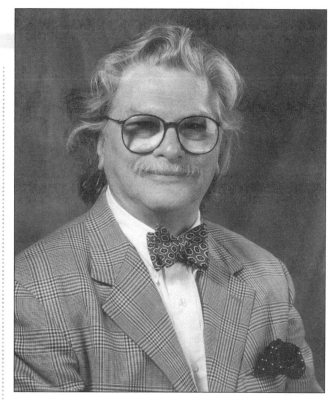

Morris Nathanson.
(Photo © Warren Jagger Photography, Inc.)

When Morris Nathanson founded his namesake firm in 1967, he already had 15 years of experience designing restaurants. He is known as a restaurant design specialist and has created many successful chain prototypes and new concept designs for a variety of operations around the world.

Q: What constitutes good restaurant design, from an operational perspective?

A: Operationally, the one thing that can make a design successful is an intelligent floorplan. The ceiling is a particularly important element but is often neglected. Ceilings are the space in the restaurant that people see the most of; chairs and tables don't cover the ceiling like they do the floor. The ceiling also incorporates lighting elements and affects the acoustics of the space.

Q: What kind of an acoustic balance do you aim for?

A: Sometimes the design demands high noise levels, like in casual restaurants where the entertainment factor is important. In more elegant restaurants, the level of sound must be lower. But if the sound levels are too soft, it doesn't work either. You don't want any restaurant to feel like housing for the elderly.

Q: What aspects of lighting are important to consider?

A: Lighting depends on the type of restaurant. Romantic lighting is different from exuberant lighting. It's important to design flexible lighting, so that the light levels can match the clientele at different times of day. The biggest complaint we hear about lighting is that there is too much overhead illumination. As much as possible, lighting should be located at a low level, using light sources like table lamps or wall sconces.

Just lighting a ceiling with recessed high hats is the worst thing to do. A person with a bald head doesn't like the lights giving him a sunbath. Of course, there needs to be enough light so that people don't feel like they are sitting in a dark hole. A good guideline is to light just enough for people to be able to read a menu.

Q: Does good design mean expensive design?

A: Absolutely not. Often it can be the opposite: Design can go too far and can try too hard. But if a restaurant concept calls for a certain amount of investment and the client is not willing to do that, it can destroy the business.

Q: What do you do when costs for a particular item come in over budget?

A: This shows who the true professionals are. Our job is to make the changes without creating any antagonism. This isn't easy. Almost every one of our recent jobs has had some budget surprises in it. The client's investment exposure is much higher today due to increases in construction costs and rapidly rising rents. Raising money has become more difficult, and cost overruns are a real problem. A one million dollar budget ten years ago was big. Today, it's not.

Q: Has restaurant design become more important to the overall success of the restaurant these days? Will this trend last?

A: Absolutely. It will never go back unless we have a serious depression. To be a good designer, you have to be aware of the social conditions and the changes to the community in which we operate. A healthy economy draws people out for entertainment and an occasion, not just to dine. And over the past fifteen years, people have changed the way they dine. Things will not change again unless women go back to being housewives. Right now, most women are in the workforce and they don't have the time to stay home and cook. Family dining is happening more as a dining-out experience than ever before. The alternative is to bring take-out food home. So the dining-out experience must be an exciting one. Food, design, and service all play a role in making the experience worthwhile.

Q: How can restaurateurs best work with designers—and vice versa—to create a successful restaurant design?

A: As much as possible, restaurateurs need to be realistic. The worst situation for a designer is to be convinced that the owner is a nice guy and then be given all the wrong information. Owners should be professional, direct, and specific, right from the start. It's important to make sure the designer understands the restaurant's intended clientele, not just the restaurateur's personal likes and dislikes. And the owner needs to have a level of confidence in the designer and allow the designer to do his work.

VIEW OF
1st LEVEL BAR
AND BALCONY

Rendering of Beacon
(Courtesy of Morris Nathanson Design, Inc.)

Designers must learn to listen to the restaurateurs. If they don't, they'll make mistakes because many important elements come out of designer-client discussions. Designers should never try to reuse a design developed for one client for another. It won't work because each client has individual preferences.

Designers must know how to ask the right questions so that their first presentation will make sense, questions like: What variety of table settings do you need? What's your budget? Who are your target markets? What's the menu? What kind and size of plates will be used to serve the menu?

Q: What does theme design mean to you? What about eatertainment?
A: Restaurants like Planet Hollywood cannot succeed over time because they are designed for tourists and cannot be tolerated for more than a few visits. As the chain grows, the problem is that tourists are seeing the same thing in every city. Why eat at a Planet Hollywood in another country if you've already been to one in the United States? The lifespan of concepts like Bugaboo Creek [outdoor-themed animatronics and grilled food items] are limited for the same reasons. The danger of doing a restaurant that is too heavily themed is that it cannot last as long as a restaurant that has a classic design because the experience wears thin too quickly.

Q: How has restaurant design changed since you've been in the business?
A: I've seen tremendous changes in restaurant design. In the 1950s, the hand of the designer was very soft, almost not there. Restaurant design wasn't even a profession. As the needs of the restaurant industry became more complicated, designers began to offer technical help, and a whole new profession was born. Design made it possible for restaurants to become a more complicated experience, one that was not just about eating food. In the 1980s, restaurants started to be about entertainment. Today, restaurants are about a multilayered experience, and design contributes to that experience in many ways.

Q: Where do you see restaurants, and restaurant design, heading in the next ten years?
A: Good food will be taken for granted. If a restaurant doesn't have good food, it won't be in business. Customers will talk more about the design and the experience. There will be fewer mom-and-pop operators who are only concerned with the cooking. Economic constraints will mean that new culinary school graduates will no longer be able to open their own business right away.

More and more people from the entertainment world will continue to get into the restaurant business. At some point, people will catch on that restaurants are as much oriented to entertainment as they are to food. Increasingly, our clients are corporations rather than individuals because it is the corporations that can afford the investment. Individuals who do get financing will quickly be bought out by corporate entities if they are successful.

Jeffrey Beers

Principal
Jeffrey Beers International
New York

Number of restaurant projects: ~60

Jeffrey Beers.
(Photo by Gwendolen Cates)

Whether he's reworking an existing restaurant interior in New York or producing a larger-than-life experience in Las Vegas, Jeffrey Beers pushes the envelope with his designs. After a six-year experience with the architectural firm I.M. Pei & Partners, he established Jeffrey Beers International in 1986 and has since gained an international reputation for his work.

Q: What does successful restaurant design mean to you?
A: Successful restaurant designs are entertaining. They create a festive atmosphere and make people want to celebrate. Successful design also supports, enhances, and embraces the food concept and supports the operational component.

Q: What is the single most important key to good restaurant design?
A: Energy. Every successful restaurant has a certain energy that is derived from many things. Design elements that create a sense of drama, like open kitchens, dramatic lighting, or elaborate wine displays, can help to create this energy.

Q: Does good design mean expensive design?
A: Not at all. Good design is about being clever.

Q: From a historical perspective, restaurant design has become more important to the overall success of the restaurant. Why? Is this a lasting trend?
A: Going to a restaurant has become an event; a kind of celebration. The experience of going to a restaurant today is like a mini vacation because people have less time to enjoy the simple things. Life has gotten harder and more demanding, and any opportunity we have to relax and escape the daily grind is appreciated. Design helps because it is part of the entertainment. It takes people out of their familiar, unstimulating day-to-day environment.

I believe that the importance of restaurant design is a lasting trend because going out to eat has become a way of life.

Q: What usually gets in the way of successful designer-restaurateur collaboration? How can the two best work together?
A: Unclear communication or undefined objectives can cause problems in designer-restauratuer collaboration. The designer needs to ask the restaurateur a lot of questions: Do you have restaurant experience? Why do you want to open this restaurant? What's driving you? What's your concept? How does it appeal to the market? Have you done your due diligence?

It's also important to identify the chef and have the location in hand. I'll agree or disagree that the location supports the food concept. At that point, the ball is in my court. I then have to process the information and present a design that enhances the chef and the owner and closes the circle.

Q: What is the relationship of design to food and service? To what extent does or should the menu influence the design?
A: The menu is integral, and so is the service flow. We are totally involved in the planning from all angles because it's key to creating a successful restaurant. The flow, entry, sequence, and operational support in the front of the house, as well as kitchen flow, is tremendously important to nail directly and put into a floorplan.

Q: How closely do you generally work with a kitchen design consultant? At what phases in the project? Do you ever interact with the chef?
A: We work with kitchen design consultants in all phases. I have to be involved in that, particularly in terms of an open kitchen. I interact with chefs on a regular basis.

Q: Do you feel that eatertainment restaurants with flashy design elements can compete successfully over time?
A: Some can, if they're good enough. I think most eatertainment restaurants that have opened to date are superficial, with somewhat two-dimensional surface treatments. They lack depth and richness. There is more to it than plastering the walls with memorabilia. That kind of treatment will just detract from the experience.

Rumjungle, a restaurant we designed in the Mandalay Bay hotel in Las Vegas, is an example of an eatertainment design that goes beyond the surface. Our goal was to add stimulation to the dining experience without detracting from it. Volcanic mountains of rum and spirits rise before guests in an illuminated bar. Conga music and dueling congas are reminiscent of the strolling guitarists who used to entertain guests in old Spanish restaurants. These are real dancers, not fabrications on a screen.

Q: What are some trends in restaurant design today?
A: Everyone's trying to be innovative and fresh and come up with new ideas. The sushi conveyor belt is an example, although it has been used in Japan for years. We're doing exciting things with fiber-optic lighting and lasers, using them both as accent lighting and dramatic features in their own right. We're also seeing food innovations that influence tabletop design and other operational elements in the front of the house, like rolling food carts with small plates of American dim sum.

Steven Pannone

Creative Director
Girvin Design, Inc.
Seattle, Washington

Number of restaurant projects: ~20

Steven Pannone spends much of his time traveling from one world capital to another, working with clients to create graphic programs for a variety of projects. He designed the graphics for most of the restaurants at Bellagio Casino Hotel in Las Vegas.

Steven Pannone.
(Photo courtesy of Girvin Design, Inc.)

Q: Why don't we see more good graphic design in restaurants?
A: In part, because the graphic designer is frequently brought in too late in the design process. We are often given very little information about the project and have to interpret the design direction rather than be an integral part of the design team from early on. Without having input into the design experience and the visual expression that resonates from that experience, we cannot contribute fully to good graphic design.

So many things go on during the design and construction of a restaurant that graphics are among the last things restaurateurs think about. But graphics are needed for the front of the menu, for inclusion in the Yellow Pages, and for the sign on the front door. We need collaborative clients who understand that good graphic design is more than the choice of a color palette and selection of typeface.

Q: How do you start a graphic design project for a restaurant? What do you consider?
A: The first thing we do is sit down with all of those who have a significant stake and drill through the process. What will be on the menu? What are the price points? What will the environment look like inside the restaurant and on the exterior facade? What's adjacent in the neighborhood, both buildings and signage? Who is the target audience the restaurant is trying to appeal to? We want more than demographics. We need insights that tell if the customers are those who are challenged by unusual cuisine and dining experiences. We also consider the seating plans and what the entry area of the restaurant will look like. From there, we begin to figure out how subtle touches in the interior can be unified with graphics.

Q: Do you consider different factors when you create graphics intended for a multi-unit restaurant operation?
A: Clients may come to us and want to roll out restaurants in dozens of locations without knowing what those locations are. Having to design a graphics program flexible enough to work for unknown buildings is probably the most difficult challenge of multi-unit operations.

For example, our program for World Wraps, a casual lunch and dinner place, had to be flexible enough to work for many unknown locations. We developed a flexible mural element that can be sized differently to accommodate the wall space of various building floorplans.

Q: Does good graphic design mean expensive design?
A: Not necessarily. The best example I can offer is the Nike logo, which was originally created by a student for thirty-five dollars. The true value of the mark obviously grew over the years. It wasn't expensive initially, but the way in which it was managed made it worth much more. So a graphic design does not have to be expensive for it to be good. It's the long-term management of the graphic identity that really gives it its value.

Q: How important is good graphic design to the success of a restaurant?
A: Consider the wine label. Wine labels express something about the product and speak to the target customer. If the customer has no experience with or knowledge of a given wine, he depends on the label to help make the purchase decision. The same holds true for the restaurant graphics and people's dine-or-don't-dine decision.

Q: How can restaurateurs best work with graphic designers?
A: Involve graphic designers at the beginning of the planning process and create a collaboration among all the members of the design team. There are many details about the graphics program—things like where they should be applied, and the cost and functionality of a preprinted versus a daily menu—that have to be considered early in the design process. The right questions, and the right answers, come out when we're charged with considering how the graphics will look over time.

David Rockwell

Principal
Rockwell Group
New York

Number of restaurant projects: ~200

The studios where David Rockwell heads a team of 150 professionals buzz with activity. Throughout the space are sketches, wall treatments, lighting fixtures, and models—samples produced for the hundreds of designs this inventive architect has created in locations all over the world. Rockwell sees restaurants as theater, and that philosophy clearly shows in his exuberant stage sets for all types of establishments. His name has become synonymous with innovative restaurant design.

David Rockwell.
(Photo by Scott Frances)

Q: What does successful restaurant design mean to you?
A: From a design perspective, it involves creating an engaging and memorable experience. We often do that with unexpected visual references—lights created from Japanese fishing baskets, a seaweed wall. But most important, successful restaurant design comes from collaboration. Trends change, but designers and owners should always collaborate. Don't just go out to eat together to react to other restaurants but also look at plays, movies, and museum exhibits to come up with fresh feelings and ideas.

Q: How can design help the restaurant work from an operational perspective?
A: It's important to understand the flow of a restaurant and the owner's priorities. Should the chairs to be comfortable to sit in for forty-five minutes or two hours? What size should the plates be? We think about what the waiters have to do in terms of a dance—the ballet of the front of the house—and how to choreograph that dance.

We also want to create spaces that engage the senses in an appropriate way. If we're designing a restaurant where fresh food counts, then we don't want to face guests with a fake brick wall.

Q: What are the keys to good restaurant design? Can you give a few examples?
A: Accurately defining the goal of the project, and the ability to keep everything in mind, including the big conceptual idea.

Next Door Nobu is related to Nobu, but it also has its own identity. It is deceptively simple. Familiar materials like mother-of-pearl and seaweed are used in surprising ways. Ruby Foo's is an Auntie Mame-like fantasy, a surreal space. But if you took away the surfaces, it is the layout that makes it work.

Each project does something different, but in each case, what makes the restaurant work is the functional layout and the fact that it suits the market.

Q: What usually gets in the way of successful designer-restaurateur collaboration? How can the two best work together?
A: Collaboration usually fails when there is not a clear vision or mission statement. Good communication is necessary for a successful working relationship and a successful restaurant design.

Q: You're known for your theatrical approach to restaurant design. What can you abstract from theater that relates to restaurants?
A: The entrance. This doesn't necessarily mean a huge space; the theatrical entrance can be a small space that opens up into a dramatic vista. It can have an element of surprise. The entrance is critical from a functional point of view, too. Does the owner want to monitor the entrance from the maître d' station? Does he or she need to see into the entire room?

Lighting is critical in both theatrical productions and in restaurants. As you sit in a theater, you see movement and transformation before you. The same happens in restaurants. This is quite different from television, which is two-dimensional.

Q: To remain competitive, must restaurants offer an architectural experience?
A: On the one hand, yes. People are becoming more and more discriminating, and the marketplace is increasingly competitive. People expect to be wowed when they go out to a restaurant. On the other hand, the design experience must go hand in hand with the food. If the food fails, then the restaurant ultimately closes.

Q: How do you get started on a restaurant project?
A: We start by relating to the client: talking about ideas, eating food together, talking about price points. We inundate ourselves with information. Research is one of the most important steps. We research the location, the specific space, spend time in the space, study the history of the building. When we sit down to design, we make sure we

understand the business strategy, the food, how many meals will be served, intended volume, what textures and colors the owner likes, the building setting, what design elements make the owner feel comfortable. We build models and collaborate with craftsmen well before the design is done.

Q: What advice would you give to restaurant owners about working with designers?

A: Carry around a tape measure. Most people don't know about dimension and its impact on a room. Work in a kitchen and behind the maître d' stand before you think about opening your own restaurant. The worst kind of client is the one who comes to us without knowing how a restaurant works. The best clients are those who have an idea of what their restaurant will be before they hire us. They are not just looking at investment opportunities.

Don't look for the design firm to have all of the answers about design at the very beginning of a project; that isn't the goal. Going in with all the answers does not allow for creativity.

Q: Your firm is known for its innovative restaurant designs. How do you keep coming up with fresh ideas?

A: A plus to having so many projects is that we can bring ideas from one project to the next. The contacts that we make help us collect a wider network of creative talent. We also have great senior people and work to create an office environment where creativity can take place. We go to the theater, movies, and museums as a group, and bring in outside speakers like sculptors and fashion designers to office meetings for a cross-fertilization of ideas. We're always traveling and keeping our eyes and minds open so we can get left-brain inspirations about materials.

Q: Does good design mean expensive design?

A: Not necessarily. Good design means making a careful decision about where the money is going to go. You pick and choose where you're going to put your money.

Q: Have acoustics become a more important element in restaurant design?

A: Absolutely. But the thing about acoustics that even acoustic engineers will tell you is that it is not a science. The trick is how and where to introduce soft surfaces that absorb sound and help shape the space—because hard surfaces are usually preferable. They have more visual appeal—everybody loves a terrazzo floor—and they last longer with less maintenance than soft materials. One solution I think

will be used in the future and that we're already starting to consider for our projects is white noise systems.

Q: What does theme design mean to you?

A: I don't think in terms of theme but rather in terms of consistency and authenticity—an authenticity within the reality you create. There is an idea of what you are doing and each design decision is weighed against that. Each choice comes back to a similar point of view.

Q: Do you aim for every restaurant to look different?

A: Yes. When clients come to us because they like a particular project and want something like it, we have to talk them into doing something different. In multi-unit situations like Nobu, there are threads that link the various restaurants together, yet each has its own personality.

Q: What are the most important directions in restaurant design today? Any forecasts for the next ten years?

A: There seems to be a trend back to the origins of what a restaurant is, and to mom-and-pop establishments. Restaurant design has become more and more sophisticated, and there is more variety. We're moving away from generic design decisions and toward design that reflects a sense of place. We're also seeing lots of lounges and areas that can accommodate singles, like bar dining and communal tables.

There's more collaboration. Chefs and owners have stronger ideas about what they want the front-of-the-house environment to look like, and designers have a greater understanding about how a restaurant works.

In the future, with an increasingly competitive marketplace, owners will have to be better educated about who their market is. All the key elements in a restaurant—food, service, and design—will be more carefully controlled.

Adam Tihany

Principal
Adam D. Tihany International Ltd.
New York

Number of restaurant projects: ~150

When Adam Tihany speaks, the design community listens. Since setting up shop in 1978, Tihany has developed a portfolio that includes some of the most celebrated restaurant designs in the world. Additionally, he has designed and licensed numerous custom items, including china patterns, chairs, cigar holders and ashtrays, flatware patterns, and what is arguably the world's most exquisite Bombay Sapphire martini glass.

Adam Tihany.
(Photo by Brian Hall)

Q: Most of your projects are elegant establishments with strong restaurateurs or chef-owners at the helm. What is the most challenging aspect of designing this type of restaurant?

A: Our design philosophy is so specific that it makes every restaurant a challenge. I'm basically a portrait artist who works in the method of a custom tailor. I design portraits of my clients. Our projects are all different from each other, but they have a common thread, which is my vision of the owner's personality. The real challenge is to define the owner's character, to find the connection with his personality, and then understand what that means in terms of space and time. Once we do that, it becomes an amusing and fun job.

Q: What do you do to arrive at a definition of the owner's personality?

A: It depends on how well a person can open up and speak in a language that translates to design. Most of the great restaurateurs and chefs that we work with do not come from a design background and cannot express themselves visually. So I will ask them to cook for me at their home, to create a dish that they would like to serve in their new restaurant. I go through the exercise of looking at the dish as a customer would, putting myself at the entry door ready to receive the food when the curtain goes up. Seeing how people cook at home helps me understand who they are, so I can create their custom portrait.

Some restaurateurs don't know what kind of food they are going to serve. I try to explain to them that the evolution of a design is a mental and creative process, a journey that we have to take together. I need to know something about the end product before coming up with the design. If they don't know the exact menu, then I ask them to explain the idea of the restaurant, to articulate the concept.

Another trick I use with clients who can't describe what they want: I ask them the question, "If I had the power and magic to produce the key to any establishment in the world and make it yours, what would you choose?" The only right answer is "None."

My goal is for our clients to go into their restaurants at the end of the day and say, "This fits me fine. It's what I am all about." To me, this is the reward.

Q: Why do you typically design just a handful of restaurants a year?

A: We work only with professional restaurateurs or chefs whose restaurants are their livelihoods. I won't take a bunch of dentists looking to make an investment, or people who want me to knock off my own designs. Our clients deserve a custom portrait. Keeping a small office enables us to do a few restaurants a year, and that supports us. By doing so, we've earned a lot of respect.

Q: How does being a restaurant owner influence your design?

A: It opens a lot of doors and cuts out a lot of rough edges. My customers view me as a colleague. They know I understand the basics of a restaurant operation; the operational details don't even need to be discussed. We can get down to the core and soul and creative aspect of the restaurant. It also gives us the edge because, given our vast knowledge of both front and back of the house, we can design very functional, clear plans for the restaurant.

Speaking as a restaurateur as well as a designer, I'm a firm believer that the front of the house is only fifty percent of the equation. If the kitchen is not friendly and usable, if the staff isn't loyal, then you can't build a great restaurant. We make it pretty clear that we want to be involved in back-of-house issues. We want to make sure that there is a seamless transition between front and back, and that the service areas for staff are clean, safe, and as aesthetic as the front of the house. Things like colored tiles in the kitchen, for example, can make it fun for the people working there. Why should a kitchen look drab? It's not much more expensive to make it look nice.

Q: What's your definition of successful restaurant design?

A: To me, a successful restaurant design is part of an equation that has to do with the least amount of surprises that people have during their dining experience. Decor, uniforms, graphics, lighting, noise levels, and so on should all express a harmonious background for the food and the service. If you can achieve that—and if the customer thinks the check is one dollar less than it should have been—you've accomplished your mission.

Q: What role does design play in attracting people to a restaurant? What makes them want to return?

A: Design assumes different roles during the life of a restaurant. When the restaurant first opens, the design is the main selling tool. It's what people see. And if there's a big-name designer, people will come to see the restaurant because it is the thing to do. When people talk about a hot restaurant in the first days of its existence, they're talking about the look. Later on, the food and service become more prominent, and design becomes the background support for everything else.

The problem is not to get people into the restaurant the first time but to get them to return. Ultimately, it takes food, service, and design together to do that.

Q: How would you characterize your design philosophy?

A: I care more about people and comfort than about image. I'm a hospitality person. I'm also a big promoter of sensuality. I love sexy. We design surfaces, treatments, and lighting to make people look sexy. When people feel good and look good, they spend money.

It has always been part of my philosophy that dining out is a special occasion. I still remember the first restaurant I went to when I was eighteen years old. The whole idea of someone serving you and cleaning up after you was a revelation. Ultimately, my concern is to create a seamless experience for the customer where the design of the room builds a level of expectation that culminates with the serving of food.

Q: From a historical perspective, has restaurant design become more important to the overall success of the restaurant these days?

A: Yes. Once it was enough to have great food: People didn't care if the restaurant was dumpy or not. But in the mid-1980s, restaurants started to become the meeting places of choice and chefs became stars. We entered into a food era, and the packaging aspect of the restaurant really started to take off and gain prominence. Now people demand not just good food and service but also good design. Why eat in dumpy surroundings? Good design has become part of the package.

Q: What advice would you give to restaurateurs about working with designers?

A: First, don't be afraid or ashamed to say what you think. Your personality is what has to come across, eventually. It's your establishment. Don't be intimidated by designers trying to sell you their look. The goal is to combine your personality with the designer's talent. But watch out for egos. Try to pick a designer who has ten percent less ego than you do.

Q: Who are your most important collaborators on a project?

A: We love to work with artists, artisans, mural artists, sculptors, metal forgers—people who can contribute ideas. We have a group of friends and artisans we take around with us. It's like being a Renaissance shop. The more people we can bring to the table with creative ideas, the better the project is. We hate working in a vacuum.

Q: What are some of the trends in restaurant design today? Any forecasts for the next ten years?

A: We've been involved with very successful chef's tables in the kitchen that basically function as private party rooms. Most restaurants benefit from being able to host a private party in a room that looks different from the dining room, so we may see more of these.

Some current trends that I think will last are open kitchens and other display cooking and preparation areas, like oyster bars. They create focal points of energy in the room and reassure customers of the cleanliness of the product.

Restaurateurs and designers will continue to pay more attention to the single diner. Once it was unheard of for a single person to sit in a restaurant unless it was at the counter, but not any more. I see more and more people eating alone. Some are business travelers who want to venture out of the hotel and go out to dinner in a restaurant to feel the beat of the city. We'll see more solo diners eating at bars, or at a communal table, or in banquette deuces, which is the European way. In Paris, half the bistros and cafés are filled with people eating alone.

Concept sketch, Le Cirque 2000, New York.
(Courtesy of Adam D. Tihany International Ltd.)

James Webb

Principal
Webb Foodservice Design Consultants, Inc.
Tustin, California

Number of restaurant projects: ~200

As a facilities design consultant for more than 20 years, James Webb gets involved with managing and designing projects from conception to completion. His firm is particularly well known for creating clean, functional noncommercial foodservice designs.

James Webb.
(Photo courtesy of Webb Foodservice Design Consultants, Inc.)

Q: What's constitutes good design from a design perspective?
A: Sensitivity to the customer's needs. Designers should not create their own monuments. They have to be sensitive to the client and to the customers. Merchandising the food in creative ways is also an important component of good design today.

Q: What's constitutes good design from an operational perspective?
A: Operationally, we need to be sensitive to food safety. We have to think of the equipment needed to support an HACCP [hazard analysis critical control] program. Many of the kitchens we design are shrinking due to budget constraints. We believe in using quality materials, so while some designers would put in basic undershelves, for a few more dollars we deliver to our clients a pristine kitchen that sends a positive message to the employees. Quality materials without nooks and crevices are also easier to clean.

Q: Does good design mean expensive design?
A: Good design doesn't have to be expensive, but it has to be smart. Real estate is too expensive to make design mistakes. An inefficient design costs the client a lot of extra money per square foot. Our approach is to make the kitchen tight and usable. We try to save money by reducing the size of the kitchen and putting the dollars into improved equipment.

It's the responsibility of the designer to go back to the client and recommend a budget adjustment, if necessary, to ensure the purchase of equipment that can go the extra mile. We consult with the client on the budget allocation for equipment and the rate of return. If smaller clients can't afford the most efficient equipment, we relent. But we want them to understand the long-term consequences.

Q: How important is good design to the success of a university or business foodservice?
A: It's important. Over the past twenty years, we've taken a lot of spaces that looked like standard institutional cafeterias and brought them to a new level of design. An operation can have great food, but

if it's served from an old, dingy straight-line servery, the perception is that it has been sitting out on the line for hours. However, a new design alone won't guarantee success. When a new menu or a new operator comes into a newly designed space, the satisfaction level goes way up.

In the B&I [business and industry] segment, the customers are more sophisticated and expect better interiors and better food presentation. Here, the foodservice is seen as an employee benefit. I think good design helps stimulate employees by giving them a break from their work. As for universities, many use their foodservices as one of the big recruitment tools, particularly for their sports teams.

Q: Do you think your noncommercial clients are paying more attention to design in an effort to attract and maintain employees?
A: Morale contributes a lot to employee retention, and well-designed kitchens and cafeterias can give operations a competitive advantage in this regard. If a kitchen incorporates positive design features, the operators have a better chance of hiring and retaining employees. A good design with good equipment also communicates a commitment to food safety, cleanliness, and quality.

Q: How can owners or contract companies best work with designers to create a successful noncommercial foodservice design?
A: First of all, it takes a lot of involvement. It begins with a commitment to having a good-quality foodservice program. Next comes the development of a strategic plan that treats the foodservice as a business. The plan must identify the market through focus groups, demographic analysis, labor availability, training capabilities, merchandising opportunities, and so on. At this point, the designers can begin to map out a design.

The detail work comes next. Once the schematic is done, we literally cook the menu with the design. How do we toast the bread and then put the mayonnaise on it? We analyze how every menu item is processed through each station. If you don't do that, you end up with employees saying, "What were they thinking of when they

Campus Market at Cal Poly.
(Photo by Dave Cook)

designed this?" The designer has to consider everything, from how the food flows from the kitchen to the customers to how the dishes are returned for washing.

Q: What critical issues must noncommercial representatives keep in mind when working with foodservice design specialists?
A: Trusting the consultant and holding to the specifications set forth in the bid documents is important. They should not allow competitive bidders to come in with cheaper alternatives. Second, they should have the designer involved throughout the construction process.

We completed one job where another firm designed a twin facility in another building. In the other building, ownership did not hold true to the specifications. We took pictures of both facilities after one year of use and the kitchen in the other facility looked like it was fifteen to twenty years old. In our facility, the kitchen still looked new, in part because ownership held to the specifications and in part because we signed on as consultants for the construction management part of the project. In the long run, the design and installation we created cost sixty thousand dollars less than in the other building, and we saved an additional two hundred thousand dollars in general construction costs.

Q: Do you ever sacrifice operational efficiency for design aesthetics?
A: Sometimes we do. The customer side is what generates the profits for the business. I'm not talking about visual design aesthetics per se but rather about aesthetics that work for the customer's benefit. Customers need to feel like they are in a professionally designed space, and they won't forgive or forget if they have a bad experience. But we won't compromise to a point where the staff has to cut chicken on the same table as they cut meat. It's important to have a balance of operational and design issues without ever compromising food safety.

Q: How do you contribute to a positive environment for employees?
A: We try to specify things like quarry tile in the kitchen. If the kitchen is well maintained, it sends a positive message to employees. If it is not well maintained, that also sends a message. Lighting helps stimulate the mind, so we create a well-lit front and back of the house. Fun accents, like whimsical colors created with paint or tile, help. Simple things can energize employees. And you always need well-maintained equipment that can be used effectively every day.

Q: Where do you get your inspiration for these projects?
A: We spend a lot of time touring and reading books and magazines. We get inspiration from our clients and their vision. We have to have the internal fire of creative ideas, but the customer has to have it as well.

Q: What are the most difficult aspects of designing foodservice spaces for noncommercial operations?
A: It's too easy to get swallowed up carrying the client's flag and become bogged down with an unrealistic agenda. For example, we can't do the job right for a client with a seven thousand square-foot space who asks for a dynamic and exciting foodservice design for five hundred thousand dollars. We try to be proactive about these kinds of problems at the beginning. We show owners our past work and the budgets for those jobs. It's amazing how many times, in a noncommercial environment, the budgets will open up. But steering the client can be tough, especially in B&I. Some administrators can't imagine how much a cafeteria will cost. But it is crucial to paint the picture for them.

Q: What trends do you see for the future?
A: More emphasis on food and display, just-in-time (JIT) cooking, and fresher cooking. The servery marketplace concept will expand. A more European style of food and lots of customer interaction at the servery order stations will become even more popular. We see a high amount of service, good food quality, more home meal replacement offerings, menu flexibility, and increased sanitation.

Andrew Young

Principal
Andrew Young & Co., Inc.
New York

Andrew Young is an international restaurant developer and consultant. His projects range from the famed Gundel restaurant in Budapest, where he worked with George Lang to restore one of Hungary's important national monuments, to master planning for the foodservice in the Deira City Centre, which is the largest shopping center in Dubai, United Arab Emirates. Young brings a seasoned knowledge of food and beverage operations to each of his projects, along with a team of associates, each with his own area of foodservice expertise.

Andrew Young.
(Photo courtesy of Andrew Young & Co., Inc.)

Q: How important is design to the success of restaurants today?

A: Design is an integral part of the restaurant's success. The owner/operator must determine at the beginning of the project how design is going to be used. Do you need design to make the restaurant pleasant or ergonomically efficient? Or is design going to be used as a marketing tool? Successful design creates an environment that suits the concept.

Q: What is the relationship of design to food and service? To what extent does or should the menu influence the design?

A: Food is one of the elements that drives the design. The draft of the menu should be communicated to the designer to ensure that the plates and the food work together. Any discordant, out-of-place tones, and the restaurant fails. Everything must fit together, like a big puzzle.

Q: When you set out to design a concept, what are the questions you ask?

A: First, you have to understand the market. Coral Gables, Florida, for example, is a very particular, clearly defined market, while in New York, the market is so large that you need to define just a piece of it as your target clientele. No single restaurant menu could possibly appeal to everyone in the New York market.

Next, you have to prepare a written concept brief that includes an explanation of the basic concept, the menu, how many seats, how big a bar, how many and how big the service stations should be, and the feeling that you want to create in the space. The menu description should identify the number of appetizers, the number of main course items, and their price points. The brief should also include ideas about interior surfaces and furniture, like requests for a hard-surfaced floor or plush upholstered seating, and a sense of what the space should feel like. Should the atmosphere feel energized and boisterous or quiet and elegant? Spacious or intimate? The same kind of brief goes to the kitchen designer.

Q: What elements do kitchen and interior designers need to collaborate on?

A: It is important that the interior and kitchen designers work together on the impact of lighting. Fluorescent lighting in an open kitchen negatively affects the front of the house, for example.

Q: Are there ways to save money on a kitchen design?

A: So many places opt for the cheap way out by getting the equipment supplier to provide the design free of charge. The owner ends up getting charged no matter what. If you pay a good designer a good fee, you can get a better price and product because the design will meet your best interests. It can actually save money.

Q: Is it fair to say that design helps attract people to the restaurant but the food keeps them coming back?

A: Absolutely. The component that is most overlooked is ongoing management. You can have a great design, a great chef, and a great menu but, at the end of the day, you need to manage the restaurant properly and provide a level of service that keeps guests coming back. It's not just about food and design.

Q: Does good design mean expensive design? How expensive?

A: Most designers charge a flat fee. Good design does not necessarily mean expensive. You can get interesting, well-designed custom pieces created for a reasonable price. Sometimes custom furniture can be built for less than the price of furniture from a showroom. Part of my role is to control costs by looking at the design specifications and deciding what is necessary. If a $40-per-square-foot floor treatment is specified, I may ask for something that is less expensive but that gets across the same feeling.

Q: Can you give us some ideas of the construction and FF&E [furniture, fixtures, and equipment] costs that you've dealt with recently?

A: Construction costs averaged about $400 per square foot in London, $300 per square foot in New York, $260 per square foot in Sydney, Australia, and less than $225 per square foot in Coral Gables. Of course, these costs are before FF&E. In general, FF&E runs about $50 per square foot in the front of house.

Q: What was your most challenging restaurant project?

A: Our most challenging project was Monty's, a private club in London, where we served as the overall project manager. There were a lot of functions to cram into the ten thousand square feet of space: a dance floor and bar, a lounge and bar, a private dining room, a cigar bar, and a high-end dining room. Getting this design to work on a four-level facility was like putting together a Swiss watch. The key to success was design coordination.

Q: What usually gets in the way of successful restaurateur-designer collaboration? What do you do to ensure that this doesn't happen?

A: Ego is the biggest problem. Both designers and restaurateurs have big egos that can clash. I choose my clients and keep my business small so that I work with people I like, in places I like, and on projects that are challenging.

I'll admit that I'm quite opinionated, but ego is something different. I've made mistakes. And I always try to be open to new ideas. I've worked closely with Adam Tihany on many projects, and we've developed a mutual level of respect for one another. With a new designer, I try to find a way to express myself that respects the design but also gets my message across.

Q: Certain restaurant designers, like Adam Tihany, have become famous names in their own right. How important is the name designer as a marketing tool?

A: As a marketing tool, using a famous designer with a name really helps. Both name designers and name chefs help owners get press for their restaurants. There's a cachet that comes from an Adam Tihany design, and it attracts people. But the name has to go hand in hand with the skills to succeed.

Q: What are the most important trends in restaurant design today? Will they last? Any forecasts?

A: Open kitchens have become very popular lately. I don't think this

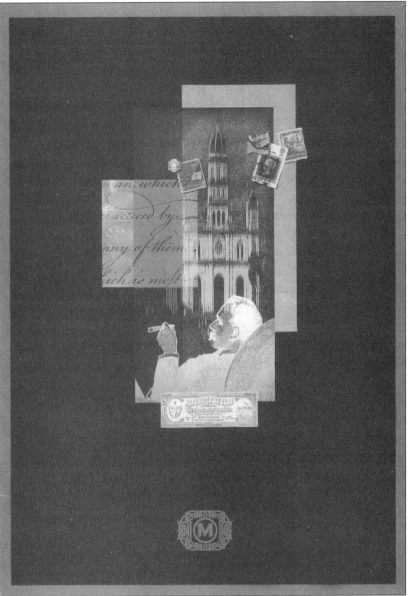

Menu cover from Monty's.
(Courtesy of Andrew Young & Co., Inc.)

trend will last, even though I like it. The open kitchen evolved because people grew to want more than just a dining experience; they wanted theater. When the action and excitement of the kitchen is brought to the front of the house and people can watch the chefs at work, it fulfills their desire for theater. But I believe that trends are cyclical, and soon we'll bounce back to the point where people want to experience elegance, not a working kitchen.

A lasting trend, one that has been evolving over the last fifteen years, is that design will continue to be a important element in the restaurant. This doesn't necessarily mean more extravagant design—just good design. Some restaurant designers today are trying to be creative in ways that are too off the wall, with too much stuff, so that the interior does not feel comfortable. But I think we'll be seeing restaurateurs and designers working together to create a cohesive mix that works.

Notes

Design for the New Decade

Only in the past twenty years has restaurant design come into its own. The 1970s had fern-bar restaurants, plasticized fast-food restaurants, stuffy hotel restaurants, slick contemporary restaurants, and instant-history theme restaurants. Few establishments reflected original design treatments, and it often took years before fashion and furnishing trends influenced the restaurant interior.

In the 1980s, everything changed. The momentum that began then has catapulted forward to where today's restaurants not only reflect the latest design directions but often create them. Here's a look at past trends still shaping restaurant design today.

The 1980s and 1990s

Starting in the early 1980s, restaurants began to reflect an overall lighter look and a clean aesthetic hand: Neon replaced hanging plants, bentwood café chairs supplanted molded plastic seating, and walls were stripped bare of theme memorabilia. No single style prevailed. The 1950s diner came back into vogue, art deco influences were seen in restaurant furniture and accessories, and the decorative embellishments of postmodernism manifested themselves in restaurant interiors. Theme didn't die, but it often became more subtle and more complex, with evocative references rather than stock clichés. Theatrical lighting helped create dramatic stage sets, and hard-surfaced materials contributed to the loud noise levels that were associated with the large, see-and-be-seen theatrical restaurants. Murals and other commissioned artwork individualized interiors. Color was newly appreciated as a design tool. Intricate color schemes ranging from muted pastel hues to bold primary accents formed the decorative shell of many restaurants, and along with the new palette came a variety of new light sources that made the colors come alive.

Growing numbers of architects began to design restaurants. Their influence was evident in interiors whose decor was formed by the interior architecture—

restaurants where materials, form, color, space, and light took the place of decoration. The building itself became important and, often, surface coverings were stripped away to reveal the building structure, whether ventilation ductwork in the ceiling or structural columns. Some architects created buildings within buildings, using architectural objects instead of applied decoration to break up space and create visual interest. Many solutions were metaphorical as well as functional in an effort to stimulate people's perceptions. Straightforward architectural treatments, such as the use of levels to define seating areas, became commonplace in restaurant interiors.

The gap between fashion and restaurant design grew smaller. Style was crucial, but the restaurateur had many choices. Just as one person's wardrobe might contain many styles of clothing, any given U.S. city sported many styles of restaurant design. Like fashion, restaurants often reflected a kind of mix-and-match mentality.

A new sensuality and playfulness emerged in the 1990s. Texture became an important design element. Building walls were often stripped down to their rough-textured, unfinished state. Rough, natural materials such as concrete, stone, and wood, plus all sorts of metals, dominated the architectural toolbox. Increasing numbers of artists and craftspeople were hired to create special pieces for restaurants. As food became more important to the clientele, so did comfort. Many restaurants scaled down and became quieter. At the same time, theatrical restaurants continued to expand across the country, and open kitchens became more common in many types of restaurants. Theme returned, and the first eatertainment restaurants opened. Design diversity increased as design took cues from the building style, or the cuisine, or fashion trends. Even hotel restaurants, formerly unexciting, became high-design destination places. Cookie cutter was out, fashion was in, and a new generation of restaurant-goers avidly sought the most stylish new places.

By the end of the 1990s, restaurant design had blossomed into a bona-fide profession. Design was a critical marketing tool in virtually every type of establishment. Restaurant reviews described the decor as well as the food, and preeminent restaurant designers became celebrities in their own right: Sometimes their name alone was enough to generate a buzz that drew people to try a new or redesigned restaurant.

In the back of the house, restaurateurs responded to the public proclivity for fresh food. Wholesale cuts of meat were vacuum packed, which significantly extended their shelf life, and delivered in refrigerated form to operators. Fabrication areas for meat and fish, with items such as fish files, came back into vogue, as increasing numbers of à la carte restaurants catered to the health-conscious American consumer. Fresh, natural ingredients were essential to the production of every type of fare.

Concurrent with the interest in fresh food was the advent of American cuisine. This new wave of grassroots food featured on-premises gardens and locally grown meat and fowl. Chefs scoured the width and breadth of the country to find all manner of American-grown exotica. Some operators installed hydroponic gardens in their restaurants to serve fresh herbs at the peak of flavor.

Food presentation reflected the aesthetic sensibility, but not the small portions, of nouvelle cuisine. In gourmet restaurants, American chefs combined ingredients in ways that no European chef would dream of, then paired plates with food in artful arrangements of form, color, and texture. Towering vertical food presentations became dramatic focal points.

In more casual restaurants, the kitchen also gained stature, often moving to the front of the house so that guests could watch the cooks at work. Open kitchens infiltrated all types of restaurants, from Italian to Mexican to American. What better way for people to know what they were eating than to watch it being prepared? All manner of kitchen references—wood-burning pizza ovens, rotisseries, theatrically lit grill stations—became integrated into the front of the house in the 1980s. By the 1990s, increasing numbers of fine dining restaurants allowed glimpses into the back of the house as well, often through glass walls. By the turn of the century, the prevailing wisdom was that food and service had to match the standards expressed in the design, and that design alone could not ensure a restaurant's success.

2000 and Beyond

What design changes should we expect to see through 2010? Numerous factors will shape restaurant design in the near future, including big-picture or macro issues, and micro factors that reflect restaurant and design industry trends.

MACRO FACTORS

DEMOGRAPHICS Demographic changes will significantly affect restaurant design, as aging boomers enter an era of changing physical abilities and their offspring, alternately called the echo generation or Generation X, become active restaurant customers with their own design preferences. As boomers move into their fifties, they will expect certain elements of comfort and convenience from the dining environment. High light levels that make it easy to read the menu and move around the restaurant, seating that is easy to get in and out of, acoustic treatments that allow for comfortable conversation, and take-home packaging for leftovers will be the norm for restaurants targeting this huge demographic segment. Starting in 2006, the first generation of boomers will begin early retirement, many with sizable retirement incomes that will allow them to continue to dine out often. As adults, boomers spearheaded the move to frequent dining out, and there are no indications that they will not continue this trend.

The offspring of the boomers who entered the new millennium as 15- to 24-year-olds represent the age group that restaurants typically rely on for hourly labor. However, these potential workers will have better earning opportunities in other industries, such as the technology sector. They have grown up accustomed to dining out because many of them were raised in two-income homes where away-from-home dining was more a rule than the exception, and will become an increasingly strong market segment. Unlike their parents, they are likely to tolerate high noise levels and low light levels. Most significant, they will look for each restaurant to provide more than a good meal in comfortable surroundings; they will want an experience more exciting than the last.

By 2005, the number of people 25 to 34 years old will be significantly lower than it has been in over two decades (Figure 8.1). The decrease of population in this group will have a negative impact on the entry-level labor pool and on the pool of college-trained managers who serve as the backbone management staff in many types of restaurant operations. By 2010, the smallest population group will be the 30- to 39-year-olds (Figure 8.2). This is the group from which businesses will draw their midlevel managers and whose members will have reached an income level where they can spend money on frequent dining-out activities.

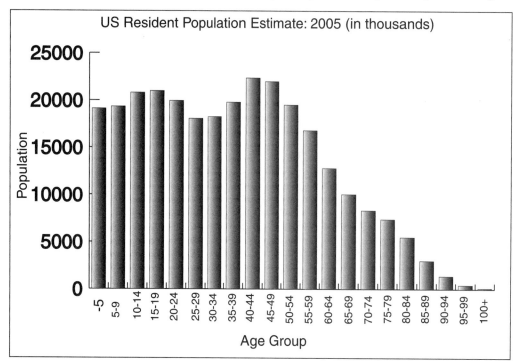

FIGURE 8.1 *In 2005, the population dip in the 25-34-year-old age group represents a diminished labor pool in the age groups from which the restaurant industry draws many of its employees.*

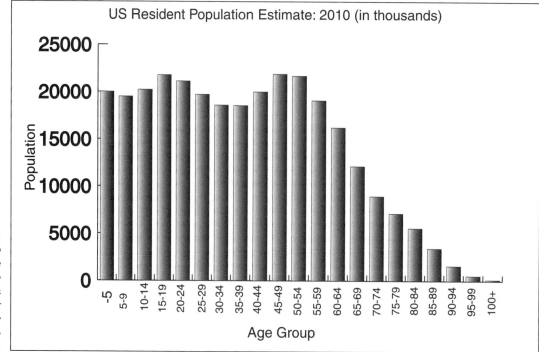

FIGURE 8.2 *In 2010, the population dip will reach the 30-39-year-old age group, and this decreased customer base will negatively affect sales in the restaurant industry.*

BOOMING ECONOMY If good economic times continue, unemployment rates will remain low, continuing to cause labor shortages in the restaurant industry. Those shortages will drive up the cost of labor when the federal government enacts laws that increase the minimum wage. Young workers will continue to have the freedom to find less demanding employment at higher salaries in other industries. Restaurateurs will increasingly rely on immigrants for whom English is not a first language, so equipment from the point of sale (POS) to the convection oven will have to incorporate multilingual operating features.

The booming economy will also lead to more disposable income—which has always been good news for the restaurant industry. A feature of the current economy not seen in other boom times is a relatively flat inflation rate. If inflation remains under control, disposable income levels will continue to grow. A boom economy makes consumers comfortable and willing to spend money on restaurant meals, even if those meals are charged to a credit card.

THE EXPERIENCE ECONOMY In their 1999 book, *The Experience Economy: Work Is Theatre & Every Business a Stage,* (Harvard Business School Press), coauthors Joseph Pine II and James H. Gilmore say that we are entering a new age of economic output in which experiences rather than goods and services will form the basis of commerce. The implication for restaurants is obvious: to succeed in this economy, they must involve people in a multidimensional experience that goes beyond food and service. Pine and Gilmore propose five principles of experience design:

1. *Theme the experience.*
2. *Harmonize the impressions with positive cues.*
3. *Eliminate negative cues.*
4. *Mix in memorabilia.*
5. *Engage all five senses.*

While theme and eatertainment restaurants seem to fit the experience economy model, they can't rest on their laurels, say the authors. "Sales are plummeting in some theme restaurants because the business fails to refresh the experience. Repeat guests see or do little different than what they saw and did on previous visits. And how many T-shirts with the same logo can you own?" they ask. Their answer is to charge admission to the restaurants and use that income to offset the cost of constantly upgrading and changing the experiences as well as to lower food prices.

Whether or not eatertainment restaurants really begin to charge admission remains to be seen, but it's an interesting concept.

ENVIRONMENTAL ISSUES Restaurants will become prime targets for antipollution efforts in the years to come. Most new refrigeration systems use refrigerants and foaming agents in their insulation that are said to have little or no impact on the ozone layer. However, the large existing base of refrigeration equipment continues to depend on CFC-based refrigerants that deplete the ozone layer. The cost of maintaining that equipment will skyrocket over the next decade as world stockpiles of CFC-based refrigerants dwindle.

Induction cooktops will improve and replace current cooktop technologies.

Restaurants will also be held accountable for the large volume of solid waste—disposables and packaging material—that they put into the wastestream. Roadside litter emblazoned with the names of local take-out restaurants will continue to remind people that restaurants produce a lot of solid waste. As landfills and trash-burning facilities are taken off line, restaurants will need to find ways to decrease waste material. Using biodegradable or recyclable packaging, or installing recycling equipment in the back of the house, will become more commonplace.

Air pollution will be an increasing concern for restaurateurs. The plume of grease-laden smoke emerging from a restaurant's ventilation system will be controlled by smoke-reducing ventilation filters, and menu items that rely less on grilling may also help to reduce smoke emissions.

Smoking will continue to be a hot environmental issue. More states will enact complete bans on indoor and outdoor smoking in public spaces. For those that don't, one alternative will be the installation of smoking rooms in the restaurant that allow no smoke carryover from one space to another. Properly designed ventilation and air-filtering equipment may make it possible for restaurateurs to accommodate both smokers and nonsmokers.

Water supply and the disposal of wastewater will become major issues facing restaurateurs. The industry will be forced to use water-saving dish- and potwashing equipment. While dishwashers in the 1990s were far more efficient than their predecessors, the next generation will use less water per dish washed and rely on cleaning agents that are friendly to the environment. Automated potwashers that can use a single batch of water and cleaning agent for up to 30 days will save enormous amounts of water and pollute much less than conventional potwashing equipment.

Rising electrical costs will cause lighting to become more energy-efficient. Incandescent lamps will often be replaced with more efficient fluorescent lamps: Fluorescent lamp manufacturers will introduce new lines of lamps that rely less on mercury and other environment-polluting metals. They will also produce a wider variety of energy-efficient lamps that deliver spectral qualities similar to those of natural sunlight.

Electrically powered kitchen cooking equipment will become more efficient. Induction cooktops will improve and replace current cooktop technologies. Ovens will be produced with better insulation and temperature controls that minimize waste heat. Steam kettles will have insulation around the exterior jackets. Waste heat from refrigeration systems and dish machines will increasingly be captured to heat water before it flows into hot water tanks. In some instances, the tanks will be eliminated and replaced with instant-on water heaters.

GREEN DESIGN Environmental concerns will increasingly drive designers and restaurateurs to incorporate green design elements into restaurants. Recycling programs and the equipment they require will be integrated throughout the industry. Environment-conscious designers will stop using wood harvested from old-growth forests. Softwoods and farmed hardwoods will become increasingly popular, and wood from old structures and all kinds of recycled materials will be used to add character to restaurant designs. Even common disposables like styrofoam cups and clamshells will be recycled into seating, tables, and structural components.

FOOD SAFETY A 1999 release from the International Food Safety Council revealed that consumers view food safety as a greater threat than crime or water purity. During the 1990s, consumers read and heard about numerous major food poisoning outbreaks from contaminated meat, both in the United States and abroad, and the restaurant industry was held accountable for some foodborne illness problems.

As a result, restaurateurs will have to become increasingly vigilant about food safety. Those operators who have not already adopted a hazard analysis critical control point (HACCP) program may be forced to do so. The HACCP programs themselves will point out the need for new equipment or modified designs in the back of the house. In the front of the house, design elements that are hard to keep clean will be minimized.

MICRO FACTORS

REDESIGNED CHAINS Restaurant chains that expanded rapidly in the 1970s and 1980s will undergo redesigns at an even faster rate than seen in the late 1990s, when Burger King changed its graphic, interior, and exterior design; McDonald's changed its back-of-the-house production techniques in an effort to appeal to customer demands for higher-quality meals; and smaller chains such as Steak and Ale, Coco's California Café, Pizzeria Uno, Red Lobster, Chili's, and Luby's upgraded interior and exterior designs. To keep up with the competition, chains, like the Outback Steakhouse, that were introduced in the 1990s may be forced to make interior upgrades.

The impetus for chain redesigns will be to update stale themes and decor and to reposition the restaurants for developing target markets. These redesigns will require both back- and front-of-the-house modifications. In addition, new chain restaurants that hit the market in the early 2000s will reflect stylish front-of-the-house design schemes and efficient kitchens carefully targeted to specific markets.

LABOR SHORTAGES Labor shortages will force restaurateurs to modify the layout and equipment in their operations to increase staff productivity. Environmental improvements that make the kitchen a comfortable workplace will help minimize employee turnover. Processing equipment that increases worker productivity, automated cooking equipment, and programmable controls will all help minimize challenges brought on by labor shortages. Technology will be integrated with the front of the house to speed order entry, and service stations will incorporate elements that improve server efficiency. Equipment readouts will be in multiple languages to accommodate non-English-speaking employees.

The first fully automated kitchen was built in the 1960s, but it didn't fly because it wasn't a practical solution. However, today's improved robotic systems and computer-based technology make it possible to build more efficient automated kitchens that can help alleviate the labor shortage. They're especially practical for fast-food restaurants.

PREPROCESSED FOODS Restaurateurs will increasingly seek out and use preprocessed foods, like washed and bagged salad greens that are ready for plating, to minimize the need for labor-intensive on-site prepreparation work. In some cases, the salads will be prepared to the exact specifications of the restaurateur and vacuum-packed to ensure a seven-day shelf life. Onions, shallots, and garlic will arrive peeled, along with carrots and potatoes that will be peeled, cut, and ready for cooking. While the per-pound cost of these processed foods will be higher, they will not only save labor but also eliminate the need to make the capital investment in equipment and space that would normally be required.

INCREASED SALES Restaurant sales, in general, will continue to expand due to an increased number of two-income families and singles who would rather socialize in a restaurant than cook and clean up at home. Fewer people are growing up with cooking skills, and dining away from home and take-out will be their only food options. While some freestanding home meal replacement (HMR) operations will be built, significant HMR sales will also occur as take-out sales from established restaurants.

COMMISSARY OPERATIONS Increasingly, chain restaurants, even regional chains, will develop commissary operations to take advantage of automated labor-saving equipment that will decrease the cost of labor per portion of food served. These centralized facilities will also contribute to improved consistency. By centralizing production of bakery products, sauces, soups, produce, and other items that can be preprepared, packaged, and held without loss of quality, chain operators will be able to decrease capital investments and labor costs at the individual restaurant level.

COOK-CHILL SYSTEMS For those operators who cannot take advantage of commissary operations, cook-chill systems will afford a means to save labor, improve food consistency, and minimize stress in the kitchen. Cook-chill systems enable restaurateurs to produce sauces, soups, stews, and braised foods in bulk. The foods are then packaged in either bags or pans and refrigerated. Packaged foods are rethermalized as needed. The system helps decrease stress levels because work is spread more evenly over a shift rather than concentrated at fever pitch during serving times.

CODE REQUIREMENTS Building, fire, and health code regulations and the bureaucracies that oversee them will become increasingly more challenging to deal with. Permit applications that once took several hours to complete and a day to receive now require dozens and, in some cases, hundreds of pages of documentation, review by attorneys, and weeks or months of waiting for approval. Inevitably, the trend toward greater complexity in the permitting process will continue to expand, along with the associated costs.

Increasingly, designers and restaurateurs will turn to experts who specialize in code expediting. Their role is to understand the nuances of the building, fire, health, and other codes for each jurisdiction in which they practice. They will fully understand the exact format for needed documentation, the lead time required to file each piece of documentation, and they will be able to work with designers to ensure that final inspections go smoothly.

FRONT-OF-THE-HOUSE DESIGN

What will the guest contact area of restaurants look like? Without doubt, fashion will continue to influence the aesthetics of restaurant design. The colors, shapes, and forms that we find in restaurants will mirror the fashions of the time. Architectural trends will also influence design, and interiors will be inspired by their architectural shells. Designers will continue to become more and more creative, both in response to an experience-hungry public and to shrinking budgets. As designers become increasingly knowledgeable about restaurant operations, interiors will be as practical as they are pleasing to the eye.

SMALLER SPACES Land costs, rent, and the price of materials will continue to escalate. At the same time, restaurateurs will be expected to maintain selling prices. The only solution is to pack more customers into smaller spaces. That may pose a problem in some settings because the percentage of Americans classified as obese continues to increase—meaning that larger seats with more space between them are needed to accommodate customers comfortably.

FASTER TURNOVER "Get 'em in and get 'em out" will become the mantra of the decade in fast-food and casual restaurants. While the size of chairs may increase to accommodate larger people, they will not become so comfortable that customers will extend their experience beyond the intended dining period. Guest pagers will be used throughout the industry to call people from the bar to the host stand when their table is ready. Sophisticated front-of-the-house-table management software will manage the dining room even more efficiently than a good maître d', alerting floor supervisors of delays in serving guests. In some settings, order-entry screens will be placed on the tabletops so diners can order without waiting for their server. At the end of the meal, they can insert their credit card into the order-entry device to take care of the charges.

LABOR-SAVING FEATURES A short supply of front-of-the-house labor will force designs to incorporate as many labor-saving features as possible, including the order-entry technology mentioned above. Display cooking areas that shorten the distance between the kitchen and the tabletop will also be thought of as a way to save labor. Service corridors will be incorporated into most banquet spaces to help speed service and to maximize the number of diners who can be served by a single waitperson. These service corridors and, in some instances, the banquet spaces themselves will incorporate water and waste hookups, along with electrical connections, to support mobile side stations designed specifically for banquet facilities.

EASY MAINTENANCE In part to save labor but increasingly because of a demanding clientele, front-of-the-house materials will be easy to clean and highly durable. Metals that tarnish quickly or show fingerprints, and upholstery materials like pale silks that show stains, will be used only in restaurants that can afford to maintain them. In general, hard-surfaced materials are easier to maintain than soft materials, and we'll continue to see them proliferate in restaurant interiors. Newly developed synthetic materials that are durable yet easy to shape and install will also come into vogue.

REST ROOM SANITATION AND DESIGN As with the kitchen, sanitation in rest rooms will rely, in part, on improved construction. Seamless floors and walls with self-closing and self-cleaning drains will speed cleanup. In some instances, auto-sanitizing toilet stalls will be used to clean and sanitize the toilet and seat between users. One-piece molded sinks and counters will eliminate cracks and crevices where dirt and germs can breed. All faucets will have infrared sensors, toilets and urinals will auto-flush, and rest room doors will have auto-open features on the inside to prevent guests from recontaminating their clean hands when grabbing a door handle.

Increasingly, rest rooms will be considered part of the total design scheme, particularly in high-ticket tableservice restaurants. Their design will incorporate decorative elements that tie in with the restaurant interior.

ENVIRONMENTAL COMFORT Designers and architects will pay more attention to the human dimension when creating restaurant spaces. They will design with greater attention to sound and light levels, choose appealing materials, and work with the back-of-the-house design team to improve the dining experience offered guests from the moment they walk in the restaurant. With more customers packed into smaller spaces, sound control systems will become paramount. Improved temperature controls will be installed to help keep guests as comfortable as possible. In some restaurants acoustic, lighting, and temperature controls will be installed at individual tables.

DESIGN DIVERSITY The trend of design diversity will continue—sometimes with a vengeance, as restaurateurs try to outdo the competition with new and exciting designs that lure customers. The hard part will be to keep people coming back. That will require a consistent experience where food, service, and design work in concert. In some instances, designs will incorporate personal dining spaces within a larger space (Figure 8.3).

PREDICTIONS BY RESTAURANT TYPE

FAST FOOD Consumers will increasingly demand accuracy and efficiency from fast-food drive-throughs. Voice-activated order-entry kiosks will shift the order-input responsibility to customers themselves. In extremely noisy drive-through locations, customers will be able to punch in their orders on a touch-screen unit that lines up with a vehicle window using a laser distance finder. For quickest service, credit-card-only drive-throughs will be installed. Double and triple drive-throughs will become popular, with orders being delivered via a conveyor system.

Eat-in customers will frequently be faced with order-entry kiosks at which they can place their order and pay for their meals via credit card. Counter staff will spend most of their time assembling food rather than keying in orders and handling cash.

In fast-food dining spaces, seating will become more flexible. Fewer chairs

will be bolted to the floor and some booths may be upsized to accommodate larger diners. Acoustic treatments on walls and ceilings will help reduce noise levels. Increasing numbers of fast-food restaurants will add game rooms and play areas for younger children. Tabletops and other surfaces will become more resilient and easy to clean. Trash stations will be fitted with compactors to decrease the number of trips needed to empty receptacles during meal periods.

TABLESERVICE Many tableservice restaurants will be brighter and quieter, with creative acoustic ceiling treatments that blend with the room or make design statements in their own right. Tabletops will get smaller wherever possible. Natural and synthetic hard-surfaced materials, especially recycled materials, will add layers of texture to interiors. Open kitchens and bar or table seating designed for single diners, both trends that began in the 1990s, will continue to be seen in many types of tableservice restaurants. Designers will pay more attention to food and wine merchandising, and create spaces for HMR displays and sales areas. More and more hotel restaurants, both casual and formal, will be given a distinct design identity geared to attract clientele other than hotel guests. Fine dining establishments will reflect the same high level of attention given to food, service, and design—or they won't survive.

Theatrical restaurants will continue to attract and dazzle customers with attention-getting design treatments, many of which will use new technologies. Theme, often expressed in nonclichés, will tie together the design in all areas of

FIGURE 8.3 *Individual dining environments, like these proposed by the Rockwell Group for installation in the Pod Restaurant in Philadelphia, will incorporate separate environmental controls that customers manipulate themselves.*
(Concept sketch courtesy of Rockwell Group)

285

the restaurant, from entry to rest room. We will also continue to see lavish eatertainment restaurants, often designed to appeal to families. These may incorporate changing animatronic or other design elements in order to attract repeat business, or they will be intentionally designed for a short lifespan.

CAFETERIA Cafeteria spaces in business settings will shrink as telecommuting becomes more common and the number of employees working in the central office decreases. However, in those corporate offices that continue to offer foodservice, as well as in other noncommercial sectors, like hospitals, cafeteria design will be upscale, with scatter-style serveries, display cooking, and lots of food and HMR merchandising. Similarly, cafeteria-style eateries in retail settings will sport serveries designed like mini-open kitchens, with cooks making everything from made-to-order fries to grilled fish in front of the customer.

BANQUET Banquet spaces will become increasingly flexible and multifunctional. Growing numbers of restaurateurs will allocate space for private banquet rooms, sometimes with their own kitchens, for parties and events that range from birthday celebrations to corporate meetings. These will be designed to be stylish as well as functional, with hidden screens for audiovisual presentations and floor ports for Internet connectivity.

TAKE-OUT In the past, designers didn't pay much attention to take-out in the front of the house, but that's going to change. Dedicated space will be allocated for HMR and designed so that the flow of traffic into the restaurant won't intersect with the flow of traffic to the HMR area. The HMR area will receive the same attention to design detail as the rest of the restaurant, with some elements that carry through the overall look integrated with visually attractive food displays. In addition to a pickup counter, space will also be added for beverage refrigerators and the sale of meal accompaniments such as bread and cheese.

BACK-OF-THE-HOUSE DESIGN

We've discussed design changes that will result from macro and micro factors and how front-of-the-house design will change. Let's now take a look at back-of-the-house design changes that we will see in every type of restaurant operation, then specific directions for particular types of restaurants.

SMALLER SPACES Construction and rental costs will continue to escalate, so back-of-the-house spaces will become smaller even as restaurants increase their sales dramatically. The drive to increase productivity per square foot of space will be stronger than ever. This will lead to the development of new and increased use of multipurpose equipment. Storerooms will become increasingly compact, and rolling shelving that shares an aisle with several sets of shelves will become the norm. A shift to foods preprepared off site will decrease the need for on-site preprep equipment. Preprocessed fresh vegetables will eliminate deliveries of such items as bulky boxes filled with lettuce heads (from which 20 percent of the leaves would be discarded). Many of these prepared foods will arrive in puncture-proof biodegradable packaging that takes up much less space in the trash. This decreased wastesteam will mean less space set aside for trash storage.

IMPROVED WORK ENVIRONMENT With a shortage of labor, the age-old adage, "If you can't stand the heat, get out of the kitchen," will become a vestige of the past. Increasingly, kitchens will be air conditioned and ventilation systems will be reconfigured to improve the ambient working environment for all kitchen staff. Sound levels will also be improved with modifications to ceiling treatments and noisy ventilation systems. Noise-producing preparation equipment either will no longer be needed or will be modified to produce less noise when in operation.

SANITARY ENVIRONMENT Restaurant equipment and architectural elements in the kitchen will be chosen to ensure the most sanitary conditions possible. Floors and walls will be fashioned from resin-based materials to prevent cracks where dirt can build up and where insects can lay eggs. Sloping floors will lead to auto-closing floor drains. These will help to drain away water used during high-temperature pressure cleaning and sanitizing of floors, walls, and equipment and to prevent insects from entering the kitchen from the waste lines.

Kitchen equipment will be built with watertight electronic modules that will not short out during cleaning. Equipment like ranges will be redesigned to facilitate cleaning. Hand sinks will be equipped with knee, foot, or autosensing faucets to eliminate the chances of cross-contamination, which is a problem with conventional faucet handles.

Refrigerators will be equipped with air curtains to prevent a rise in the cavity temperature when doors are left open. When doors are left open for longer than the preset time, an alarm will sound. Temperature probes embedded in foods will broadcast readings to a monitoring system that will continually record internal temperatures. When temperatures fall in the danger range—40 to 140 degrees Fahrenheit—management will be notified.

MODULAR EQUIPMENT COMPONENTS AND CONSTRUCTION Equipment will be constructed with an on-board diagnostics program that continually monitors its status and phones anomalies to a service agency that will take remedial action. In some cases, management will be told to take the equipment off line. In others, the equipment will be kept in service and modular replacement parts that can be quickly and easily replaced without help from a service technician will be sent to the restaurant via same-day mail.

Upgrade components will also be available for certain pieces of equipment. For example, a range fitted with 15,000-Btu gas burners can be upgraded with 35,000-Btu burners to provide extra heat in support of a new menu item. Convection ovens will be upgradable to combination ovens with the addition of a plug-in steam generator unit and a new control panel.

Restaurants will also be constructed using modular units (Figure 8.4) that are built off site. This practice will significantly decrease installation time and minimize the on-site supervision needed with conventional construction. Specialty food stations can be constructed and installed in a single working day.

FIGURE 8.4 *Modular stations with multiple pieces of equipment assembled for quick installation will decrease the time and cost of labor needed to open during the construction phase.*
(Photo courtesy of Perlick Corp.)

IMPROVED COMMUNICATIONS Communications between the front and the back of the house will improve in all types of restaurants. In à la carte restaurants, order printers will be included in every kitchen. Some kitchens will incorporate television screens that provide cooks with an instant view of the number of portions and the status of every item in production. In fast-food operations, production software will help kitchen staff build food inventories to meet peak demand periods. The software will automatically update itself based on the number of persons entering the restaurant and the exact items ordered. Managers and supervisors will stay in touch at all times with lightweight radio frequency-based earphones. Servers will also use the earphones to relay messages to the kitchen and to receive updates on the availability of certain dishes.

AUTOMATED TASKS Automated equipment will be found extensively in fast-food operations, where the limited menu and high volume of customers make it possible to automate many tasks. Burger patties will be automatically dispensed onto conveyor grills or griddles. Robot arms will turn burgers on griddles and place the cooked burgers on waiting buns. Carbonated beverages will be poured by robot dispensers with far greater accuracy than humans. Fries will be automatically portioned by weight into fry baskets and, as needed, dropped into fryers and then lifted to drain bases. All these automated tasks will be based on input from the POS terminal. In full-service operations, automated equipment will be used to preprepare some ingredients, to package foods prepared for a cook-chill program, and to package foods for HMR offerings.

PREDICTIONS BY RESTAURANT TYPE

FAST FOOD As mentioned above, increased automation will play an important role in the design of fast-food kitchens in the new decade, and not only for burgers. Fast feeders will integrate automation for all sorts of menu items. Pizzas will be auto-assembled and fed directly into conveyor ovens. High-heat burners for such items as prepared-to-order Asian dishes will be integrated to afford a broader menu that can be cooked in a minimal amount of time. Single-portion steamers will be introduced to appeal to the health-conscious customer who chooses to dine in a fast-food setting.

All griddles will be equipped with clamshell tops. The clamshells shorten cooking times, help conserve energy, and prevent vapor loss for a moister and more flavorful product. These batch-style griddles will be used in fast-food operations where a conveyor cooking system is not appropriate. Fryers will increasingly incorporate autolift features as fewer kitchen staff oversee more work. In high-volume fast-food restaurants, operators will use convection fryers that continuously filter the fry medium: A single convection fryer can replace as many as six conventional fryers.

TABLESERVICE Higher-output ranges, the increased use of steamers, and the incorporation of high-speed ovens will head the list of design changes in tableservice hot food areas. In cold food areas where salad greens and vegetables are cleaned in-house, automated washing, drying, and bagging equipment will save labor. Cook-chill equipment will be chosen to prepare and package small batches of stocks, soups, and sauces during off hours in order to lessen the need for labor during peak hours. Pull-out refrigerated drawers will replace the under-range oven. In addition to batch steamers, an increasing number of single-portions steamers will be used to reheat cook-chill foods. The move to rethermalizing foods will decrease dependence on steam tables. High-speed ovens for single portions or small batches will become popular. Combinations of light energy, impinged air, and microwaves will shorten oven cooking times by as much as 80 percent over technologies used in the 1990s. As we approach 2010, we may even see pulsed lasers or other new technologies used in ovens.

Theatrical restaurants will move toward more visual stimulation in display kitchens. Well-insulated rotisseries will cook not only chicken but also such items as whole fish and vegetables seasoned with regional spice blends. Charbroiling will become popular again, with exhaust filters removing much of the smoke particles before they are exhausted outdoors. Banks of equipment such as compact steamers will be stacked to create both a visual focal point in a display kitchen and a low-fat cooking alternative. The wood-fired oven will be joined by an increased number of tandoori ovens and other specialty ovens once associated solely with Indian or other ethnic cuisines.

CAFETERIA Cafeteria back-of-the-house kitchens will continue to shrink as more of the food preparation is moved to the serving lines. We may even see some back-of-the-house kitchens with nothing more than refrigeration and warewashing. Display kitchens will become increasingly complex. Few foods will be cooked in bulk, so high-speed cooking equipment will become the norm on most cafeteria serving lines. Wok ranges with multiple burners of 30,000+ Btu will become popular for creating individual portions of Asian-style foods. Induction cooktops will be chosen for safety and efficiency, but their kilowatt ratings will increase significantly to shorten cooking times. Banks of high-speed, small-capacity ovens will be installed on back counters to bake individual items in 90 seconds or less. Some cafeterias will incorporate automated equipment to save labor and to create a focal point in the servery. For example, one such piece of equipment produces perfectly formed rice cylinders for sushi and sushi rolls. Presliced sushi toppings can be added to the rice cylinders by counter staff rather than highly trained sushi chefs.

FIGURE 8.5 *Computerized control panels will enable management to input the exact temperature, humidity level, and cooking time for different menu items. This will save labor and ensure that foods are prepared consistently.* (Photo courtesy of Rational Cooking Systems)

Banks of small steamers will also be used extensively. The quick-cooking steamers will afford customers a low-fat cooked-to-order option rarely available in the 1990s. In some cases, precooked portions of food ranging from chicken breasts to vegetables will be held in a cold table—rather than a steam table—and rethermalized with steam, microwave, or other heating technology when ordered.

Cafeteria serveries will sport a wider variety of HMR offerings, particularly in upscale installations. Customers will be able to choose from a variety of precooked and packaged meals that can be reheated in a microwave oven, toaster oven, or conventional oven. Upright reach-in display cases will hold foods below 40 degrees Fahrenheit no matter what the ambient temperature. Insulated packaging will help keep foods in a safe temperature zone during transport.

BANQUET Banquet operations will continue to rely on large-volume cooking equipment for initial cooking. However, due to labor shortages, cook-chill programs will be implemented wherever feasible. Programmable combination ovens (Figure 8.5) will play a major role due to their high-output capability and flexibility. In many cases, foods will be cooked, chilled, plated, and held in rethermalizers under refrigeration. The rethermalizers can be programmed for time, temperature, and humidity levels depending on the menu item. Semi-automated equipment will be used to portion soups, salad dressings, and other liquid ingredients.

TAKE-OUT The kitchen equipment that supports the take-out/HMR market will, by necessity, be quick cooking. With increased labor costs and tighter profit margins, restaurateurs from every market segment and service style will incorporate take-out/HMR offerings in an effort to boost overall sales without adding seats. The most successful take-out operations will shift from large batch to small batch to individual portion production.

HMR foods will be prepared using cook-chill equipment. Semi-automated portioning equipment will be used to package foods for reheating at home. Most dedicated HMR operations will also incorporate rethermalizing equipment on site so that customers can reheat their meals for immediate consumption.

Small steamers will also play an increasingly important role in this service segment. Refrigerated drawers containing the mise en place for an evening's worth of cooking will sit below the bank of steamers. As ordered, the ingredients will be placed into heat-stable packaging and then cooked in the steamers. Those items that are best cooked in dry heat will be similarly assembled and baked in quick-cooking ovens.

Conclusion

The strong economy should continue to fuel a growing restaurant industry, save for those affected by shifting lifestyles. However, a booming economy inflates real estate prices and construction costs. The result is that restaurateurs will have to allocate more revenues to support their occupancy costs. As mechanical and electrical systems—the essential installations behind the scenes—become more costly, front- and back-of-the-house budgets will be increasingly scrutinized. A final point of concern is that many markets have become oversaturated with dining availability that exceeds dining demand. In those markets, highly creative designs and management excellence will be needed for restaurants to succeed.

Notes

Index